Ben Nevis
Rock and Ice Climbs

Including
Creag Meagaidh, the Aonachs and Central Highlands

Simon Richardson
Alastair Walker
Robin Clothier

Series Editor: Roger Everett

SCOTTISH MOUNTAINEERING CLUB
CLIMBERS' GUIDE

Published in Great Britain by the Scottish Mountaineering Trust, 1994

British Library Cataloguing in Publication Data
Richardson, Simon
Ben Nevis: Rock and Ice Climbs
I. Title
796.5220941185
ISBN 0-907521-42-8

Maps drawn by Jim Renny and Noel Williams
Diagrams drawn by Jeremy Ashcroft
Production by Scottish Mountaineering Trust (Publications) Ltd
Typeset by Westec, North Connel
Colour Separations by Par Graphics, Kirkcaldy
Printed by St Edmundsbury Press, Bury St Edmunds
Bound by Hunter and Foulis, Edinburgh

Distributed by Cordee, 3a DeMontfort Street, Leicester, LE1 7HD

The Great Tower, Ben Nevis

Contents

List of Illustrations

Additional photography by Peter Hodgkiss and Donald Bennet

List of Diagrams and Maps

The Climber and the Mountain Environment

With increasing numbers of walkers and climbers going to the Scottish hills, it is important that all of us who do so should recognise our responsibilities to those who live and work among the hills and glens, to our fellow climbers and to the mountain environment in which we find our pleasure and recreation.

The Scottish Mountaineering Club and Trust, who jointly produce this and other guidebooks, wish to impress on all who avail themselves of the information in these books that it is essential at times to consider the sporting and proprietary rights of landowners and farmers. The description of a climbing, walking or skiing route in any of these books does not imply that a right of way exists, and it is the responsibility of all climbers to ascertain the position before setting out. In cases of doubt it is best to enquire locally.

During stalking and shooting seasons in particular, much harm can be done in deer forests and on grouse moors by people walking through them. Normally the deer stalking season is from 1st July to 20th October, when stag shooting ends. Hinds may continue to be culled until 15th February. The grouse shooting season is from 12th August until 10th December. These are not merely sporting activities, but are essential for the economy of many Highland estates. During these seasons, therefore, especial care should be taken to consult the local landowner, factor or keeper before taking to the hills.

Climbers and hill walkers are recommended to consult the book HEADING FOR THE SCOTTISH HILLS, published by the Scottish Mountaineering Trust on behalf of the Mountaineering Council of Scotland and the Scottish Landowners Federation, which gives the names and addresses of factors and keepers who may be contacted for information regarding access to the hills.

It is important to avoid disturbance to sheep, particularly during the lambing season between March and May. Dogs should not be taken onto the hills at this time, and at all times should be kept under close control.

Always try to follow a path or track through cultivated land and forests, and avoid causing damage to fences, dykes and gates by climbing over them carelessly. Do not leave litter anywhere, but take it down from the hill in your rucksack.

The number of walkers and climbers on the hills is leading to increased, and in some cases very unsightly erosion of footpaths and hillsides. Some of the revenue from the sale of this and other SMC guidebooks is used by the Trust to assist financially the work being carried out to repair and maintain hill paths in Scotland. However, it is important for all of us to recognise our responsibility to minimise the erosive effect of our passage over the hills so that the enjoyment of future climbers shall not be spoiled by landscape damage caused by ourselves.

As a general rule, where a path exists walkers should follow it and even where it is wet and muddy should avoid walking along its edges, the effect of which is to extend it sideways. Do not take short-cuts at the corners of zigzag paths. Remember that the worst effects of erosion are likely to be caused during or soon after prolonged wet weather when the ground is soft and waterlogged. A route on stony or rocky hillside is likely to cause less erosion than on a grassy one at such times.

Although the use of bicycles can often be very helpful for reaching remote crags and hills, the erosion damage that can be caused by them when used 'off road' on soft footpaths and open hillsides is such that their use on such terrain must cause concern. It is the editorial policy of the Scottish Mountaineering Club that the use of bicycles in hill country may be recommended on hard roads such as forest roads or private roads following rights of way, but it is not recommended on footpaths or open hillsides where the environmental damage that they cause may be considerable. Readers are asked to bear these points in mind, particularly in conditions when the ground is wet and soft after rain.

The proliferation of cairns on hills detracts from the feeling of wildness, and may be confusing rather than helpful as regards route-finding. The indiscriminate building of cairns on the hills is therefore to be discouraged.

Climbers are reminded that they should not drive along private estate roads without permission, and when parking their cars should avoid blocking access to private roads and land, and should avoid causing any hazard to other road users.

Finally, the Scottish Mountaineering Club and the Scottish Mountaineering Trust can accept no liability for damage to property nor for personal injury resulting from the use of any route described in their publications.

The Mountaineering Council of Scotland is the representative body for climbers and walkers in Scotland. One of its primary concerns is the continued free access to the hills and crags that we now enjoy. Information about bird restrictions, stalking and general access issues can be obtained from the National Officer of the MCofS. Should any climber or walker encounter problems regarding access they should contact the National Officer of the MCofS, whose current address is published in Climber and Hillwalker magazine.

Acknowledgements

A great many people have contributed to this guidebook over several years. First we must thank the authors of the previous SMC guides, Colin Stead and Jimmy Marshall. These thorough texts have provided the backbone for this edition, and made our task considerably easier than it might otherwise have been. Our knowledge of Creag Meagaidh and Meall Garbh was supplemented by the privately published guides written by 'Bugs' McKeith and Pete Webster. Other useful information came from *The Central Highlands* District Guide by Peter Hodgkiss (SMC 1984), *The Climbing Guide to Scotland* by Tom Prentice (Crowood 1992), *Winter Climbs Ben Nevis and Glen Coe* by Alan Kimber (Cicerone 1990), and *Rock Climbing in Scotland* by Kev Howett (Constable 1990).

The SMC Journal and personal communications have been the primary reference source for historical material, but considerable use was made of *Ben Nevis* by Ken Crocket (SMC 1986), which is the essential reference for anyone interested in the history of climbing on the mountain. Further historical details were gleaned from *One Man's Mountains* by Tom Patey (Gollancz 1971), and the Alpine Journal.

Roger Everett and Donald Bennet provided continuous assistance, advice and encouragement, and their professionalism has contributed greatly to the guide. The crag diagrams by Jeremy Ashcroft and maps by Jim Renny and Noel Williams add a touch of class to the book. Special thanks are also due to Graham Dudley for the chapter on Ski Descents, and Rod Burt for his scholarly, but very readable, geology section. Thanks are also due to John Ashbridge for his assistance with the geology.

Ken Crocket, Dave Cuthbertson, Mal Duff, Con Higgins, Alan Kimber, Jimmy Marshall, Colin Stead and Roger Webb freely contributed their in-depth knowledge and experience of Ben Nevis, and Noel Williams provided assistance with the chapter covering the Mamores and Glen Nevis gullies. Considerable help with the text was given by Tom Prentice.

One of the greatest pleasures in writing this guidebook has been the contact with the many climbers who have been asked to provide photographic material, verify route descriptions, and comment on the graded lists. Some have been chased by letters all over Europe, or disturbed by late night phone calls. People have been stopped in the street or cornered in bars to be quizzed on obscure first ascent details, whilst others have even been questioned while climbing on nearby routes! Without exception, the response has been both warm and encouraging, and we offer our sincere thanks. A full list of contributors follows. We are indebted to them all.

Sandy Allan, Rab Anderson, John Ashbridge, Jeremy Ashcroft, Donald Bennet, Geoff Birtles, Jim Blyth, Rod Burt, Martin Burrows-Smith, Alastair Cain, Robin Campbell, Rab Carrington, Chris Cartwright, Mark Charlton, Andy Clarke, Ken Crocket, Dave Cuthbertson, Pete Drummond, Graham Dudley, Mal Duff, Roger Everett, John Fowler, Ian Fulton, Allen Fyffe, Doug Hawthorn, Dave Heselden, Con Higgins, Peter Hodgkiss, Geoff Hornby, Ken Johnstone, Steve Kennedy, Alan Kimber, Dai Lampard, Doug Lang, Alan Leary, Graham Little, John Lyall, John Mackenzie, John Main, Jimmy Marshall, Charlie Martin, Darryl Milne, Keith Milne, Alan Moist, Guy Muhlemann, Andy Nelson, Willie Nicol, Grahame Nicoll, Andrew Nisbet, Paul Nunn, Arthur Paul, Godefroy Perroux, Tom Prentice, Bob Reid, Jim Renny, Christine Richardson, Dave Ritchie, Dave Roberts, Victor Saunders, Klaus Schwartz, Douglas Scott, Alan Shand, Andy Slater, Colin Stead, Greg Strange, Terry Sullivan, Ian Sykes, Andy Tibbs, Willie Todd, Stephen Venables, Roger Webb, Andy Wielochowski, Roger Wild, Dave Wilkinson, Simon Yates.

Finally, we extend our gratitude to our wives and families who have allowed us countless hours away, whether it be on the hill checking out a remote corrie, or sitting behind the word processor at home.

Introduction

By a happy coincidence of geology, altitude and location, Ben Nevis is not only the highest mountain in Britain, it also contains some of the finest climbing in the British Isles. The magnificent cliffs on the northeast face are alpine in stature, and offer mountaineering on a grand scale. Routes such as Tower Ridge, The Long Climb, and Minus One Direct will be high on any climber's list, and on the Great Buttress of Carn Dearg, Centurion, The Bat and Titan's Wall, provide some of the best rock climbs of their standard in Britain.

It is in winter though that the mountain really comes into its own. By virtue of its height and position, it is exposed to the full force of Atlantic weather systems. The resulting high level of precipitation, and frequent changes in temperature and wind direction, allow ice to build rapidly. This, combined with the superbly articulated character of the mountain's great ridges and gullies, produces a winter climbing ground without equal in the country. The classic ice routes are sought after, not only by British climbers, but by mountaineers from all over the world. In peak season during February and March, the mountain can take on a cosmopolitan air, and you are as likely to meet a climber from France or Spain on the summit plateau, as you are someone from Glasgow or Manchester.

Good conditions on the harder routes can be very elusive, and some climbers have waited in vain for many years to realise their ambitions. When conditions are good, a single-minded approach is necessary, for ice which can take weeks to form, can disappear in the space of a few hours once the weather turns. The transitory nature of ice climbs only adds to their appeal, and success on a major Nevis winter route is an experience to treasure, to be relived again and again.

This guide covers the area of the Central Highlands north of Glen Coe and south of the Great Glen. Although Ben Nevis dominates the region in terms of altitude, the other cliffs in the area are a worthy match in terms of the quality of their climbing. Creag Meagaidh is one of the highest cliffs in the British Isles and has a huge variety of easy, classic and extreme winter climbs. The recently developed ski area at Aonach Mor has transformed this once quiet backwater into an important climbing centre. There are many excellent middle grade climbs here, and some of the mixed routes can rival any others in Scotland for quality. For those looking for seclusion, solitude can be virtually guaranteed if you visit the remote corries on Meall Garbh and

Ben Alder. In so vast an area there are, without doubt, other undeveloped cliffs and corries which will provide plenty to intrigue those with an exploratory urge for many years to come.

It has been both a pleasure and a privilege to write this guidebook. We have been acutely aware of our responsibility in not only accurately describing this important climbing ground, but also in maintaining an accurate historical record. Undoubtedly however, errors and omissions will have occurred, and we strongly urge climbers to record their discoveries, new and old. Any information should be sent to the New Routes Editor of the SMC Journal which is published annually in July.

The authors have been visiting this area for over 20 years. The mountains continue to provide an intoxicating mix of pleasure, adventure and excitement, whether it be revisiting an old classic, looking round new corners, or fighting through a blizzard after a long and gruelling winter climb. We wish users of this guide every bit as much enjoyment as we have had, in climbing and exploring in this magnificent area.

Simon Richardson, Alastair Walker and Robin Clothier

December 1993

Geology *by Rod Burt*

The spectacular scenery of Ben Nevis and the Central Highlands is formed from one of the most complex areas of geology in the British Isles. The region has fascinated geologists for centuries, and many fundamental geological principles were first worked out here, although a full understanding of the area is still far from complete. Before reviewing some of the more interesting geological features, it is worth considering the broader picture into which the Central Highlands fits. The Earth is believed to be 4600 million years old. The first traces of life are found in rocks that are 3000 million years old, although fossil remains are relatively uncommon until the evolution of organisms with hard shelly or bony parts at the end of the Precambrian 590 million years ago. The magnitude of geological time is difficult to comprehend, but if the entire history of the Earth is compressed into one year, then the oldest rocks we know of date from mid-March and the earliest known life forms appeared in May. The first land plants and animals evolved during late November, at about the same time as the rocks forming Ben Nevis were crystalising from molten magmas. Dinosaurs became dominant during mid-December but were extinct by Christmas. Man-like creatures appeared during the evening of Hogmanay (impeccable timing!), and the last Ice Age ended just 1 minute and 15 seconds before midnight.

The oldest rocks in Scotland, Lewisian Gneisses, are 2900 million years old. The Earth at this time was very different from the blue and green planet familiar to us today. Photosynthesis had yet to make a significant impact on the composition of the atmosphere, and consequently the ozone layer was practically non-existent. To escape from harmful ultra-violet radiation, life (algae) was confined to the oceans. During the period of Torridonian sandstone deposition (1000 million years ago), oxygen was sufficiently abundant to oxidise (rust) the iron in these sediments to give the Torridonian sandstones their distinctive red hue. Despite the age of the Torridonian rocks, they are surprisingly little affected by folding or metamorphism and geologists refer to the area of Torridonian and Lewisian outcrop as the North-West Foreland. The Foreland represents the continental interior against which the sediments of the Moine (Northern Highlands) and the Dalradian (Central Highlands) were squashed during the Caledonian Orogeny (mountain-building phase).

A fundamental concept in modern geology is the theory of plate tectonics. The Earth's crust is not a rigid inflexible layer but a thin veneer 'floating' on a much thicker layer known as the Mantle, and made up of several interlocking segments known as plates. The movement of the continents across the surface of the Earth is known as continental drift. Continents can split or drift apart and the intervening gap will become an ocean, whereas collision of two continents results in the formation of a mountain belt. The collision of India with Asia, for example, formed the Himalayas. This process is still continuing today, and Nanga Parbat is rising at a rate of 9cm per year, although erosion is removing material at a similar rate. The speed at which the continents move across the face of the Earth is about as fast as your finger nails grow. However, even a rate of 5cm per year can produce large movements over geological time. After 10 million years, 5cm per year will equal a distance of 500km.

Scotland's geology, and therefore any form of mountaineering, be it ice climbing on the Ben or ticking Munros, is dominated by the effects of the Caledonian Orogeny, a major period of mountain-building which ended around 390 million years ago. Modern ideas for the development of this orogeny are based on the movements of three ancient continents known as Gondwana (Europe and Africa), Baltica (Scandinavia) and Laurentia (the Americas and Greenland). The Iapetus Ocean (Iapetus, father of Atlantis in Greek mythology) separated Laurentia from Gondwana and Baltica. Closure of the Iapetus Ocean led to the development of the Caledonian orogenic belt.

Scotland is normally considered to be part of the Laurentian continent, and was separated from England and Wales (Gondwana) by the Iapetus Ocean until the end of the Caledonian. The Caledonian Orogeny is associated with upheaval and violent volcanic activity. However, recent work in Scotland has suggested that the Central Highlands was formerly part of Gondwana, and not Laurentia. It is now recognised that orogenic belts are composed of a number of far-travelled 'terranes' and the Central Highlands forms part of the British Isles known to geologists as the Grampian Terrane. A terrane is a fault-bounded area or region, characterised by a geological history distinct from that of adjacent areas. This process can be seen acting today in the United States, where California is moving northwards at a speed of 8cm per year, along the San Andreas Fault. If the Pacific Ocean were to close 100 million years in the future, then California will have travelled 8,000km and its geology will bear no relation to that of adjacent regions. Such a movement would place California on the opposite side of the Pacific, so the Grampian Block represents what California may look like 100 million years in the future!

Volcanic activity, granite intrusion, metamorphism, folding and faulting, characterise orogenic episodes, and it is these features that have made Central Highland geology so difficult to unravel. During metamorphism, the mineralogy of a particular rock type changes in a predictable way. This allows geologists to work back from the mineral composition of a rock and estimate the pressures and temperatures of metamorphism that a rock has suffered. From such work, it has been suggested that during the Caledonian, the present day land surface was buried under a substantial thickness of rock, up to 35km in some cases, although 20km is a better average. This gives a total crustal thickness approaching that of the Alps or even the Himalayas, and the Grampian Block represents the roots of a now vanished mountain belt at least as high as the Alps. Towards the end of the Caledonian, the orogenic belt underwent uplift and erosion, reducing crustal thicknesses to values little different from today.

Geologically, the rocks exposed at the surface of the Central Highlands are usually placed into one of three major units, these being the Central Highland Division, the Grampian Group and the Dalradian Supergroup. Division, Group and Supergroup, all being terms used by the geologist to define packages of sediments with similar geological histories.

The Central Highland Division is believed to have undergone an earlier episode of mountain building and continental collision known as the Grenvillian Orogeny. Temperatures and pressures were high enough to induce partial melting of these rocks during this earlier episode. The Grampian Group and Dalradian Supergroup sediments were deposited in small marginal basins, possibly similar to the North Sea and English Channel today. The Grampian Group forms a monotonous series of psammite (meta-sandstone) and semi-pelite (meta-muddy-sandstone). Creag Meagaidh, much of Glen Spean and the Monadh Liath are formed from this particular rock formation. On Creag Meagaidh, in contrast to much of the Central Highlands, the strata is horizontal, providing good holds and protection, and the great gullies or 'Posts' are formed from eroded intrusive dykes.

The mountains south of the A86 (Spean Bridge to Dalwhinnie) are formed from the Dalradian Supergroup. This group of sediments is further subdivided into three groups, these being the Appin, Argyll and Southern Highland Groups. The Appin Group dominates the geology of the Grey Corries and Mamores. The most obvious rock formations in this group are the white quartzites that form much of the Grey Corries, the summit of Stob Ban and the waterfall at Steall. Structures within the quartzite formations suggest that the sediments were deposited in deltas or offshore bars. Creamy white to green metalimestone formations indicate shallow water marine conditions. Periodic stagnation and isolation of the Dalradian basin led to the deposition of black pyritiferous slates such as the Ballachulish Slates.

At the base of the Argyll Group a sequence of glacial deposits (tills) indicates a period of glaciation. The tills exposed in Scotland are believed to be comparable with similar deposits exposed in Norway. This glacial episode occured some 650 million years ago. Interestingly, the Argyll Group also includes deposits, such as the Aberfeldy Baryte deposit, that indicate warm tropical conditions. Consequently, this glacial episode must have covered much of the globe. Ice climbing in the Bahamas?

Towards the end of the Caledonian, approximately 420 million years ago, magma rose towards the surface from deep in the crust. The granite bodies or plutons of Cairngorm, Lochnagar, Glen Etive, Ben Starav, Ben Nevis, Mullach nan Coirean and Strontian, to name but a few, were formed at this time. Most of these granites were emplaced below the surface of the Earth, by a process known as cauldron collapse. This is when a subterranean block of country rock fractures and subsides, creating space into which the magma flows. In the case of Lochnagar, repeated subsidence of the cylindrical block resulted in the intrusion of nine separate magmas. Very likely, the land surface was spectacularly peppered with volcanoes located above the granite plutons.

Both mountaineer and geologist alike find Ben Nevis and its associated mountain group fascinating, and it is this area that this account now concentrates on. Geology, like any other science, has developed its own terminology and before launching into a discussion of Ben Nevis the following explanations may be useful to those not familiar with geology and its definitions. Igneous rocks fall into two categories. Intrusive rocks such as granite, are emplaced into the Earth's crust without reaching the surface. Extrusive igneous rocks are found on the surface, either as lava flows, or as pyroclastic deposits. Lava is molten, or partially molten rock whereas pyroclastic deposits consist of fragmented volcanic material that has been blown into the atmosphere by explosive volcanic activity. If the deposit is composed of angular-shaped fragments it is called a breccia, and the term conglomerate is used when the fragments are rounded.

At the bottom of the tourist path, a short description of Ben Nevis can be found in which the mountain is described as an extinct volcano. This is not so, but the most important feature of Ben Nevis is the occurrence of both extrusive and intrusive igneous rocks in the same locality.

The geology of Ben Nevis is composed of a central core of volcanic rocks overlying an older metamorphic basement. This core is completely enclosed within the Inner Granite, which is in turn partially enclosed along two-thirds of its circumference by the Outer Granite. Together these components form the Ben Nevis Volcanic-plutonic Complex. The lowest exposure of Outer Granite in Glen Nevis and the highest on Aonach Mor represents a height difference of over 1,350m (3,900ft) making this intrusion the largest vertical thickness of granitic rock exposed anywhere in the U.K. In addition, Aonach Beag is the highest mountain in the U.K. composed of metamorphic rock.

Conventionally, Ben Nevis is divided into two granite units, the Inner Granite and the Outer Granite. In fact, the Outer Granite is made up of three separate intrusions, these being the Outer Quartz Diorite, the Inner Quartz Diorite and the Porphyritic Outer Granite. Quartz Diorite is an igneous rock richer in iron and magnesium and poorer in silicon, potassium and sodium than granite. The term 'porphyritic' refers to the presence of large crystals known as phenocrysts. In the case of the Porphyritic Outer Granite, the most distinctive phenocrysts are large salmon pink feldspar crystals. This rock forms an attractive granite and is exposed over much of Aonach Mor and on the lower slopes of the Ben Nevis range.

After the Outer Granite, but prior to intrusion of the Inner Granite, a series of dykes were injected laterally. A dyke is a sub-vertical sheet-like intrusion of igneous rock cutting across earlier structures. Several examples of the these dykes can be seen to the side of the tourist path above the second zigzag.

A second episode of subsidence allowed the intrusion of the Inner Granite to invade the space created by the downgoing block. Being later than the dyke swarm, the Inner Granite cross cuts and truncates the earlier dykes. Only a few dykes were injected after the intrusion of the Inner Granite. From the simple relationships between the dykes and the two granite intrusions it is possible to tell that the Outer Granite is the older of the two intrusions.

Several deep gullies and chimneys cut into Carn Dearg (the southwest top of Ben Nevis), into Meall an t-Suidhe and into the cliffs of Coire an Lochain on Aonach Mor. Small faults have broken up the granite in these localities, accelerating the rate at which they are eroded. A similar fault-related mechanism is the cause of many of the gullies on the north face of Ben Nevis. Douglas Gap is one such example. Adjacent to the zone of fracturing, the rock is relatively sound and devoid of natural crack lines, which explains why protection can be hard to find on the sidewalls of many of the gully lines.

Shortly after the intrusion of the Inner Granite, a section of the magma chamber roof failed, collapsing into the still largely molten Inner Granite. Part of the Inner Granite was then vented in an extremely violent and powerful eruption. On the surface this would have formed a circular depression known as a caldera. If a similar eruption occurred today in London, much of the city would be totally destroyed and buried under a thick layer of hot volcanic ash.

Caldera formation is accompanied by exceptionally powerful eruptions. One of the more recent, Krakatau (Indonesia 1883), resulted in the deaths of 36,000 people, mainly due to drowning from tsunamis (tidal waves). Some 18 cubic kilometres of material were ejected out of the vent and the explosion could be heard as a thunder-like rumble some 1,000km away. So much ash reached the upper atmosphere that the following year was known as the year without a summer. Many artists painted spectacular red sunsets, again an effect of the ash in the atmosphere. This eruption, though powerful in human terms, was quite small on a geological scale. Some caldera-forming eruptions in the United States (where everything is bigger than anywhere else) have ejected at least 1000 cubic kilometres of material in the space of a few days.

A large eruption column develops over the caldera site. Gravitational collapse of this column generates large volume pyroclastic flows known as ignimbrites. Close to the source, ignimbrites contain enough energy to surmount any topography. At greater distances flows are confined into pre-existing drainage channels. A depression forms above the collapsed block, into which material from the eruption column may pond. Crater Lake in the United States is one example of a partially-filled caldera depression. The block that subsides into the chamber is bounded by a ring fault that may or may not contain remnants of the erupted magma.

At roughly the same time as the Outer Granite was crystalising below the surface, the rocks of the volcanic pile were forming. The volcanic pile can be conveniently subdivided into three units; a pre-volcanic basement, a unit dominated by volcanic breccias, and a dominantly andesite lava unit. Andesite is a type of volcanic rock with a particular chemical composition and it is the extrusive equivalent of quartz diorite.

The base of the volcanic pile is formed from Dalradian metapelites (metamorphosed mudstones); this is exposed in the west bank of the Allt a'Mhuilinn some 200 metres upstream from the C.I.C. hut. An outcrop of Dalradian rock can also be found in Five Finger Gully. Both Dalradian outcrops form part of an ancient land surface that was buried under volcanic rocks 420 million years ago. Overlying the Dalradian in the Allt a'Mhuilinn, and also exposed beneath North-East Buttress and the Little Brenva Face, is a sequence of fine-grain muds and silts interbedded with much coarser sedimentary breccias. These fine-grain sediments have none of the sedimentary structures associated with deposition in a marine environment, and a freshwater lake is therefore the most likely setting. Into this lake flowed a series of mass flow units or landslides, represented today by heterolithic and poorly sorted breccias. Heterolithic and poorly sorted are terms that give the geologist some idea of the way in which a breccia is made up. A heterolithic deposit is one in which a large variety of clast types (stones) occur, and sorting refers to the distribution or range of clast sizes encountered. Whilst clasts of up to 25cm in diameter can be found in the breccias, no igneous clasts are present, leading to the obvious conclusion that igneous activity had not yet begun in the Ben Nevis area. Movement of the breccias was gravity-driven and controlled by an ancient topography, confining the breccias into natural drainage channels.

Similar volcanic breccias to those found on Ben Nevis have been described from Mount Pelee, the eruption of which devastated Martinique in 1902. Here angular to sub-angular andesite blocks rarely larger than 6m across, and supported in a matrix of smaller andesite clasts and ash, were deposited by fast moving gravity-driven pyroclastic flows. This type of deposit is termed a 'block and ash flow'. On human scales these eruptions are very violent, but in geological terms, block and ash flow eruptions are rather small compared to a caldera-type eruption. The source for the Ben Nevis block and ash flows may have been several kilometres from the site of the ancient lake.

Thin, finely laminated muds and silts are found sporadically throughout the Volcanic Breccia sequence. Of limited lateral extent, these sediments appear to fill small localised depressions and probably represent remnants of much larger lake-like bodies of standing water.

The sediments are highly distorted, indicating that the area was tectonically active (earthquakes), possibly caused by the subterranean movement of magma.

The absence of sediments above the Dalradian rock exposed in Five Finger Gully could be explained by the location of this area above the lake, whereas Coire na Ciste and the area around the C.I.C. hut are located within the topographic depression infilled by the lake. Such a hypothesis may also explain the low volume of block and ash flows in the vicinity of Five Finger Gully. Block and ash flows, being gravity-driven, are restricted to valley floors and other low-lying areas.

Between the volcanic breccia and andesite subdivisions, on the northern side of Coire na Ciste and on the Orion Face above the Basin, yet another type of breccia deposit is exposed. This is known as the Ledge Route Breccia, where it is particularly well exposed. In contrast to previously described breccias, the Ledge Route Breccia is moderately well sorted and it is suggested that it represents a pyroclastic airfall deposit. The most extensive sedimentary band occurs at the base of the Ledge Route Breccia and its thickness (20m and over) implies a substantial period of quiet before deposition of the breccias.

The great bulk of the andesite lavas form the steep vertical cliffs of the Orion Face and North-East Buttress, as well as the cliffs around Castle Corrie. The lavas are fine-textured for the most part, offering reasonable friction. Although individual sections of cliff vary from slabby and fairly featureless to steep and dramatically sculpted, the climbing is always well detailed, with individual features and climbs following distinct and clean-cut features.

Each lava is of high aspect ratio (height to length) compared with typical plateau lavas such as those found on Skye, Mull and other islands of the Inner Hebrides. This feature is controlled by the viscosity of the lava, and the thickness of individual flows ranges from a few metres to possibly several tens of metres. The andesite is normally brecciated throughout the entire thickness of a flow. Brecciation has been caused by the way in which the lava flowed, and not because of explosive vulcanism or sedimentary processes.

The andesite lavas above the volcanic breccias may represent the migration of the source for the Ben Nevis pile to a site closer to the Ben. Evidence for this is based on the occurrence of Felsite Dykes at the base of the volcanic pile in Five Finger Gully. This type of dyke was intruded very early on in the intrusion of the Ben Nevis Granites, and it is possible that as the granite was being intruded below the surface, a volcano was located above which generated the andesite lavas.

Near source andesite lavas dominate the succession again, suggesting that the source of these rocks must have been fairly close. Sporadic horizons of volcanic breccia occur through the andesite sequence, representing bursts of explosive volcanism. Both types of deposit can be produced from the same volcano. Plugging of the vent allows the build up of magmatic pressure until the plug fails, producing a violent eruption and a block and ash flow. Such an eruption clears the vent and allows relatively quiet effusions of viscous, gas-poor lava until the vent becomes blocked again and the cycle is renewed. It is not known how long this cycle of events went on for, as the thickness of the volcanic pile before erosion is unknown.

Several intrusions are found cross-cutting the Volcanic Pile and two of these are worthy of further discussion. On the right wall of Number Four Gully, a 15m by 20m ellipsoidal vent intrudes the andesite. The strong vertical fabric of this rock unit and its fragmentary nature suggest that this may be a feeder pipe to a small explosive vent. In thin section, rounded clasts of Dalradian quartzite and pelite can be identified along with a suite of andesite fragments, all contained within a very fine grain matrix. A small dome-like intrusion is extremely well exposed where Ledge Route flattens out above the amphitheatre of Number Five Gully. This example is perhaps 12m thick by 50m wide and has its feeder pipes exposed.

No trace of the ancient volcano, caldera, or roof of the granite magma chamber (except for small inliers on the eastern side of Aonach Mor) have survived. The pyroclastic flows and lavas of Ben Nevis survive because the collapse of the magma chamber roof allowed the volcanic pile to subside into the magma chamber. Thus the rocks of the volcanic pile were formed one to two kilometres above its present location and represent deposition in a depression surrounded by high ground. At around this time the Great Glen Fault, north of Ben Nevis, was active. This fault, similar to the San Andreas Fault in California, still causes weak earthquakes today.

During the Cretaceous and Tertiary periods, the Atlantic Ocean began to open and the Americas separated from Europe and Africa. Igneous rocks associated with this event form the Cuillin Ridge of Skye and much of Mull, Rum and Ardnamurchan. The Giant's Causeway and the rocks of Fingal's Cave were also formed at this time. On the Ben Nevis tourist track a thin black dyke can be located above the second aluminium bridge. Unlike any of the dykes in the Ben Nevis Dyke swarm, this dyke is believed to be part of the igneous activity associated with the opening of the Atlantic.

At the end of the Tertiary the climate of the Earth cooled and glaciers formed in the high mountains of the British Isles. The Ice Age was not one single event, and the glaciers advanced and melted several times. Warm interglacial periods, when temperatures were warm enough for hyenas and jackals to live in the south of England, punctuated the Ice Age. In the colder glacial episodes the ice reached as far as London and the Severn Estuary. Vast quantities of rock were removed from the Highlands and carried south across the border. The spectacular Highland scenery we see today results from the sculpting during the Ice Age.

In Scotland, the glacial episode which exerted the major influence on shaping the landscape was the Devensian, which was the last major advance of ice in Northern Europe. This episode began 120,000 years ago, and culminated in an ice-sheet which covered all of Scotland and much of England and Wales some 18,000 years ago. The greatest thickness (1800m) of ice lay above Rannoch Moor. A series of major glacial troughs radiate from this area including Glen Coe, Loch Etive, Loch Earn, Loch Rannoch, Loch Ericht and Loch Treig, suggesting that this area was a persistent source of glaciation from which ice flow radiated throughout the Quaternary, imposing a dominant 'grain' on the landscape. It is clear that even then precipitation in the west was greater than in the east, and greater snowfall gave rise to more powerful glacial action. The effects are clearly evident when driving along the A86 from Newtonmore to Spean Bridge as the broad rounded mountains of the Monadh Liath give way to more deeply eroded mountains with pronounced aretes, corries and U-shaped valleys in the Aonachs and Grey Corries. The majority of the corries face north or east due to the protection of snow accumulation on these slopes from direct sunlight.

About 18,000 years ago the Earth's climate began to gradually warm and the glaciers retreated. A short cold snap 11,000 years ago (the Loch Lomond Re-advance), led to a short period of ice-sheet growth, but 1,000 years later the ice had largely disappeared. It is estimated that the last of Scotland's glaciers lay in Coire Leis below the Little Brenva Face, and only finally disappeared about 8000 years ago.

The British Isles are still suffering from the after-effects of the last glacial episode, for the great mass of ice that once covered much of Scotland depressed the land surface, and to counter-balance this Southern Britain rose. Now that the ice has gone, Scotland is rising and Southern Britain is sinking. There may be more Munros yet!

History *by Simon Richardson*

In 1892, some 27 years after his celebrated Matterhorn ascent, Edward Whymper visited Ben Nevis to conduct a series of pressure experiments with aneroid barometers. He was clearly very impressed by the mountain and later wrote of the northern cliffs - *'This great face is one of the finest pieces of crag in our country, and it has never been climbed, though every now and then adventurous ones go and look at it with wistful eyes.'* Within days of Whymper's visit however, the brothers John, Bertram and Charles Hopkinson had made two major first ascents - Tower Ridge and North-East Buttress. These significant events went unnoticed for three years until the routes were recorded in the Alpine Journal as a note in 1895.

The SMC Easter meet of 1894 was based at the Inveroran Hotel, which could be conveniently reached from Tyndrum station on the partially completed West Highland Railway. The hotel was crowded, so Norman Collie persuaded Lake District climbers Godfrey Solly and Joseph Collier to move on to Fort William. After several new routes in Glen Coe *en route*, they were rewarded with the first winter ascent of Tower Ridge (III), climbed in a very respectable time of five hours. Collie was so delighted with the climb that he repeated it the next day with Geoffrey Hastings. On hearing of the ascent, Willie Naismith (regarded as the father of the SMC) was furious - *'The Sassenachs have indeed taken the wind out of our sails ... Flodden or even Culloden was nothing to this ...'*

In the autumn of 1984, the West Highland Railway was opened, and the 1895 and 1896 SMC Easter Meets were held in Fort William. Castle Ridge (III 1895) was climbed and Tower Ridge saw several repeats, but the most significant event was Naismith's ascent of North-East Buttress (IV,4 1896), a long and sustained undertaking which is still well respected today. To climb such a long and committing route, with sections that were difficult to retreat from, seems remarkable for the time, but by the end of the 1890s such ascents were becoming commonplace. Many mountaineers active in Scotland were also accomplished alpinists, and Collie for example, compared his winter ascent of Tower Ridge to the Italian Ridge on the Matterhorn.

Exploration then continued at a more leisurely pace, with Ben Nevis firmly established as the major centre for Scottish winter climbing. Activity consisted primarily of repeating existing lines until the redoubtable Harold Raeburn came on the scene. Although he had already taken part in first ascents of the fine Direct Route on the Douglas Boulder (Very Difficult 1896) and The Castle (Very Difficult 1898), his first major contribution was the first ascent (solo) of Observatory Ridge (Difficult 1901). The following June he soloed Observatory Buttress (Very Difficult) and then made an inspirational lead of the brilliant Raeburn's Arete (Severe) on the Minus Face with Dr and Mrs Inglis Clark.

Raeburn was equally at home on snow and ice, and his ascent of Green Gully (IV,4 1906) with Eberhard Phildius (a Swiss climber Raeburn met in Fort William) was nothing short of remarkable. The route was so far ahead of its time (unequalled in difficulty for at least 30 years), that the ascent was unrecognised until the 1970s. Crowberry Gully (III 1898), Raeburn's classic Glen Coe route, also suffered a similar fate, no doubt due to his modesty in recording climbs. After Green Gully, Raeburn concentrated on other areas, resulting in a string of fine ascents such as Central Buttress (III 1907) on Stob Coire nan Lochan, The Great Ridge (III 1908) on Garbh Bheinn, and the Spigolo Inglese (D 1910) on the North Face of Monte Disgrazia.

The First World War brought exploration on Ben Nevis to a virtual standstill, and it was not until 1920 that the 55-year-old Raeburn returned to make a hard-won first winter ascent of Observatory Ridge (IV,4) with W.Mounsey and Frank Goggs. Sadly it was Raeburn's last route on the mountain, for he contracted dysentery the following year whilst leading a reconnaissance party to Everest, and died in 1926. Observatory Ridge was the outstanding Scottish winter ascent of the decade, but with no-one to take Raeburn's place, Scottish winter climbing went into decline.

The only other significant event of the 1920s was the erection of the C.I.C. Hut in memory of Charles Inglis Clark who was killed in the First World War. His parents, Dr and Mrs Inglis Clark, were mountaineers with a great passion for The Ben. Splendidly situated at the head of the Allt a'Mhuilinn under the north face, the C.I.C. Hut is the closest thing to an alpine refuge in the British Isles, and its erection was to act as a catalyst for summer exploration of the mountain through the 1930s.

Jim Bell and Graham Macphee were the two dominant climbers that stand out from this period. Macphee was charged with writing a new guidebook, and he developed a considerable knowledge of the mountain. From a base in Liverpool, he repeated nearly all the existing climbs and added many new summer routes. Of these, the chimney line of Route I (Severe 1931), the first climb to breach the great

The C.I.C. Hut

buttress of Carn Dearg, was the most significant. Macphee was partnered by Lake District climber Alan Hargreaves on this ascent, who later added the bold Rubicon Wall (Severe 1933) on Observatory Buttress.

Macphee's few winter climbs were more significant. Glover's Chimney (III,4 1935), climbed with George Williams and Drummond Henderson, had an inspirational effect on an emerging generation of climbers who realised that many summer climbs were winter possibilities given a good coating of snow and ice. Macphee also climbed the fine lines of Cousin's Buttress (III 1935) and Good Friday Climb (III 1939), and made a bold solo of the exposed South Gully (III 1936) on Creag Coire na Ciste.

Bell was considerably more selective over his climbs. He pioneered several fine routes on previously untouched faces on the mountain, such as West Face Upper Route (Severe 1937) on Observatory Ridge, but his outstanding contribution was the exploration of the Orion Face with a series of fine mountaineering rock climbs. These culminated in The Long Climb (VS 1940), which by virtue of its length and complex route-finding, is one of the few rock climbs in the British Isles to assume an alpine stature.

In winter, Bell repeated Green Gully, and in 1936 made an audacious attempt at Zero Gully with Colin Allan. After 30m they were forced to climb several icy pitches on Slav Route before regaining the gully higher up. Today's climbers would have considered this a route in itself rather than a failure! In 1938, inspired by the Glover's Chimney ascent, Bill Murray, Bill MacKenzie and Archie MacAlpine repeated Observatory Ridge, 18 years after Raeburn's first ascent. Later that winter, Dick Morsley and Percy Small (who had partnered Bell on Green Gully) climbed the fine Comb Gully (IV,4) with Gardner Stangle. Whilst Scottish winter climbing in the 1930s was still catching up with Raeburn's achievements of 30 years earlier, ice climbing in the Alps was developing at a fast pace, with Willo Welzenbach's audacious series of north face routes which included the Grands Charmoz (TD 1931) and the Gletscherhorn (TD+ 1931).

By far the most active climber during the Second World War was Brian Kellett, a conscientious objector who was assigned to forestry work at Torlundy just north of Fort William. In 1942 he made the first summer ascent of the difficult Number Two Gully (VS), and the following year he set about exploring the mountain in earnest. Climbing after work, and often solo, he repeated 74 of the existing 89 routes, and added 17 new routes and variations including the classic Route

II (Severe) on Carn Dearg Buttress. The following summer he made 15 more first ascents, many of them of outstanding quality. Left-Hand Route (VS) and Right-Hand Route (VS) on Minus Two Buttress, climbed solo and on sight, were huge leaps into the unknown, and his solo ascent of Kellett's Route (HVS) on Gardyloo Buttress was a quantum jump in technical difficulty, not to be superseded for over 10 years. Kellett met his death later that summer while climbing on the North Wall of Carn Dearg with Nancy Forsyth. Ironically, this time Kellett and his companion were roped, and both climbers died in the fall.

Kellett's death and the aftermath of the Second World War left a void that took several years to fill. The only route that stands out from the late 1940s was The Crack (HVS 1946) on Raeburn's Buttress by H.Carsten and Tommy McGuinness. This rarely climbed and daunting route was to give a young Robin Smith an epic ten years later, and it continues to intimidate leaders to the present day. In the early 1950s attention focussed on a direct ascent of the front face of Carn Dearg Buttress. The most natural line of weakness, the great chimney line in the centre of the face, is guarded by an overhanging base. It had been tried by at least four different parties who had attempted to traverse above the roofs. After failing on Point Five Gully in April 1954, Joe Brown and Don Whillans aided through the overhang, and then fought their way through the loose chockstones in the great chimney above.

The much-prized ascent of Sassenach (E1) was greeted with dismay by the Scots, but the English onslaught continued with North-Eastern Grooves (HVS 1955) and Minus One Direct (HVS 1956) by a Cambridge University team including Bob Downes and Mike O'Hara. Whillans returned with Downes at the end of August 1956 to add a second route on Carn Dearg. The final two pitches of the classic Centurion (HVS), which find their way through the overhangs at the top of the face, were a masterly piece of route-finding. Scottish pride was dented further when the same pair climbed The Shield (HVS) two days later. It was not until 1959 that the Scots eventually climbed a route on Carn Dearg that they could call their own, when Robin Smith and Dougal Haston fought their way up the imposing corner of The Bat (E2) to the right of Centurion. This route, equal in stature and technical difficulty to Shibboleth (E2 1958) on Buachaille Etive Mor, stands as a testament to Smith's vision and rock-climbing genius. The other important first ascent of the 1959 summer was the little-known Subtraction (E2), on the Minus Face, by John McLean and Willie Smith.

In March 1952, the Edinburgh University pair of Dan Stewart and Bill Foster climbed the rather obscure Observatory Buttress Direct (IV,4), the first new winter route on the mountain for 15 years. Winter standards elsewhere in Scotland were beginning to rise. Tom Patey was at the forefront of developments in the East with first ascents of Douglas-Gibson Gully on Lochnagar (IV,4 1950) and Scorpion (V,5 1952) on Carn Etchachan, while in Glen Coe, Hamish MacInnes climbed a fine series of routes including Raven's Gully (V,5 1953) and Agag's Groove (VI,6 1953). On Ben Nevis, the great gullies of Zero and Point Five were the main challenge, but before the Ballachulish bridge was built, it was easier to climb in Glen Coe or the Cairngorms rather than make the longer journey to the Ben. By February 1957 competition was intense, and with pressure from the rival Creag Dhu team of John Cunningham and Mick Noon, MacInnes teamed up with Tom Patey and Graeme Nicol at the C.I.C. Hut to attempt Zero Gully. Conditions were excellent, and the route succumbed in the very respectable time of five hours. It was a busy day on Nevis that day, with Len Lovat and Donald Bennet making the first ascent of the now classic Number Three Gully Buttress (III), and Malcom Slesser and Norman Tennent adding a direct finish to Cresta (III), the first route on the Little Brenva Face, which Patey, Lovat and Nicol had climbed two days earlier.

No routes the following winter could match Zero in terms of technical difficulty, but there was a healthy level of activity. Jimmy Marshall climbed his first new winter routes on the mountain with Number Two Gully Buttress (III), Italian Climb (III) and Direct Route on Douglas Boulder (IV,4). Ian Clough, a young English climber from RAF Kinloss, explored the Carn Dearg Summit Gullies, climbed the all too obvious Garadh Gully (III), and added Frost Bite (III) to the Little Brenva Face.

1959 came in with a roar with the young Edinburgh pair of Robin Smith and Dick Holt climbing the Tower Face of the Comb (VI,6). Long shrouded in mystery, this demanding mixed route was not repeated for over 25 years, and brought mixed climbing standards on the Ben level with Lochnagar and Tom Patey's hard classics of Eagle Ridge (VI,6 1953) and Parallel Buttress (VI,6 1956). Later in the month, Smith and Holt stunned the Nevis cognoscenti by climbing the first winter route on the Orion Face. The Smith-Holt Route (V,5) was based on the line of The Long Climb, but avoided the Great Slab Rib on the left and finished up Epsilon Chimney above the Basin. Their bold 12-hour ascent was a major step forward in breaking down the psychological barriers of the great unclimbed Nevis walls and faces.

Whilst Smith and Holt were making their ascents in perfect classical style, Clough was adopting a more clinical approach. After a two-day siege of Waterfall Gully (IV,4), he turned his attention to the great prize of Point Five Gully. Partnered by John Alexander, Don Pipes and Robin Shaw, Clough fixed 300m of rope in the gully with an armoury of 60 rock and ice pegs. It took 40 hours of effort spread over six days before the team was eventually successful. The Scots were aghast that the Ben's greatest gully should fall in such a way, but Clough and his team genuinely believed that their approach was justified. Shaw wrote in the Glasgow University MC journal of that year - *'I have no doubt that Point Five will be climbed in less time, but a party will be very lucky to find it in suitable condition to climb in one day.'* He was soon to be proved very wrong!

On the SMC meet two weeks later, activity continued at a frantic pace. Marshall, Patey and Bill Brooker were responsible for first ascents of The Winter Girdle (IV,5), West Face Lower Route (IV,5) and Raeburn's Buttress (IV,4), and Ronnie Sellars and Jerry Smith climbed the delightful Pinnacle Arete (IV,4). Marshall was on a roll, and in February, buoyant from ascents of Smith's Gully (V,5) and 1959 Face Route (V,4) on Creag Meagaidh, he cut his way up Minus Two Gully (V,5) with Dougal Haston and James Stenhouse barely managing to follow. Marshall's outstanding eight-hour lead resulted in the hardest gully climb on the mountain for 15 years.

The climax of the step-cutting era came the following February when Smith and Marshall teamed up for their now legendary week at the C.I.C. Hut. Conditions on the mountain, and the matching of Marshall's skill and experience with Smith's youthful drive, were perfect. They made six outstanding first ascents and repeated Point Five Gully (V,5) in a mere seven hours. Minus Three Gully (IV,5), The Great Chimney (IV,5), Observatory Buttress (V,5) and Pigott's Route (IV,5) are still very much respected today, and Smith's Route on Gardyloo Buttress (V,5) and Orion Direct (V,5) were so advanced that they had to wait over ten years and a revolution in ice climbing technique before they were repeated. In the space of seven days, the standard of Nevis ice climbing had not only overtaken the rest of Scotland, but was now comparable with anywhere else in the world. The Cornuau-Davaille on the North Face of Les Droites (ED1 1955) was the only route of equivalent technical difficulty in the Alps at the time.

Smith's death in the Pamirs in 1962 slowed the pace of development, and the next ten years were characterised by an increased level of rock climbing activity rather than a rise in standards. On Carn Dearg,

Marshall added the elegant rising traverse of The Bullroar (HVS 1961) with Stenhouse, and The Shield Direct (HVS 1962) with George Ritchie. The Creag Dhu team of John McLean, Willie Smith and Willie Gordon climbed the brilliant Torro (E2 1962), and Brian Robertson and Jimmie Graham forced their way through the overlapping slabs to the right of Centurion to give the unlikely King Kong (E2 1964). Several years later, Rab Carrington and Ian Nicolson breached the slabs to the left of Torro to give Cowslip (E2 1970), but although the route looks good from below it is rarely dry and possibly still unrepeated.

Exploration of other cliffs on the mountain resulted in the development of the Central Trident Buttress by several Glasgow-based climbers including Norrie Muir, Stevie Docherty and Ian Nicolson. The best routes here were Steam (HVS 1970) and Metamorphosis (E1 1971). On Number Three Gully Buttress, the Marshall brothers climbed the prominent groove of The Knuckleduster (HVS 1966), Nicolson found the excellent Sioux Wall (HVS 1972), and Ken Crocket and Ian Fulton climbed the delightful Serendipity Variation (HVS 1972) to Minus One Direct.

In winter during the 1960s, nothing could quite match the Smith-Marshall highpoint, but Vanishing Gully (V,5 1961) by Ronnie Marshall and Graham Tiso, and The Curtain (IV,5 1965) by Dave Bathgate and Jock Knight, were later to prove two of the mountain's most popular routes. By 1970 however, the world ice climbing scene was on the brink of change with the development of front-pointing and the 'curved axe revolution'. Mike Geddes, a Scot studying at Cambridge University, was the first to apply seriously the new technique on Ben Nevis, with quick repeats of Smith's Route and Point Five Gully in March 1971. Later that month, terradactyls were used by Hamish MacInnes, Ken Spence and Allen Fyffe on a winter ascent of Astronomy (VI,5). In April, Geddes climbed the prominent icefall of Hadrian's Wall Direct (V,5) and next winter made the long-awaited second ascents of Minus Two Gully and Orion Direct with fellow student Al Rouse. They climbed the latter route with sacks full of their weekend gear so they could rush back down and start the long hitch back to Cambridge that night!

Conditions on the Minus Face during the winter of 1972 were excellent, and several teams used them to good effect. Wagroochimsla (IV,4) by Stevie Docherty and G.Adam was the first route to fall, although Docherty nearly came to grief when his crampon came off as he was pulling over the top and he fell back down the final pitch. A week later Docherty and Norrie Muir added Left-Hand Route (VI,6) on Minus Two Buttress, soon to be joined by a winter ascent of the neighbouring Right-Hand Route (VI,6) by Al Rouse and Rab Carrington. These routes were only slightly steeper than the Smith-Marshall masterpieces of Smith's Route and Orion Direct, but they are more serious with long runouts on thin ice. In a different vein, Dave Knowles and D.Wilson fought their way up the chimneys and vegetation on the technical Route I (V,6) on Carn Dearg.

The 1973 season was quiet with only Boomer's Requiem (V,5) by Con Higgins and Dougie McArthur being of note, but the big event the following year was Minus One Gully (VI,6) by Ken Crocket and Colin Stead. This was the last of the Nevis gullies to be climbed in winter, and had seen many previous attempts which had failed below the great chockstone. Doug Lang and Neil Quinn recorded two excellent routes with Left Edge Route (V,5) on Observatory Buttress, and the outstanding Slav Route (VI,5), which has become one of the great classics on the Orion Face.

The following year Gordon Smith and Terry King just beat Lang and Quinn to the first ascent of Indicator Wall (V,5). The Lang-Quinn ascent differed somewhat from the original line, so it is now recognised as a (slightly harder) route in its own right - Indicator Right-Hand (V,5). In March, D.Kirtley and D.Montgomery climbed the deceptively steep Two-Step Corner (V,5) on Number Three Gully Buttress. It was originally graded IV, and has continued to unnerve leaders ever since! Other important ascents were the difficult Left Edge Route (VI,6) on Gardyloo Buttress by Rab Carrington and Al Rouse, and the fine Harrison's Climb Direct (IV,4) by Ken Crocket and Chris Gilmore.

The pace now began to hot up. In December 1976, Con Higgins and Alan Kimber were quick off the mark with Astral Highway (VI,5), a steep left-hand exit above the Basin on Orion Face. They later climbed the impressive, but rarely repeated Lobby Dancer (VI,6) on the North Wall of Carn Dearg. The route of the winter however was Minus One Buttress (VI,6) by Norrie Muir and Arthur Paul. This superlative line has rarely been in condition since, and was a superbly timed ascent with good snow-ice on the final tower. It had a second ascent a few days later by Jerry Smith and Graham Little, but despite being high on the tick list of many Nevis regulars there have been no further complete repeats. Muir and Paul finished off a good April with the icy corner-line of Rubicon Wall (V,5) on Observatory Buttress.

During the 1978 season, modern winter climbing on Ben Nevis came of age. Excellent conditions prompted a high level of activity which resulted in a series of outstanding face routes. Muir and Paul were first on the scene with Abacus (IV,4) and Antonine Wall (IV,4) on the west flank of Observatory Ridge, and Mike Geddes and Brian Hall squeezed in Sickle (V,5), a fine parallel icefall to the right of Hadrian's Wall Direct, just before New Year. In January, Geddes and Higgins ventured onto the steepest part of Indicator Wall with the serious and sustained Albatross (VII,6), and the following day Muir and Paul climbed the now classic Psychedelic Wall (VI,5) a little to the right. On Gardyloo Buttress, Tut Braithwaite and Paul Moores tip-toed up The Great Glen (VI,5), a bold exercise in thin ice climbing to the right of Smith's Route.

Good conditions persisted throughout February, and competition for the major lines was intense. Geddes and Rouse just beat Gordon Smith to the excellent Route II (V,6), the first winter climb to venture onto the front face of Carn Dearg Buttress. Smith repeated the route with the difficult Direct Start (VI,6) three days later with Ian Sykes. Spurred on by Geddes's interest in the area of blank icy slabs to the left of Point Five Gully, Smith then succeeded on the serious Pointless (VII,6) with Nick Banks after several failed attempts. Geddes returned with Con Higgins at the end of the winter to add a companion route, Galactic Hitchhiker (VI,5), which is now one of the more popular modern thin face routes on the mountain.

British climbers, well practised on Ben Nevis ice, applied their skills with great effect in the Alps and elsewhere throughout the 1970s. Perhaps the best example was the Colton-MacIntyre Route on the North Face of the Grandes Jorasses (ED3 1976). This very narrow couloir, totally Scottish in character and similar to Minus One Gully in technical difficulty, was undoubtedly the hardest ice climb in the Alps at the time. Another example, was the application of Nevis-style thin face climbing to the North Face of the Pelerins (ED2) by Rab Carrington and Al Rouse in February 1975.

By the summer of 1977, no new rock routes had been climbed on the mountain for five years, but the worldwide rise in rock climbing standards arrived with a jolt with the free ascent of Titan's Wall (E3) in June. This spectacular route on the smooth right wall of Carn Dearg Buttress was originally climbed as an aid route by Ian Clough and Hamish MacInnes in 1959. A free ascent had been attempted as early as the 1960s, but the plum fell to Mick Fowler and Phill Thomas who just beat Dave Cuthbertson and Murray Hamilton by a matter of days. Phill Thomas had cleaned the route earlier, but Fowler's on-sight lead of the crucial second pitch was impressive. The other major unclimbed line on Carn Dearg was the great 'Banana Groove' to the right of The Bat corner. Cuthbertson returned the following summer with Willie

Todd and Dougie Mullin, and attempted the route on sight, but moss and lichen forced them out of the groove onto the right wall, resulting in Caligula (E3). A few days later Willie Todd was joined by Ken Johnstone on Adrenalin Rush (E3), a sustained line through the overlaps left of Cowslip.

By 1978, 45 new winter routes had been added to Ben Nevis in the space of eight hectic years. The leading activists were now venturing out of the main gully and corner lines onto thinner ice on the steep faces in between. Their routes were not significantly steeper than anything climbed before, but they demonstrated what was possible if front-point technique was seriously applied to thin face routes. In March 1979, there was a further leap in technical difficulty. On the steep right flank of Carn Dearg Buttress, Mick Fowler and Victor Saunders took advantage of the excellent icy conditions to climb The Shield Direct (VII,7), a stupendous line up a series of soaring chimneys, which combined steep ice with several technical mixed pitches. The following weekend Arthur Paul and Davy Sanderson broke left out of Waterfall Gully to create Gemini (VI,6), a steep ice line based on the summer route Evening Wall. A few days later, Alex MacIntyre and Alan Kimber completed the line by climbing a steep direct start, which avoided Waterfall Gully completely. Also on Carn Dearg, but more mixed in nature, was The Shadow (VII,6), a companion line to Route II climbed by Paul Braithwaite and Dave Pearce. The trend for steep ice continued with Arthur Paul's ascent of Kellett's Route (VI,6 1980) on Gardyloo Buttress, and Mega Route X (VI,6 1982) by John Murphy and Alastair Cain.

By the early 1980s many Ben devotees had ticked their way through the classic Smith and Marshall routes, but there was considerable reticence to try the more recent face climbs. A keen group of climbers based around Glasgow and Strathclyde Universities, including John Murphy, Roger Webb, Robin Clothier, Alastair Cain, Ronnie Bruce and Alan Shand, were responsible for breaking down many of the psychological barriers. It was soon realised that routes such as Astral Highway, Psychedelic Wall and Slav Route were quite reasonable given good conditions. Galactic Hitchhiker only succumbed after John Murphy took a huge fall from the second pitch. He returned the following weekend to find his axes, complete with gloves in the wrist loops, still sticking out of the ice! Other routes however, such as Albatross and Pointless, retained their reputations for long runouts and poor belays, and were left unrepeated for longer. On two occasions, Pointless repelled strong teams when the leaders fell off the crucial third pitch. On one occasion, the long fall onto the belay ripped the anchors, pulling the second to the ground, although fortunately everyone survived to tell the tale!

Carn Dearg has provided the focus for high standard rock-climbing over the past ten years. The Banana Groove was eventually climbed in 1983, after cleaning, by Murray Hamilton and Rab Anderson to give a fine and sustained E4. The same pair also managed to free the initial overhang of Sassenach at E3. The most impressive lead of the 1980s however, was the well named Agrippa (E5 1983) by Pete Whillance, on the left arete of Titan's Wall. Again this route required extensive cleaning, but was a bold lead in very cold and windy weather. Other new routes on Carn Dearg include Willie Todd's fine Boadicea (E4 1989), a sister route to the right of Titan's Wall, and the intricate Red Rag (E2 1991) by Guy Muhlemann and Simon Richardson which wends its way up the grooves and overlaps to the right of Torro. Exploration of other crags on the mountain by Hawthorn, Paul, Muir and Adam resulted in 15 new routes in the summer of 1984 including the fine lines of Last Stand (HVS), The Banshee (VS), The Urchin (E1) and Orient Express (E2). Recent exploration by Con Higgins and Tam McAuley of the steep wall beneath Castle Ridge has yielded Prodigal Boys (HVS 1991) and Camanachd Heroes (E1 1992).

In February 1983, the development of thin winter face routes took a step forward when Dave Cuthbertson and Rudi Kane ventured onto the steep uncharted territory between Albatross and Psychedelic Wall to create Stormy Petrel (VII,6). This bold and committing undertaking has only been repeated once, and tales of long unprotected traverses on thin ice with only psychological belays has put off all subsequent ascents. The following month, Robin Clothier and Alastair Cain climbed the Second Slab Rib above the Basin to give Long Climb Finish (VI,5). Arthur Paul and Doug Hawthorn then made a true winter ascent of the lower part of The Long Climb by climbing the crest of the Great Slab Rib. Paul had made several attempts on this outstanding pitch over a number of years, before finding optimum conditions in April 1983. They finished up the groove system to the right of Astronomy, having climbed Urban Spaceman (VII,6), one of the finest winter routes of the decade.

Mal Duff contributed a string of good winter routes throughout the 1980s including Diana (V,5 1985), Bydand (V,5 1986) and the sensational Ring the Alarm (VI,6 1986), which traverses above the overlaps on Carn Dearg Buttress before finishing up the 'Weep' of Cowslip. His finest contribution however, was the left edge of Observatory Buttress overlooking Point Five Gully. He first attempted the route in February 1984 with Jon Tinker, but after climbing the initial groove they were forced into Point Five to avoid a crucial blank section guarded by an overhang. The climb was now flawed, but they managed to regain the edge higher up. It took Duff several attempts, spread out over the next four years, before he eventually managed to straighten out the line to record Point Blank (VII,7 1988).

The big event of the 1986 winter was Ken Spence and Spider McKenzie's ascent of the much-prized Centurion (VIII,8). They made a planned bivouac before finishing up Route II, to create the most technically sustained undertaking on the mountain. In April the Ben came into excellent condition, and Fowler and Saunders were again first on the scene to make the long-awaited second ascent of Point-less. Several good new routes were added later that month. Of particular note were Riders on the Storm (VI,5) on Indicator Wall by Hawthorn and Euan Todd, The Black Hole (VI,6) on the Minus Face by Fowler and Saunders, and Match Point (VI,6) on Observatory Buttress by Simon Richardson and Ed Hart. All these routes showed that, given the right conditions, there were still new routes to do. Robin Clothier and Chris Cartwright continued to plug gaps the following winters with Tramp (IV,4 1987), Lost the Place (IV,4 1988) and Satanic Verses (V,5 1989). Clothier also added the fine Pinnacle Buttress Direct (V,5 1989) with George Armstrong. Throughout the late 1980s Clothier was the most active winter climber on the mountain, repeating almost all the routes and adding a number of important variations.

Few pure mixed lines have been climbed on Nevis, since the rock does not run to protection as easily as the Cairngorms or Glen Coe. In 1979 Andy Nisbet and Brian Sprunt climbed the summer HVS Central Route on Minus Two Buttress, and although they used some aid, their ascent demonstrated what was possible. More recent examples are John Main and Andy Clarke's Cutlass (VI,7 1989) and The Groove Climb (V,6 1992), Clefthanger (V,6 1985) by Hawthorn and Paul, and the serious Kellett's North Wall Route (VII,7 1991) by Mark Charlton and Martin Burrows-Smith.

Winter activity on Ben Nevis will always focus on climbing ice however, and the active 1993 season showed that there is still scope for more lines when conditions are good. The Shroud (VII,6), the impressive hanging icefall to the left of Harrison's Climb, was a notable coup by Main and Clarke, and Simon Richardson and Roger Everett found The Good Groove (VII,7), an elegant icy mixed line on the headwall of The Comb. In April, Robin Clothier and Jim McGimpsie chased Richardson and John Ashbridge across the serious rising traverse of The Flight of the Condor (VI,5) on Indicator Wall, before being deflected by the imposing Mickey Mouse Finish (VI,6). Visiting French guide Godefroy Perroux roped in Clothier and Bruce Goodlad for an ascent of Le Panthere Rose (VI,6), a companion route to his Upper Cascade (IV,5 1991) on the icy headwall above Raeburn's Easy Route. Perroux then added the prominent icefall of Une Journee Ordinaire (VI,6) to the left of Central Gully in Coire na Ciste, to be swiftly followed by Dave Cuthbertson and Joanna George who climbed the technical Levitation (VI,6) just to the right.

CENTRAL HIGHLANDS

Following completion of the long-awaited West Highland railway in 1895, the SMC held its Easter meet in Fort William. Until then, Scottish mountaineering had focussed on more easily accessible areas such as Skye and the Southern Highlands, and Ben Nevis and its surrounding mountains were largely unexplored. Twenty seven members attended the meet, and attention was not only on Ben Nevis, but the surrounding peaks as well. This appears surprising today, but at that time there were no guidebooks, and climbers had to explore the hills as thoroughly as possible for themselves. It was clear that The Ben held plenty of of opportunities, but how about the surrounding mountains?

Fortunately, Norman Collie had *'spent several seasons exploring the ridges and corries of the district'* and *'provided a perfect encyclopaedia of information regarding possible and impossible routes.'* On a tip-off from Collie therefore, J.Maclay, Willie Naismith and Gilbert Thomson set off early from Spean Bridge bound for the North-East Ridge of Aonach Beag. During the long walk across the peat bogs, the weather closed in and the party mistook the North-East Ridge for the easy north-bounding spur of An Cul Choire on Aonach Mor. Whilst the party were questioning Collie's mountaineering judgement, the skies cleared to reveal their objective to the south. They made a swift descent, completed the ridge in four hours, which was in full winter condition, before returning over the summit of Aonach Mor on their way back to Fort William. William Tough and William Brown repeated the route three days later, and added the East Ridge to Stob Ban the following day with Lionel Hinxman and William Douglas. The meet had been a great success, and made a major impact on the exploration of the area.

It was not surprising, given the exploratory appetite of these Victorian mountaineers, that Coire Ardair on Creag Meagaidh was soon recognised as having enormous potential. Attention initially focussed on the Post Face when in April 1896 the formidable team of Raeburn, Tough and Douglas attempted Centre Post. In thawing conditions they reached the base of the impressive icefall at half-height, but then made a swift retreat when the cornice collapsed. The following day they attempted the edge of Pinnacle Buttress, but left it for a *'more favourable opportunity - or for a more favoured party'*, although they did record an ascent of Easy Gully by way of consolation. Raeburn was eventually successful in climbing the Post Face in the autumn of 1903 with a partial ascent of the Central Pillar, which was gained by a traverse from Centre Post from below its crux pitch. Three years later he climbed the South Pillar with Frank Goggs.

The corrie was then neglected for over 20 years until Jim Bell began to take an interest in the place. As Bell himself explained, he was equally at home on bad rock as good - *'Any fool can climb good rock. It takes craft and cunning to get up vegatatious schist and granite'*. In June 1930, in favourably dry conditions, Bell succeeded where Raeburn had failed, and climbed Edge Route on Pinnacle Buttress with D.Macdonald. This was the beginning of a successful summer campaign spread out over the next seven years which included the complete ascent of Central Pillar and North Post. Without doubt, Bell's most impressive summer contribution was Red Scar Route (Severe 1936) on the front face of Pinnacle Buttress, which he climbed with Sandy Wedderburn. It was later described as *'typical of the very best of Scottish climbing'* - a sentiment which few climbers would share today, but nevertheless it was a bold ascent of a daunting face.

Bell's winter explorations on the crag have the greatest significance today. In April 1934, he made a matter-of-fact ascent of Staghorn Gully (III) on the Post Face, and the following January climbed the South Pipe (III). His finest ascent however was Centre Post (III) with Colin Allan in March 1937. At the foot of the great icefall they traversed right, with Allan in the lead. Techniques were already becoming advanced - *'A new technique was adopted by Allan. With his left hand he secured himself with his ice axe, while his right wielded a small hatchet, a most adaptable step cutter in such a position of precarious balance. It proved equally useful for hammering in belays. Allan's lead was a magnificent piece of work.'*

Although pitches of comparable difficulty had already been climbed on Ben Nevis and elsewhere (Raeburn had led Green Gully (IV,4) some 30 years earlier), Bell's concept of what was possible was visionary. He returned to Centre Post two winters later with an anxious Bill Murray to attempt the great icefall direct. Murray later recounted that Bell *'arrived armed with a big bagful of sawn-off brass curtain rods....Tubular pitons, he had correctly discovered, gave better grip in water-ice. He had ringed their tops and filed their bottoms....My inward dismay at the thought he may want me to lead....was relieved next day when we found insufficient ice in the gully. I had grim forebodings for next winter, when the attempt must be renewed, but was saved by that eleventh hour outbreak of war.'*

Although exploration of Ben Nevis continued throughout the war, little of note was recorded in the Central Highlands until 1946 and 1947 when the long Glen Nevis gullies were climbed. The most impressive of these, Surgeon's Gully (VS), was named after Dr Donald Duff, the father of Scottish mountain rescue, who was also responsible for installing the abseil posts at the head of Coire Leis.

After another gap of nearly 20 years, interest was resumed in Creag Meagaidh when Malcom Slesser and Norman Tennent climbed South Post (III 1956). A three day wait was rewarded by good freeze conditions allowing them to avoid the opening steep pitch by traversing in from the right. Jimmy Marshall first visited the cliff in the summer of 1951, and noted the winter possibilities of the gully lines on the front face of Pinnacle Buttress. He returned with George Ritchie on a fine but windy day in February 1957, to find Robin Smith already at work on what was to become Smith's Gully - *'We sat and jeered, watched him for a spell, comforted by the cataracts of powder thundering on his head, then moved on to traverse into the left-hand gully above the icefall.'* Marshall made a shrewd decision, for although they had a difficult battle with deep powder they were eventually successful on Ritchie's Gully (IV,4), whilst Smith was forced to retreat in the snowy conditions.

Fresh from success on Parallel Gully B (V,5 1958) on Lochnagar, Marshall returned to Meagaidh the following winter, but intense cold precluded any climbing. In February 1959 he was back again with the strong team of Jimmy Stenhouse, Dougal Haston and Graham Tiso. After a heavy snowfall followed by a period of freeze-thaw, conditions were perfect, and the gullies were choked with ice. Whilst Haston and Stenhouse attempted what was later to become Centre Post Direct, Marshall and Tiso cut their way up Smith's Gully (V,5). The following day, Marshall joined forces with Haston and Stenhouse to climb the long and open 1959 Face Route (V,4). Smith's Gully was an outstanding ascent, and comparable in difficulty with Minus Two Gully (V,5) on Ben Nevis which the same trio had climbed two days later. They were considered the hardest gully climbs in Scotland until 1972, when Labyrinth Direct (VI,6) was climbed on Creag an Dubh Loch.

This was the start of the golden years on Meagaidh, with Tom Patey recording many fine routes through the 1960s such as Last Post (V,5), Diadem (V,4) and North Post (V,5). His explorations culminated in the magnificent Crab Crawl (IV,4), a complete girdle traverse of the cliffs. In 1964, the huge icefall of Centre Post Direct (V,5), which had repelled many previous attempts, was climbed by Brian Robertson, Fred Harper and E.Cairns. Throughout the 1960s, the Inner Coire was developed, with Patey being particularly active. The best lines however fell in 1968 and 1969 to Dundee climbers including Neil Quinn, Doug Lang and Graeme Hunter who put up a fine trio of ice routes with The Pumpkin (V,4), The Wand (V,5) and Trespasser Buttress (IV,5). The pace slackened in the early 1970s, although several worthwhile routes were climbed. In 1972 the strong Aberdeen team of Dougie Dinwoodie, Mike Freeman, Brian Lawrie and D.Stuart added Nordwander (IV,4) on Pinnacle Buttress, and in 1975 Lang and Quinn made their final contribution to the cliff with Easter Pillar (IV,4), the first route to venture onto Great Buttress, on the right side of the Post Face.

February 1976 was cold and snowy, and access to the high crags was difficult. Several climbers from the Joint Services Mountain Training Corps (JSMTC) visited the remote, but relatively low-lying Creagan Coire na Cnamh on Meall Garbh, which had been found by Philip Tranter in the early 1960s but had never been developed. Pete Webster and Andy Wielochowski were the most active, recording several fine routes such as Broad Gully (III), The Frozen Vice (IV,4) and Ping Pong (III). The JSMTC also rediscovered the remote Glen Roy crags which had been explored by Klaus Schwartz, Brian Chambers, R.Schipper and J.Mount in 1972. Here, Wielochowski and Dave Nottidge climbed the fine icefall of Fox Trot (V,5). Meall Garbh saw further activity the following winter when Paul Moores overcame the huge chockstones in Central Gully (IV,5), and Huw Davis added several routes, including Little Spider (IV,4).

The most significant event of the 1976 winter was on Meagaidh. Like Raeburn, Bell and Marshall before him, Wielochowski had become fascinated by Pinnacle Buttress, and resolved to climb The Fly, the narrow parallel fault to the right of Smith's Gully on the front face. Initial forays with John Nash resulted in ascents of The White Spider (IV,4) and Vanishing Ledge (IV,5), but the correct combination of conditions, weather and partners eluded him. In March, Wielochowski teamed up with Dave Nottidge, and they were eventually successful in climbing the line from Vanishing Ledge, although they used a fixed rope on the steep first pitch and atrocious weather forced them to climb the upper section in two instalments. It was a determined attempt at an audacious line that would have been one of the hardest ice routes in the country at the time. Wielochowski was clearly disappointed by the style of their ascent, but the harsh comments in the SMCJ could only have rubbed salt into the wound - '....the manner this line was assaulted we find impossible to accept....siege tactics are out of place in Scotland.'

Mick Fowler and Victor Saunders fulfilled Wielochowski's vision in February 1983, by climbing the entire gully from the bottom to give The Fly Direct (VII,6). Fowler, displaying his uncanny knack of being in the right place at the right time, found the gully choked with ice and the bottom pitch complete. Andy Nisbet and G.Harper also took advantage of the great conditions that weekend, by climbing The Midge (VI,5), a line of weakness up the huge wall to the right. On a previous attempt with Brian Sprunt, Nisbet had climbed to within 15m of the top when darkness forced retreat along Appolyon Ledge. The following year, John Sylvester and Kevin Howett completed a fine trio of difficult routes on the front face of The Pinnacle by climbing the prominent icefall of Pinnacle Buttress Direct (VI,5).

The mid 1980s saw a general increase in exploration throughout the Central Highlands. Noel Williams spearheaded the winter development of Stob Ban with Bodice Ripper (IV,5 1984) and Triad (III 1986) and later Roger Webb added the elegant Skyline Rib (IV,4 1987). John Lyall and James Grosset discovered the remote Loch Dubh Crag in the Monadhliath with the fine Wee Team Gully (IV,4). In 1987, Lyall also climbed several routes on the lonely Creag Dhubh crag above Loch Ericht with pride of place going to the impressive icefall of The Hex Factor (V,5). Conditions were good low down in January of that year, and the Newcastle team of Kevin Howett and Alan Moist exploited the cold conditions on Binnein Shuas with Eastern Chimney (IV,5). In February, Roger Everett and Simon Richardson made the long approach to the remote Ben Alder to check out the rumours of vast unexplored corries and crags. Their reward for the 60km of walking that weekend were three routes on separate cliffs, the best being Alderwand (III) and Ice Maiden (V,5). The following year they were joined by Roger Webb, Chris Rice and Colin Grant to add Witchwhite (V,4) and Nightshift (V,4) to Maiden Crag.

Credit for initiating the thorough exploration of Aonach Beag must go to Roger Webb, who in November 1985 persuaded Simon Richardson to take a look at the north face. Conditions were poor, but Whiteout (II) hinted at the future potential. They returned in February 1987 to find the cliff draped in ice, and climbed the gully line of King's Ransom (VI,6). Conscious that they had evaded the main challenge of the crag, they returned mid-week to climb the prominent ice smear of Royal Pardon (VI,6). This gave Webb a testing time when the pins in his axe sheared while he was on the crux moves, and the pick bent flat against the ice! Later that winter Richardson and Roger Everett climbed Raw Egg Buttress (IV,4), a prominent feature on the west face of the mountain. Exploration of the west face continued the following winter with the discovery of Broken Axe Buttress and the fine mixed line of Twinkle (IV,5), while an attempt to climb the true crest of Raw Egg Buttress resulted in the technical Aonach Wall (V,6).

Few high mountain cliffs in the Central Highlands are either steep or clean enough for good quality rock climbing, but the 90m vertical south facing wall of Raw Egg Buttress looked a likely exception. It had been discussed many times, but it was a great surprise when two Glasgow teams independently arrived at the foot of the virgin face early one warm June day in 1988. The honours that day went to Roger Everett and Chris Rice for their on sight leads of the crux pitches of Chandelle (E3) and Pirates (E2). The wall lived up to expectations, and the routes compare favourably with the very best of Scotland's high mountain rock climbs.

Without doubt the snow gullies and couloirs in Coire an Lochain on the east face of Aonach Mor had been played in for many years, but it was not until January 1988, when Roger Everett and Simon Richardson climbed Morwind (III,4), that anything was ever recorded. Conditions were thin, but it provided a pointer for the following poor winter when the corrie was often the only cliff in condition in the area. After climbing several of the obvious gullies, the pair concentrated on the buttresses. Of particular note were Typhoon (IV,4), Grooved Arete (IV,5), Force Ten Buttress (III,4) and the difficult Hurricane Arete (VI,7). Chris Rice and Roger Webb discovered the delightful Hidden Gully (II) and George Armstrong and Sue Richards led a party up the prominent cleft of Temperance Union Blues (III).

Steve Kennedy and Dave Ritchie took over the development of the crag in 1990, recording over a dozen new routes, with the best discoveries being Stirling Bridge (VI,7), The Guardian (IV,5), and Gondola with the Wind (IV,5). With its easy access from the ski gondola, friendly granite and sunny aspect, Coire an Lochain has now become a playground for the middle grade climber, with gully lines such as Left Twin (III 1989) and Jet Stream (IV,4 1989) proving especially popular.

With Aonach Mor rapidly reaching worked-out status, the focus swung back to the more serious schist crags on Aonach Beag. Following up earlier exploration in 1989, Steve Kennedy and Dave Ritchie developed the remote buttress of Stob Coire Bhealach on the east face with Sideslip (IV,4 1991) and Helter Skelter (IV,4 1993). Mixed climbing standards in the Aonachs saw a significant rise in technical difficulty when Richardson and Everett clawed their way up the very technical and forbiddingly steep Salmonella (VII,8 1991). On the icy north face, Robin Clothier and Chris Cartwright succeeded on the short but steep Stand and Deliver (V,5 1989) after Richardson and Webb had failed the day before, and further left, Everett and Richardson eventually found the icicles complete on Camilla (V,5 1993) on their third visit to attempt the route.

Perhaps nothing better illustrates the untapped potential of the Central Highlands than Postman Pat (VII,7) on Creag Meagaidh. This impressive route, which takes the fine groove cutting through Great Buttress above Staghorn Gully, was climbed by Mal Duff and Andy Perkins in February 1991. Long recognised as a last great problem, its hanging icicle start is rumoured to be one of the steepest ice pitches in the country. For such a prominent line to have remained unclimbed for so long on the best known crag in the area more than hints at what is still waiting to be discovered elsewhere. Future generations of climbers are sure to be rewarded as richly as the pioneers of the last hundred years.

Notes on the Use of the Guide

Classification of Routes

Summer

The normal British grading system of Easy, Moderate, Difficult, Very Difficult, Severe, Very Severe (VS), Hard Very Severe (HVS) and Extremely Severe has been used. The Extreme grade is sub-divided into E1, E2, E3, E4, E5, and so on.

Technical grades are given for routes of VS and above where known. Much effort has been made to elicit information from active climbers about routes, some of which will have all the relevant pitches graded, while others will have only the crux pitch so described. The normal range of technical grades expected on routes of the given overall grade are as follows: VS - 4b, 4c, 5a; HVS - 4c, 5a, 5b; E1 - 5a, 5b, 5c; E2 - 5b, 5c, 6a; E3 - 5c, 6a; E4 - 5c, 6a, 6b; E5 - 6a, 6b. Routes with a technical grade at the lower end of the range will be sustained or poorly protected, while those with grades at the upper end of the expected range will have a short and generally well protected crux section.

Although the British system is thought second to none by those who use it, it is known to confuse visitors from abroad. For their benefit, it can be assumed that 5a, 5b, 5c and 6a correspond approximately to the American grades of 5.9, 5.10a/b, 5.10c/d and 5.11a/b respectively. Eurocraggers should note that there is little or no fixed protection on most of the climbs here, and that if they are used to cruising bolted French 6c, they may suffer some distress while attempting the corresponding 6a pitches here, with their sometimes spaced and fiddly protection.

Winter

Winter climbs have been graded using the two-tier system, in which the roman numeral indicates the overall difficulty of the climb and the accompanying arabic numeral represents the technical difficulty of the hardest sections of climbing. Since its introduction in 1991, this sytem has gained widespread acceptance amongst the majority of the leading winter climbers in Scotland, and almost all new climbs reported in the SMC Journal and the specialist magazines are now given two-tier grades. The aim of the two-tier system is to grade modern mixed routes to indicate their high levels of technical difficulty, while taking into consideration the frequently greater seriousness of the older-style ice routes. Two-tier grades were published for the harder climbs in appendices in the preceeding SMC guidebooks to Glen Coe and the Northern Highlands. However, this is the first SMC guidebook to use this system in the main body of the text, and it is necessary to describe its essential elements in some detail.

(i) Nearly all grades up to and including grade IV retain their original overall grades.

(ii) Climbs of grade IV and above (and some of grade III) have two grades, an overall grade in roman numerals, and a technical grade in arabic numerals.

(iii) The overall grade takes into account all factors affecting the difficulty of reaching the top of the climb, including its technical difficulty, seriousness (frequency of protection and reliability of belays) and sustainedness (length of hard sections of climbing and number of hard pitches).

(iv) The technical grade reflects the actual difficulty of the hardest section(s) of climbing, without reference to seriousness. It is not intended to be used as a technical pitch-by-pitch grading. On a climb of overall grade V, a technical grade of 5 indicates relatively straight-forward, steep ice climbing; a technical grade of 6 generally indicates more technical mixed climbing; technical grades of 7 and 8 indicate much more intricate and harder snowed-up rock moves.

(v) The technical grade normally varies by not more than two below or two above the overall grade. Thus V,5 can be taken as an average grade V route of the old system. A higher technical grade than the overall grade would indicate greater technical difficulty, offset by better protection (as frequently found on mixed routes); a lower technical grade would indicate greater seriousness. Thus the system has some parallels with the E-grade system for summer rock climbs.

(vi) The previous artificial ceiling of grade V (and reluctant VI) has been removed, so as to reflect more realistically the differences between the old classic climbs of grade V and the current state-of-the-art routes.

(vii) The overall difficulty is reflected in the overall grade, and just as an E1 5a can be a more serious proposition than an E1 5c, a V,4 is not necessarily easier overall than a V,6. Examples are given in the graded list.

Some degree of variability undoubtedly occurs according to the prevailing conditions. While some climbs will nearly always be possible at close to the given grade, others require special (or even extraordinary) ice build-up, and the grades apply to such favourable situations. At other times these climbs may simply be non-existent. Although the two-tier grading system is new, the grades given to the climbs in this guide book have been decided after extensive consultation.

A complete list of the new grades for all the harder Scottish winter climbs in this and other areas (where information is available) has been published in the 1992 SMC Journal.

Equipment and Style

It is assumed that a good range of modern nuts and camming devices will be carried for the harder climbs, both summer and winter. The summer climbs described in this guide do not require the use of pegs, and their use on new climbs should be extremely sparing; please keep to the Scottish tradition of bold climbs with leader-placed protection. On occasion it might be necessary to use pegs on winter climbs for belays or runners; please make all efforts to find a safe alternative before resorting to pegs, especially on winter ascents of summer climbs (on which pegs would be most unwelcome).

Bolts

After extensive consultation with all interested parties, the Mountaineering Council of Scotland has issued a policy statement on the use of bolts in Scotland. This policy is endorsed by the Publications Sub-Committee of the Scottish Mountaineering Club.

"The MCofS acknowledge that there is a place for bolts in the future development of Scottish climbing. However, to ensure that the highly regarded ethos of, and future development of, traditional climbing (involving the use of leader-placed and second-removed protection) is not threatened, it is felt that the use of bolts should be limited to the production of sport climbs. There should be no retrospective bolting of established climbs for protection or belays, and there should be no minimalist bolting.

The production of sport climbs with bolts is acceptable on natural rock only when all the following conditions have been satisfied:

(1) On low-lying cliffs, provided that such development is not against the wishes of the landowner. Bolts are inappropriate on mountain cliffs and sea-cliffs.

(2) On routes where natural protection is absent or is inadequate for the repeated falls that such routes necessitate.

(3) Where the rock is steep and provides climbs of a high order of difficulty, at the forefront of developments of the day.

(4) Where there is no historical or local anti-bolt ethic.

Concerning quarried rock, it is felt that any future development should be constrained only by points (2) and (4) above.

Finally, it is felt that bolts should be located to ensure minimum visual impact and should be placed according to current best practices.

It is intended that these principles are not seen as simply restrictive rules, but as a guide to promote the positive development of Scottish climbing, where sports climbing, rather than becoming a substitute for traditional climbing, grows alongside it."

In practice, these guidelines indicate that the use of bolts is inappropriate on all of the cliffs and crags described in this guidebook. It goes without saying that the use of bolts on winter climbs is entirely unacceptable.

Terminology
Left and right refer to a climber facing the cliff or facing downhill in descent. In cases of potential ambiguity a compass direction is also given. Pegs and other fixed gear are for protection only, except where specifically stated that they are for direct aid. Do not assume that they will either be in place or in a safe state of repair.

Pitch Lengths
Pitch lengths are given in metres, to the nearest 5m (except for very short distances). Ropes of 45m should be adequate for the majority or routes, though 50m ropes are useful (and sometimes essential) in winter.

Diagrams
Where climbs have been numbered, this indicates that there is a diagram depicting the line of the climb, and the numbers in the text correspond to the numbers on the diagrams. Climbs on illustrated cliffs that do not have numbers are not shown on the diagram, but they will be found in the relevant order (left to right, or right to left) in relation to the numbered climbs on either side. For routes that have been climbed in both summer and winter, it is the summer line that is shown, except where the winter line is specified by a marked (W) in the legend.

Recommended Routes

No list of recommended climbs is given, instead a star grading system for quality has been used. Three stars indicates a route of the highest quality. If a route has no star this does not necessarily mean that it is poor, it may also indicate that insufficient is known about that route properly to assess its quality. Every effort has been made to make the star ratings consistent, but the great variety of climbing in the area means that comparisons from crag to crag are difficult. For example, a long and serious ice route on Ben Nevis will give a very different experience to a short mixed route on Aonach Mor.

First Ascensionists

The year of first ascent, where known, is given in the text. The full date and pioneers are listed in chronological order, area by area, at the back of the guide. Further relevant details of the first and subsequent ascents where known are also listed in this section. Whether the route was climbed in summer or winter conditions is indicated by an S or W at the left end of each line. The abbreviations used in this list are standard and self-explanatory.

Maps and other sources of information.

Place names and map references have in general been taken from the OS 1:50000 Landranger Series maps. The following Ordnance Survey maps cover the area of this guide:

1:50000 Landranger Sheet 41 (Mamores, Ben Nevis, Aonachs and Meall Garbh).
1:50000 Landranger Sheet 34 (Creag Meagaidh and Binnein Shuas)
1:50000 Landranger Sheet 35 (Monadh Liath)
1:50000 Landranger Sheet 42 (Ben Alder)
1:25000 Mountainmaster Sheet 32 (Mamores, Ben Nevis and Aonachs)

Occasionally information in the 1:25000 series has been used, but these maps are not necessary to navigate to and from the climbs. The 1:250000 OS Routemaster Series maps of Scotland are very useful to put into context the whole of the area described in this guide. The meanings and pronunciations of local place names can be found in *Scottish Hill and Mountain Names* by Peter Drummond, published by the Scottish Mountaineering Trust (1991).

Mountain Rescue

In case of an accident requiring rescue or medical attention, contact the Police. If a victim has to be left, be sure that the exact location is known before leaving the site of the accident, and that if possible the nature of any injuries can be reported. Try to leave someone with the victim, who should in any case be made as comfortable and as sheltered as the injuries allow. Some knowledge of rudimentary first aid is a desirable thing for a climber to have, so it is wise to consult one of the large number of suitable books on mountaineering first aid, rescue techniques and rescue helicopters.

Avalanches

Avalanche conditions are common in many of the areas covered by this guide, and climbers have been caught in them. To minimise the risk of exposure to avalanche it is sensible to avoid icefalls and gullies during periods of thaw and immediately following a heavy snowfall. The buttress climbs can provide alternatives in these conditions.

Avalanches occur most often following heavy snowfall or during thaw. All gullies and most slopes between 22 and 60 degrees should then be suspect. The greater the amount of fresh snow, the higher the risk. Fresh snow can include wind-blown deposits, so that stormy weather can maintain an avalanche risk for prolonged spells. Past and present weather conditions are very important. Climbers preparing for winter climbing should familiarise themselves with basic avalanche theory, using one or more of several useful books available on the subject. In the field, much can be learned by digging a hole and examing the snow profile, looking especially for different layers of snow with different degrees of bonding. Slab avalanches, for example, will be caused when a weakly cohesive layer of snow collapses underfoot. Such a weak layer is usually hidden under a firmer layer, hence its great potential as a killer. The top layer will often break into slabby fragments, the first warning.

If avalanched, try and either jump free or anchor yourself for as long as possible, depending on circumstances. If swept down protect your access to oxygen by 'swimming' to stay on the surface, by keeping your mouth closed, and by preserving a space in front of your face if buried. Wet snow avalanches harden rapidly on settling, so try and break free if possible at this point. If trapped try to stay calm, which will reduce oxygen demand.

If a witness to an avalanche it is vital to start a search immediately, given it is safe to do so. Victims will often be alive at first, but their chances of survival lessen rapidly if buried. Unless severely injured, some 80% may live if found immediately, but only 10% after a three-hour delay. Mark the burial sight if known, listen for any sound, look for any visual clue, search until help arrives if possible. Again, a working knowledge of first aid may save a life, as many victims may have stopped breathing.

SKI DESCENTS *by Graham Dudley*

This section lists ski descents of graded climbs that are known to have been accomplished in Ben Nevis area. Any ski mountaineer who is contemplating a ski descent will no doubt be fully aware of the seriousness of such an activity. The following points should be always be carefully considered:

1. Acquire perfect technique and skill on safe slopes with good runouts. The scarp wall of a Nevis gully is no place for experimentation.
2. Develop a thorough understanding of snow from the point of view of avalanche risk and skiability.
3. Unless absolutely sure of the snow quality, climb the gully first to assess its condition.
4. Be aware of any climbers and avoid skiing above them as much as possible.
5. Be flexible, keep options open; the descent does not have to be skied the whole way. Remember the gully should only be a straight-forward snow climb in ascent, so keep an ice axe handy and revert to climbing mode as required.

There are no written rules regarding the claim of a particular descent. However for complete personal satisfaction the gully should be descended by making ski turns with minimal side-slipping or side-stepping. Clearly any abseiling or down-climbing will also degrade the quality of the descent.

BEN NEVIS

Skiing on Ben Nevis can be a magnificent experience. With good snow cover, the run back down into Glen Nevis via the Red Burn gives the longest continually steep descent in Scotland. The gullies on the north-east face are very popular with climbers, and this clearly provides problems for the skier with steps and lumps interrupting the slope. Also the cornices and scarp walls on Nevis tend to be more impressive than elsewhere, to the skier's disadvantage. The descents mentioned below are those that are known to have been done, so the list does not claim to be complete. The average angles of the slopes have been estimated from the 1:10000 Ben Nevis map.

Bob-Run
This needs a good fill to cover a short ice pitch low down. The cornice is usually mild.

Cresta
An unsatisfactory descent has been made of most of the central snow gully with a traverse to Bob-Run to finish. The upper section appears improbable without a long abseil.

Good Friday Climb
This has been skied by a Chamonix guide for a TV film. A long abseil was required to gain entry.

Gardyloo Gully
A very good fill is required to cover the main pitch. Only the lower section beneath a very steep scarp wall and cornice is known to have been skied (55 degrees).

Tower Gully
This gully is often well corniced, and has a serious feel in the upper section when traversing under Gardyloo Buttress. An uncontrolled fall might be fatal. (48 degrees).

Number Two Gully
Only the lower section beneath the scarp wall has been skied (47 degrees).

Garadh Gully
With a good fill to cover the short lower pitches, this gully can be relatively straightforward with no entry difficulties.

Number Three and Number Four gullies
Both these gullies give a good introduction to ski descents, but the cornices are often prohibitive (36-41 degrees).

Number Five Gully

A fine long descent sustained at a reasonable angle. Moonlight Gully can give an alternative to the lower section if there is enough snow (39 degrees).

South Castle and North Castle gullies

These two finely situated gullies need a good fill to cover various short pitches, particularly in the lower section of South Castle Gully. Stable snow conditions essential as this is one of the most avalanche-prone areas on the mountain (40 degrees).

AONACH MOR

An easily accessible ski mountain, with the top of Coire an Lochan reached from the top ski tow of Nevis Range in 5 minutes.

Easy Gully

This wide gully provides the only obvious descent direct into the corrie, but large cornices can sometimes be a problem.

CREAG MEAGAIDH

This is a popular mountain with ski mountaineers, and the Coire Ardair gullies can also give some excellent sport. In general there are fewer cornice problems than on Ben Nevis, but if anything, the area is more prone to avalanche.

Raeburn's Gully

The tight upper section can be avoided by the more open slopes on the right. A fine descent (45 degrees).

Easy Gully

This gully is of moderate angle and is a good introduction to gully skiing. It has plenty of width and good atmosphere (35-38 degrees).

Cinderella

A tight and technical descent centrally positioned in the Inner Corrie (47 degrees).

Amenities

Accommodation

Camping

There are several roadside campsites in Glen Nevis and alongside the A86 Spean Bridge to Newtonmore road which have traditionally been used without any restriction, although it should be remembered that camping and lighting fires in the Scottish countryside without permission is an offence. This traditional freedom to camp should be treated as a privilege and respected by considerate behaviour for local inhabitants, other campers, tourists and the wildlife which inhabits the countryside. Most of all one should respect the environment. The Highlands of Scotland are a beautiful place; please help to keep them that way by leaving no trace of your passing.

Unfortunately, a small minority of campers create problems for those who do behave with due care and consideration. The area covered by this guide has become extremely popular with a large number of outdoor enthusiasts, and as a result the environment can only suffer under the considerable strain. Rough camping, although free, has one major drawback in that there are no sanitary facilities. For this reason it is strongly recommended that where possible an official campsite should be used. These are as follows:

Glen Nevis Campsite, Fort William (Map Ref 125 722); Open mid-March to mid-October. (Tel: 0397 702191)

Lochy Caravan and Camping Park, Fort William (Map Ref 126 764); Open all year. (Tel: 0397 706172)

Invercoe Caravans, Glen Coe (Map Ref 098 594); Open Easter to mid-October. (Tel: 08552 210)

Forestry Commission Site, Glen Coe (Map Ref 112 577); Open April to September. (Tel 08552 397)

Red Squirrel Campsite (Map Ref 574 119); Open all year. (Tel: 08552 256)

Corran Caravans and Camping, Onich (Map Ref 021 632); Open all year. (Tel: 08553 208)

Bunroy Holiday Park, Roy Bridge (Map Ref 274 806); Open mid-March to October. (Tel: 0397 712332)

Bunkhouses

Since the skiing area at Aonach Mor opened, the pressure on winter accommodation in the Fort William area has increased considerably. A catalogue of accommodation can be obtained from the tourist information Office in Fort William (Tel: 0397 703781). Many climbers base themselves in Glen Coe and make a daily foray to Ben Nevis. Convenient bunkhouses (open all year) are:

Ben Nevis and Aonachs Area

Glen Nevis Youth Hostel, Fort William (Tel: 0397 702336)
Calluna, Fort William (Tel: 0397 700451)
Achintee Farm Bunkhouse, Fort William (Tel: 0397 702240)
Fort William Backpackers, Fort William (Tel 0397 700711)
Snowgoose, Corpach (Tel: 0397 772467)
Inchree Bunkhouse, Onich (Tel: 08553 287)
Mamore Lodge, Kinlochleven (Tel 08554 213)
West Highland Lodge, Kinlochleven (Tel 08554 471/396)
Glen Coe Youth Hostel, Glencoe (Tel: 08552 219)
Glen Coe Bunkhouse, Glencoe (Tel: 08552 256)
Glen Coe Outdoor Centre (Tel: 08552 350)

Creag Meagaidh and Ben Alder Area

Aite Cruinnichidh, Roy Bridge (Tel 0397 712315)
Grey Corrie Lodge, Roy Bridge (Tel: 0397 712236)
Craigellachie Lodge, Newtonmore (Tel: 0540 673360)
Glen Feshie Hostel, Kingussie (Tel 0540 651323)

Climbers' Huts

There are eight climber's huts in the area available for booking to members of clubs affiliated to the MCofS or the BMC. Addresses and phone numbers of current hut custodians can be obtained through your club or by contacting the MCofS, who issue an annually revised hut list covering all the huts in Scotland. The huts of interest to the users of this guide are as follows:

Ben Nevis and Aonachs Area

C.I.C. Hut (Map Ref 168 722) SMC Hut; on the west bank of the Allt a'Mhuilinn, under the north face of Ben Nevis. Altitude 680m.

Steall Hut (Map Ref 177 684) JMCS Hut; on the south bank of the River Nevis, reached by 3km walk through Steall Gorge from the car park at the head of Glen Nevis.

Alex MacIntyre Memorial Hut (Map Ref 046 612) BMC and MCofS Hut; on the A82 roadside adjacent to the Creag Mhor Hotel, Onich.

Manse Barn (Map Ref 033 613) Lomond MC Hut; on the A82 roadside adjacent to the Onich Hotel.

Creag Meagaidh and Ben Alder Area

Jock's Spot (Map Ref 667 947) JMCS Hut; on the north side of the A86 Laggan to Newtonmore road, 2km west of Creag Dubh.

Milehouse (Map Ref 839 043) LSCC Hut; Kincraig, 2km from the village on the road to Insh.

Mill Cottage (Map Ref 844 047) MCofS Hut; Feshiebridge, 500 metres towards Kincraig.

Raeburn Hut (Map Ref 636 909) SMC Hut; 8km from Dalwhinnie and 5km from Laggan, on the A889.

Climbing Shops

Fort William is well serviced by climbing shops. All hire some winter climbing gear.

Ellis Brigham, Fort William; next to the railway station.

Nevisport, Fort William; at the east end of High Street.

West Coast, Fort William; near the west end of High Street.

Glen Coe Guides and Gear, Glen Coe village.

Fort William Services

There is a large Safeway supermarket on the An-Aird development at the east end of town. It is open until 8pm during the week and 6pm at weekends. For those coming off the hill very late, the Spar shop at Claggan, on the road leading to the start of the Tourist Track up Ben Nevis (Map Ref 117 743), is open until 11pm every night. The railway station, Leisure Centre and Marco's An-Aird all have showers available for public use. Petrol is obtainable around the clock from two garages outside town on the Inverness road.

Fort William Wet Weather Alternatives

Leisure Centre (Tel: 0397 703881); a few hundred metres from the town centre on the Inverness road (Map Ref 109 742). It has a climbing wall, swimming pool, fitness suite and squash courts. Some equipment can be hired.

Marco's An-Aird (Tel: 0397 700707); a new leisure facility with concert hall, snooker tables and ten pin bowling.

Cinema (Tel: 0397 705095); in the Information Centre building on the High Street.

Pubs; the most popular climber's bars are the Nevis Bank, near the entrance to Glen Nevis, and the Nevisport Bar.

Skiing at Nevis Range, Aonach Mor (Tel: 0397 705825); equipment can be hired from Nevisport and Ellis Brigham, or from the Nevis Range base station.

Avalanche and Weather Forecasts

All the climbing shops display mountain forecasts, either inside the shops or in their windows. Notice boards giving weather details and avalanche reports are placed at strategic locations, such as the start of the Ben Nevis approach from the golf course, and at the Nevis Range base station on Aonach Mor. The Scotsman newspaper publishes an excellent forecast for the Lochaber area, and a detailed mountain forecast. On Sunday, they are given in the Scotland on Sunday newspaper along with a forecast for the following week. Avalanche predictions are given alongside the weather forecasts in winter. If all else fails, it may be necessary to resort to the expensive telephone forecasts:

Mountain Call: 0898 500 441 for the west (442 for the east).
Climbline: 0891 654 669 for the west (668 for the east). This forecast also includes the Scottish Avalanche Service prediction.
Scottish Avalanche Service (mid-December to mid-April): 0463 7131921. This is an excellent report, with the Lochaber predictions based on observations on Ben Nevis and Aonach Mor. A brief forecast for the following day is also given. The call is charged at standard rates.

Ben Nevis

Ben Nevis

INTRODUCTION

Ben Nevis (1344m) is a mountain of superlatives. As the highest massif in the British Isles, with the tallest and most extensive cliffs, it attracts some of the most severe winter weather. This unique combination produces probably the best snow and ice climbing of its type in the world, matched during the short summer by a host of rock climbs of excellent quality. Long recognised for its outstanding climbing, Ben Nevis is steeped in history, a crucible where influential climbers of the past and present have forced new standards and techniques.

The sheer number of quality winter climbs, in all grades, is unequalled anywhere else in Scotland. Some have gained justified international recognition. Proximity to the western seaboard results in large and frequent variations in temperature which, coupled with high precipitation, leaves even the steepest faces plastered white. Deep thaw followed by rapid freeze transforms the hoar to climbable neve, with runnels of white ice in the grooves and cracks. Such conditions allow exhilarating climbing on very steep ground, and the consequent lack of easily accessible protection adds bite to the experience.

The Ben provides a wide variation in style of climbing. There are the snow and ice gully climbs, some straightforward, others complicated by bulges or long pitches on hard ice. These contrast to the face routes — long, bold and exposed, much dependent on conditions and exact choice of line. Then there are the icefalls, some sweeping down unlikely walls of almost vertical rock. Finally there are the buttresses, not only the classic ridges (which are without equal in Britain), but also mixed climbs in the modern idiom, snowed up rock routes with high technical difficulty. This feast of opportunities provides climbs of all styles at all grades, but if you just feel like a walk, the traverse of the Carn Mor Dearg Arete gives a stupendous view of it all.

Although Ben Nevis is rightly famous for its winter climbing potential, it is also an important venue for rock climbing. The short summer season reveals huge crags of solid rock. The classic ridges provide extremely enjoyable expeditions in the lower grades, while the steep walls of Carn Dearg Buttress hold some of the most sought-after high mountain E-grade rock climbs in Scotland. Perhaps less well known are the increasing number of excellent climbs on less prominent crags, hidden in the corners of the extensive corries. It is a measure of the scale of the place that some of these 'smaller' crags are considerably larger than many a high mountain crag elsewhere.

To climb on the northern flank of Ben Nevis is to experience the best mountaineering that Britain has to offer. In winter it can be a serious place, especially in poor weather. Technical proficiency, good navigation, fitness and strength are all required to enjoy the experience to the full. A seasoned mountaineer once commented that 'if you can climb safely on Ben Nevis, you can climb safely anywhere else in the world'. An apt note of respect with which to describe our highest mountain.

SEASONAL CONSIDERATIONS

Records show that it can snow at any time of year on the summit plateau of Ben Nevis. However, good winter climbing conditions usually appear only from around early January onwards. Unlike the Cairngorms or some of the crags on the nearby Aonachs, there is insufficient turf on the volcanic rocks to provide much early season climbing. Before there is a reasonable build up of snow, even the easy gullies may have steep pitches on unconsolidated snow. However, the ridges can give enjoyable struggles on rocks plastered with powder as early as October. After a few good snow falls and periods of freeze-thaw, conditions become reliable. It is pertinent that the altitude of the foot of the Orion Face is higher than the summits of many other Scottish mountains, and that the whole of Indicator Wall and Gardyloo Buttress lie above 1200m. Once the major ice lines have formed, they are very resilient to thaw and some routes may remain in good condition until late April. In contrast, some of the ice smear routes, such as Gemini on Carn Dearg Buttress, require prolonged periods of frost to form, and they can collapse with alarming rapidity during a thaw. Some of the harder buttress routes require an exceptional plating of snow-ice on the underlying blank slabs, and such conditions may occur only in occasional winters.

The summer season is short. The snowfields of winter are slow to disappear, and they can form huge bergschrunds guarding the foot of the Minus and Orion Faces, and make descent of the gullies (particularly Number Five Gully) very precarious in rock boots. However, the big routes of Carn Dearg Buttress may be climbable (in a dry spring) from May onwards. The best months are probably June and July, because the climate becomes wetter later in the summer. The season continues into September, but by then the freezing level may already be hovering close to the summit.

TOPOGRAPHY

Ben Nevis is situated 7 km east-south-east of Fort William and has three subsidiary tops: Carn Dearg (1221m Map Ref 158 719), the highest point on the north-west spur, lies 1.2 km from the summit; Carn Dearg SW (1020m Map Ref 155 701) is the highest point on the south-west spur and lies 1.6 km from the summit; Meall an t-Suidhe (711m Map Ref 139 729) overlooks Fort William and lower Glen Nevis, and lies 3.2 km north-west of the summit. The main summit and subsidiary tops form the massive bulk of the mountain, topped by an extensive and wild plateau.

The western and southern aspects of the mountain, overlooking Glen Nevis, consist of steep grass slopes cut by long gullies. There are a few excellent exposures of rock, but they are short. By contrast, the north-east face falls abruptly from the plateau to present a complex and magnificent series of cliffs overlooking the upper part of the Allt a'Mhuilinn glen. It is the most impressive and continuous mountain cliff in the British Isles, being over 3km in extent and reaching a height of 500m. The scale is so huge that it can be difficult to appreciate, particularly on first acquaintance.

Approaching the north-east face by the Allt a'Mhuilinn, one first passes the huge broken North Wall of Castle Ridge, and then Castle Ridge itself which projects low down into the glen. Between Castle Ridge and the Great Buttress of Carn Dearg lies Castle Corrie which contains the buttress of The Castle, well demarcated by the North and South Castle gullies. Raeburn's Buttress lies left of The Castle and above is the flake-like Cousin's Buttress, which joins the North Wall of Carn Dearg Buttress. To the left, less steep rocks extend to the impressive front face of Carn Dearg Buttress.

Beyond Carn Dearg, scree slopes lead up to Number Five Gully, followed by the complex of Moonlight and the Trident buttresses which extend to Number Four Gully. Left of this is the castellated Creag Coire na Ciste and Number Three Gully, which is the arbitrary dividing line between Carn Dearg and Ben Nevis proper. Here, the cliffs turn through a wide bend until they face almost due north. Adjoining Number Three Gully is Number Three Gully Buttress, then the jagged buttress of The Comb, Number Two Gully and numerous minor buttresses which lead round to Tower Ridge. This projects north-east, far into the glen to terminate in the Douglas Boulder. This section of crags from the Great Buttress of Carn Dearg to Tower Ridge encloses Coire na Ciste with its tiny green lochan set amid splendid mountain scenery.

East of Tower Ridge lies the huge Observatory Gully, which branches in its upper third to form Gardyloo Gully on the left, Tower Gully on the right, and Gardyloo Buttress in between. Further left lies Observatory Buttress, then Point Five Gully and Observatory Ridge. This is followed by Zero Gully, which divides Observatory Ridge from the great mass of North-East Buttress which projects far into the glen to end in a rocky platform, not unlike the Douglas Boulder in formation. Beyond lies Coire Leis and the Little Brenva Face, which is bounded to the south-east by the crescent-shaped Carn Mor Dearg Arete. The climbs are described from left to right, starting with the Little Brenva Face.

The summit plateau is a large area with comparatively gentle slopes. Deeply incut by the gullies of the north face, it can be a confusing place in poor weather. The south-facing hillside below the summit itself is steep and dotted with crags and smooth slabs, falling 800m into the remote Coire Giubhsachan. The slopes descending north-east into Glen Nevis comprise the biggest and steepest hillside in Britain. It is a dangerous place, rent by deep gullies. The only easy ground to the plateau is taken by the Tourist Track, sandwiched between the the treacherous Five Finger Gully and the avalanche-prone Red Burn. The north-west slopes of Carn Dearg are strewn with huge boulders, scree and other small crags, which produce unpleasant going. These features conspire to make descent from the climbs a tricky business in all but the most perfect weather. It is essential to follow the detailed descriptions which follow.

A good idea of the configuration of the mountain can be gained by following the edge of the plateau. From the top of Castle Ridge to the top of Carn Dearg is about 400m. It is a further 800m from its cairn to the top of Number Three Gully, sloping gently down, then up and down. Thereafter, about the same distance and a rise of 150m leads to the summit of Ben Nevis. The Observatory lies a few metres from the cairn, just behind the top of Observatory Buttress, about midway between the tops of Tower Ridge and North-East Buttress, which are respectively 250 and 300m distant.

The Arete leading to Carn Mor Dearg leaves Ben Nevis about 300m beyond the top of North-East Buttress, gradually curving round to the left, until its direction is due north leading to the summit of Carn Mor Dearg. Magnificent views of the Ben Nevis cliffs may be obtained from this peak and from the continuation ridge to Carn Beag Dearg. On the south-east side of the Carn Mor Dearg Arete, Coire Giubhsachan leads down to Steall in Upper Glen Nevis.

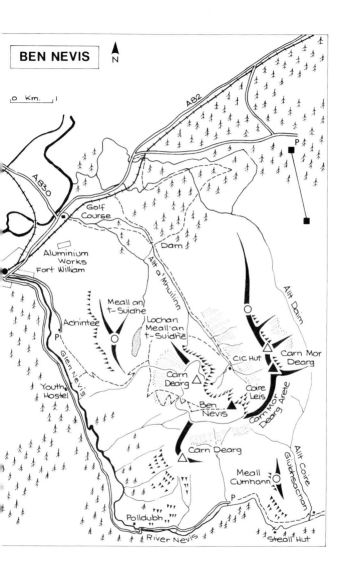

APPROACHES

The ordinary route to the summit is the Tourist Track which follows the pony track built for the old Observatory. Leave Fort William by the north (A82), cross the Nevis bridge and take the Glen Nevis road on the right to reach Achintee Farm (Map Ref 126 730) where the pony track begins. The track climbs steeply to the col between Meall an t-Suidhe and Carn Dearg. From the Glen Nevis Youth Hostel (Map Ref 128 718), cross the River Nevis by a foot bridge, then continue up the steep slope of Meall an t-Suidhe to join the pony track near the first zigzag on this section. Rising above Lochan Meall an t-Suidhe (also known as the Halfway Lochan) at 600m, the path turns back across the distinctive Red Burn to ascend a series of zigzags up the scree slopes and gain the plateau near the top of Number Three Gully.

On the final slopes, the track passes close to the cliff edge where some of the gullies cut far into the plateau. It is essential to keep a watchful eye open, particularly in mist, or in winter when large cornices project far over the edge.

Approaches to the climbs on the north-east face of Ben Nevis all aim initially for the C.I.C. Hut (Map Ref 167 723), which is situated at 700m below the Douglas Boulder. This hut is privately owned by the SMC, and it is normally full throughout the winter season. Bookings must be made well in advance through the hut custodian. There has been some friction in the past between hut occupants and other visitors to the mountain, but it should be obvious that such a small hut cannot be open to all, so please be considerate. There are four possible approaches to the Hut from the valley:

1. Glen Nevis Approach

From Achintee Farm, or the Glen Nevis Youth Hostel, follow the Tourist Track to the broad col between Meall an t-Suidhe and Carn Dearg. Leave the track above Lochan Meall an t-Suidhe, and continue northwards, keeping almost level to the far slopes of the col. Here a path can be found which, after descending 30m, bears north-east to contour under the North Wall of Carn Dearg. A large boulder, known as the Lunching Stone, lies to the left of the path. The Hut is located some way beyond at a height of 670m, close to the Allt a'Mhuilinn, just above its junction with the burn from Lochan na Ciste (2 to 2¹/₂ hours). This is not the best approach after heavy snowfall as contouring down into the glen can be difficult with drifting snow, and the path is threatened by avalanches from Castle Corrie.

2. Distillery Approach

Start from the distillery near Victoria Bridge on the A82 (Map Ref 124 756). Walk through the premises of the distillery and cross the main railway line, where a well-defined track leads to the line of a disused narrow gauge railway. Follow this to the left for a few hundred metres, cross a small bridge and turn diagonally left up the slope on the right to reach the Allt a'Mhuilinn at a small dam (Map Ref 147 751). Cross the burn and follow the boggy track on the left to reach the Hut. Excellent views of the cliffs are obtained on this approach (1½ to 2 hours).

3. Golf Club Approach

Parking is available at the Golf Club car park (Map Ref 136 762), but please respect this privilege. Walk under the main railway line by a small bridge, then go south-east across the golf course, taking care to keep off the greens, to reach the disused narrow gauge railway. Above, steep and muddy slopes on the left side of the burn lead to the dam where the distillery approach comes in from the right. Continue up the left bank of the Allt a'Mhuilinn to the Hut (1½ to 2 hours).

4. Approach via the Carn Mor Dearg Arete

Although this approach is not a very logical way to reach the C.I.C. Hut, it is useful for North-East Buttress and the routes on the Little Brenva Face. From the car park at the end of the public road up Glen Nevis gain the Bealach Cumhann by following the true right bank of the small stream which descends from the col. The best starting point is where it cuts the upper minor path through the Glen Nevis gorge. From the col, follow the ridge in a north-westerly direction until it merges with easier angled slopes, then bear slightly right to gain the Carn Mor Dearg Arete at the Abseil Point Sign (Map Ref 171 710). Descend into Coire Leis by the easiest line, or traverse left from the col to reach the left end of the Little Brenva Face (2 to 2½ hours).

It is also possible to reach the Carn Mor Dearg Arete by climbing the steep right bank of the Allt Coire Eaghainn, known as the Water-slide. Once over the lip of the corrie, head up right (north-east) to join the previous route on the ridge about 200m below the Carn Mor Dearg Arete (2 to 2½ hours). Care should be taken in icy conditions, as there have been many accidents on the slabs above the Waterslide. It is not a route for mountain walkers.

5. Approach from Steall

The best approach from the Steall Hut is to gain the Bealach Cumhann from Glen Nevis as described above. Alternatively, continue along Glen Nevis to the ruins of Old Steall (Map Ref 187 688) and take the west branch of the Allt Coire Giubhsachan to gain the Carn Mor Dearg Arete. This approach can be difficult in icy conditions due to the great area of slabs below the Arete.

From the C.I.C. Hut, the approach to Coire Leis continues up the valley on a faint path, while Observatory Gully and Tower Ridge are reached by heading diagonally up the hillside. Coire na Ciste is approached by heading over the domed rock east of the Hut, then negotiating a short vegetated wall at the foot of the main corrie. The approach to the butresses in the region of Number Five Gully and Carn Dearg Buttress starts up towards Coire na Ciste, then heads diagonally right below the short vegetated wall. Castle Ridge, Castle Corrie and the North Wall of Carn Dearg are all easily reached from the foot of Carn Dearg Buttress. It may take over an hour to reach the foot of some routes from the C.I.C. Hut, and longer for Gardyloo Buttress and Indicator Wall, which are 500m above the hut.

After a heavy snow fall, the slopes of Observatory Gully and the upper part of Coire na Ciste may be dangerously avalanche-prone, so the snow should be carefully monitored in such conditions. An equal hazard is when hard neve covers the mountain. It is never too early to put on crampons — a long slide down even the seemingly innocuous slopes of Observatory Gully can prove fatal.

DESCENTS

The summit plateau of Ben Nevis is surrounded on nearly all sides by steep and difficult ground. It is a serious place, especially in winter, and many accidents have occurred in descent. It should be remembered that conditions may dictate descending a different route from that originally planned, and it is strongly advised that the following descent routes are studied carefully before leaving the valley. The summit of Ben Nevis in a gale and a whiteout is no place to learn how to navigate, and every member of a party climbing on the mountain should carry a map and compass and know how to use them. The most useful map is the O.S. Outdoor Leisure 32, Mountainmaster 1:25000, which has an enlarged 1:10000 detailed plan of the summit plateau. A detailed map of the summit plateau and the descent routes is shown opposite and at the back of this guidebook.

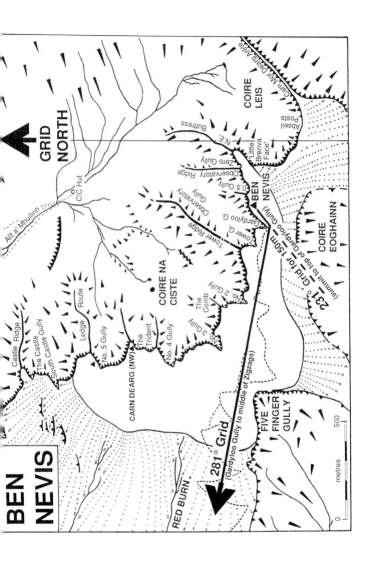

In a hard winter the summit cairn and triangulation point can be completely buried by snow. However, the ruined Observatory a few metres from the summit is an unmistakable landmark, and it is topped by a survival shelter which can be used in an emergency. There are two other emergency shelters on the mountain, one on the plateau at Carn Dearg (Map Ref 158 719), and the other in Coire Leis (Map Ref 173 713). Neither are much use in winter, as they are very difficult to locate and are normally very badly snowed up. If at all possible, descend the mountain, rather than waste time finding and digging out these shelters.

1. The Red Burn
This is the safest and easiest descent. From the summit follow a bearing of 231 degrees grid for 150m to a point just left of Gardyloo Gully, then continue downhill on a bearing of 281 degrees grid for 800m to reach the Tourist Track and the Red Burn area. Continue down an easy slope for about 1km, then turn north towards Lochan Meall an t-Suidhe. From here either descend the Tourist Track to Glen Nevis, or contour round into the Allt a'Mhuilinn as for the distillery approach. It is essential to follow the bearings exactly, as there have been many accidents on this route in the vicinity of Five Finger Gully, when parties have headed towards Glen Nevis too early. The exact line of the Red Burn itself should be avoided, as it can avalanche.

If completing a climb away from the summit area, it is safest to follow the plateau rim to the metal indicator post at the top of Number Four Gully (described below). From here a bearing of 270 degrees grid leads to the Tourist Track and the Red Burn.

2. Number Four Gully
This descent is commonly used by those returning to the C.I.C. Hut or the Allt a'Mhuilinn. Follow the line of the plateau, keeping clear of the cornices, and giving the deeply incut Gardyloo and Tower Gullies a wide berth, to reach the top of Number Four Gully which is marked by a metal indicator post (Map Ref 158 717). Descend this to Coire na Ciste. Sometimes the cornice is impassable, but it is often possible to gain the gully by descending steeper ground to the north. If all else fails, descend by the Red Burn (270 degrees grid from the top of Number Four Gully) and contour round into the Allt a'Mhuilinn from Lochan Meall an t-Suidhe.

3. Carn Mor Dearg Arete

Although this descent is the fastest means of losing height from the summit, it should only be used with care. There have been many fatalities to parties who have strayed too far north (left) of the summit, and for those unfamiliar with the route it is not recommended in bad visibility.

From the summit follow a bearing of 134 degrees grid. The ground is flat for the first 100m, and then steepens abruptly. There are several short posts on this section which should be kept to the left (north-east). After 200m of descent a slight col is reached on the left which lies about 500m from the summit.

At this point is a metal sign (Map Ref 171 710) with information relating to the Abseil Posts. Only two of these now remain, and it is best to descend the 150m Grade I slope, to the left of the post as one looks downhill, which leads down into Coire Leis. There have been many accidents on this slope, as it catches the sun so the snow is often extremely icy. This descent should be avoided in windslab conditions after a period of heavy snowfall and high winds.

COIRE LEIS

North-East Buttress, the first of the great ridges of Ben Nevis, extends east-north-east from near the summit cairn, and divides Coire Leis from Observatory Gully.

Coire Leis lies at the head of the Allt a'Mhuilinn, under the crescent-shaped Carn Mor Dearg Arete, the well-defined ridge extending from Carn Mor Dearg to Ben Nevis. Access to the Arete from Coire Leis is by its south-west slopes, over scree or snow. In winter, considerable icing can occur here, and a line of abseil posts have been erected to assist the descent into the corrie. Their usefulness is now doubtful, and only two remain. It is normally better to descend the slope to the left of the posts, looking downhill. The cornice may be large, but it is usually avoidable. There is a small emergency shelter on the floor of the corrie at Map Ref 173 714. It is often covered by snow in winter, so in an emergency it would be preferable to head for the C.I.C. Hut.

Beyond the line of the abseil posts, the rocks steepen into the east flank of North-East Buttress, named The Little Brenva Face due to its open alpine character. The lower rocks of the front face of North-East

Buttress form a subsidiary buttress topped by the First Platform, a large grassy easement. Above this, the crest of the buttress rises in a great sweep to the summit plateau. The right (north-western) flank of the buttress extends to Zero Gully over the magnificent Minus and Orion Faces, an area of slabs and gullies, encompassing some of the best climbing in the British Isles.

THE LITTLE BRENVA FACE

This is solely a winter climbing area. The climbs are not technically hard, but they are generally long and, if visibility is poor, route-finding may be difficult. Most routes are open to much variation, but there are few easy passages through the headwall, and the lines converge on these. The face is exposed to the sun, and while this may make the prospect of climbing here more pleasant, it increases the risk of falling ice and avalanche.

Final Buttress   55m   III
Climb an icy gully in the centre of the short buttress at the left end of the face.

1   Bob-Run   120m   II *   (1959)
The gully right of Final Buttress is the easiest route on the face and often banked up with snow. Climb easy-angled ice for 30m, then continue up snow to the bifurcation (30m). Either fork can be taken. Each contains a short ice pitch, then finish up snow.

2   Moonwalk   260m   IV,3 **   (1973)
An interesting route up the open face right of Bob-Run. Start just right of a small rocky spur (about 10 metres left of Cresta) below a short ice pitch. Climb this and continue up the snow slope above to the foot of an ice pitch formed by a rock corner (100m). Climb this (spike runners) to a snow slope (45m), then move up to a steep ice wall (45m). Climb this for 15m, then continue up an ice groove to another snowfield. Cross this trending right and belay below a steep rock wall. Traverse horizontally right below the wall until a steep rocky arete leads to the summit snow slopes.

THE LITTLE BRENVA FACE

1 Bob-Run
2 Moonwalk
3 Cresta
4 Slalom
5 Frost Bite
6 Route Major
7 North-East Buttress
m Mantrap
p First Platform

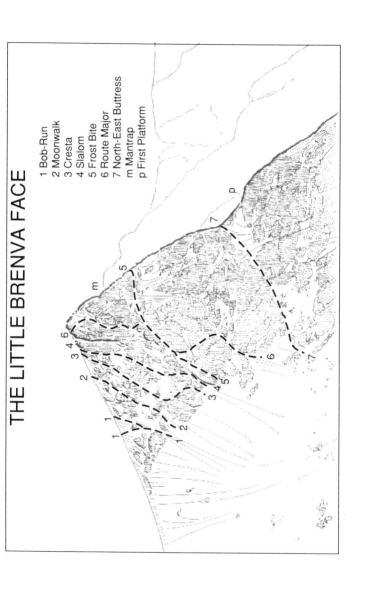

3 Cresta 275m III *** (1957)

This popular route is a climb of great character, and was the original route on the face. It follows a hanging snow gully which in its lower reaches ends at a rocky spur after 90m. Start well right of this spur and climb a left-slanting ice shelf for 75m to gain a small gully which runs up the right side of the rocky spur. Continue up the snow gully above for 185m to a large ice pitch, traverse right across steep rocks for 30m, then break through to easy ground above.

Variation Start: 90m II (1959)

Follow Moonwalk for a pitch, then traverse right across a snow shelf to the foot of the main snow gully.

Direct Finish: 60m IV,4 (1957)

Climbing straight up through the exit cliffs.

4 Slalom 275m III * (1959)

Start from a snow bay to the right of Cresta and follow a shallow gully on the left. Climb up towards a rocky spur, making occasional traverses to avoid rock walls. Below the spur traverse 30 metres left to an easy snow slope which leads to the final rocks overlooking the top of the Cresta gully. Climb these to easier ground and the top.

5 Frost Bite 275m III * (1958)

Starting from the snow bay right of Slalom, climb a steep snow and ice groove to a large snowfield. Follow this for 120m to beneath a rocky spur. Traverse up right to the crest of a ridge under the steepest part of the spur. Descend on the other side to the bed of a gully, and climb this rightwards for 30m. Follow the shallow gully to the left and climb an ice pitch (30m), then continue up iced slabs on the right for 30m to reach the crest of North-East Buttress just below the Mantrap.

6 Route Major 300m IV,3 *** (1969)

A fine and sustained mountaineering route with difficult route-finding. The winter line approximates to a poor summer route, **The Eastern Climb** (300m Severe 1935). Start slightly left of the approach ramp to North-East Buttress, and climb mixed ground to join Frost Bite after the large snowfield. Follow Frost Bite towards the rocky spur, then stay left of the spur and follow a left-slanting gangway, broken by an awkward corner, into a big snow bay. Break out to snow shelves on the right, and follow these horizontally left for a short distance to reach a groove which leads to the upper slopes.

NORTH-EAST BUTTRESS

7 North-East Buttress 300m Very Difficult *** (1892)

One of the easier classics on the mountain, sure to be enjoyed by all who climb it. Start by traversing below the rocks of the lower section of the buttress, until a broad ledge can be followed rightwards across the face to the crest of the ridge. This leads to the first level section of the buttress, the First Platform. This point can be reached more enjoyably by an ascent of one of the routes below the First Platform, such as Raeburn's Arete. Now follow the narrow ridge to a steepening, and turn this by a shallow gully slanting up left. Trend right by short chimneys and walls to gain the Second Platform, a sloping shelf on the crest of the ridge. Above, the ridge is narrower and well defined, and it presents no real obstacle until a smooth overhanging wall is reached. This is turned on the right by a corner with large steps, or it can be climbed directly by working from left to right along a ledge until a bulge can be climbed on good holds. A short distance higher is the infamous Mantrap. Although this is only a short step on the ridge, it is the most difficult pitch on the route. It can be turned on either side, but a direct ascent is recommended as both variations are inferior. Beyond the Mantrap is the '40ft corner', which is climbed directly or can be turned on the left, to enter a small gully which leads to easier rocks above the corner. Reach the summit plateau above without further difficulty.

A number of variations have been climbed on the ridge. From just above the First Platform it is possible to traverse onto the right wall of the buttress, regaining the crest by a series of slabs and grooves (75m Very Difficult 1929). It is also possible to climb the steep section of the ridge above the First Platform directly (60m Very Difficult 1930). The Mantrap can be avoided on the right by following the Tough-Brown Variant which descends onto the right wall of the buttress, then crosses slabs to gain a gully which leads up to the foot of the '40ft corner' (20m Difficult 1895).

Winter: 300m IV,4 *** (1896)

One of the finest mountaineering expeditions in the country. Depending on conditions, all degrees of difficulty may be found, with success in the balance until past the Mantrap. The start of the climb proper can

NORTH-EAST BUTTRESS TO GARDYLOO BUTTRESS

8   Newbigging's 80 Minute Route
8a Newbigging's Route, Far Right Variation
9   Raeburn's Arete
10 Green Hollow Route
11 Bayonet Route
12 Ruddy Rocks
13 Green and Napier's Route
14 Slingsby's Chimney
17 Platforms Rib
18 Minus Three Gully
19 Left-Hand Route
21 Right-Hand Route
23 Minus Two Gully
24 Minus One Direct
25 Minus One Gully
26 Astronomy
29 The Long Climb
30 Orion Direct

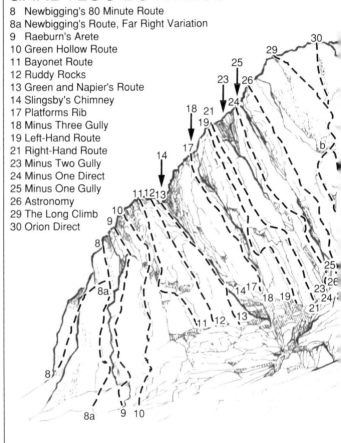

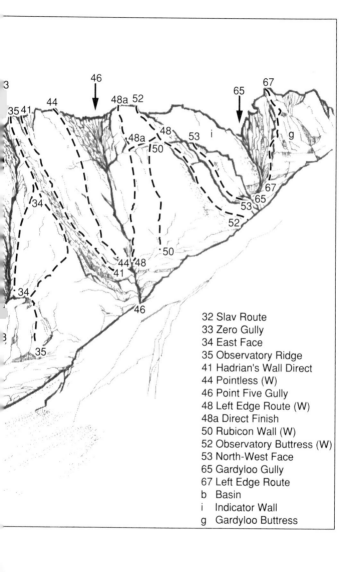

32 Slav Route
33 Zero Gully
34 East Face
35 Observatory Ridge
41 Hadrian's Wall Direct
44 Pointless (W)
46 Point Five Gully
48 Left Edge Route (W)
48a Direct Finish
50 Rubicon Wall (W)
52 Observatory Buttress (W)
53 North-West Face
65 Gardyloo Gully
67 Left Edge Route
b Basin
i Indicator Wall
g Gardyloo Buttress

be reached by the traverse to the First Platform from Coire Leis, or by an ascent of Slingsby's Chimney. Both the original line or that via Slingsby's Chimney are on steep snow to the First Platform. After this, the route takes the easier of the summer lines. From the First Platform follow the easy ridge to a steepening of the buttress. Turn this by a shallow gully slanting up to the left, then trend right and left by steps and grooves to reach a snowfield on the left side of the ridge (90m). This is the Second Platform. Climb the snowfield easily to its top, where the way is barred by an overhanging wall. Turn this on the right by a corner and large step, and follow the ridge above to the notorious Mantrap. This can be extremely exposed and awkward, but it is short and well protected. Climb the '40ft corner' which lies directly above, (or avoid it on the left by a small gully) to reach the summit snows. The Mantrap can be avoided by taking the Tough-Brown Variant on the right flank of the buttress, by stepping down and moving into a groove which leads up to the foot of the '40ft corner'.

Below the First Platform is a subsidiary 150m buttress. The front face of the buttress lies opposite the slopes of Carn Mor Dearg, with a large steep section right of centre. The slabby right-hand face consists of very friendly rock, and faces down the Allt a'Mhuilinn. It is defined at its right-hand side by Slingsby's Chimney, the messy gully leading up to the First Platform. The rock climbs on the right-hand face include some of the finest lower grade routes on the mountain, and there is scope for additional routes on the front face. Most of the summer routes have been climbed in winter, but they are only rarely in good condition. The easiest descent is to reverse the initial right-slanting ledge taken by North-East Buttress.

8 Newbigging's 80 Minute Route   230m   IV,4   (1967)

About 45m down to the right of the start of the broad easy ledge leading to the First Platform on North-East Buttress, a series of raking grooves and ledges lead up rightwards beneath a steep triangular wall. Climb the rake on mixed snow and ice (100m) to the first step, and turn it on the left by a large groove (20m). Continue up the groove above to a narrow chimney which leads to easier ground (40m). Continue up this to the top (70m). The original summer route is poor and messy (200m Very Difficult 1902), and is not recommended. In summer, it is best to take the Far Right Variation which is essentially a distinct route in its own right, and is described as such later.

Orient Express   90m   E2 *   (1984)
This route takes the slabby left-rising ramp close to the left edge of
the steep part of the buttress. Scramble up to some blocks at the start
of a rising traverse leading up to the slab.
1. 45m 5c   The rising traverse leads to a good belay, but poor stance,
on the slab.
2. 45m 5a   Continue up the slab to finish.

Steam Train   100m   HVS   (1984)
The main feature of this route is the large corner in the middle of the
face. Scramble up to the base of some short grooves leading into the
main corner.
1. 40m 5a   Climb the initial grooves, stepping right at the top into the
line of the main corner.
2. 30m 5a   Continue up the corner to its top.
3. 30m   Easier climbing leads to a ledge. Traverse off to finish.

   The Ramp (150m Very Difficult 1984) traverses the face from right
to left below the previous route.

   The final two routes on the front face of the buttress are variations
to Newbigging's 80 Minute route. The first of these, the **Right-Hand
Variation** (200m Severe 1938), begins about halfway between the
start of the original route and the right edge of the buttress. It goes first
left, then right to join the great groove on the right-hand side of the
face. It is of poor quality. The second variation is a better and more
interesting climb.

8a   Newbigging's Route, Far Right Variation   (1938)
     230m   Very Difficult **
The best line hereabouts and really a distinct route in its own right
rather than just a variation. The overhang on pitch two, and the corner
above, can be climbed direct (40m Severe 1945). Start at the foot of
the great corner at the right-hand side of the front face of the buttress.
1. 15m   Climb a slab and move into the corner to a thread belay.
2. 25m   Continue up the slab, pass an overhang by grooves on the
left, then climb a series of ribs to a belay.
3. 45m   Follow the grooves above.
4. 45m   Continue in the groove line to a belay on more open ground.
Easier ground now leads up and left to the First Platform.

Winter: 230m   IV,4 **   (1972)
The natural winter line up the front of the lower buttress, but unfortunately it is only rarely in condition. Difficulties are confined to the first half of the route, which takes thinly iced corners and slabby grooves.

The following routes lie on the clean slabby face looking down the Allt a'Mhuilinn. Most dry fairly rapidly after rain.

9   Raeburn's Arete   230m   Severe ***   (1902)
The arete formed by the north and east faces of the buttress provides one of the cleanest Severes on The Ben. A superb route.
1. 20m   Start at the lowest rocks directly under the arete. Climb up to a black overhang, turn this on the right, and reach a grass ledge and belay.
2. 35m   Follow the arete above to a stance.
3. 40m   Traverse right for 6 metres, then climb up to regain the arete at the earliest opportunity.
4 to 6. 135m   Follow the arete, with minor deviations, to the First Platform.
1931 Variation: 45m   Severe *   (1931)
After turning the initial overhang, ascend directly from the ledge by delicate slabby grooves to rejoin the original route.
1949 Variation: 55m   Severe *   (1949)
Start just right of the 1931 Variation. Follow a crack to a niche with a chockstone floor, and climb a delicate 6m slab leading left to a big ledge on the original route.
Winter: 235m   IV,5 ***   (1986)
An excellent winter climb, unfortunately only rarely in condition. Start left of the arete. Traverse right below the initial roof and climb a deep groove to a stance (45m). Climb up and slightly right by grooves until a left traverse below the overhangs leads to a block belay on the edge of the arete (100m). Climb the arete (now easier), to the First Platform (90m).

10   Green Hollow Route   215m   Very Difficult   (1933)
A rather grassy route, but not unpleasant.
1. 20m   From the lowest point of the rocks, work diagonally up and right by easy slabs to a grass ledge.
2. 35m   Take a crack on the right, then traverse right to a grass platform. Traverse up from the right end of the platform by slabs to gain a groove leading to a small overhang.

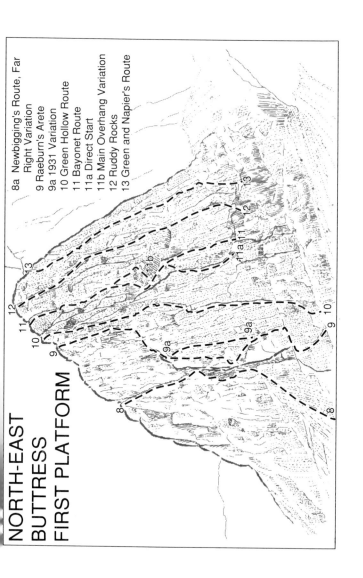

NORTH-EAST
BUTTRESS
FIRST PLATFORM

8a Newbigging's Route, Far
   Right Variation
9 Raeburn's Arete
9a 1931 Variation
10 Green Hollow Route
11 Bayonet Route
11a Direct Start
11b Main Overhang Variation
12 Ruddy Rocks
13 Green and Napier's Route

3. 20m   Climb a crack to the left of the overhang, traverse right, and belay on top of the overhang.
4. 50m   Continue up the cracks above to a belay.
5. 20m   Move up and right by a slab and groove. Exit the groove on the left to reach a parallel groove and belay.
6. 25m   Climb the groove to an overhang and exit right to the Green Hollow (a large grassy bay).
7. 45m   Climb up the bay for 25m and leave it on the left to reach the arete. Continue easily by the crest to reach the First Platform.
Winter: 215m   IV,4 *   (1965)
Follow the slabs and grooves as for the summer route to reach the snow-filled Green Hollow. From its top, climb an iced slab to gain the final arete, and follow this with little difficulty to the First Platform.

11   Bayonet Route   185m   Very Difficult **   (1935)
One of the most enjoyable climbs of its grade on the mountain. A combination of the original line and the two variations is recommended. Start from a large grass platform which lies about midway between Raeburn's Arete and the foot of Slingsby's Chimney.
1. 45m   Climb a rib of rough rock trending slightly left for 20m to a grass niche. Traverse left across a rib, and continue up a grass groove to a belay.
2. 20m   Move left onto the rib and climb to below the left edge of the main overhang.
3. 25m   Gain the rib on the left, and follow it until a right traverse leads into a grassy bay.
4. 35m   Take the rib on the right of the bay to a belay.
5. 20m   Continue up the rib in the same line.
6. 40m   Climb a corner, exit on the left just above a prominent square-cut overhang, then continue by easier rock for 25m to the crest of the buttress.
Direct Start: 35m   Severe **   (1959)
Climb the obvious corner from the left end of the large grass platform, to join the original route below the overhang.
Main Overhang Variation: 35m   Hard Severe 4b **   (1943)
A bold and committing pitch which has caused the occasional quiet thought! From the grass groove of the original route, climb a slab to a point below a V-notch in the main overhang. Reach this by cracks and exit on the right. Trend left above the overhang to join the original route after 30m.

Winter: 185m   III   (1982)
In winter the Direct Start forms into a steep icy groove. Climb this, then follow the original line, but avoid the final part of the rib by a traverse onto the left arete.

12   Ruddy Rocks   180m   Very Difficult *   (1935)
Start a metre or so to the right of Bayonet Route. Above and to the left is a large overhang, defined on its right by twin chimney-cracks.
1. 35m   Climb directly above the ledge to reach the cracks.
2. 45m   Continue, mainly by the left crack, to grooves which lead to easier ground.
3. 30m   Continue in the same line to a small black overhang.
4. 20m   Turn the overhang on the right by a chimney, using a smooth slab on the right wall.
5. 50m   Easier climbing now leads to the First Platform.
Winter: 180m   IV,4   (1967)
Approach by steep snow, then climb the grooves, which hold snow and ice well. A sustained route, especially over the lower 100m.

Rain Trip   180m   Severe *   (1978)
This route climbs good rock to the right of Ruddy Rocks.
1. 40m   Start just right of Ruddy Rocks and make a series of mantelshelves to gain a thin grass ledge. Climb the black wall above, turning an overhang on the right. Flake belays on the right.
2. 20m   Go up left into a corner and climb to a stance.
3. 45m   Climb ribs trending left to a huge flake, then move up and left to a bay.
4. 40m   Climb past a spike to the roof above, step left to flakes, and continue to a steep headwall. Flake belay on the right.
5. 35m   Climb the overlap above, then follow the corner, finishing by a crack.
Winter: 180m   IV,4   (1987)
Follow the summer line throughout, taking a series of snow and ice-filled grooves.

13   Green and Napier's Route   150m   Difficult   (1895)
Another grassy but pleasant route. Start 30 metres left of Slingsby's Chimney. Climb difficult slabby rocks, trending slightly right, to grass ledges (15m). Continue more easily by a series of short walls and corners. Considerable variation is possible.

Raeburn's 18 Minute Route   135m   Moderate   (1901)
Follow the series of short walls and corners immediately to the left of
Slingsby's Chimney, starting about 7m left of the gully bed. One of the
easiest routes to the First Platform, and a convenient descent for
competent parties.
Winter: II   (1952)
Take the easiest line of grooves and ledges to the First Platform. Under
heavy snow cover much of the climb can bank out.

14   Slingsby's Chimney   125m   II   (1950)
The obvious gully bounding the right side of the subsidiary buttress is
a Moderate climb (1895) of no merit and poor belays in summer. The
Chockstone Variation (45m Very Difficult 1904) takes a more direct
line above a chockstone at 80m by following a line of mossy cracks
slightly left of centre. In winter the lower gully gives a straightforward
ascent on steep snow. The easiest line trends left where the gully fans
out. If the top section is not snow-covered, it will provide a sustained
mixed pitch (Grade III). The route is often climbed as an alternative
start to North-East Buttress, and if combined with descent by the
North-East Buttress approach ledge, it provides an easy outing for a
short day.

OBSERVATORY GULLY

Contained within this broad, corrie-like gully are some of the finest and
most famous winter climbs in Scotland.

THE MINUS FACE

The Minus Face is the impressive wall of slabby buttresses and long
gullies between Slingsby's Chimney on the left and Minus One Gully
on the right. Minus Three Buttress is the shortest buttress immediately
right of Slingsby's Chimney, and is flanked on its right by Minus Three
Gully, which has an overhanging right wall. Minus Two Buttress is
easily identified by the huge undercut nose at about one-third height,
and the gully to the right is Minus Two Gully. Minus One Buttress is
the slim buttress between Minus Two Gully and the deeply-cut Minus
One Gully.
   The Minus Face provides summer and winter climbs of considerable
quality and length. The summer climbs on Minus Three Buttress tend
to be of a lesser quality than those on the rest of the face. All the routes

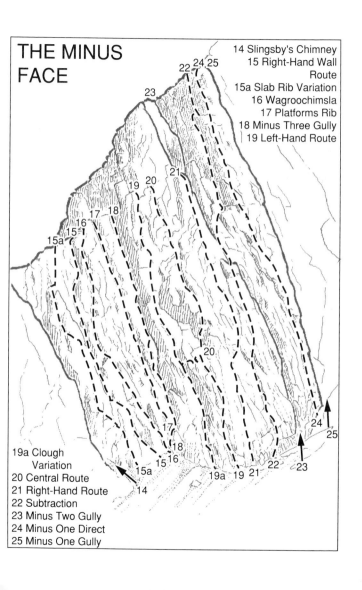

THE MINUS FACE

14 Slingsby's Chimney
15 Right-Hand Wall
Route
15a Slab Rib Variation
16 Wagroochimsla
17 Platforms Rib
18 Minus Three Gully
19 Left-Hand Route

19a Clough
Variation
20 Central Route
21 Right-Hand Route
22 Subtraction
23 Minus Two Gully
24 Minus One Direct
25 Minus One Gully

finish on North-East Buttress, which can be descended or followed to the summit as desired. In summer, the routes require around two to three days to dry after prolonged rain, and after a winter of heavy snow there can be occasional bergschrund problems.

MINUS THREE BUTTRESS

15   Right-Hand Wall Route   150m   IV,5   (1972)
Start below the chimney line immediately right of Slingsby's Chimney. Follow the initial groove to a cave where the way is barred. Traverse briefly left into an icy groove, then regain the natural line above. Climb the final pitch on the left (as for the Slab Rib Variation). In summer, the route is vegetated and often wet (150m Difficult 1929).

15a   Slab Rib Variation   150m   IV,5 *   (1982)
This route climbs the rib immediately right of Slingsby's Chimney; it is a distinct climb in its own right. Under powder or unconsolidated snow it provides a good hard climb. In summer, it is cleaner and slightly better than the original line (150m Difficult 1935).

16   Wagroochimsla   150m   VS   (1964)
Reasonably good climbing, but a bit vegetated and dirty. The route follows the crest of the broad rib between Right-Hand Wall Route and Platforms Rib. Start below a small left-slanting slab to the left of a dirty loose fault.
1. 35m 4b   Climb the slab to a short overhung corner, which leads to easier ground. Belay well above.
2. 40m 4b   Continue up and left into the large corner, and climb it to an exit on the right. Belay above and right of a grassy bay.
3. 45m   Climb up and slightly right by grooves and slabs to a belay below and left of a large raised crest.
4. 30m   Gain the crest of North-East Buttress via a slab.
Winter: 150m   IV,5   (1972)
Follow the summer line throughout. On the first ascent a sling was used for aid on the overhung corner. The climb lacks seriousness as escapes can be made onto adjacent routes at various points.

17   Platforms Rib   130m   Very Difficult   (1934)
Start at the foot of Minus Three Gully.
1. 25m   Climb the bed of the gully for a short distance, then move onto the rib on the left and follow this by a shallow groove to a belay.

2. 20m   Continue by the rib to below a steep wall.

3. 15m   Climb the left edge of the wall to regain the grooves above, then move up to a belay.

4 and 5. 70m   Follow the line of grooves and chimneys above to reach the crest of the North-East Buttress between the First and Second Platforms.

Winter: 130m   IV,4 *   (1959)

Start just left of Minus Three Gully and climb snow trending left (crux) to a short iced wall. Climb this, and continue by a series of grooves to the crest of North-East Buttress.

18   Minus Three Gully   150m   IV,4 ***   (1960)

The shallow gully close under the left flank of Minus Two Buttress is one of the best gully climbs of its grade on the mountain. The right wall is overhung, but it is possible to escape to the left at several points to more broken ground on Platforms Rib. It comes into condition less readily than Minus Two and Minus One gullies. In summer it is wet and loose and not recommended (150m VS 1964).

1. 30m   From the base of the gully climb mixed snow and ice to a deep cave.

2. 25m   Exit by a short icicle on the left to gain a groove leading to a stance.

3. 40m   Climb the groove above, with a short difficult wall at 25m, and continue up snow to a belay.

4. 15m   Climb the ice pitch above to easier mixed ground.

5. 40m   Mixed climbing leads to the crest of North-East Buttress.

MINUS TWO BUTTRESS

19   Left-Hand Route   275m   VS **   (1944)

An excellent route. The original line follows the prominent cracks splitting the raised crest on the front face, then traverses across the top of the corner-groove on the left side of the buttress, and climbs the superb-looking slab at about one-third height. While providing fine climbing, the slab is unfortunately slightly messy and out of character with the best pitch of the route. There are two variations: the first follows the great corner-groove on the left of the crest (usually wet); the second takes the edge of the buttress overlooking Minus Three Gully. This is the recommended route, giving sustained climbing in a magnificent situation.

1 and 2. 65m 4a   Climb the cracks which split the front of the raised crest of the buttress to a ledge at the foot of a slab which lies left of some stepped roofs.

3. 10m 4b   The crux pitch. From the left end of the ledge, descend a slab then traverse left to a second slab which is climbed on small holds to a belay. The belay can also be reached by a direct ascent of the slabs above the ledge (4c).

4. 45m 4b   Climb the slab above, keeping close to its left edge, until it is possible to reach a rib on the right and a belay. A memorable pitch.

5 to 8. 155m   Climb easier and more broken ground to the crest of North-East Buttress (better to the left).

Clough Variation: 60m   VS *   (1963)
The huge groove to the right of Minus Three Gully gives a fine start to the route, but unfortunately it is often wet. Start at the foot of a V-groove below the main corner. Climb this and continue up the corner, turning the overhang on the right, to join the original line below its crux.

Left Edge Variation: 80m   VS ***   (1988)
The edge of the buttress overlooking Minus Three Gully gives excellent climbing, in keeping with the best on the original line. Start at the foot of the V-groove of the Clough Variation.

1. 30m 4b   Move out onto the left rib and climb left via slabs and grooves to a flake belay in a niche on the edge of the buttress.

2. 40m 4c   Descend to the right for a short distance, then move up and right and climb a bulging groove. Continue up a further groove on the very edge of the buttress to reach a superb stance below an imposing wall.

3. 10m 4b   Turn the wall on the left, then move up right to join the original line above its crux.

Winter: 275m   VI,6 ***   (1972)
A fine winter line up thinly iced slabs, which require a delicate touch. Follow the summer route, starting with the Clough Variation.

20   Central Route   275m   HVS *   (1960)

Little more than a direct variation to Left-Hand Route, but a worthwhile climb nevertheless. Start below the prominent cracks on the raised crest on the front face of the buttress.

1 and 2. 60m 4a   Climb the cracks to reach the nose of the raking belt of overhangs.

3. 40m 5a   Traverse right and climb the nose by a thin crack to a slab. Turn the overhang above on the left, and continue to easier climbing.

4 to 8. 175m   Continue to the crest of North-East Buttress.

Winter: 275m   VI,7   (1979)
A difficult exercise in technical mixed climbing, and probably unrepeated. Follow the summer line to the nose, and climb the thin crack (one nut and one peg for aid). Turn the overhang above on the right (one peg for tension) to reach the crest immediately above.

21   Right-Hand Route   275m   VS **   (1944)
A slightly harder partner to Left-Hand Route, following the line of cracks just right of the well defined right-facing corner bounding Central Route on its right.
1. 10m   Climb cracks to a belay in the corner.
2. 40m 4b   Continue delicately by the slab or cracks to a small stance and belay.
3. 40m 4b   Climb the steepening wall above for a metre or so, then traverse 4 metres right. Surmount a bulge, then traverse left to a groove and climb this to a belay.
4. 20m   Continue to easier ground.
5 to 8. 165m   A choice of lines leads the crest of North-East Buttress.
Winter: 275m   VI,6 **   (1972)
A worthwhile route which deserves more ascents. Start at the foot of the prominent right-facing corner. Climb iced slabs up the corner, then make a difficult exit via a short steep corner to gain the easier upper section of the buttress. Continue by slabs and grooves to the left of Minus Two Gully to the crest of North-East Buttress.

22   Subtraction   275m   E2 **   (1959)
Unjustifiably neglected, this fierce climb sees little traffic. Start about 10 metres right of Right-Hand Route.
1. 35m   Climb the well defined groove to a belay below the leftward trending overhanging continuation of the groove.
2. 25m 5b   From the rib on the right surmount the overhang above, and climb up to a belay.
3. 40m   Climb the arete above to a belay under a corner.
4. 40m   Continue by the corner to reach Minus Two Gully and a belay.
5. 30m   Cross the gully and climb up right on Minus One Buttress to the second obvious groove. Climb this to a belay on a grass ledge on the right wall.
6. 45m 5c   Climb the overhanging groove and continue to a belay.
7 and 8. 60m   Easier climbing leads to North-East Buttress.

Minus Two Buttress   275m   V,5 **   (1974)

In good conditions the obvious corner-gully line midway between Right-Hand Route and Minus Two Gully forms a fine icefall.

1. 50m   Climb iced slabs, then move up right to enter an open book corner which leads to a ledge and belay.

2. 50m   Continue up the corner to its end on a snow crest.

3. 45m   Traverse left across a snow ramp to enter an icy gully.

4 to 6. 130m   Climb the gully, finishing by a choice of lines to reach North-East Buttress.

23   Minus Two Gully   275m   V,5 ***   (1959)

A magnificent and classic climb, the finest of the Nevis gullies. In summer the route is often wet and rarely climbed (275m Severe 1950).

1. 45m   Climb steep snow and ice to an overhang. Belay on the right.

2. 50m   Turn the overhang by traversing left to enter the main chimney line, then follow this with less difficulty to a good belay on the left. It is possible to avoid the left traverse by continuing directly over steep iced mixed ground, then stepping back into the gully to join the original route below the next pitch, harder than the original line.

3. 30m   Continue easily up the gully to the foot of a steep ice pitch. Belay on the right.

4. 50m   Turn the steep ice pitch by the walls on the left, then continue more easily to where the gully forks.

5 and 6. 100m   Climb the easy-angled chimney on the left, or make a difficult step right to finish up the right-hand chimney.

MINUS ONE BUTTRESS

There are two excellent rock climbs on this elegant and slender buttress. Although they share the same lower section, both are well worth climbing.

North-Eastern Grooves   295m   VS *   (1955)

The original route on the buttress. At one-third height it crosses onto Minus Two Buttress, climbs this for a short distance, and then moves back right onto Minus One Buttress for the steep upper section. Start in the centre of the lowest point of the buttress.

1. 25m   Scramble easily to a belay under a corner.

2. 25m 4b   Climb the corner, then exit right onto a glacis and belay.

3. 45m 4c   Ascend a shallow groove in the wall above to a block at 6m. Pass this by a crack on its right (it is also possible to climb on its

left), then climb by short walls, moving left to a niche. Step right and climb to the top of a vast plinth.

4. 25m   Traverse left under a steep nose and climb the groove above to arrive on large ledges level with the overhangs on the right.

5. 10m   Descend into Minus Two Gully and climb easy rocks on its far side. Emerge onto a glacis where the gully lies back.

6. 35m 4b   Traverse along the obvious line back right onto Minus One Buttress and climb up to a 'stook of perched bollards'.

7. 35m 4c   Step past the bollards and climb the chimney-groove on the right for 10m. Move right along a ledge on the open crest of the buttress, then bridge strenuously up a groove to a spacious terrace.

8. 45m 4b   Climb to the top of a 12m pinnacle, and move easily up to a leaning pedestal.

9. 50m   Finish up the delightful knife-edge arete to join North-East Buttress above the Second Platform.

24   Minus One Direct   260m   HVS **   (1956)

An outstanding climb, one of the finest of its grade in the country. It combines superb rock with interesting route-finding, and has a distinct alpine feel. The best line follows the original route for four pitches, then takes the Serendipity and the Arete variations, to rejoin the original route close to the top. Following the original route in its entirety provides a fine, but less demanding alternative, although it does involve a poor section in Minus One Gully and the traverse of a horribly shattered wall. The original line is described first, followed by the Serendipity and Arete variations. Another alternative, the Plinth Variation (1967), leaves the plinth at the end of the third pitch as for North-Eastern Grooves, then makes a rising traverse back right above the crux groove to rejoin the buttress at the end of the first pitch of the Serendipity Variation. Start as for North-Eastern Grooves, in the centre of the lowest rocks of the buttress.

1 to 3.   Climb North-Eastern Grooves to the huge plinth.

4. 30m 5b   The crux pitch; a sustained and committing lead on perfect rock. Traverse right onto a nose above the overhang and climb up to a ledge. At the right-hand end of the ledge is an undercut groove. Pull into this (crux) and climb it until it is possible to follow a ramp rightwards, to finish at a block belay on a platform overlooking the lower chimney of Minus One Gully. (The Serendipity Variation moves up left from this belay).

5. 25m 4b   Move up to a wide crack. Climb the overhang at its foot, then continue up the crack into Minus One Gully to a grassy depression (The Meadow). Belay beside a great detached flake.

6. 40m 4a   Climb grooves on the left-hand side of the gully until it is possible to regain the buttress by traversing across the loose left wall to a fine niche.

7. 45m 4b   Step left onto the crest of the buttress and climb cracks and slabs above to the great terrace.

8 and 9. Finish as for North-Eastern Grooves.

Serendipity Variation: 85m   HVS ***   (1972)
Start from the block belay at the end of pitch 4 of the original route.

1. 25m 5a   Traverse up and left, until a hard move leads to a recess (crux). Make some devious moves up this, then climb up to a small grassy niche. (The Arete Variation steps left from here).

2. 20m 4c   Continue directly above the niche by the prominent crack.

3. 40m 5a   Continue by slabs and grooves to the great terrace.

Arete Variation: 80m   HVS ***   (1983)
Start from the small grassy niche at the top of the first pitch of the Serendipity Variation.

1. 20m 4c   Step left into a further recess and climb its slabby left wall. Climb the steeper rocks above until it is possible to break out onto right-trending slabs. Belay at a stack of detached blocks.

2. 20m 5b   On the left is a prominent slab capped by a long narrow overhang. Gain a foothold in the centre of the slab (crux), move up to the overhang, then traverse left on underclings to the arete. Follow this to a small exposed stance.

3. 40m 4c   Climb a crack in the crest above, then continue more easily to a groove. Bridge strenuously up this to reach the great terrace.

Minus One Buttress   290m   VI,6 ***   (1977)
One of the finest thin ice routes on the mountain. It is rarely in condition, and as a result there have been very few ascents to date. Follow North-Eastern Grooves on thinly iced slabs to the plinth. Take the groove on the left and make a difficult step right past an overhang. Move up and right across slabs to join the original summer line below the snow-filled basin of the Meadow in Minus One Gully. Climb snow and ice ramps on the left side of the gully until it is possible to break out left to reach the fine niche at the top of pitch 6 of the original route. Continue up the summer line to reach North-East Buttress.

25 Minus One Gully   275m   VI,6 ***   (1974)
A magnificent climb, the hardest of the Nevis gullies. It is not often in
condition and consequently it is a much-prized route. The conspicuous
overhang at one-third height is the crux. Enter the gully and climb
easily to an awkward ice wall which leads to a cave below the
overhang. Turn this on the left, then regain the gully above. Continue
up steep ice followed by a fine corner to reach a snow bay (The
Meadow). A choice of two snowy grooves lies above. Either may be
climbed, but the right-hand one is the more natural line. It leads to a
groove which bears left to the final arete of Minus One Buttress. In
summer Minus One Gully is wet and best avoided (275m VS 1958). It
traverses onto the face on the right at one point.
Direct Finish: 50m   V,5 **
Instead of bearing left towards Minus One Buttress, continue straight
up the steep icy chimney above.

THE ORION FACE

Shaped like an inverted wedge, the Orion Face fans out from Minus
One Gully on the left to Zero Gully on the right. The depression in the
centre of the face is known as The Basin. It holds snow well into
summer, and is a place of intersection for many routes on the face.
The name Orion derives from a fancied resemblance of the original
routes on the face to the configuration of the stars in the constellation
Orion, with The Basin corresponding to Orion's belt.

Access to or from The Basin is possible via the **V-Traverse** (90m
Difficult 1943), which follows a slabby weakness leading left towards
a prominent notch on North-East Buttress. If desired, the traverse can
be continued from The Basin, across Zero Gully, to Observatory Ridge.
The short narrow chimney at the back left-hand corner of The Basin
is **Epsilon Chimney** (110m Difficult 1943). The chimney, followed by
a left-slanting line, gives the easiest exit from The Basin, and is also
the best line for escape from the face in winter conditions (Grade IV).

26 Astronomy   300m   VS *   (1962)
A fair route, and climbed fairly regularly. It starts from a grass ledge 15
metres right of the foot of Minus One Gully, and follows a line of cracks
and grooves parallel to and right of the gully.
1. 35m 4b Climb diagonally right to a slabby crest and follow grassy
grooves to a flake belay.
2. 20m Move up, then right, to a large spike belay below twin grooves.

3. 35m 4b Climb the right-hand groove, then trend right to the corner bounding the Great Slab Rib on its left. Climb this to a spike belay.

4. 25m 4a Continue up the corner, then traverse left to a chockstone belay above a smooth groove.

5. 35m 4a Climb cracks to the foot of a big slab-corner, then continue by a crack in the slab to a stance and chockstone belay.

6. 40m Surmount the flake-chimney and corner above. Move up 4m, traverse right and climb a groove to a stance under an overhang.

7. 10m Turn the overhang on the right and follow a crack to an overhanging corner.

8. 40m Traverse right for 6m, then trend back left and continue more easily to grassy ledges and a chockstone belay.

9. 60m Trend up and left to a grassy corner, then continue moving left to the crest of North-East Buttress.

Winter: 300m   VI,5 ***   (1970)

A first class winter route, never particularly hard, but it requires a good plastering of snow and ice and can take a while to come into good condition. Although the entire summer route has been climbed, the best winter line follows the summer route only in part, then takes the Direct Finish. Start at the toe of the right wall of the buttress right of Minus One Gully. Climb up to twin cracks and onto sloping snow shelves slanting leftwards to a small snow bay. Climb up right by grooves to a large left-facing corner (the left bounding corner of the Great Slab Rib). Follow the corner and exit right by a wide, shallow flake-chimney above the Great Slab Rib. Climb up, move right into a thin ice groove, then trend back left by walls and grooves until under the steep upper rocks near the top of the buttress. Make a short descent into the steep chimney at the top of Minus One Gully and climb this to the top.

Direct Finish: 120m   VI,5 ***   (1986)

At the top of the thin ice groove trend slightly right to a belay below the right-hand end of the steep upper section. Gain the crest of the buttress on the right, then continue up an iced slab trending right to reach a fine ice groove near the crest of the buttress. Follow this steeply to an easier arete leading to North-East Buttress.

27   The Black Hole   235m   VI,6 **   (1986)

This route takes the slanting corner formed by the left wall of the Great Slab Rib and follows the continuation fault line in its upper reaches.

Start at a right-facing corner approximately 15 metres left of the chimney at the start of Orion Direct.

1. 50m Climb the corner (awkward) to gain the left side of the Great Slab Rib (common to the Smith-Holt Route).

2. 45m Climb up the corner on the left side of the rib for 20m. Continue steeply in the same line for 10m, traverse left 3m and climb an obvious ice-choked overhanging crack (poorly protected and serious) leading to a snow patch above.

3. 35m Leave the top of the snow patch with difficulty where the fault line overhangs. Continue to a second snow patch and climb this to belay above its top left edge.

4. 45m Move 3m back right into the fault line and continue directly to join Astronomy where the original route traverses left to join Minus One Gully.

5 and 6. 60m Continue in the same line up thinly iced grooves.

Urban Spaceman   350m VII,6 ***   (1983)
A magnificent route, but rarely in condition. Its lower section follows the Great Slab Rib, and above it takes a series of icy grooves to the left of Epsilon Chimney. Start at the same point as Orion Direct.

1. 35m Move out left to below the Great Slab Rib.

2. 30m Climb the crest of the rib to a stance.

3. 40m Continue in the same line to a belay.

4. 30m Move up and right to reach a set of open grooves.

5. 50m Climb the grooves to below the steep upper section.

6. 30m Move up right over slabs to a stance.

7. 45m Climb a steep ice-filled chimney (overlooking The Basin) followed by steep mixed ground.

8 and 9. 90m Continue to the crest of North-East Buttress.

28   Smith-Holt Route   420m V,5 **   (1959)
This route was the result of an attempt on The Long Climb in winter, and although the Great Slab Rib was not climbed, it is a fine climb with a different character from Orion Direct. Start as for the first pitch of The Black Hole by climbing snow and ice to the Great Slab Rib, which is turned on the left with difficulty. From here, follow Astronomy until above the Great Slab Rib. Now go up and right to The Basin. At the top left-hand corner of The Basin is a steep gully, Epsilon Chimney. Climb this and continue by grooves to the crest of North-East Buttress.

29 The Long Climb 420m VS *** (1940)

An outstanding route of alpine proportions. It is one of the finest mountaineering expeditions in the country, but its relatively lowly grade means that it can be enjoyed by climbers of all standards. The climb is neither totally clean or solid, and in anything but perfect dry conditions the route is likely to be significantly harder. Choose a dry sunny day to savour the situation, and watch out for falling rocks from other parties! Start to the left of the foot of Zero Gully.

1 and 2. 60m Climb an easy-angled ochre rib left of Zero Gully to a small platform.

3. 45m 4a From the left end of the platform, a rib leads steeply up to the base of the Great Slab Rib, an easily identifiable feature. Step round the rib on the left, then move up to the foot of the Great Slab Rib. Alternatively, climb the rib direct or the groove on its right side. Both variations are harder than the original line.

4. 30m Traverse right onto the crest of the Great Slab Rib and climb it by parallel cracks to reach a recess and belays. A superb pitch.

5. 45m Move out and up right, then climb more easily to The Basin.

6. 40m Cross The Basin and climb to the foot of the Second Slab Rib, a prominent feature which bounds the top right-hand side of The Basin.

7. 40m 4b Climb the rib by its slabby left edge. High up, turn a steepening on the left wall (4c if climbed direct), then regain the crest above. Climb an awkward wall on either the left or right side to a stance.

8 to 11. 160m The climb now continues on easier rocks, with much variation possible. The original route trends up left aiming, for the base of yet another great slab, some 60m high. This is not climbed, but the rocks to its right are taken to a niche near the top, where a short difficult pitch leads to the top of the slab. Easier climbing then leads to the crest of North-East Buttress.

Variation Alpha: 150m Severe (1940)

1. 45m Above the Great Slab Rib, continue directly by a slabby rib, then move right to the crest of the left edge of The Basin, just below an overhanging section.

2. 25m Climb a slanting groove, then make an awkward exit to a stance above.

3 to 4. 80m Continue more easily to the crest of North-East Buttress.

Variation Zeta: 110m Very Difficult (1935)

Climb the left rim of The Basin to the overhang, traverse right, then move obliquely up left to easier ground. Continue moving left to the crest of North-East Buttress.

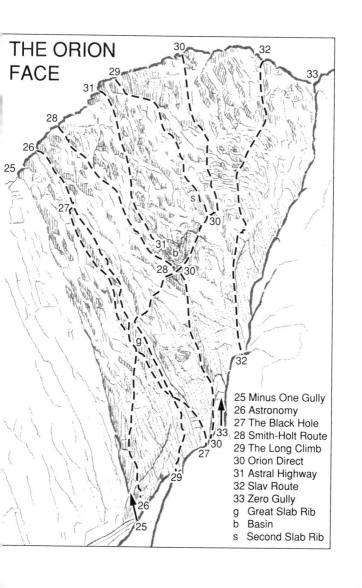

THE ORION
FACE

25 Minus One Gully
26 Astronomy
27 The Black Hole
28 Smith-Holt Route
29 The Long Climb
30 Orion Direct
31 Astral Highway
32 Slav Route
33 Zero Gully
g Great Slab Rib
b Basin
s Second Slab Rib

30 Orion Direct 400m V,5 *** *9.3.02 c̄ Ben.* (1960)
One of the finest winter climbs in Scotland, with all the atmosphere of
a major alpine face. The route is sustained, open, and exposed, but it
is nowhere technically difficult, although both belays and runners can
be hard to find. Start left of Zero Gully, where a broad ledge leads to
the foot of a prominent chimney-line leading up towards The Basin.
Climb the chimney for two long pitches until an upward traverse leads
left into The Basin. Move up and right across snow to the foot of the
Second Slab Rib. Descend a little, move round the right side of the
rib, then climb up to and across a steep icy wall on the right (crux).
Above, follow left-trending snow and ice grooves to the snow slope
under the final tower. This can either be climbed directly on steep ice
or turned by following a groove and chimney-line on the left to reach
the plateau at the top of North-East Buttress. If time is pressing there
are a number of escapes: Epsilon Chimney (taken by the Smith-Holt
Route) is the quickest exit from The Basin; it is also possible to traverse
easily left from the foot of the Second Slab Rib to reach North-East
Buttress. If conditions are poor on the upper section, it may be
necessary to make a long traverse to the right in order to find a feasible
route to the plateau.
Direct Start: 75m V,5 * (1971)
In good conditions, a line of icy grooves forms on the front of the
buttress between Orion Direct and Zero Gully. Start just left of Slav
Route and climb the grooves to reach The Basin in two pitches.
Steeper and more sustained than the original route.

31 Astral Highway 240m VI,5 ** (1976)
An excellent ice route, taking a direct exit from The Basin up the steep
line of grooves right of Epsilon Chimney. It is often in condition and
quite popular. Follow Orion Direct to The Basin and climb a shallow
groove which trends left to the main groove-line a few metres right of
Epsilon Chimney. Climb the main groove over bulges (crux), then
continue by grooves on the right (the steep groove-line on the left can
also be climbed). Continue by successive grooves to exit on the crest
of North-East Buttress above the 40ft corner.

Orion Direct, Ben Nevis (Climber, Nick Halls)

Zybernaught   240m   VI,5   (1980s)
This steep ice route follows the set of zigzag grooves between Epsilon
Chimney and Astral Highway.
1. 45m From the foot of Epsilon Chimney move up right to below a
steep bulge.
2. 45m Climb the bulge and continue to a left-trending groove.
3. 45m Follow the groove to an open corner.
4 to 6. 105m Climb the corner and continue more easily above to
reach North-East Buttress.

Journey into Space   240m   VII,6 **   (1980)
An intricate route taking a complex line between Astral Highway and
the Second Slab Rib, directly up the centre of the Orion headwall. It
is rarely in condition, and has seen very few repeats. Start midway
between Astral Highway and the Second Slab Rib. Climb directly to
the right of a short corner where a delicate traverse right on steep
ground leads to easier climbing and a block belay. Continue diagonally
leftwards by an obvious iced slab until a break onto the upper section
of the wall can be made after 20m. (The section after the first belay is
believed to be part of the diagonal line taken by J.H.B.Bell from the
Second Slab Rib on the first summer ascent of The Long Climb. Bell's
route continues traversing diagonally leftwards to Astral Highway and
North-East Buttress). Climb a slab, move right beneath an overhang,
then continue up a groove to the right end of a prominent snowfield.
Move diagonally left up the snowfield (it is possible to finish direct from
here), and climb the obvious corner passing an overhang on the left
to finish.

Long Climb Finish   240m   VI,5 *** 9. 3.02. ⁊ ℬℯ⋅ .   (1983)
An excellent but steeper alternative finish to Orion Direct, which
approximates to the upper section of The Long Climb. From The Basin
climb a steep ice groove just left of the Second Slab Rib. Regain the
summer line above, and follow this up a series of icy grooves to the
top.

Point Five Gully and Observatory Buttress

Beta Route   100m   VS   (1940)
This route links the lower reaches of Slav Route to The Basin. Climb
to the top of the second steep pitch of Slav Route, then traverse to the
left end of a large platform overlooking the lower reaches of a deep
chimney. The route starts properly here.
1. 30m 4b Climb the rib to the right of the chimney to a stance.
2. 15m 4c Move up right over difficult smooth slabs to easier climbing
and a belay.
3 and 4. 55m 4a Turn the steep rocks above on the right, then climb
directly to The Basin.
Direct Variation: 45m   VS 4c   (1944)
Climb the rocks directly above the belay at the end of the second pitch.
Winter: 90m   V,5
A direct entry to the right-hand side of The Basin. Start just left of Slav
Route and climb steep grooves and icy slabs to The Basin.

32   Slav Route   420m   Severe   (1934)
A pleasant enough route, but not in the same class as The Long Climb.
Start a short distance up Zero Gully, where a rock rib rises from the
bed of the gully. Scramble up the rib until the rock steepens. Climb up
to a small stance at 15m, step out right, then move up to a belay (35m).
Continue up and right to the edge of a slab overlooking Zero Gully,
then move up left to a platform. Follow the scoop left of the rib to a
shallow cave, then move right to a further platform. From the right end
of the platform climb directly to easier ground (45m). Continue by the
rocks close to the left of Zero Gully. Near the plateau, bear left to finish
by chimneys and corners.
Winter: 420m   VI,5 ***   (1974)
This excellent route maintains its interest throughout, and is one of the
longest winter climbs of its standard in Scotland. Climb a groove
immediately left of Zero Gully, then move up right into an iced groove
to belay below a steep icefall (50m). Climb the icefall (crux), or avoid
it on the left (easier), then continue up grooves to a snowfield (50m).
Move up and right and belay below a snow arete overlooking Zero
Gully (50m). Continue by steep steps and grooves for four long
pitches, keeping close to but left of Zero Gully, to emerge on a snow
slope below a wide square-cut chimney immediately right of a steep
buttress. Traverse right across a groove and wall for 30m, then climb
a steep corner to a belay (50m). Finish by the groove on the left to
emerge on the crest of North-East Buttress, well left of Zero Gully.

33 Zero Gully V,4 300m *** 22. 4. 01 Hamish R. (1957)
This historic route was the first Grade V gully on Ben Nevis. It rarely achieves the character of a deep gully, being more of a great open groove. Although technically easy for the grade, it is a serious climb with poor belays and it is exposed to spindrift. In summer it is rarely climbed (300m Hard Severe 1955).

1. 50m Climb the central ice groove to the foot of a little rib (possible stance), continue up a short groove on the left, then traverse right below a steep wall to a snow bay. It is also possible to climb steep ice on the right wall of the gully to the same stance.

2. 40m Continue more easily to a stance below the next steep section.

3. 40m Climb a short steep ice wall, then move right into a groove which is followed to a belay.

4 to 7. 170m Continue easily above by snow and occasional short pitches to the plateau.

OBSERVATORY RIDGE

Observatory Ridge is the long narrow buttress right of Zero Gully. For the purposes of this guide, the Observatory Ridge area covers the routes between Zero and Point Five gullies. There are several short climbs on either side of the ridge; the three short winter routes on the left side of the west flank are worth considering in bad weather, since they can be descended by abseil. To their right is the prominent wide icefall of Hadrian's Wall Direct, and further right is a steep wall bounding the left side of Point Five Gully. This contains some of the finest hard winter routes on the mountain. The top of the wall is crossed by a great curving ledge taken by The Girdle Traverse.

34 East Face 170m IV,5 * (1974)
Below and right of Zero Gully, a prominent groove strikes leftwards for the entire length of the east face of Observatory Ridge. When the groove is completely iced up, several bulges will normally be encountered before gaining the crest of the ridge. The route has also been climbed in summer (170m VS 1978).

Silverside 120m IV,4 (1977)
Start about 15m below and right of East Face. Climb rightwards up snow and ice grooves to the left end of a large ledge. Traverse left and climb under a bulge to gain a line leading up and left to a steep snow bay. Continue easily to the crest of Observatory Ridge.

35   Observatory Ridge   420m   Very Difficult ***   (1901)
A really splendid route, a must for everyone. From the lowest rocks
climb easily to the right end of an obvious grass terrace (65m).
Continue by slabs and walls, a little left of the crest, to steeper rocks
which are turned on the right flank. Climb cracks and grooves to the
easier-angled crest of the ridge, and follow this with occasional
difficulties to the plateau.
Left-Hand Start: 70m   Moderate
Start from the foot of Zero Gully. Climb easy slabs to gain the left end
of the grass terrace.
Direct Variation: 80m   Very Difficult   (1930)
Climb the steep front face of the buttress, which is avoided by the
normal route on the right flank.
Winter: IV,4 ***   (1920)
This, the most difficult of the classic Nevis ridges, gives a superb climb
which can be very awkward under powder. The easiest line starts up
the shelf on the left flank and works up obliquely rightwards to the
crest. The upper ridge is normally straightforward, but it can be time
consuming under heavy snow conditions. Many parties avoid it altogether and move left into the easier upper section of Zero Gully.

36   Observatory Wall   90m   IV,4   (1985)
The first of the three short climbs on the west flank of Observatory
Ridge. Start about 20 metres left of the obvious bow-shaped chimney-
groove in the centre of the face, below a crack-line with a prominent
cave at half-height. In summer the route can be used as an alternative
start to Observatory Ridge (90m Very Difficult 1984).
1. 45m Climb slabs to below the cave.
2. 45m Climb to the cave and exit out left. Finish up cracks leading to
the crest of the ridge.

37   Abacus   105m   IV,4   (1977)
Follow the obvious bow-shaped chimney-groove in the centre of the
face to the crest of the ridge.

38   Antonine Wall   150m   IV,4 *   (1977)
To the right of Abacus is a steep ice-filled groove which leads to a slab
capped by a huge roof. Climb the groove to below the roof, move right
over slabs to a snow-filled groove and follow this to the crest of the
ridge.

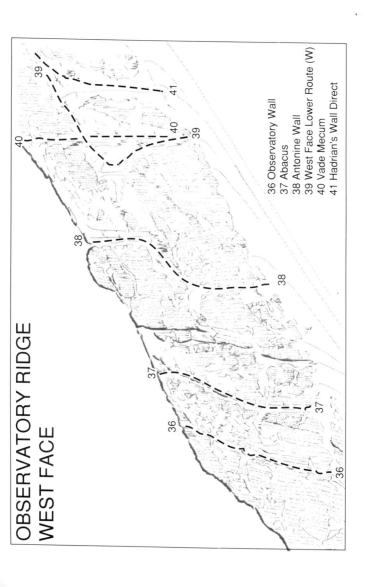

OBSERVATORY RIDGE
WEST FACE

36 Observatory Wall
37 Abacus
38 Antonine Wall
39 West Face Lower Route (W)
40 Vade Mecum
41 Hadrian's Wall Direct

39   West Face Lower Route   325m   Very Difficult   (1944)
Start about 35 metres left of Point Five Gully. Climb to a pointed block, then follow grooves to a vertical wall below the crest of Observatory Ridge. Continue by slabs and a mossy rake on the right to a deep chimney. Climb this to the upper section of the buttress, then continue up a shallow gully on the right to the plateau.
Winter: 325m   IV,5 **   (1959)
A good route, hard for the grade and worthy of more ascents, taking an interesting line across a major face of the mountain. It is also known as Hadrian's Wall, which can cause confusion with the better known Hadrian's Wall Direct. Start just left of the huge icefall of Hadrian's Wall Direct, and climb up to the base of twin ice grooves. Enter the left-hand groove and climb to a steep snow bay under the vertical upper wall. Traverse snow and iced slabs up right under the wall to enter a deep icy chimney. This leads to the easier upper section of the buttress. Follow the shallow scoop above, then negotiate awkward slabby walls under the plateau edge to finish.

40   Vade Mecum   190m   V,5 **   (1974)
A fine climb. Start as for West Face Lower Route by climbing up to the belay at the base of the twin ice grooves. Take the right-hand groove to a steep snow bay under the vertical upper wall. Belay to the left of a vertical ice pillar. Climb the pillar and continue more easily to the crest of the ridge.

41   Hadrian's Wall Direct   300m   27.3.10 E Harwal.   V,5 **   (1971)
This popular ice climb, which comes into condition early and remains so until late in the season, goes up the large prominent icefall on the right flank of Observatory Ridge. Climb the ice smear, bulges and all, to a belay near steep rocks on the left (50m). Continue very steeply for 10m, then climb easier snow to a belay (50m). Follow the snow (trending slightly right) to a deep icy chimney, which leads with interest to a large snow field (50m). Follow this for four long pitches to the upper section of the cliff. Take the shallow scoop above, then negotiate slabby walls under the plateau edge to finish.

42   Sickle   300m   V,5 ***   (1977)
This excellent ice route takes the curving slabby groove right of Hadrian's Wall Direct. Start a few metres right of the previous route below a small icefall.

1 and 2. 90m Climb over a steep ice step to gain a groove leading up and left close to Hadrian's Wall Direct, then curve back right to a steep icy corner and belay.

3 and 4. 100m Follow the icy corner, and exit right up grooves to reach the snow slope below the headwall.

5 to 7. 110m Climb the obvious break in the headwall to the top.

43   Galactic Hitchhiker   300m VI,5 **   (1978)

This serious route starts up the ice-glazed slabs and corners between Sickle and Point Five Gully, then continues up the steep right-trending corner system above. Start 15 metres right of Sickle below an icy groove.

1. 50m Climb the groove for 10m, step into another on the right and follow this over thinly iced slabs to an overhang. Exit right to a belay.

2 and 3. 70m Climb the corner and snow shelves to a point where a choice of lines can be made. Either move left up a snow bay, then traverse right past a distinctive pointed block to the base of a corner, or descend slightly right into an icy corner and climb directly to the same corner. Belay on the right-hand side of the snow bay.

4. 45m Climb the iced wall right of the corner with difficulty, then move back into the next corner and follow it to easier ground and the Girdle Traverse ledge.

5 to 7. 135m Continue directly to the plateau.

Left-Hand Start: 100m   V,5

Easier than the original way and more often in condition. Climb slabs and grooves just right of Sickle, then traverse right to the pointed block.

44   Pointless   355m VS   (1966)

This seldom-climbed route takes a central line up the slabs left of Point Five Gully. The crux section and the slabs below are often wet. Start a metre or so left of Point Five Gully.

1. 35m Climb a groove leading to a large scree patch.

2. 40m Continue by the crest of a broad rib, aiming for the foot of the obvious corner. Climb slabs slightly right of centre to the foot of the corner.

3. 30m 4c Climb the corner and break out right to belay under another corner on the right (crux).

4. 35m Follow the steepening corner to a belay.

5. 35m Continue in the same line towards a narrow chimney and belay.

6. 20m Climb the chimney to the Girdle Traverse ledge.

7. 40m Continue directly by slabs and grooves.

8 to 10. 120m Continue to the plateau, occasionally climbing.

Winter: 330m   VII,6 ***   (1978)

A serious thin face route guaranteed to provide a memorable experience! The climbing is hard and sustained, and protection is difficult to find. Start below an icy slab some 5 metres left of Point Five Gully.

1. 50m Climb the slab to a groove, then break out right through a short overhang to reach the upper slab. Trend left across this to a large spike and peg belay.

2. 30m From the top of the spike (peg runner on left wall), climb the difficult corner above (crux), then move right into a small alcove and spike belay.

3. 30m Climb an ice smear just to the left, and continue above to a narrow overhanging chimney.

4. 20m Follow the chimney to easy ground.

5 to 8. 200m Continue more easily to the plateau.

Variation Start: 50m   VI,5   (1986)

From the foot of Point Five Gully climb a short corner (8m), then traverse up and left across the top of the prominent steep slab to the spike belay at the top of pitch 1.

West Face Upper Route   300m   Severe   (1937)

Start as for Pointless and take a left-trending line before heading up towards the upper part of Galactic Hitchhiker.

45   Interstellar Overdrive   330m   VI,5 *   (1980)

Another serious thin face route taking the ribs and grooves between Pointless and Point Five Gully. Climb the left-hand rib of Point Five Gully to below a wall (belay), then move right across the wall until immediately above the gully. Follow a groove running left to a chimney, and climb this to a belay on top of an enormous jutting block. Climb a corner to reach a ledge running left, then take the icefall on the right wall to a stance. Continue by a groove on the right, then trend back left to join Pointless above the chimney. Easy ground leads to the summit.

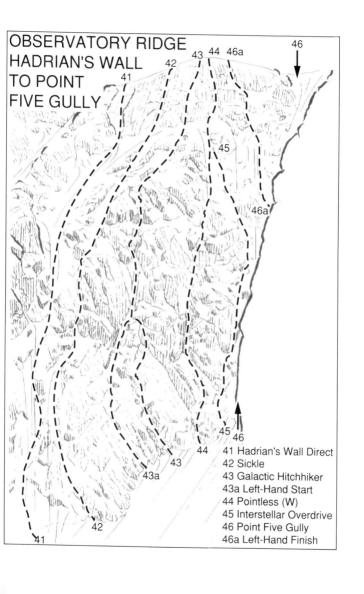

OBSERVATORY RIDGE
HADRIAN'S WALL
TO POINT
FIVE GULLY

41 Hadrian's Wall Direct
42 Sickle
43 Galactic Hitchhiker
43a Left-Hand Start
44 Pointless (W)
45 Interstellar Overdrive
46 Point Five Gully
46a Left-Hand Finish

23.2.0## coligem

46   Point Five Gully   325m   V,5 ***   *26.2.98 i then*   (1959)

An outstanding climb, and probably the most famous ice gully in the world! Belays are good and the route is often in condition. With the major difficulties concentrated in the first four pitches, the route is an excellent introduction to the Grade V classics and it is not uncommon for the gully to have several ropes of climbers stretching (often literally) from top to bottom. In windy conditions, the upper funnel collects vast quantities of spindrift which causes mini-avalanches to funnel down the lower narrow section. The gully is a wet VS in summer (1955), and probably best avoided.

1. 40m Climb easily up iced slabs to a stance on the right below a steep ice wall. Either continue straight up, or move left a few metres, and climb a steep icy bulge to a snow bay and belay.

2. 45m Climb the narrow ice-choked chimney to a stance.

3. 30m The Rogue Pitch. Continue up the gully and climb the bulging icy wall to the easier upper section.

4 to 8. 210m Follow the gully past the occasional short pitch to the plateau. The cornice is normally avoided on the right.

Left-Hand Finish: 150m   IV,4   (1988)

From the top of pitch 4, a groove and ice walls lead out leftwards to the plateau.

1. 50m Leave the gully and climb up and left to a snow slope. Follow the groove above to a belay.

2. 25m Continue by a further groove and wall on the left to a snow slope below the headwall.

3 and 4. 75m Climb the headwall on the left-hand side, then continue more easily to the top.

Right-Hand Finish: 75m   IV,4

From above the fourth pitch continue up the gully, and climb the next short ice section. Above this, exit right and climb iced slabs to a steep wall. Climb the wall with difficulty to a snow crest, and follow this to the plateau.

Right-Hand Escape: 100m   III

Useful in the dark, in worsening weather, or if the spindrift becomes too unbearable! From halfway up pitch 3, just below the bulging wall, move out right onto a steep ramp and a blunt spike belay. Continue traversing right along the Girdle Traverse ledge to the foot of Good Friday Climb and the shelf that leads into Observatory Gully. Beware of avalanche risk here, especially if snowfall has driven you out of Point Five Gully.

OBSERVATORY BUTTRESS

Observatory Buttress is the broad mass of rock extending from Point Five Gully on the left to Gardyloo Gully on the right. It rises steeply to a great ledge at half-height, which is taken by the Girdle Traverse and narrows towards its left end. On the right, the ledge finishes at the foot of Gardyloo Gully at its junction with the top of Observatory Gully. The ledge is a useful but very exposed means of escape should conditions on the plateau make the prospect of a visit too daunting.

The buttress is characterised by an open left-facing corner which separates the steep wall to the right of Point Five Gully from the easier angled spur on the right. This is a peaceful part of the mountain in both summer and winter, with generally good rock. The high standard winter climbs to the right of Point Five Gully are most likely to be in condition towards the end of the season.

47   Point Blank   350m   VII,6 **   (1988)
A difficult and serious route taking a direct line up the edge of the buttress immediately right of Point Five Gully.
1. 40m Start 4m below and right of Point Five Gully. Climb a steep groove left of Left Edge Route to the left end of a snow patch. Move up to belay at its top right corner.
2. 30m Above are twin wide cracks, 3m high. Climb the left-hand crack, then continue directly up slabs to gain a left-facing groove on the right. Move briefly up the groove to below a small overlap and semi-hanging stance in slings.
3. 40m Descend 3m and pull steeply into a corner on the right, which leads to the foot of a narrow chimney-crack. Climb this to a roof and move left beneath a small overhang overlooking Point Five Gully (5m). Take a steep ramp through the overlap (4m) and continue up steep snow to belay on a rounded spike.
4. 40m Climb a slanting groove a little to the left of the spike for 5m, then continue up a series of easier corners which lead up to the crest of the ridge.
5 to 8. 200m Follow the line of corners and steps on the crest right of the upper funnel of Point Five Gully.

48   Left Edge Route   125m   Severe   (1936)
Start at the foot of the rib bounding Point Five Gully on its right.
1. 45m Climb the rib for 30m, continue by steeper rocks, then move right to a belay.

2. 40m Climb the shallow groove on the left, then move up and right. Gain a flake on the right, then move up into a groove and slab. Follow a grassy rake up to the right to a belay.

3. 25m Climb the steep water-worn groove above, then move right to finish at a ledge and block.

4. 15m Surmount the corner, then continue up a further corner leading left to the Girdle Traverse ledge.

Winter: 360m   V,5 **   (1974)

A climb of great character, especially if followed by the Direct Finish. Start at the foot of Point Five Gully and climb the rib to a snow patch. From its right end, climb the left-hand of two grooves to a hidden traverse line leading right to beneath twin icefalls. Climb the left-hand icefall to the easy terrace. Move right along the Girdle Traverse ledge and finish as for Observatory Buttress.

Direct Finish: 200m   V,5 **   (1980)

Instead of traversing right along the terrace, climb directly up a series of sustained icy grooves just right of the crest, overlooking the upper section of Point Five Gully. Excellent climbing.

49   Match Point   335m   VI,6 **   (1986)

A direct line between Left Edge Route and Rubicon Wall. Start below the right-hand of two left-facing corner systems.

1. 50m Climb the corner (good spike runner at 25m) to a steep snow patch.

2. 40m From the top of the snow patch, traverse left below an inverted triangular overhanging rock wall and climb an icicle fringe on its left-hand side. Belay on the snow terrace above.

3 45m Take the right-hand of the two prominent icefalls above to reach the Girdle Traverse ledge.

4 to 7. 200m Continue as for the Direct Finish to Left Edge Route.

50   Rubicon Wall   160m   Severe *   (1933)

A fine route on good rock taking the open left-facing corner on the right side of the steep wall which bounds Point Five Gully on the right. Start about 15 metres from the left edge of the buttress.

1. 30m Climb easy yellow slabs to a large ledge. From the left end of the ledge climb a rib to a further ledge and block belay.

2. 40m Move right and climb into a groove leading to a large ledge. Traverse almost horizontally into the incipient gully on the right, and follow this until a move out right leads to a block belay.

OBSERVATORY BUTTRESS

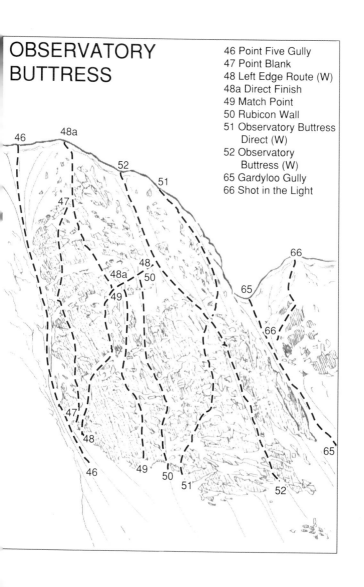

3. 25m Continue the traverse past a little buttress to a V-shaped corner. Move out right then up, and climb a corner or rib to a ledge.
4. 30m From the right end of the ledge climb slightly left to a higher ledge, then continue by a thin crack and small groove to a stance. Climb the corner on the left to sloping ledges and an inconspicuous flake belay.
5. 25m Climb grooves, make an awkward move right onto a rib, then climb up to a flat ledge. Surmount some blocks to reach a recess, then move delicately right to a small ledge and belay.
6. 10m Move up right into a corner containing a large block. Climb this to the Girdle Traverse ledge.

Winter: 325m   V,5 **   (1977)
In good conditions a prominent icefall forms the down the left-facing corner masking the summer line. Climb the icefall in three pitches to the Girdle Traverse ledge. Move right along the terrace and finish as for Observatory Buttress, or continue up the upper buttress as for the Direct Finish to Left Edge Route. If the upper part of the left-facing corner is insufficiently iced, it is possible to traverse left and finish to the right of the inverted triangular wall of Match Point.

51   Observatory Buttress Direct   340m   Very Difficult   (1931)
Start about 30 metres right of the lowest rocks, in a shallow bay. Move up to awkward short walls, then climb these to a large platform (45m). Traverse left and climb a difficult corner to a platform and belay. Follow a series of walls and corners leading up right to a ledge with a large slab leaning against the left wall. Continue above by steep slabs, trending right to an overhang close to the obvious chimney. Turn the overhang on the left and climb up to a recess. Easier climbing leads to the Girdle Traverse ledge. Scramble up to the right for 60m to an obvious crack topped by an overhang. Climb the crack, turn the overhang on the right, and continue to easier slabs. Gain the crest on the left by a chimney and climb to the plateau. The Slab Variation (45m Very Difficult 1936) starts from the ledge with the large slab leaning against the left wall, and climbs the slabs on the left.

Winter: 340m   IV,4 *   (1952)
Start a little right of Rubicon Wall, then ascend the buttress trending right by snow ledges and short walls, crossing the icefall on the Ordinary Route at about 110m. Finish by easier climbing on the upper section of the buttress to reach the Girdle Traverse Ledge. Follow the crest of the buttress to the top.

52   Observatory Buttress   340m   Very Difficult *   (1902)
A good route, and a much sought-after problem prior to Raeburn's inspired solo first ascent. Start well right of the lowest rocks, directly below the obvious chimney splitting the buttress high up and just right of a large rib.

1. 30m Gain a small shelf at 10m, traverse up right, then go back left to a large ledge and a spike belay.
2. 40m Climb to a large block in a square corner. Move right a short distance, then go up left to a corner with a flake belay high up on the wall below the obvious chimney.
3. 15m Continue close to the chimney to a thread belay behind a large fallen block.
4. 20m Climb the groove above, traverse right, then make an awkward step across the chimney to a large platform.
5 to 9. 235m Easier climbing leads to the Girdle Traverse ledge. Finish by a square-cut buttress with giant steps to gain the plateau a short distance from the site of the old Observatory.

Winter: 340m   V,5 ***   (1960)
A fine and interesting climb, with one short hard section just before the chimney. Start in the centre of the buttress, climb a short snow runnel and continue on steep snow with short ice steps. Follow a shallow depression to the chimney (normally well choked with ice), then continue up an easier groove to the Girdle Traverse ledge. It is possible to traverse right from here into Observatory Gully, but it is preferable to continue up and slightly left to the crest of the buttress, which leads with little difficulty to the plateau.

53   North-West Face   75m   IV,4 *   (1975)
Further up the right flank of the buttress is a large bay with a chimney at the back. This short and sustained climb is a useful approach to the routes on Indicator Wall. Start 25 metres right of the chimney and climb a series of steps on the left to the icy upper continuation groove. In good conditions it may be possible to climb the lower chimney. The route is poor and messy in summer (75m Difficult 1938).

Two short icy lines have been climbed further right. These can be used as an approach to the Indicator Wall area. The first climbs the steep ice wall 25 metres right of North-West Face (50m V,6 1989), and the other takes the short corner-groove at the right end of the buttress (30m III 1989).

INDICATOR WALL

The steep slabby face above and to the right of the Girdle Traverse ledge extends from the narrow gully of Good Friday Climb on the left to the deep cleft of Gardyloo Gully on the right. In winter, after an extended cycle of freeze-thaw, the slabs become coated with a thin layer of ice and provide a number of excellent routes, which are mostly hard and serious with infrequent belays and limited protection. Starting at an altitude of 1200m they are the highest ice climbs in the British Isles, and are often in condition late into the season.

In summer the routes are rarely climbed, which is not surprising considering the purgatorial scree approach up Observatory Gully. The easiest and quickest approach in summer is to climb Tower Ridge, and continue beyond the Eastern Traverse into Tower Gully. If approaching from the valley in good weather, it is best to take the Tourist Track to the plateau, then descend Tower Gully.

54 Good Friday Climb 150m III *** (1939)
This enjoyable and popular climb is especially good early in the winter before snow banks much of it out. From the foot of Gardyloo Gully traverse left along the easy terrace to the foot of a narrow gully. Climb this for 60m to a steep rock wall. Traverse right on ice to a small gully, then climb up and slightly left to easier ground leading to a further small gully. Climb this for 15m, before moving up and right to the summit cornice. The indicator post no longer exists, but tradition still dictates taking the highest belay in the country, round the triangulation pillar on the summit!
Left-Hand Finish: 90m III,4
Instead of traversing right at the top of the initial gully, climb the rock wall directly, then trend up and left to the top.

55 Indicator Wall 165m V,4 *** (1975)
This excellent climb is often in condition, and takes the prominent ice sheet on the left side of the face. Start the base of a groove not far right of the gully of Good Friday Climb. In summer the route is dirty and not recommended (110m Very Difficult 1941). The Direct Variation (45m Severe 1943) climbs a steep rib to the right of the original route.
1. 30m Climb an icy chimney-groove to the right of a prominent rib, over ice bulges to a small snow scoop.

INDICATOR WALL

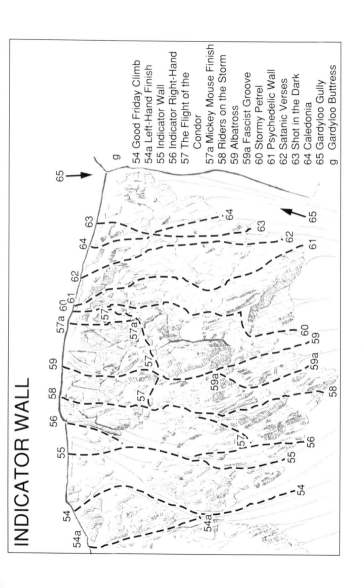

54 Good Friday Climb
54a Left-Hand Finish
55 Indicator Wall
56 Indicator Right-Hand
57 The Flight of the Condor
57a Mickey Mouse Finish
58 Riders on the Storm
59 Albatross
59a Fascist Groove
60 Stormy Petrel
61 Psychedelic Wall
62 Satanic Verses
63 Shot in the Dark
64 Caledonia
65 Gardyloo Gully
g Gardyloo Buttress

2. 45m Take the steep ice bulge on the right and continue up the ice ramp above, then move up and right to the base of a short chimney. (It is also possible to climb the groove directly above the snow scoop).
3. 45m Climb the chimney and follow a line leading out left through bulges to the snow slope above.
4. 45m Either climb straight up, or bear left on steep snow and ice to the cornice. An easy pitch in a superb situation.

56   Indicator Right-Hand   160m   V,5 **   *13. 4.02 ō Bret.*   (1975)
A steeper and more direct version of the original route, but not so often in condition. Start below the steep groove 15 metres right of the normal start, and climb straight up through the bulging ice flow to the belay at the base of the short chimney. Climb the chimney and follow a line leading out left through bulges (as for the original line) to the snow slope above. Finish by the gully to the right of the steep headwall and turn the cornice on the right.

57   The Flight of the Condor   200m   VI,5 **   (1993)
This superb and committing expedition climbs the steep buttress to the right of Indicator Wall, then takes the natural rising traverse line which cuts across the steep central section of the face. Start at the foot of Indicator Wall.
1. 45m Climb up and right and a follow a ramp to the groove of Indicator Right-Hand (20m). Surmount a short icy wall to reach the buttress crest. Climb a groove on the left side of a prominent block, then step across it and move up and right to a stance below the prominent slabby groove taken by Riders on the Storm.
2. 25m Continue up the groove (as for Riders on the Storm), to the start of the stepped right-trending line of weakness which cuts across the face.
3. 45m Step down, cross the corner-line of Albatross and continue traversing right. After 25m climb thinly iced slabs to the upper traverse line, and follow it to its end.
4. 45m Continue in the same line by moving first right, then up on thinly iced slabs to a ledge situated directly below an overhanging chimney. Climb a shallow corner to the base of the chimney, then step down and right to a stance below and left of the exit chimney of Stormy Petrel.
5. 40m Climb the ice wall above for 15m, then continue up snow slopes to the top.

Mickey Mouse Finish: 50m   VI,6 **   (1993)
This impressive exit takes the corner which cuts through the impending
headwall between Albatross and Stormy Petrel. Start at the stance at
the end of the third pitch of The Flight of the Condor. Move up and
right on iced slabs to the base of the corner. Climb the thinly iced
vertical left wall, continue over ice bosses to the top of the headwall
and finish easily up snow to the cornice. A spectacular pitch.

58   Riders on the Storm   165m   VI,5 ***   (1986)
The prominent buttress to the right of Indicator Wall is cut by a
bow-shaped corner system on its left side. Gain the first corner by an
icy slab just up and left from the lowest point of the buttress, and
continue by a series of icy stepped grooves for four pitches to the top.

59   Albatross   170m   VII,6 ***   (1978)
An excellent route up thinly iced slabs - a modern classic. The line
follows the prominent shallow corner in the centre of the wall which
runs the full height of the crag. There are three separate starts, but
the original line is usually followed. Start in the centre of the open bay
to the left of Psychedelic Wall, about 30 metres right of the rock spur
on the left.
1. 30m Follow a shallow ramp trending up and right, then move
directly up to a rock spike in a corner which runs into an overlap.
2. 50m Climb the twinned groove above, and make an interesting
move left onto the top of the overlap. Continue above on steep slabs,
avoiding an overhang on the right, to a snow bay and belay.
3. 50m Exit the bay on the right by a ramp, then traverse left into a
shallow corner and follow this over an icy bulge to a snowfield below
the cornice.
4. 40m Continue easily to the cornice.
59a   Fascist Groove   55m   VI,6 *   (1983)
This left-hand start to Albatross is less often in condition than the
original line. Start left of Albatross, in the top left-hand corner of the
bay, below a groove running up to a large roof.
1. 25m Climb the groove to belay at the foot of a large hanging slab
below the roof.
2. 30m Cross the steep thinly iced slab to its top right corner, and pull
round into a narrow iced groove above the overlap on the second pitch
of Albatross.

Right-Hand Start: 90m   VI,6   (1989)
Start as for Albatross, but instead of moving up to the rock spike in the
corner, climb further right to belay to the left of Stormy Petrel. Climb
the short chimney above and exit left onto the crest. Follow this to join
Albatross on the left traverse on pitch 3.

60   Stormy Petrel   170m   VII,6 ***   (1983)
A superb but very poorly protected thin face route. The climb starts up
the central slabs and moves right under a series of undercut roofs
before breaking out directly to finish left of Psychedelic Wall. Rarely in
condition. Start at the foot of the open corner as for Albatross.
1. 30m Follow a shallow ramp trending right, then move directly up to
a rock spike belay under an overlap.
2. 20m Traverse horizontally right under several rock ribs to belay at
the foot of an impressive corner.
3. 40m Climb the steep left wall of the corner and gain a big slab
above. Continue steeply up and right to another open area of slab.
Belay in a shallow runnel.
4. 20m Ascend rightwards, turning a corner and roof on the right, to
belay at the foot of another corner.
5. 45m Climb the corner and trend left through bulges. Move back
right and go up a steep chimney to belay on the final slope.
6. 15m Easy climbing leads to top.

61   Psychedelic Wall   185m   VS   (1967)
Probably the best summer route on the wall. Be wary of summit visitors
dropping boulders down the climb! The technical grade is 4c. Start
about 20 metres left of Gardyloo Gully, below a large detached flake.
1. 35m Gain the flake from the right, then move up and right to a ledge.
Continue by the slabby arete on the left to a ledge and belay.
2. 30m From there climb the arete to the left end of a mossy ledge.
3. 20m Climb the corner above for 3m, move left 3m, then climb a 6m
wall to a ledge. Continue by the corner-crack above to belay on top of
an enormous block.
4. 25m Continue up grooves and cracks leading up right to a ledge
beneath a prominent corner.
5. 30m Climb the deep crack above to a large block at 6m, move out
right, and climb the right edge of a loose chimney to a belay.
6. 45m Gain good slabs, then finish by one of three corners in the
final wall. Scrambling leads to the plateau.

Winter: 165m   VI,5 ***   (1978)
This popular route, the established classic on the wall, takes a direct
line starting from the lowest rocks opposite the left edge of Gardyloo
Buttress.
1. 50m Start up icy slabs to a snow bay, then continue up steeper ice
to a left-trending snow ramp leading to a large plinth. Belay below and
to the left.
2. 40m Climb slabs to an open corner which leads onto a large area
of thinly iced slabs. Climb these slightly right to a corner high on the
right.
3. 45m Continue up the corner and short chimney above to below a
steep wall. Step left through bulges and climb the rightmost of three
corners to an easy snow slope.
4. 30m Follow the snow to the cornice, which is best breached on the
left.
Direct Finish: 100m   VI,5 **   (1989)
From the large plinth, climb directly up the large area of iced slabs to
a poor belay below an overhang (50m). Take the steep thinly-iced wall
to the left of the overhang (good runner below the roof), and exit right
with difficulty into an icy groove. Continue over two bulges and climb
a steep icy wall to a snow field (45m). Climb the cornice to the plateau.

62   Satanic Verses 115m   V,5   (1989)
Start immediately right of Psychedelic Wall, where four parallel ramp
lines slant up right across the lower part of the wall.
1. 50m Take the left-hand ramp line and follow this up and right to a
snow patch (25m). Continue up the next ramp to a second snow patch
and belay.
2. 35m Climb straight up, following grooves to a large snow bay. Belay
in the corner formed by the obvious rectangular slab on the right and
a buttress on the left.
3. 30m Surmount the steep left wall, then the groove above, and
continue directly to the cornice. If this is large, an exit can be made 15
metres to the left.

63   Shot in the Dark 120m   V,5 **   (1978)
The easiest climb on the wall, but still a serious route nevertheless.
Start below the left wall of Gardyloo Gully, about 30m up and right from
Psychedelic Wall. Climb a shallow ice groove, aiming initially for a

distant rectangular roof near the top of the face. Cross several right-slanting overlapping grooves to reach a short corner. Climb the corner to where it forks, then traverse right and cross a shallow groove below a large overhang. Finish by a steep slab and short ridge some distance to the right of the rectangular roof.

64   Caledonia   100m   V,5 *   (1978)
A good route up the bulbous icefall some 60m right of Psychedelic Wall. Climb the corner to a snow bay, then move up a right-trending snow ramp. From its top, finish up steep slabs, turning bulges on the right.

Observatory Gully (300m Easy), which is more like a small corrie, separates Observatory Ridge and Observatory Buttress from Tower Ridge. Starting as an easy scree slope, the gully gradually narrows and steepens to terminate beneath a high rock barrier. On the left, this barrier is breached by Gardyloo Gully (170m Severe 1935) which cuts through some very impressive rock scenery with the added bonus of antique trash from the old observatory!

To the left of Gardyloo Gully, a broad terrace continues left below Indicator Wall to join the Girdle Traverse ledge on Observatory Buttress. To the right the terrace extends below Gardyloo Buttress, past Tower Gully and joins the Eastern Traverse of Tower Ridge.

In winter, Observatory Gully is a simple snow ascent (300m I) which gives access to the routes on Indicator Wall and Gardyloo Buttress. After heavy snowfall it is prone to avalanche, and great care should be taken in icy conditions. The easiest exit from its top is to traverse 50 metres right and finish up Tower Gully.

65   Gardyloo Gully   170m   II *   (1897)
Originally called Tin Can Gully, this deep cleft was used as a rubbish chute for the old Observatory. The difficulty largely depends on the amount and condition of the snow. Start up a uniform snow slope above the narrows in Observatory Gully to reach an ice pitch. Climb this, and continue up steep snow to the cornice which can be very large, and is often double. The gully can almost totally bank out in a winter of heavy snow, but lying high on the mountain and being a natural drainage line, it is one of the first routes to freeze up. Under these conditions it provides an interesting Grade III,4 ice climb.

GARDYLOO BUTTRESS

This steep and compact buttress dominates the head of Observatory Gully, and consists of two ridges, with a shallow depression between them. The left-hand ridge is well defined, and the upper part of the depression opens out into a wide funnel. In winter the funnel takes the form of a snow chute, which drains into two icefalls. The most prominent is the left-slanting icefall of Smith's Route, and the steeper line to the left is taken by Kellett's Route. Being high on the mountain, the climbs stay in condition until late in the season, but good ice on the harder routes such as Left Edge and The Great Glen is rare.

66   Shot in the Light   100m   IV,5   (1983)
Start 50m up Gardyloo Gully at the first break on the right wall.
1. 40m Traverse diagonally up and right along a series of sloping shelves to a stance.
2 and 3. 60m Climb up and back left via a series of delicate mantel-shelf moves (crux), then continue more easily to the top.

67   Left Edge Route   160m   VS *   (1962)
Undoubtedly the best summer line on the buttress. The many decrepit pegs testify to the close attention of those chasing the first ascent in the 1940s. The technical grade is 4c. Start at the lowest left-hand point of the buttress, at the foot of Gardyloo Gully.
1. 35m Climb the crest by awkward tilting grooves to belay by an old peg.
2. 20m Gain the slab above, turn a rib on the right, then climb directly to belay beneath a crack and flake.
3. 30m The crux pitch. Climb the crack, move up right, and mantel-shelf onto a sloping shelf. Move round a rib on the right to enter a shallow groove. Climb this for 3m, move right to gain the left edge of a slab and follow this to a belay.
4. 30m Continue up the edge for 3m, then traverse horizontally right to a groove. Climb this for a short distance until a crack leads back left to the edge and belays.
5. 45m Follow the crest by steep walls and steps to the plateau.
Winter: VI,5 *   (1976)
Start at the left edge of the buttress and climb the arete up and right until level with the upper chute of Smith's Route. Move across into the chute and finish up this. The route requires a good plating of snow and ice, and is not often in condition.

68   Kellett's Route   140m   HVS   (1944)

This direct line up the front face was the first route on the buttress. Its first ascent was a remarkable solo performance by Kellett, on what at the time was the hardest route on the mountain. Start about 25 metres left of the lowest rocks.

1. 35m 4b Climb easily to the foot of a corner, then climb the left wall to a belay.

2. 45m 5a Traverse right beneath an overhang, then climb a bulge to gain a recess. Climb the corner with difficulty to easier rocks below three parallel grooves.

3. 20m 4c Climb into the right-hand groove and follow it to a belay beneath a right-angled corner.

4. 40m Climb the corner. then move left to climb an easier corner leading into the lower rocks of the upper gully. Follow the gully with little difficulty to the top.

Variation Finish: 60m   Severe   (1958)

Leave the final gully bed at its lowest point and follow the left-hand ridge to the top. Better than the normal way.

Winter: 140m   VI,6 ***   (1980)

An excellent steep climb following the prominent icefall on the front face of the buttress. Start below the obvious right-facing corner, 30 metres left of Smith's Route.

1. 45m Climb the groove and step right over bulges to gain a shallow depression.

2. 30m Continue by an open groove on the right to belay at the foot of the final chute.

3. 50m Climb the chute to the top.

Augean Alley Finish: 50m   V,5   (1981)

From the top of the second pitch, gain the left-hand ridge and follow it to the top.

69   Smith's Route   125m   V,5 *** 8. 4. 00 i colwyn.   (1960)

A very popular ice route. Although short, it is a sustained climb with impressive exposure, and is often in condition from December until May. The Icicle Variation is slightly easier than the original route, and has now become the standard line. Start directly below the lower end of the slanting grooves.

1. 30m Follow the ice groove to a good belay on the right about 10m below a cave with a large icicle to its right.

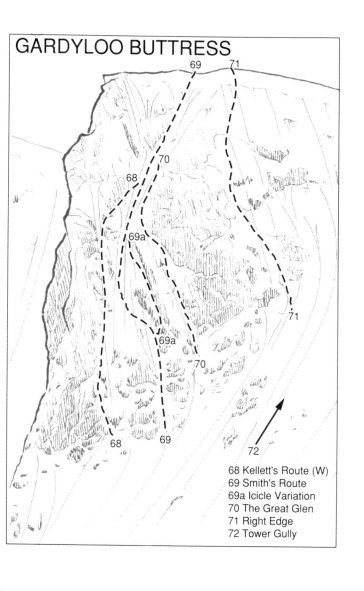

GARDYLOO BUTTRESS

68 Kellett's Route (W)
69 Smith's Route
69a Icicle Variation
70 The Great Glen
71 Right Edge
72 Tower Gully

2. 45m Climb up to the cave (possible belay), move out left up the steepening groove and break out right on steep ice to gain the left edge of the upper slab-groove. Climb up into the funnel. Belays here can be hard to find.

3. 50m Continue easily up the gully above and exit on the left.
Icicle Variation: 45m   V,5 ***   (1975)
From the belay at the top of pitch 1 move up to the cave, climb the icicle on its left side, then continue up the ramp above into the funnel. Peg belay on the right wall.

70   The Great Glen   120m   VI,5 *   (1978)
A difficult and serious route up the steep shallow groove right of Smith's Route. Climb the groove with increasing difficulty and exit left across a sloping gangway to belay right of Smith's Route (55m); long rope essential! Re-enter the groove and follow the steep arete on the right to a snowy finish.

71   Right Edge   120m   III *   (1977)
From the start of The Great Glen move up and right to gain the right arete of the buttress. Follow this to the top.

72   Tower Gully   120m   I   (1897)
The gully defines the right, or west flank of Gardyloo Buttress, and starts from the broad terrace above the rock barrier at the head of Observatory Gully. Climb the snow slope easily to a large cornice, which can usually be passed on the right. In winter, if the cornice is not too large, this is a useful, but steep, descent route down into Observatory Gully. Great care should be taken to locate the top of the gully correctly, and a traverse left is required below the level of Gardyloo Buttress to avoid the steep rock barrier taken by Tower Scoop. In summer the gully consists of loose scree and is not recommended for descent (120m Easy).

About halfway up Tower Gully, on the left wall, is a conspicuous crack. This is **Tower Face Crack** (30m Moderate 1944). The buttress bounding Tower Gully on its right often has a prominent ice-fall close to the mouth of the gully. This provides a pleasant Grade III climb leading to Tower Ridge.

73   Eastern Traverse from Tower Gully 120m   II/III   (1904)
The continuation of the broad terrace under Gardyloo and Tower
gullies leads almost horizontally to the base of the Great Tower on
Tower Ridge. From about halfway along the shelf, climb the easy
prominent gully to reach Tower Gap, then continue up Tower Ridge to
the top. This route provides an easy means of gaining Tower Gap, and
can also be used as an escape from Tower Ridge or as an easier
access to Tower Gap when the harder routes are impracticable.

TOWER RIDGE
EAST FLANK

The east flank of Tower Ridge consists of a series of steep and
forbidding walls which see little sun. In spite of this, there are some
worthwhile summer climbs here, although they do have a distinctly
serious air about them, partly due to stonefall caused by parties on
Tower Ridge.

74   Tower Scoop 65m   III **   (1961)
This excellent short and very popular ice route climbs the obvious icy
scoop in the rock barrier at the head of Observatory Gully. Climb an
ice pitch to gain the scoop, and finish by an awkward corner to reach
the terrace below Tower Gully. Some variation is possible depending
on conditions. The thin groove to the left is a worthwhile variation (60m
III,4).

75   Tower Cleft 75m   III **   (1949)
An interesting route following the deep cleft in the angle formed by the
cliff containing Tower Scoop and the east flank of Tower Ridge. The
difficulty depends largely on the quantity of snow present. Alternatively,
climb the steep icy left wall to break out left to easy ground (Grade III).

Clefthanger 90m   HVS   (1984)
The corner system to the right of Tower Cleft. Start at the foot of Tower
Cleft.

1. 20m Climb up to a large belay ledge below a large mossy corner.

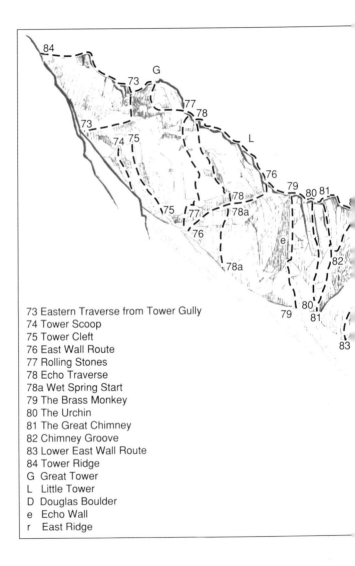

73 Eastern Traverse from Tower Gully
74 Tower Scoop
75 Tower Cleft
76 East Wall Route
77 Rolling Stones
78 Echo Traverse
78a Wet Spring Start
79 The Brass Monkey
80 The Urchin
81 The Great Chimney
82 Chimney Groove
83 Lower East Wall Route
84 Tower Ridge
G Great Tower
L Little Tower
D Douglas Boulder
e Echo Wall
r East Ridge

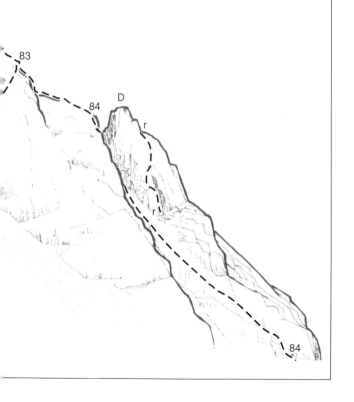

83

84

D

r

84

2. 45m 5a Traverse right round an arete to a clean corner with a large dubious flake at mid-height on the left wall. Climb the corner, then move up and left over slabs and continue by a small chimney to a belay ledge.

3. 25m Continue by left-trending grooves to the top.

Winter: V,6 *   (1985)

A good technical mixed route following the summer line.

76   East Wall Route   110m   II/III   (1966)

About 60m up and right of Tower Cleft, a ledge leads out right towards Tower Ridge. Start a few metres right of Tower Cleft and climb snow and ice for 60m to the ledge below a steep rock wall. Traverse right on snow to the crest of Tower Ridge. In summer the route is started up slabs from just right of Tower Cleft (110m Difficult 1929).

77   Rolling Stones   135m   HVS   (1965)

A good route, but rarely climbed. Start about 30 metres right of Tower Cleft.

1. 25m Climb easily to rock shelves and a belay.

2. 10m Traverse horizontally right along a good ledge beneath an overhanging wall. At the end of the traverse climb a broken wall to a large ledge.

3. 25m From the right end of the ledge traverse 20m to an overhanging recess just over a metre wide. Climb this to a small ledge on the left.

4. 45m Climb the corner above, traverse right to a wide crack, then move up to a good belay.

5. 30m Continue by easier rocks to the foot of the Great Tower.

78   Echo Traverse   135m   III   (1966)

Follow East Wall Route to the traverse ledge, then move along it for 25m to the base of a chimney-recess. Climb a groove left of the chimney to a large spike (6m), traverse the slab on the left (Grade IV under thin conditions), then climb a short chimney-groove to a snow bay. Continue by the left-trending fault above for two pitches to the crest of Tower Ridge, just below the Great Tower. In summer the route is a mediocre Severe (1956).

Wet Spring Start: 50m   V,6   (1993)

The obvious icefall provides a steep start.

79   The Brass Monkey   130m   HVS   (1961)
A worthwhile climb, but a bit slow to dry. About halfway up the east
flank of Tower Ridge is a huge recess, defined on the left by the
impressively steep Echo Wall and on its right by The Great Chimney.
Start at the foot of the slabs below the corner formed by Echo Wall
and the main ridge.
1 and 2. 65m Climb the slab to its apex beneath the corner.
3. 10m 5a Move up the corner for 3m, then traverse right to the base
of the crack (crux).
3. 40m Climb the crack directly.
4. 25m Continue to the crest of Tower Ridge.

80   The Urchin   60m   E1   (1984)
The first left-facing corner-crack left of The Great Chimney.
1. 30m 5a Climb a thin crack directly below the corner to a small grass
ledge. Continue up the corner to a belay at a large detached flake.
2. 30m 5b Follow the corner-crack to the top.

81   The Great Chimney   65m   IV,5 ***   (1960)
This atmospheric mixed route takes the large, conspicuous, deeply
cut chimney about 70 metres right of Echo Wall. The rock scenery in
the chimney is impressive. In summer the route is a rattling Severe
(65m 1935), which has certain character building elements.
1. 30m Climb a steep snow slope into the icy chimney which leads to
a belay under a vertical block.
2. 35m Climb the left crack on verglassed walls, followed by mixed
snow and ice to the crest of the ridge.

82   Chimney Groove   90m   IV,6   (1993)
An uneven route with a short and fierce crux. Start by traversing right
from the foot of The Great Chimney and climb up to a flake belay below
a bulge. Climb the bulge (crux), then continue up easy ground to Tower
Ridge. In a good build up the bulge can be avoided by slabs to the
right (Grade II). The route is vegetated in summer (110m Difficult).

83   Lower East Wall Route   125m   III   (1974)
Start about 60m down and right from The Great Chimney. Surmount
a short overhang, then follow ledges rightwards to the crest of Tower
Ridge at the top of the first steep section above the Douglas Gap. Yet
another loose summer climb (125m Difficult 1943).

TOWER RIDGE

Probably the best known feature on Ben Nevis, Tower Ridge is the third of the great buttresses on the mountain, projecting northwards from the main line of the cliffs towards the Allt a'Mhuilinn. Starting a short distance above the C.I.C. Hut at a level of 700m, the ridge rises for 200m to the top of the Douglas Boulder, a gigantic rock pinnacle separated from the main ridge by the deep cleft of the Douglas Gap. The ridge beyond narrows and rises to the Little Tower after an almost level section. A short distance above this is the Great Tower, which rises steeply for some 30m. From its top a short descent leads to the Tower Gap, after which easy rocks lead to the plateau at a height of almost 1340m.

On the first summer ascent the party climbed the ridge to the foot of the Great Tower, where they were defeated by a steep pitch. The following day they descended the whole ridge from the summit, including the Great Tower by Recess Route and the Douglas Boulder by its north-east face.

The party on the first winter ascent gained the ridge via the easy rocks just above the foot of Observatory Gully and reached the crest of the ridge a short distance above the Douglas Gap. They turned the Great Tower on its right-hand side via the Western Traverse, a line which may often prove difficult and is seldom followed now.

Tower Ridge itself is described first, followed by the Great Tower variations, and lastly, the routes on the Douglas Boulder.

84   Tower Ridge   600m   Difficult ***   (1892)
A time-honoured classic by virtue of its great length and the scale of its rock architecture. Strictly speaking, an ascent of the Douglas Boulder should be included as part of the climb, but many parties go round the foot of the Boulder to its east side, and climb the rocks above a grassy bay into East Gully and so to the Douglas Gap. It is easy to miss this lower section in mist, but the grassy bay is a good landmark. The crest of the Ridge can also be gained from almost any point in the lower reaches of Observatory Gully, but some careful route-finding may be necessary.

From the Douglas Gap, climb a moderate but well-polished 20m chimney, to the crest of the Ridge. The crest here is quite narrow and

The Great Tower and the upper part of Tower Ridge, Ben Nevis

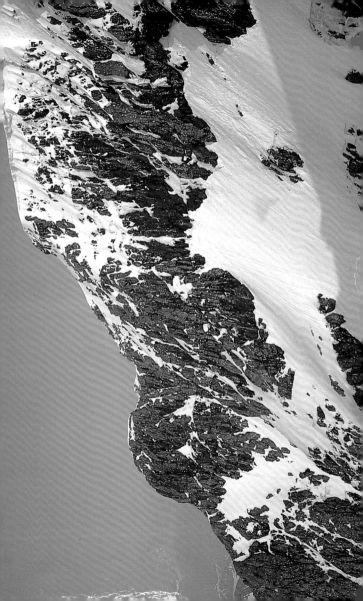

almost level, but soon steepens to a short overhanging wall. Turn this by a ledge leading up to the right. Above, moderate scrambling leads to a further level section, on which two small depressions are crossed, the second being the top of The Great Chimney. Some 50m beyond this lies the Little Tower, which is in reality little more than a step in the Ridge. Climb it on its left edge, then follow an awkward ledge leading right to a corner. It is also possible to climb straight up the face.

From the top of the Little Tower, follow a mostly level section for 100m, then scramble up easy ground to the vertical rocks of the Great Tower. Go left round the north-east corner, and follow a level ledge about a metre wide (The Eastern Traverse). Cross an exposed groove, round some rocks, and enter the foot of a tunnel formed by a huge fallen block. From the top of the through-route, steep but easy climbing leads to the top of the Great Tower. It is also possible to continue The Eastern Traverse to the terrace at the foot of Tower Gully.

From the top of the Great Tower, make a slight descent and traverse the narrow crest to Tower Gap. The descent into the Gap is quite tricky, but getting out the other side is straightforward. Easy rocks beyond the Gap lead to a final steepening. Turn this on the right by a ledge and groove, to reach the plateau. *Ben Harused 13.2.10*

Winter: 600m III *** *4.3.06. Tom + Paul*   (1894)
One of the finest mountaineering expeditions in the British Isles. Depending on the conditions, all degrees of difficulty may be encountered, with many of the major obstacles being met high on the route. The Ridge has repulsed strong and experienced parties, and should not be under-rated. Benightments occur with monotonous regularity and 6 to 10 hours should be allowed for an ascent. Early in the season, when coated in powder snow and verglas, the Ridge may be very time-consuming and possibly a grade harder.

The normal approach is to follow East Gully to the Douglas Gap. The chimney above the Gap can be tricky, but thereafter the ridge is quite straightforward as far as the Little Tower. In dry or good icy conditions this is best climbed on the left, but under heavy powder variants further right may be easier. Above, easy but spectacular ground leads to the foot of the Great Tower. The best route is to take the Eastern Traverse, which is sometimes banked out to an alarming angle. This leads to the (usually buried) fallen block chimney, above which tricky short walls lead to the top of the Great Tower. Follow the

Spindrift in Vanishing Gully, Ben Nevis (Climber, Graeme Livingstone)

knife-edge ridge to Tower Gap. The descent into the Gap is difficult, and it is best to take some care over the belay once down. The climb out the other side is a little easier, but still good sport. Now the ridge eases until the final steepening, which is best taken by a groove on its right-hand side.

If time, energy or proficiency run short, there are a number of variations which avoid many of the difficulties. In good conditions, the ridge may be gained by taking the slopes left of East Gully, thereby avoiding the tricky chimney. The ascent of the Great Tower can be avoided by a rather devious continuation of the Eastern Traverse, which leads into Tower Gully close to Tower Gap. The climb out of the Gap can be avoided by moving round to its left, then climbing back to the crest of the ridge. Obviously, it is possible to escape into Tower Gully from Tower Gap, but remember that the slopes leading across to Observatory Gully can be steep and icy, and below lie the cliffs of Tower Scoop. Purists will avoid all these temptations.

Great Tower Variations:

The following routes lie on the Great Tower, and may be used as an alternative to the normal route. They are described from left to right.

Macphee's Route   45m   Very Difficult   (1935)
This lies some 10 metres along the Eastern Traverse, below the second slanting slab. Climb up 8m to a block in the crack close to the overhanging right wall. Continue to some large blocks and a flake, then traverse left to the outer edge of the slab and climb to a large block under an overhanging wall. Pull up on overhanging blocks, then continue on easy ground to the top of the Tower.

Ogilvy's Route   45m   Very Difficult   (1940)
Start some 6 metres along the Eastern Traverse, below the first line of slanting slabs. Climb steep rocks to the foot of a steep slabby corner leading up left. Climb this, then finish more easily to the top of the Tower.

Pigott's Route   45m   Very Difficult *   (1921)
A worthwhile variation, but very imposing for the grade. Start at the foot of the north-east corner of the Tower. Climb a slab on small holds to a ledge, then traverse left onto the east wall and climb a short chimney to exit by an overhanging block (35m). From a loose flake,

climb the slab to the left of the right corner-crack to the top (10m). An easier alternative is to climb from above the overhang by a shallow chimney in a corner on the left.
Winter: 45m   IV,4   (1958)
A worthwhile finish to the ridge in winter.

Bell's Route   45m   Very Difficult *   (1929)
Another impressive route. Climb the initial slab of Pigott's Route, then traverse up on good holds across the north face of the Tower, making for the obvious block on the right. Make a difficult stride to reach the crack on top of the block, then climb a steep scoop on good holds to the top of the Tower.

Recess Route   45m   Difficult   (1894)
From the foot of the north-west corner of the Tower climb up to a broad platform. Step off a large block into a chimney-recess above, and continue on good holds to the top. In winter this variation gives a good finish to the routes on the Pinnacle Buttress of the Tower (45m III,4).

Cracked Slabs Route   45m   Very Difficult   (1896)
This route lies a short distance to the right of Recess Route. Start from a broad platform and climb steep cracked slabs (20m) followed by a shallow gully to the top.

The Western Traverse   70m   Difficult *   (1894)
The was the line taken on early ascents of the Ridge. It is harder than the Eastern Traverse, and has a totally different character. It is loose in places, but the climbing is good. From the foot of the north-west corner of the Tower traverse right, negotiate an awkward corner, and reach a broad ledge. This point can be reached more easily by taking a lower traverse line. Follow the ledge to a chimney with a projecting far wall. Cross the chimney (exposed) to reach a further ledge, and follow this to a corner. Continue by cracks and grooves to the top of the Tower.
Winter: 70m   III,4 **   (1894)
A more serious proposition than the Eastern Traverse, and seldom climbed. A little cunning and nerve may well be required!

Rotten Chimney   45m   Difficult   (1940)
The chimney, which lies some 15 metres along the Western Traverse, is steep, exposed and well named. In winter it can give a hard climb, Grade III or more, depending on conditions.

THE DOUGLAS BOULDER

The Douglas Boulder dries quickly after rain and is often clear when the rest of the mountain is shrouded in mist. There are several worthwhile summer routes on the front face, but Direct Route provides the finest start to Tower Ridge. In winter there are a number of good mixed lines, which can provide absorbing climbing after a heavy snowfall before the higher routes have come into condition. Routes are described from left to right.

From the top of the Boulder, it is necessary to either down-climb or abseil to reach the Douglas Gap. Route-finding can be awkward, and it is easiest to descend to the right as one looks into the Gap.

The obvious gully defining the east side of the Boulder, which leads into the Douglas Gap, is **East Gully**. It is a scramble on scree and gravel in summer, and a Grade I snow slope in winter. The right-hand rib is **East Ridge**, a poor summer climb (60m Difficult 1896). The Variation Start climbs a vertical corner to gain the ridge from within the gully (20m Very Difficult 1931).

85   Direct Route   215m   Very Difficult **   (1896)

This fine climb takes the great groove in the centre of the front face of the Boulder and is the recommended way to start an ascent of Tower Ridge. Start at the foot of the lowest rocks, well left of a smooth slabby wall which is an obvious feature of the lower section of the face. Climb up easily by a large shallow groove to a point where the groove steepens to form an open chimney. Climb the chimney for some 60m to a well-defined ledge. Traverse right along this and climb steep but broken rocks to the top.

Winter: 215m   IV,4 *   (1958)

Follow the summer line throughout.

Down to the Wire   220m   V,6   (1993)

A well protected mixed climb.

1. and 2. 80m Follow Direct Route to the base of the chimney.
3. 40m Continue up the groove on the right.
4. 30m Move up and left, cross Direct Route, and continue up the curving corner on the left to a ledge.
5. 30m Continue up the corner to a large spike, then pull out right onto a slab.
6. 40m Surmount a leaning block and continue up icy grooves to the top.

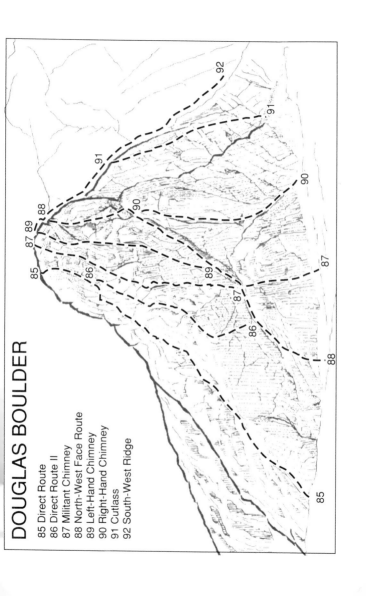

DOUGLAS BOULDER

85 Direct Route
86 Direct Route II
87 Militant Chimney
88 North-West Face Route
89 Left-Hand Chimney
90 Right-Hand Chimney
91 Cutlass
92 South-West Ridge

Direct Route III   200m   Very Difficult   (1984)
An indifferent climb to the left of Direct Route, starting just left of the open chimney.

The Black Douglas   280m   Severe *   (1986)
Start at the lowest rocks, just right of Direct Route. Climb easy rock (sometimes used as an approach to Direct Route) for 120m up the rib until below a steep wall of excellent grey rock, just a little right of the chimney of Direct Route. Climb a crack up and left through a niche to a ledge and belay (4b). Continue up grooves and walls to the top.

86   Direct Route II   185m   Severe *   (1967)
A pleasant route on good rock. Start under the right edge of the smooth slabby wall which is a prominent feature of the lower rocks of the Boulder. Climb the slab just right of a sickle-shaped scoop to a terrace above. Scramble to the foot of the steep upper section and climb this direct. The crux is at the top of the wall where easier rock is gained from the top of a leaning block. Continue more easily to the top of the Boulder.

87   Militant Chimney   180m   Very Difficult   (1984)
The chimney-crack between Direct Route II and Left-Hand Chimney. Climb a small buttress directly to a grass terrace and belay. Continue straight up a knobbly wall, then follow grooves to a belay on the right side of a ledge. Climb the chimney-crack to a further ledge, above which smooth slabs lead to a junction with other routes on the Boulder.

88   North-West Face Route   215m   Very Difficult *   (1936)
As viewed from the hut, three chimneys in the form of an inverted 'N' are a feature of the north-west face. This route follows the central chimney. Start right of the prominent smooth slabby wall on the lower rocks.
1. 45m Climb an easy-angled groove to a short wall barring access to Left-Hand Chimney.
2. 25m Climb the wall to enter the chimney, follow it for 6m, then traverse across the slabs on the right to the central chimney.
3. 25m Climb the chimney to its final section, which narrows and contains a chockstone. Some 6m below the chockstone, traverse slabs to the rib on the right, then climb up and left to finish at the top of the chimney.
4 to 6. 120m A choice of routes lead to the summit of the Boulder.

Winter: 215m   IV,5   (1980)
Follow the summer line without the diversion into Left-Hand Chimney. The chimney and the traverse below the chockstone provide sustained difficulties. Thereafter, snow ramps and grooves lead to the South-West Ridge one pitch from its top.

89   Left-Hand Chimney   215m   Difficult   (1944)
Start as for North-West Face Route and climb up to the base of the left-hand chimney. Climb the chimney to a large ledge, and continue in the same line to the top of the Boulder.
Winter: 215m   IV,4   (1972)
Gain the defined section of the chimney by a long traverse over snow from the lowest rocks on the left. The chimney provides several difficult mixed pitches.

90   Right-Hand Chimney   150m   Severe   (1944)
Start in a small bay directly under the right-hand chimney of the inverted 'N'.
1. 45m Climb easy rocks to the foot of the chimney.
2. 15m Surmount the first overhang by bridging, then climb to a belay on the left edge.
3. 40m Continue up the chimney, turn an overhang on the right rib, and climb up to a recess. Exit left and climb slabs to belay at the right end of a second large recess.
4. 50m Easier climbing by a choice of routes leads to the top of the Boulder.

Nutless   145m   Severe   (1971)
The groove system between Right-Hand Chimney and the dirty chimney taken by Gutless. The groove consists of four progressively harder sections. Climb up to a large ledge some way to the left of, but level with, the chimney of Gutless. Climb the groove system, using a rib on the right to avoid partly an overhanging section, then continue by an overhanging chimney-crack, followed by a further crack to reach easier ground. Finish directly above.

Gutless   130m   Severe   (1970)
Some 40 metres left of the South-West Ridge, and fairly high up, is a huge dirty chimney. This gives a good pitch. Skirt the steep wall above to reach easier ground.

Winter: 130m   IV,5   (1979)
Climb the chimney to a right-sloping ledge at 90m. Move along the ledge to the buttress edge, and finish up the snow grooves of North-West Face Route.

Western Grooves   195m   IV,5   (1979)
Start in the snow bay left of Cutlass. Climb up for 45m, trending left to the base of a shallow groove. Follow the steep corner-groove for two pitches to a flake belay. Move left round a rib, and climb a ramp to belay below a semi-detached flake. Climb the groove above, then follow a right-trending ramp which leads to the final snow grooves of North-West Face Route.

91   Cutlass   135m   VS *   (1963)
A reasonable route in a good situation, and worth doing when the higher routes are cloud-covered. It follows the clean-cut corner which lies some 30 metres left of South-West Ridge.
1. 40m Climb easy slabs to the foot of the clean-cut corner.
2. 25m 4b Climb the corner to a ledge and belay on the right wall.
3. 30m Continue up the chimney above, followed by a cracked wall, to reach the South-West Ridge.
4. 40m Follow the crest to the top.
Winter: 145m   VI,7 *   (1989)
A good steep mixed climb with a surprising amount of turf. Follow the summer line exactly. The crux is the steep corner on pitch 2.

92   South-West Ridge   180m   Moderate *   (1904)
The crest of the well-defined ridge overlooking West Gully is the easiest of the face routes to the top of the Douglas Boulder.
Winter: 180m   III **   (1934)
A great little climb, good value for money, and at its best when other routes on the mountain are out of condition under deep snow. Follow the summer line, with continuous interest and fine situations. An excellent start to the winter ascent of Tower Ridge, if time permits.

   West Gully leads to the Douglas Gap, and is both steeper and more direct than East Gully. It is a straightforward scramble on gravel and scree in summer (140m Easy), and steep snow in winter (140m I). A traverse of the Douglas Gap by climbing up West Gully and descending East Gully is a fine scenic excursion.

SECONDARY TOWER RIDGE

Secondary Tower Ridge lies on the west flank of Tower Ridge, some distance below its crest. For the most part it rarely attains the status of a distinct ridge but takes the form of a parallel slanting shelf, which is separated from the main ridge by a well defined depression which holds snow until late in the season. Pinnacle Buttress of the Tower lies at the right end of the shelf, and rises steeply to just below The Great Tower.

On completion of a route on this part of the mountain, it is usually possible to descend Tower Ridge or the lower part of 1934 Route to reach Douglas Gap West Gully. In winter, for routes right of 1931 Route, it is best to cut down right and descend Broad Gully. This is a useful option to avoid being exposed to bad weather on Tower Ridge and the summit plateau.

There are a number of icefalls to the right of Douglas Gap West Gully. At least three routes have been climbed but only one has been recorded.

93   Fawlty Towers   155m   II *   (1980)
The first icefall just right of Douglas Gap West Gully provides a good route for a short day. Climb the obvious icy chimney and gully, then trend slightly right and climb a steep gully to the crest of Tower Ridge.

94   1934 Route   185m   II   (1934)
Start about 50 metres right of Douglas Gap West Gully. Climb snow, then traverse right to a slabby groove which often holds ice and provides the only real difficulty on the route. Now follow the snow shelf to the upper reaches of Tower Ridge. This is a useful descent route from climbs finishing on the Secondary Tower Ridge in both summer (185m Moderate) and winter.

95   Beggar's Groove   175m   Very Difficult   (1959)
Start mid-way between 1934 Route and Vanishing Gully.
1. 20m Climb a chimney to a grass ledge and belay.
2. 30m Follow the groove above to a large block, step down and right, then traverse up right along a groove to a stance.
3. 25m Cross a groove, climb a wall trending left, then move up to a platform above the lower tier of slabs.
4 and 5. 100m Follow grooves and cracks to the crest of Tower Ridge.

SECONDARY TOWER RIDGE

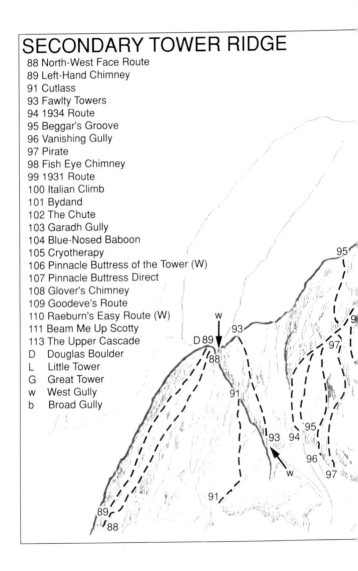

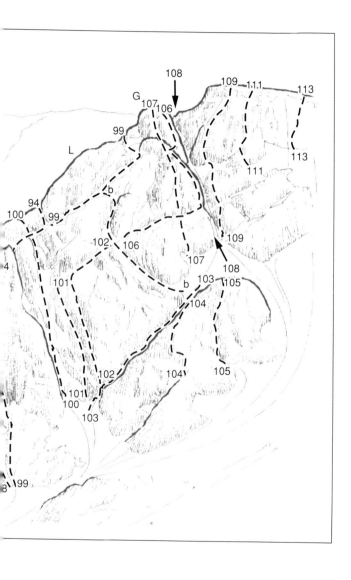

Vagabond's Rib   200m   Severe *   (1959)
A worthwhile climb with some fine slab climbing. Start about 70 metres
right of Douglas Gap West Gully, directly below the slabs bounding
Vanishing Gully on its left-hand side.
1. 15m Climb easily to a belay centrally placed below the steep slabs.
2. 45m Climb the slabs to a niche, move out right, and continue up
the steep crest by a groove and crack.
3 to 5. 140m Continue more easily to the crest of the ridge by grooves
and cracks, as for Beggar's Groove.

Running Hot   120m   V,5   (1986)
Start just left of Vanishing Gully. Climb iced slabs to reach a leftward
traverse, follow this for a few metres, then move up a second iced slab
to a recess and roof. Surmount the roof on the right, then head
diagonally left to a corner and short wall leading to a corner stance.
Move right into a groove, descend 3m, then move right to another
groove which is climbed to a spike. Exit left, and climb to the top.

Lady's Day   120m   Very Difficult   (1959)
A poor route taking a rising traverse across the wall to the right of
Vanishing Gully. Start 10 metres right of Vagabond's Rib, just left of
Vanishing Gully. Climb up to a stance (20m), then traverse right across
the gully and move up to a belay (20m). Climb a steep slab, then trend
right to a spike belay (20m). Traverse up and right to gain the slabby
groove of 1934 Route (20m). Follow this to the crest of Tower Ridge.

96   Vanishing Gully   200m   V,5 *** *13.2.10 C alwyn* (1961) -
A classic Grade V ice climb with good belays and protection. The gully
is deep and well-defined in its upper reaches. Lower down it narrows,
eventually becoming a crack before finally disappearing. It forms ice
well, and under normal conditions it presents a steep ice runnel over
the lower 70m. Lying low on the mountain however, it can be quickly
stripped bare after a thaw.
1. 50m Start up mixed snow and ice to reach the narrow steepening
gully, and climb it to a snowy horizontal ledge with a belay in an ice
cave (occasionally buried).
2. 45m Continue by the bulging ice wall, passing a cave at mid-height
(which may also be buried), to easier ground. Belay on the left.
3 to 5. 105m Finish up the easier upper gully to the crest of Tower
Ridge, or descend 1934 Route to reach Douglas Gap West Gully.

Reprobate's Rib   155m   VS *   (1989)
A good route up the right-bounding rib of Vanishing Gully, with an interesting crux on the steep tower. Start just right of the gully.
1. 30m Climb the rib to a belay 10m below a huge clean slab.
2. 45m 4b Climb straight up, then move slightly right to below a steep dirty wall. Climb this to belay on a large ledge.
3. 10m Move back left and go up to belay on a further large ledge below an overhanging corner.
4. 25m 4b Climb the corner to easy ground.
5. 45m Scramble up to the crest of Secondary Tower Ridge.

97   Pirate   150m   IV,4   (1986)
Start about 20 metres right of Vanishing Gully.
1. 30m Climb easily up a snow ramp slanting left, then pull over its retaining wall and move up into a small left-facing corner.
2. 45m Climb slabs just left of the corner to a smooth, steep wall bounded on the right by a large corner. Traverse right under it, climb the right rib of a second corner, then slant left into a vertical corner.
3. 30m Climb the corner and move right to follow a shallow chimney.
4. 45m Follow grooves to the crest of Secondary Tower Ridge.

98   Fish Eye Chimney   150m   V,5   (1987)
This route takes the striking parallel-sided slot a little to the right of Pirate. Start just left of 1931 Route and make a difficult left-rising traverse on mixed ground to the foot of the chimney. Climb the chimney (50m) and follow a large groove to the crest of Secondary Tower Ridge.

99   1931 Route   125m   III   (1961)
Some 150 metres along the flank of the ridge from Douglas Gap West Gully is a bay formed by a steep projecting buttress, from which twin chimneys lead up to the crest of Secondary Tower Ridge. This route takes the right-hand chimney. Climb steep snow into the chimney and follow this for three short pitches to the snow shelf of 1934 Route. Either continue up the easier upper gully to the crest of Tower Ridge, or descend 1934 Route to reach West Gully.

Two variations have been climbed in the vicinity of the twin chimneys of the summer route (125m Difficult 1931). Left-Hand Chimney Variation (55m Difficult 1943) climbs the left-hand chimney, and Central Rib Variation (40m Severe 1959) takes the steep rib which divides the twin chimneys.

Rogue's Rib   215m   Severe   (1956)
Although this route looks superb from below, it does not live up to
expectations. It lies on the steep two-tier buttress projecting from the
west flank of the ridge, just left of the deeply-cut gully of Italian Climb.
On the first ascent, the lower pitches were avoided by climbing Italian
Climb, which was still in winter condition. Soon after this a complete
ascent was made from the lowest rocks. Start immediately left of Italian
Climb, and take the crest for 20m to a belay, then continue by the right
flank to a large platform (30m). Continue up the shallow chimney
above (25m) to easier climbing leading to the base of the upper tier of
the buttress. Climb by thin cracks for 10m, then traverse left into the
obvious chimney and belay (20m). Follow the chimney to some huge
perched blocks, traverse right, then climb up behind a large flake to a
chockstone belay (25m). Continue by the chimney above, or the ridge
on the right, to the top of the buttress (30m).
Winter: 220m   IV,4   (1960)
Follow the line of the original ascent, using the lower section of Italian
Climb, then continue by cracks and grooves to the top of the buttress.

100   Italian Climb   180m   III *   (1958)
The deeply-cut gully which defines the right flank of the steep two-
tiered buttress of Rogue's Rib provides a good and popular winter
climb. Care should be taken assessing snow conditions before attempting this route, since the large snowfield at the head of the gully
lies on slabs, and is avalanche prone. The lower gully normally
contains two good ice pitches, above which the angle eases to snow
slopes and occasional ice leading to the crest of Tower Ridge below
the Little Tower. In summer Italian Climb gives a typically loose gully
climb (180m Severe 1943).

Italian Right-Hand   IV,4 ***   (1973)
Better climbing than the original line, but harder. Follow the first pitch
of the original route, climb the icefall on the right, and rejoin the parent
route on the easier upper section.

101   Bydand   150m   V,5 *   (1986)
A fine route. Start just right of Italian Climb and follow two steep icy
corners to below the obvious sharply-defined curving groove. Climb
this in two pitches, exiting left at the top.

102   The Chute   220m   V,4 **   (1965)

This excellent route starts 30 metres right of Italian Climb and follows a prominent line of icy grooves directly up the face. Unusually heavy snow conditions are required for the steep initial icefall to form. On the first ascent it was avoided by a rising traverse, first left then right, to gain entry to the grooves above (IV,4). The route was originally climbed in summer and named **The Ruritanian Climb** (225m Severe 1957).

1. 30m Climb the icefall to the start of the grooves.
2. 45m Move into an icy groove on the right and follow this to a horizontal ledge which leads across a steep wall into a small gully.
3. 30m Traverse up and right to a stance below a steep ice wall.
4. 25m Climb the ice wall to the snow gully above.
5 and 6. 90m Continue above to a steep rock buttress and follow an easy snow shelf rightwards to the top of Broad Gully.

GARADH NA CISTE

To the right of Italian Climb is a subsidiary buttress separated from the main mass of Tower Ridge by the wide Garadh Gully. The buttress is crowned by a spacious platform known as Garadh na Ciste.

103   Garadh Gully   95m   II *   *ECdwyn*   *11.2.12.*   (1958)

Although this gully is sometimes climbed for its own sake, it is often used as an approach to routes starting higher up on the west flank of Tower Ridge. Under normal conditions the gully gives a straightforward climb with two short steep ice pitches. Later in the season it may bank out to a uniform snow slope. The Indirect Finish (50m III 1980) breaks out left from above the second ice pitch, and crosses slabs on the headwall, to reach the foot of Broad Gully.

The crest of the buttress just right of Garadh Gully is known as **Garadh Buttress**. It is a poor summer route (95m Moderate 1933), but in winter the buttress gives a pleasant climb, following a line of snow and ice ramps up its centre (95m III 1970).

104   Blue-Nosed Baboon   135m   Very Difficult   (1987)

Some 25 metres right of Garadh Gully is a shallow gully bounding the left edge of a pyramidal mass of rock. Start by scrambling up for 85m to the apex of the pyramid and a poor belay in a damp hollow.

1. 35m Climb the wall on the left, which is steep at first, then traverse left below overhangs to a belay by a huge block.

2. 30m Gain the ledge above and traverse a ramp to the left until it is possible to make a spectacular break-out through the overhangs. Climb grooves to a belay.

3 and 4. 70m Pleasant scrambling up ribs and corners leads to the top.

Vanishing Glories   105m   Very Difficult   (1984)
The main feature of this route is the prow of rock at the top of the Coire na Ciste face of the buttress. Start 8 metres left of a small black cave on the lower buttress.

1. 40m Climb up a fault to the terrace. Belay 10m right of a blank corner.

2. 40m Climb the left-rising fault, then continue up a mossy groove until the arete on the left can be climbed to a ledge. Move along the ledge and belay in a crack below the right-hand corner of the prow.

3. 25m Climb the corner-crack to the top.

105   Cryotherapy   75m   Very Difficult *   (1987)
A good climb with some great situations for the grade. At the extreme right end of the Coire na Ciste face of the Garadh is a steep red wall. The climb follows a line to the left of this wall. Belay just below the corner at the left end of the wall.

1. 45m Climb a mossy ramp on the left, and continue traversing across the wall with increasing exposure to a belay at the foot of a big corner.

2. 30m Climb the corner to the top.

From the top of the Garadh, **Broad Gully** (90m II 1958) leads up diagonally left across the face to join Secondary Tower Ridge, before heading back right to the crest of Tower Ridge. It is a good descent route for competent parties in both summer (90m Easy 1943) and winter, and a possible escape route from the ridge.

106   Pinnacle Buttress of the Tower   150m   Difficult *   (1902)
This route is open to much variation, but the best line is described below. Start about 50m up Broad Gully below a corner on the right wall.

1. 40m Climb the corner and continue up a steep crack with good holds. Trend up right on easier ground and follow a broad ledge which leads round right into Glover's Chimney.

2. 30m Leave the ledge under the steep upper prow of the buttress, and climb a right-slanting groove.

3. 45m Move up left by a chimney-groove to reach a ledge on the prow of the buttress. Traverse left into a groove leading through slabs to easier ground.

4. 35m Follow the crest to the foot of the Great Tower.

Winter: 150m   III,4 *   (1957)

The winter route takes a line on the right side of the buttress. From the top of the Garadh, follow Broad Gully for 50m before traversing right for 80m along a ledge above overhanging rocks and beneath the steep crest of the buttress. Beyond the crest the rocks are more broken. Follow a series of snowy grooves on the right flank until it is possible to move left to the top of the buttress. Follow a ridge to the foot of the Great Tower and traverse right until a line of chimneys can be followed to the top.

107   Pinnacle Buttress Direct   200m   V,5 **   (1989)

This good ice route tackles the steep lower section of the buttress directly before taking the deep groove-line on the right side of the front face of the buttress. Start midway between Broad Gully and Glover's Chimney, directly below the upper groove, where a break in the barrier wall is found on the right-hand side of a snow bay. Climb a ramp line rightwards, then the icy wall above to enter the main groove line. Continue by the groove, with short ice bulges, to the foot of the Great Tower. The climb can be finished by taking Recess Route, starting up the wall on the right and entering the groove, which is followed to the top of the Great Tower.

Pinnacle Buttress   140m   IV,4   (1976)

Start at the foot of Glover's Chimney, and climb the icefall on the left to easier ground left of the Chimney. Climb one of the chimneys above and continue to the top of the Great Tower.   *E Colwyn 11.2.12*

108   Glover's Chimney   140m   III,4 **   (1935)

Dropping directly from Tower Gap to the right-hand end of the Garadh is a narrow gully which provides a fine and very popular winter route. Climb the initial icefall from left to right to a stance (35m), then take mixed snow and ice back left into the gully. Follow this easily on snow to the final chimney, and climb this to Tower Gap. This spectacular mixed pitch is seldom easy, but it is well protected. In summer, the overhanging wet rock at the foot of the gully can be turned by an ill-defined ledge which slants up right (150m Difficult 1902).

The Gutter (90m Difficult 1954) starts halfway up Glover's Chimney, and climbs the right wall by a series of ribs and grooves.

109   Goodeve's Route   140m   III **   (1907)

This excellent winter climb comes into condition early and remains so throughout the season. Either start up the initial icefall of Glover's Chimney, or climb the icefall to its right, then cross a snow ramp and continue just right of Glover's Chimney to gain a snow ledge leading up right. Climb an icefall (difficult to start) to a snowfield. From its top continue up a short chimney, then take a shallow gully which leads to open snow slopes which finish at the top of Tower Ridge. Several variations are possible in the upper section.

110   Raeburn's Easy Route   110m   Easy   (1911)

Start above and well right of the Garadh, about 60 metres left of Number Two Gully. Scree and scrambling leads in a zigzag to the large ledge which traverses the buttress below the steep upper section. Gain the ledge and follow it up right to finish up a well-defined gully.
Winter: 110m   II ***   (1920)
This superb climb is reliably in condition throughout the winter. From the foot of Number Two Gully, traverse left under a steep wall to a large but easy-angled icefall. Climb this for 30m to a snow slope which leads to a long right traverse below the upper wall. At its far end gain the plateau by a shallow gully. The cornice is not usually too heavy at this point.
Direct Finish: 80m   III * 26.3.00 c Ben. *after cascade*   (1986)
After the initial icefall continue straight up, keeping close to a rib on the left and exit on the plateau at the top of Tower Ridge.

111   Beam Me Up Scotty   155m   III *   (1987)

The wall above the long traverse on Raeburn's Easy Route contains a number of icefalls. This route takes a line of grooves on the left-hand side. Start in a narrow snow bay at the beginning of the right traverse of Raeburn's Easy Route.
2. 45m Follow a ramp line diagonally right across the wall to an icy groove leading straight up to more open mixed ground.
3 and 4. 70m Climb directly to the plateau.

COIRE NA CISTE

The following buttresses and gullies lie between Tower Ridge and Number Five Gully, and are best reached by skirting Garadh Buttress to its right. It is also possible to climb Garadh Gully as a warm-up on the approach to the climbs in the left-hand part of the corrie.

NUMBER TWO GULLY BUTTRESS

Beyond the rather indeterminate wall containing Raeburn's Easy Route is a scimitar-shaped buttress, defined on the right by the wide and deeply-cut Number Two Gully. This is Number Two Gully Buttress. The bottom third of the buttress is set at a low angle, with only the upper section giving continuous climbing. It is not a good area in summer, with much loose rock, but in winter there are a number of short but very worthwhile climbs.

112   The Cascade   50m   IV,5 **   26.3 co Ē Ben (1970s)
To the right of the icefall of Raeburn's Easy Route is a steep wall, containing a second steeper icefall. This provides a superb ice climb, short but very sustained!

113   The Upper Cascade   100m   IV,5   (1991)
From the top of The Cascade, cross Raeburn's Easy Route and traverse left for 120m to the foot of a steep curtain of ice. This is vertical for the first 10m, but the angle then eases slightly (50m). Finish up snow to the cornice.

Le Panthere Rose   50m   VI,6 *   (1993)
Above The Cascade two free-standing columns of ice sometimes form. Climb the left-hand column on steep hollow ice.

Rip Off   120m   IV,4 *   (1976)
This route climbs the steep slabs and walls to the left of Number Two Gully Buttress. Start right of the obvious diagonal fault running across the walls at the left-hand of two grooves defining the left side of the buttress.
1. 45m Climb the left-hand groove until it is possible to traverse left onto steep slabs.
2 and 3. 75m Climb poorly protected slabs above to easier ground.

Five Finger Discount   135m   IV,4 **   (1978)
Start as for the previous route. Climb the groove until it steepens
(30m), then move up left onto an edge leading to a small gully. Either
finish up the gully and the snow slope above, or make an awkward
traverse right to enter the final section of Burrito's Groove.

114   Burrito's Groove   135m   IV,5 **   (1978)
This good climb takes the right-hand groove system which is often in
condition. Climb the groove throughout, passing an overhang at 45m
on the left, or continue straight up if well iced.

115   Number Two Gully Buttress   120m   III ***   (1958)
A popular and enjoyable route. Climb easy-angled mixed rock and ice
to a large snowfield where the buttress steepens. About 20 metres left
of the buttress crest, climb a steep ice groove for 20m, then trend right
on snow and ice to reach the crest of the buttress a little below the
plateau.
Variation Finish: 75m   III *   (1960)
More difficult than the original route, but with good situations. After the
easier lower section, climb a groove line close to the right-hand edge
of the buttress, then continue fairly directly to the plateau. Harder short
variations have been climbed to the left, which approximate to the line
of the summer route (120m Very Difficult 1947), which is loose and not
recommended.

116   Number Two Gully   120m   II **   (1896)
The finest of the easy gullies on the mountain, passing through good
scenery. The gully fills up well and is normally a steep snow slope with
perhaps a short ice pitch at the narrows. The cornice is often large and
difficult, and is best passed on the left. Early in the winter the route
can be very interesting, and significantly harder (Grade III). In summer
the gully has a fierce reputation and is best avoided (120m VS 1942).

High up Number Two Gully are three icefalls, which can be easily
seen to the left of Comb Gully Buttress. These provide steep single
ice pitch climbs (IV,4 to V,5).

COMB GULLY BUTTRESS

The wedge-shaped buttress to the right of Number Two Gully has an
easy-angled crest which leads to the broad middle section topped by

a steep headwall. The winter climbs lie on the western flank and follow fine groove-lines on the steep upper section. They can be reached from below, or along the obvious easy ledge cutting across from the foot of Comb Gully.

117 Comb Gully Buttress 125m IV,5 ** (1960)

This good route is normally climbed with The Variation Finish which is often in condition. Either start from just left of the lowest rocks and gain the central snowfield or, harder, climb directly up the lower chimney a little to the left (IV,4). Follow a groove on the left edge of the buttress, then make a rising traverse right to the foot of a prominent curving chimney in the steep final rocks. Climb this with difficulty, then trend left to the plateau. In summer the route has little attraction and is rarely climbed (125m Very Difficult 1943).

Variation Finish: 75m IV,4 ** (1971)

The final chimney is rarely in condition, so this variation is usually followed. After the groove on the original route, avoid the right traverse and go left to an ice column. Climb this to an ice-filled groove which narrows and steepens and leads to the top.

Roaring Forties 140m IV,5 ** (1988)

This route tackles the right side of the upper part of the headwall, first by a deep groove and then by the striking right-curving V-groove in the upper rocks.

1. 50m Climb the easy lower section of the buttress to a belay right of the deep central chimney of Comb Gully Buttress.
2. 40m Continue up the deep groove 15m right of the chimney to a ledge on the left.
3. 50m Traverse left 6m and climb the long V-groove to the top.

118 Comb Gully 125m IV,4 *** *5.4.97 c̄ Colwyn + Anon* (1938)

The prominent gully which separates Comb Gully Buttress from The Comb provides a splendid climb which is in condition for most of the winter. The belays are good when found, but protection can be sparse. Follow easy snow to the narrows where a long pitch leads to a belay. Climb a short steep ice wall on the right (crux) to easy ground which leads to the top. In summer the gully is loose with greasy rock (125m Severe 1958).

COIRE NA CISTE

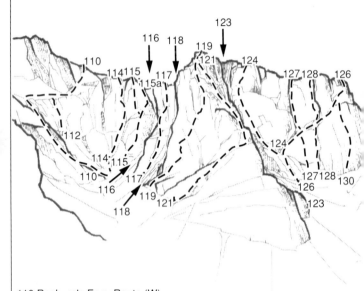

110 Raeburn's Easy Route (W)
112 The Cascade
114 Burrito's Groove
115 Number Two Gully Buttress
115a Variation Finish
116 Number Two Gully
117 Comb Gully Buttress
118 Comb Gully
119 Tower Face of the Comb (W)
121 Pigott's Route
123 Green Gully
124 Aphrodite

126 Number Three Gully Buttress (
127 Quickstep
128 Two-Step Corner
130 Sioux Wall
136 Number Three Gully
137 South Gully
141 Central Gully
143 Central Rib
145 North Gully
147 Number Four Gully
nl   North Gully, Left Fork

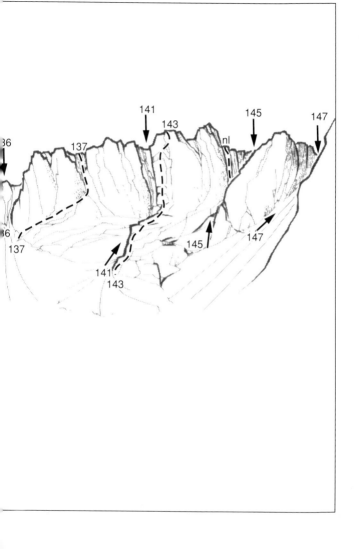

THE COMB

This great wedge-shaped buttress dominates the southerly part of Coire na Ciste. On each flank steep gullies define the buttress. To the left is Comb Gully and to the right Green Gully, which separates The Comb from Number Three Gully Buttress. It is girdled by three prominent sloping fault lines which rise from left to right. Below the lower fault, which is taken by Pigott's Route, the buttress is easy angled and slabby, whereas above it is protected for most of its length on the northern side by considerable overhangs. Until recently, these overhangs have forced all lines of ascent onto the eastern and western flanks of the buttress. The middle fault starts at the entrance to Comb Gully and crosses the buttress at one-third height. Initially it is a good ledge, but it soon disappears into a crack as it cuts above the overhangs on the north side of the buttress. The upper fault, which is not visible from below, is known as Hesperides Ledge. It passes under a steep triangular headwall cut by a distinctive curving groove.

In summer the rock on The Comb is loose and vegetated. It is unpleasant to climb on, and even worse to have to retreat from. Winter transforms the buttress, freezing the rocks into place to give first-class mixed routes which deserve more traffic.

The Comb, Left Flank   100m   IV,4 *   (1981)
This short ice route up the right wall of Comb Gully is often in condition but seldom noticed. Follow Comb Gully until just above the first narrows. Traverse right up a ramp, move left to below the obvious icefall, and climb it to enter a shallow gully which is followed to the top.

Hesperides Ledge   200m   III *   (1959)
An exposed and exciting route taking the prominent shelf leading out right. Climb Comb Gully for 70m to the obvious snow ramp leading out right onto the crest of the buttress. Follow this, past a difficult and exposed step, for two pitches to reach the crest. Continue up the crest in a fine position to the top. In summer the route is a botanist's paradise (200m Very Difficult 1940), being full of vegetation and loose wet rock – probably the ultimate tick for collectors of Bell routes!

The Good Groove   140m   VII,7 **   (1993)
This excellent icy mixed climb takes the striking curving groove which cuts the triangular headwall above Hesperides Ledge. Start by climbing Comb Gully for 70m to the beginning of Hesperides Ledge.

1. 40m The only line of weakness cutting the steep wall above Hesperides Ledge is a tiered ramp which slants up right then left. Climb delicately up to the start of the ramp, then move left with difficulty along the second narrow ramp which leads to a corner. Follow this to a belay at the left end of the curving groove, just right of the icefall of The Comb, Left Flank.

2. 25m Follow the slabs forming the right side of the groove up and right to a small stance below a steep tapering corner.

3. 25m Move up into the corner, and climb it with increasing difficulty to its top (crux). Continue up the continuation corner, then step left to a good platform.

4. 50m Climb the wall above the belay to a sharp horizontal ridge which leads to the plateau.

119   Tower Face of the Comb   230m   Very Difficult   (1940)

From the left end of the slanting fault, which splits the buttress at one-third height, move up the screes for 30m to the highest of the slabby ledges which run parallel to the main ledge.

1. 20m Traverse right along the ledge to near its end.

2. 20m Climb steep slabs on the left to a large platform with several shattered blocks.

3. 20m Gain the obvious groove above and climb its left edge until a steep section at 15m forces a left traverse to easier climbing and a flake belay.

4. 50m Climb more easily for 25m to a grassy groove. Follow this to the base of a steep wall.

5. 30m Traverse right to a large ledge with a high flake forming a window at the right-hand end. Climb over the window and round a corner on the right to a stance.

6 and 7. 90m Continue by the crest of the buttress to the plateau.

Chimney Variation: 45m   Very Difficult   (1940)
Traverse right from the flake belay at the end of the third pitch to enter a long chimney which leads to a junction with the flake and window on the original route.

Central Wall Variation: 45m   Severe   (1943)
Climb the steep wall between the original route and the Chimney Variation.

Left-Hand Variation: 60m   Severe   (1958)
Leave the original route at the end of pitch 4 and follow a groove up left by "moss bolsters and occasional rock" to join the mid-point of Hesperides Ledge. Finish as for that route.

Winter: 230m   VI,6 ***   (1959)
This route, often in condition and one of the best mixed routes on the mountain, deserves much more attention. The route-finding is intricate and the best way is slightly different from the summer line. Several variations have been climbed, which in general are harder than the original. Notably, above pitch 2, instead of traversing right, continue up the forked chimney line above. Start a little way up Comb Gully where an obvious ledge splits the buttress diagonally at one-third height.
1. 30m From the bottom left end of the ledge move up to another parallel ledge.
2. 25m Go right to the foot of an obvious groove.
3. 50m Climb the groove to a collection of broken blocks. Turn the steep wall on the left with difficulty (crux) and move up to a further ledge. Belay on the right. A fine and sustained pitch.
4. 45m Traverse right by walls and steep snow to the buttress crest.
5 and 6. 80m Continue more easily up the crest to the plateau.
Variation: *Left-Hand Start*   50m   V,5   (1987)
Climb Comb Gully for 40m to where it narrows. Leave the gully by a groove on the right and climb this for 10m. Traverse right below the barrier to a left-slanting ramp which joins the original line at the collection of broken blocks on pitch 3.

120   Don't Die of Ignorance   200m   VI,6   (1987)
This route forces a line up the steep front face of The Comb. The first pitch takes the central fault line which crosses the buttress from left to right at one-third height, then uses aid to gain the superb-looking groove line above, which provides excellent mixed climbing. From the bottom of Comb Gully follow the easy ramp right to belay.
1. 30m A2 Difficult aid climbing (large Friends) leads around the prow. Continue up the crack line above (blade pegs and RPs) to a snow bay.
2. 45m Climb the corner at the back of the basin. Belay at the base of the chimney.
3. 45m Continue up the chimney to a cave, exiting left where the gully overhangs. Follow the crest of the buttress to join the previous route.
4 to 5. 80m Finish easily up the crest to the plateau.

121 Pigott's Route   250m   IV,5 *   (1960)

A fickle climb which is not often in condition. The major difficulties are confined to the initial flake chimney, which can be very hard. Above, the route follows the largest of the grooves in the upper section of the buttress. From below Comb Gully, follow the easy ramp across the lower section of the buttress to the base of the flake-chimney, which is about 35 metres left of Green Gully. It is the first reasonable break in the overhangs, and has a large boulder just down from its base. (Not to be confused with the obvious steep corner lower down the ramp). The ramp can also be gained by climbing the lower buttress at the first possible point to the left of Green Gully. Climb the flake chimney to a ledge. Traverse 10 metres left and climb the steep ice-filled groove to the easier crest of the buttress. The route is a poor summer climb (250m Severe 1921).

122 Mercury   150m   IV,4 **   (1985)

A good route taking the furthest right of the four parallel grooves just left of Green Gully.

1. 20m Climb directly up iced grooves from the foot of Green Gully towards a chimney with a small chockstone.
2. 50m Continue up to a small overhang (often well iced), then traverse left over loose flakes to the main groove-line.
3 and 4. 80m Climb the groove and continue over steep icy walls to the buttress crest, which leads to the top.

123 Green Gully   180m   IV,4 *** *20.3.99 c ke.*   (1906)

The prominent gully defining the right flank of The Comb is a popular classic and a fine companion to Comb Gully. It is often in condition and has good belays, although they can be difficult to find on the central section of the route. Climb a steep ice pitch (which can vary depending on the snow build up) to a peg belay on the left wall (45m). Continue up the gully for two or three ice pitches with peg belays on the right wall. Above, the gully fans out and there is a choice of finishes. The easiest options are to traverse left to the ridge at the top of The Comb, or bear right up easy snow. The best finish is straight up *via* a fine direct ice pitch, but a large cornice can make this problematical. The gully has been climbed in summer, but it is not recommended (180m Very Difficult 1958).

NUMBER THREE GULLY BUTTRESS

Number Three Gully Buttress extends rightwards from Green Gully, and presents first a broad slabby wall, then a very steep buttress of excellent rock. A huge open left-facing corner, taken by the winter route Quickstep, defines the junction of the two sections of the buttress. Several good summer routes lie on the steeper right-hand section, which is split by the prominent groove of The Knuckleduster and which can be clearly seen from the C.I.C. Hut. The buttress is bounded on its right edge by Number Three Gully.

Venus   190m   V,5 *   (1982)
The well-defined arete right of Green Gully, and starting at its base, provides good mixed climbing. Climb ice just right of the gully, then continue up the arete by way of a faint open groove. After 60m, move right past a good spike and climb a groove to the top (as for Aphrodite).

124   Aphrodite   200m   IV,4 **   (1971)
This good but wandering route traverses left along the second snowy ledge system at half-height on the face to finish up mixed ground to the right of Green Gully. Start in a snowy depression just right of the centre of the base of the buttress. Climb to the foot of a slabby wall, then traverse up and left on snowy ledges until it is possible to make a hard move down and left to the foot of an open groove which is undercut by a large rock wall. Climb the groove and its continuation on the crest beside Green Gully. Move up right across snow to the cornice, which can sometimes be difficult.

Tramp   180m   IV,4 *   (1987)
A good route, but essentially just a direct start to Aphrodite. Start at the foot of the icefall right of Green Gully. Climb it diagonally rightwards to a snowy ledge. Cross this to reach a rock belay directly below a dramatic left-facing chimney, which is not visible from below. Climb the chimney and the huge pedestal above to gain a corner-crack which leads to the groove of Aphrodite and the top.

THE COMB AND NUMBER THREE GULLY BUTTRESS

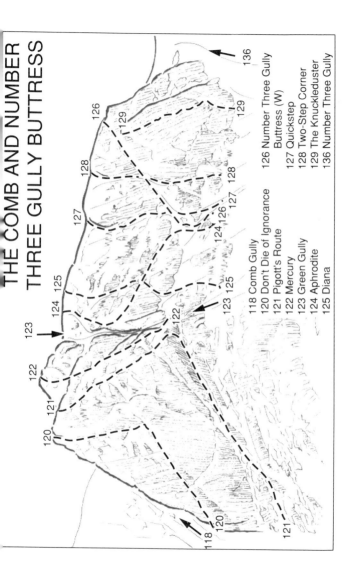

118 Comb Gully
120 Don't Die of Ignorance
121 Pigott's Route
122 Mercury
123 Green Gully
124 Aphrodite
125 Diana

126 Number Three Gully
    Buttress (W)
127 Quickstep
128 Two-Step Corner
129 The Knuckleduster
136 Number Three Gully

125   Diana   190m   V,5 *   (1985)
Start as for Tramp, at the foot of the icefall to the right of Green Gully.
1. 50m Climb the icefall, passing a horizontal snow band, to belay beneath a steep rock wall.
2. 45m Climb the chimney-groove in the centre of the steep wall. Pull over a large chockstone to reach another snow band and a huge block stance.
3. 25m Follow corners to below a huge right-facing corner.
4. 45m Pull over an overlap onto the right wall and continue up steep thin ice to easier ground.
5. 25m Follow the obvious line up snow to the top.

126   Number Three Gully Buttress   130m   Moderate * (1902)
Taking the easiest line up the buttress, this climb offers some fine situations, and is a useful descent route from the harder rock climbs. Start about 50 metres right of Green Gully and climb easily to the foot of a long groove slanting up to the right. Follow the groove for 45m to a large corner below a steep chimney-crack. Traverse right, then climb up steep but easy rocks to a large platform. Climb up to a smaller platform, then traverse right to an obvious ledge leading across the upper face of the buttress. From the end of the ledge climb slabby rock to the plateau. From the upper and smaller platform, the Chimney Variation leads out left and up a steep chimney (35m Very Difficult).
Winter: 130m   III ***   (1957)
One of the finest medium grade winter climbs on the mountain. The route is somewhat exposed in places, and the upper section can be time-consuming if the snow is not consolidated. Start as for Aphrodite in a snowy bay just right of centre of the lower part of the buttress. Climb up to a snow shelf and follow it up to the right. From its highest point traverse right over snow and ice to a large platform. Either traverse left to The Chimney Variation, and climb this on steepish ice to the top, or follow the original summer line. Both lines are exposed.

The open slabby corner which splits the buttress into two distinct sections is interrupted by the traverse line of Number Three Gully Buttress. Quickstep follows the corner and the obvious fault-line to the right is taken by Two-Step Corner.

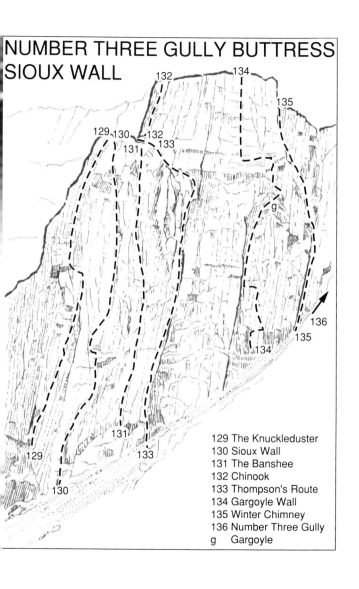

NUMBER THREE GULLY BUTTRESS
SIOUX WALL

129 The Knuckleduster
130 Sioux Wall
131 The Banshee
132 Chinook
133 Thompson's Route
134 Gargoyle Wall
135 Winter Chimney
136 Number Three Gully
g   Gargoyle

127   Quickstep   130m   V,5 **   (1983)
This excellent steep ice climb takes the huge left-facing corner directly above the start of Number Three Gully Buttress.
1 and 2. 55m Climb easily up to the traverse ledge and move up to a belay at the foot of the upper slabby corner.
3. 45m Continue up steep ice on the left wall of the corner to a belay.
4. 30m Climb into a basin below the cornice, which can be by-passed on the right.

128   Two-Step Corner   130m   V,5 ***   (1975)
Another good ice climb which is often in condition. Be warned, it has a stiff reputation and is considerably steeper than it looks. Start 20 metres right of the snow bay at the foot of Number Three Gully Buttress below an icy groove. Climb the groove to the prominent ledge which cuts the upper section of the buttress, and continue up the very steep corner to the top. There is often a large cornice which can be avoided by a traverse to the right.

The following routes are located on the steep right-hand section of the buttress. In summer the best descent is down Number Three Gully Buttress, although Thompson's Route is also sometimes used.

Arthur   140m   HVS   (1971)
This rarely climbed route follows a line to the left of the great groove of The Knuckleduster. A peg was used on the first ascent, and it is not known if the route has been climbed free.
1. 10m Climb up to a ledge below an obvious corner.
2. 40m 4b Continue up a vertical groove on the right to a pinnacle platform. Step across the cleft and continue up a short groove to an obvious left traverse. Pass behind blocks to a belay on a platform.
3. 30m 5a Climb the corner above, step left round the edge, and go up to a short overhanging wall split by a crack. Climb this (peg) and continue straight above to a tiny exposed platform.
4. 40m 4c Move up awkwardly, then continue easily rightwards into a groove which is followed to a belay.
4. 20m Continue up the groove to finish on the platform of Number Three Gully Buttress.

Number Three Gully Buttress, Ben Nevis (Climber, Alex Runciman)

129   The Knuckleduster   120m   HVS **   (1966)

A high quality route following the great groove in the steep right-hand section of the buttress. Unfortunately it is slow to dry. Start by scrambling up to a belay at the foot of the groove.

1. 40m 4c Climb the groove to a belay under an overhang.

2. 15m 5a Turn the overhang by a slab on the right. Belay on the outer edge.

3. 35m 5a Regain the groove by a horizontal ledge and continue by a crack in the right wall to a belay.

4. 30m 4c Climb the wall on the right to the large platform of Number Three Gully Buttress.

Last Stand   110m   HVS **   (1984)

The arete to the right of The Knuckleduster is a very steep and exposed route. Start below the prominent groove of The Knuckleduster.

1. 30m Follow a diagonal line of weakness up and right to the foot of the arete.

2. 40m 5a Climb by thin cracks on the right-hand side of the arete to a belay ledge on the arete.

3. 40m 5a Continue directly by cracks, surmount a bulge, and finish easily up more cracks.

130   Sioux Wall   90m   HVS **   (1972)

A superb climb and fairly popular. It follows the groove line just left of the centre of the face which, fortunately, is easier than it looks! Start below the prominent groove of The Knuckleduster.

1. 25m Follow the diagonal line of weakness up and right (as for Last Stand), then climb up past a large rock fin to a square-cut niche.

2. 30m 5a Step left onto the steep wall. Climb this to a crack, then move left onto a small ramp which leads back right to the base of an obvious corner-groove. Bridge up this to below a roof. Move left, then go back right to a belay above the roof.

3. 20m 5a Climb the steep crack above (hard to start) to a small overhang. Pull directly over this on large holds to a ledge and belay.

4. 15m Climb the continuation crack to the large platform of Number Three Gully Buttress.

Carn Dearg Buttress, Ben Nevis. Climbers on King Kong and The Bat

131   The Banshee   120m   VS   (1984)
This fine-looking route takes a line between Sioux Wall and the chimneys of Thompson's Route. The Scottish VS grade should be treated with caution! Climb a corner-chimney line to a belay on a ledge, as for Sioux Wall. Climb a narrow corner for 10m, move right a short distance, then climb grooves and walls to overlook Thompson's Route. Belay above a black corner. Continue up the broken corner above to the large platform of Number Three Gully Buttress.

132   Chinook   65m   HVS *   (1984)
The arete to the right of Two-Step Corner provides a good continuation for the routes on the lower section of the buttress. Start on the platform of Number Three Gully Buttress at a spike below a groove, 10 metres right of Two-Step Corner.
1. 35m 5a Climb the groove, trending left at about 25m, then move back right to a crack which is followed to a large belay ledge.
2. 30m Continue by a left-slanting chimney on the arete to reach the plateau.

133   Thompson's Route   110m   IV,4 ***   (1963)
The steep right flank of the buttress is bounded by a line of icy chimneys. These provide a good and sustained route which has a well deserved reputation for quality amongst Nevis regulars. Climb the chimneys in two or three pitches to the large platform above the lower buttress. Easier climbing leads to the plateau. In summer the route is rarely climbed, but it is sometimes used as a means of descent from the harder routes (110m Difficult 1941).

134   Gargoyle Wall   120m   Very Difficult   (1950)
The Gargoyle, a prominent head-shaped feature, can be well seen on the right-hand skyline when descending Number Three Gully. Start on a ledge 10m up and right of the chimney of Thompson's Route.
1. 45m Climb the steep wall above by a zigzag line to a well-defined ledge. From the left end of the ledge descend slightly and enter the first chimney. Climb this, surmount a large chockstone and gain a rocky bay with The Gargoyle now visible on the right.
2. 30m Cross a groove and follow a short gangway to reach The Gargoyle. Climb the ridge above, passing a perched block, to a ledge.

Traverse right into a corner and climb this to a stance and block belay below a steep wall.

3. 30m Continue by the steep crack above to a rock platform. Traverse 6m left to a chimney-crack and climb this on good holds to a stance and belay.

4. 15m Climb the chimney with difficulty (it can be avoided on the left), then continue easily to the top of the buttress.

Winter: 120m   IV,6 *   (1977)

A good route deserving more ascents. Climb the icy chimney of Thompson's Route, traverse onto the Gargoyle, and follow the summer route to the top. The climb is not sustained, but the upper cracks can be very difficult.

135   Winter Chimney   60m   IV,5 *   (1963)

Rarely climbed, this route ascends the chimney lying in the back of the bay which defines the right edge of Gargoyle Wall. Start 30m up the gully from the previous route. The chimney contains three or four shortish ice pitches, and can provide a sustained and hard climb. The ice wall to the right can be climbed at Grade IV.

136   Number Three Gully   90m   I *   (1895)

This is the large gully situated at the back of Coire na Ciste, separating Number Three Gully Buttress from Creag Coire na Ciste. It can be easily identified from above by a pinnacle standing as a flat topped blade of rock at the head of the gully. This is a useful landmark when trying to locate the gully when the plateau is shrouded in mist. The gully is a straightforward snow slope, although the final 10m may be quite icy. If using the gully for descent, start to the right of the pinnacle. In summer the gully is a scree slope, with about 10m of loose rock at the top, but it does pass through some impressive rock scenery.

CREAG COIRE NA CISTE

The series of buttresses which lie between Number Three and Number Four gullies is known as Creag Coire na Ciste. The left end of the cliff is set at a high angle, and is seamed by a number of steep gullies. The rock is very poor, and this is not an area to visit in summer, despite some interesting-looking lines. In winter the cornices may be a formidable problem.

137   South Gully   120m   III *   (1936)
Start from the foot of the narrow section of Number Three Gully, level
with the lowest rocks of Number Three Gully Buttress. Climb an
obvious slanting ledge leading right to the foot of a steep gully which
turns back left. Under heavy snow it can be a straightforward snow
climb, though normally there will be a couple of short ice pitches.

138   Lost the Place   140m   IV,4   (1988)
The buttress between South and Central Gullies is cut by a groove
system which starts to the left of Central Gully. Follow this trending
right to a point overlooking South Gully, then traverse right along a
ramp line to reach a loose chimney which leads to the cornice.

139   Une Journée Ordinaire dans un Enfer Quotidien   (1993)
          105m   VI,6 **
A good steep ice climb. Start by climbing Central Gully for 10m, then
traverse 10 metres left to the foot of a steep icefall.
1. 45m   Climb the icefall, exit left, then continue up a further short steep
section to belay on the left.
2. 45m   Continue up easy snow to a steep 8m wall of hollow ice, which
leads to the cornice.
3. 15m   Traverse left and exit through the cornice at the easiest point.

140   Levitation   115m   VI,6 **   (1993)
A varied climb with difficult mixed moves followed by steep ice.
1. 30m   Climb Central Gully for 10m, then traverse across the left wall
beneath an overlap to a steep hanging icicle on the prow of the
buttress. Climb this to easier ground and good belays.
2. 35m   Continue easily up the snow basin on the left to belay below
the steep upper section.
3. 50m   Climb ice, then traverse left to break through cornice at its
narrowest point (as for the previous route).

141   Central Gully   120m   III **   (1959)
A very fine climb but quite hard for its grade. Start at the lowest rocks
and climb via a series of snow patches to the left of a rib to reach the
foot of two parallel ice gullies. Climb the left-hand gully on steep ice
(strenuous but with good protection). After 35m, cross into the right-
hand gully and continue up snow to the plateau.

CREAG COIRE NA CISTE

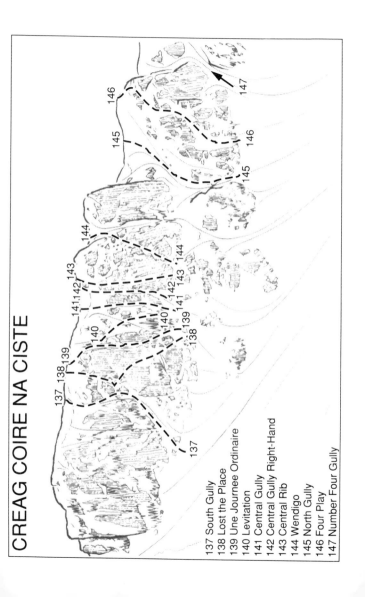

137 South Gully
138 Lost the Place
139 Une Journee Ordinaire
140 Levitation
141 Central Gully
142 Central Gully Right-Hand
143 Central Rib
144 Wendigo
145 North Gully
146 Four Play
147 Number Four Gully

142   Central Gully, Right-Hand   120m   IV,4 ***
Start as for Central Gully and climb the right-hand chimney throughout. An excellent and sustained ice pitch with good belays. An independent start can be made by climbing the right-slanting icefall to the left of North Gully, then traversing left to the foot of the chimney.

143   Central Rib   120m   III,4 *   (1970)
A good early season route. Start at the lowest point of the crag and climb up to where the rib becomes well defined. This section is often well banked out. Continue steeply up the left edge overlooking Central Gully Right-Hand, and finish on a large ledge which runs round left under the final tower. It is a fair climb in summer (120m Difficult 1941). The final tower can be climbed by following right-slanting grooves (15m Very Difficult 1943).

144   Wendigo   110m   IV,4 **   (1963)
An enjoyable climb, consisting of steep ice in its lower section, and interesting mixed ground in its upper reaches. Start in a bay right of Central Rib, at the foot of an icefall. Climb a steep icy right-slanting rake up the steep buttress (overlooking North Gully) to a large ledge. Climb mixed ground above by the line of least resistance to a snow bay just under the cornice.

145   North Gully   110m   II **   (1934)
The obvious narrow gully close to the entrance to Number Four Gully gives a great little climb. The first section is often full of ice, and the route is reliably in condition early in the season. Climb the initial gully, then traverse up and right to a large snow fan leading to the plateau. Beware of avalanche danger on the final slopes. The gully has been climbed in summer but is not recommended (110m Very Difficult 1935).
Variation: The Left Fork   35m   III   (1964)
Climb up into a steep scoop from the snow basin, then take a steep ice groove at the back of the scoop to the plateau. Harder, but better than the original line.

146   Four Play   110m   IV,4   (1993)
The buttress between North Gully and Number Four Gully is split by a thin V-groove. Start just left of where Number Four Gully widens at its base, well to the right of North Gully. Climb the chimney and bulge above to a snow bay. Continue up an icy groove to a short ice arete which leads to the top. The route is often well banked out (Grade III).

147   Number Four Gully   100m   I   (1895)

The most straightforward of the Nevis gullies, and the best descent route from the plateau. There is a marker post at the top. The gully is a simple snow slope and the cornice can always be turned on the right towards the upper slopes of Number Four Gully Buttress. About halfway up the gully, a chimney splits the left wall (Grade III). In summer the gully is a scree slope and is a useful descent route, but it is very loose.

Number Four Gully Buttress is the broken mass of rock immediately to the right of the mouth of the gully, above South Trident Buttress. It is Moderate in summer, and gives a straightforward winter climb (100m II 1929).

SOUTH TRIDENT BUTTRESS

The most southerly and best defined of the three Trident Buttresses is bounded on the left by Number Four Gully, and on the right by Central Gully. The buttress comprises three tiers. The lowest is steep, with routes leading to the upper reaches of a broad grassy ledge. This point can also be easily reached from the screes at the foot of Number Four Gully. The middle tier commences above the ledge, and is defined by a similar, though smaller ledge, slanting up from the narrows of Number Four Gully. An obvious feature of the right-hand end of the middle tier is the huge corner of The Clanger. The upper tier is a narrow shattered ridge which gives scrambling to the summit plateau. The buttress provides very pleasant rock climbing in the lower and middle grades. The easiest descent is to traverse left across the ledges at the top of each tier to reach Number Four Gully.

The following routes lie on the lower tier of the buttress.

1934 Route   100m   Very Difficult   (1934)

Start at the lowest point of the buttress.

1. 25m Climb up to a dark corner below a rotten chimney. Descend slightly, then traverse left round a rib to a shallow gully and belay.
2. 30m From a metre or so up the gully, climb the right wall to a stance. Continue over large blocks to a well-defined ledge.
3. 30m From the left end of the ledge climb a bulge to slabs which lead to the foot of a clean-cut corner.
4. 15m Traverse left and move up to the top of the lower tier. Alternatively, take the Direct Finish up the crack at the back of the clean-cut corner (15m Severe 1954).

1936 Route   110m   Severe   (1936)
A poor route; only the final section is worthwhile. Start left of the lowest rocks. Climb up left of a shallow gully, then traverse across it after 10m. Climb the steep rocks above to a stance and belay. Continue for about 6m, then traverse right by a series of shelves to a grassy ledge and a block belay. Above the block, climb up right on steep rock to the foot of an obvious groove which leads to the top of the lower tier.

148   1944 Route   125m   Severe ***   (1944)
An excellent climb, which is best followed by one of the routes on the middle tier to provide a fine combination.
1. 30m Scramble to the foot of the steep wall about 30 metres right of the lowest rocks.
2. 25m Climb left of the steep chimney, then trend left to a ledge and belay.
3. 25m Move up from the foot of a large leaning block to the foot of the second groove from the left. Traverse right under the third groove to a point beneath the fourth and final groove.
4. 35m Climb into the groove, then using a crack in the right wall reach a system of ledges and follow them to a steep corner.
5. 10m Finish by the corner to gain the middle ledge near its northern end.

Eastern Block   125m   VI,6   (1987)
A hard mixed climb. Climb the first two pitches of 1944 Route (bold), then traverse the ledge to some stacked blocks. Climb the bulging wall above to a belay ledge some 15m higher, then continue more easily to the top of the buttress.

The Minge   105m   VS   (1981)
To the right of 1944 Route, just right of a curving black crack, is a prominent crack in the centre of the face.
1. 30m Climb the lower buttress to a grass ledge.
2. 35m 4c Step left into the crack and follow it onto a slab. Belay in the crack.
3. 40m 4b Climb the slab, traverse right into another crack, and move up to a belay.

The following routes ascend the middle tier of the buttress. They can be reached either by the lower routes, or by traversing the terrace from the screes below Number Four Gully.

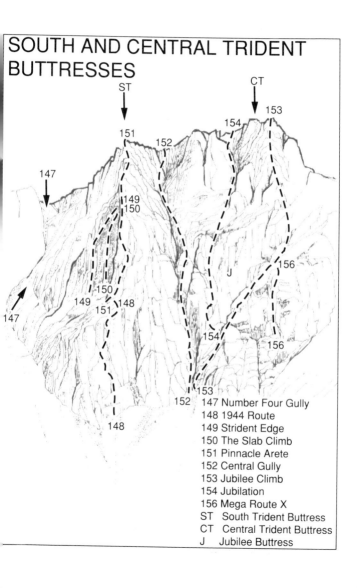

SOUTH AND CENTRAL TRIDENT BUTTRESSES

ST

CT

153

154

151

152

147

149
150

156

J

150
149   148

151

154

147

156

154

153

152   147 Number Four Gully
148   148 1944 Route
      149 Strident Edge
      150 The Slab Climb
      151 Pinnacle Arete
      152 Central Gully
      153 Jubilee Climb
      154 Jubilation
      156 Mega Route X
      ST   South Trident Buttress
      CT   Central Trident Buttress
      J   Jubilee Buttress

The Rattler   75m   Severe   (1984)
Above the left end of the screes under the middle tier is a deep
chimney-groove which can be easily identified by a small pinnacle at
its top. Start 15 metres left of the chimney-groove.
1. 25m Climb a chimney to a ledge.
2. 35m Step over the top of the chimney into a groove-crack and follow
this to a ledge. Climb the steep wall above on large holds to a second
ledge.
3. 15m Climb the corner-flake to the top.

The Groove Climb   75m   Very Difficult   (1943)
Start beneath the deep chimney-groove 15 metres right of The Rattler.
1. 30m Climb the groove to a deep cave.
2. 10m Make an awkward exit, then move up to a belay.
3. 35m Continue up to the right by easy cracked slabs to the crest of
the buttress.
Winter: 80m   V,6 *   (1992)
A good short mixed route, ideal for a short winter's day. Follow the
summer route to the end of pitch 2, but instead of trending right up
cracked slabs take a left-slanting icy ramp to the top.

Sidewinder   100m   VS *   (1964)
About 15 metres right of The Groove Climb is a triple-tiered corner
rising steeply leftwards across the face.
1. 25m Scramble from the ledge to the foot of the corner.
2. 25m 4c Climb the corner.
3. 20m 4b Continue in the line of the corner to an easy slab.
4. 30m Finish directly by a crack and large flake to reach the crest of
the buttress below the final tier.

149 Strident Edge   100m   VS **   (1972)
The formidable looking arete to the right of the triple-tiered corner gives
fine exposed climbing, but it is a little rattly in places.
1. 25m Scramble up to base of the wall 6 metres left of Sidewinder.
2. 15m 4b Climb up to a belay in the corner of Sidewinder.
3. 35m 4c Move out right and climb a steep crack immediately to the
left of the crest of the arete.
4. 25m 4b Follow the left edge of the arete to the top of the middle
tier.

Spartacus   100m   VS *   (1962)
Traverse the middle ledge below the arete of Strident Edge to a corner
some 20 metres left of the huge corner of The Clanger.
1. 30m 4b Climb the corner, surmount the overhang, then traverse
right to a stance.
2. 15m 4b Follow a small groove on the right to a flake. Descend a
little across a steep wall to an arete and climb this to a large flake belay.
3. 25m 4b Continue directly, then move left above the overhang to a
flake crack. Follow this for a short distance, then traverse right to a
belay on the arete.
4. 30m Climb the groove above to the top of the tier.

150   The Slab Climb   90m   Very Difficult *   (1944)
A good route, but not recommended in the wet! Start midway between
Spartacus and the great corner of The Clanger.
1. 25m Climb the right-hand of two cracks to an overhang. Traverse
into the left-hand crack to a stance.
2. 25m Continue up the crack to a conspicuous chimney.
3. 15m Climb the chimney (strenuous).
4. 25m Follow the continuation of the chimney to the top of the tier.

The Clanger   90m   IV,5 **   (1967)
The chimney-groove at the back of the large corner near the right end
of the middle tier gives a sustained and difficult mixed climb. It is not
a route for the over-weight climber! Start at the foot of the groove, and
climb mixed rock and ice to a steep cave pitch (35m). Escape from
the cave by the right wall, where a narrow through-route leads behind
a large flake onto the crest of the buttress. Easier climbing leads to
the top. The summer route follows the chimney-groove all the way to
its top and finishes directly up a very loose wall (90m VS 1964).

151   Pinnacle Arete   150m   Very Difficult **   (1902)
This excellent route is often combined with one of the routes on the
lower tier. Start from the right end of the middle ledge at a point
overlooking the steep north wall of the buttress. Climb sloping ledges
for 3m, then continue up an awkward corner on the right, followed by
10m of difficult rock to reach easier ground. Trend left onto the crest
and climb to the foot of a steep wall. Climb this directly on good holds,
or by joining the chimney about mid-height on the left. A further short
steep section gives access to the narrow shattered crest leading to
the final tier of the buttress.

Winter: 150m IV,4 **   (1959)
Follow a snowy traverse across the middle ledge, then climb a series
of snow and ice grooves immediately right of the crest to the easier
upper section of the buttress.

Joyful Chimneys 180m III   (1971)
This route follows the obvious series of four icy chimneys on the right
flank of the buttress about 50 metres left of Central Gully. Start just
right of a distinctive long thin rib and climb the first chimney. The
second chimney is bottomless and entered from a flake on the left,
and the third is best avoided by grooves to its left. These lead to a
further series of grooves and the crest of South Trident Buttress. The
summer route takes a line just to the left (170m Severe 1972).

152 Central Gully 360m III *   (1904)
A fine climb with an alpine feel. It lies almost directly above Lochan na
Ciste, separating the right-hand end of South Trident Buttress from
several subsidiary buttresses to the right. The lower gully is well
defined, and the upper half consists of large snowfields which can be
avalanche-prone after heavy snowfall. Follow the lower gully to a steep
ice column. Turn this by a traverse left on mixed snow and ice, and
return to the original line as soon as possible. Climb the snowfields
with some short difficult steps, to reach the plateau beside the top of
Number Four Gully. The ice column can be climbed direct (30m III,4
1956).

JUBILEE BUTTRESS

The following two routes lie on the steep diamond-shaped buttress
between Central Gully and the rake taken by Jubilee Climb.

Nosepicker 90m Severe   (1972)
This climb takes the line of least resistance on the buttress. Start below
the 3m pitch of Jubilee Climb and make a left-rising traverse below
the vertical central section. Traverse right onto the nose and follow this
to the top.

Gutbuster 100m HVS *   (1972)
This sustained route tackles the front of the buttress as directly as
possible, and involves some awkward moves and fine situations. Start
just right of the toe of the buttress.

1. 40m 4c Gain the toe of the buttress and traverse 5 metres left to a groove ; follow this to below a wide open corner-ramp. Climb this for 10m to a stance where two huge ledges breach the steep central part of the buttress.

2. 20m 5a Traverse the lower ledge to its end and move round onto the right-hand face. Move down and across to a rib, and climb this to a rotten fault rising rightwards below a roof. Enter this and stomach traverse below the roof to emerge at a foothold.

3. 40m 4c Traverse a thin wall on the left between roofs to the crest of the buttress. Follow a gangway to the left, then the ensuing ramp, to finish up the nose of the buttress.

153   Jubilee Climb   240m   Very Difficult
Although this is not a particularly good rock climb, its lower section is sometimes used as a descent route from the harder routes on Central Trident Buttress. From the bifurcation in the lower reaches of Central Gully, take the shallow right-hand branch over easy slabs and scree for 75m to a steep corner-crack. Climb this for 3m, then traverse right over blocks to a belay. Climb the slabs above for 10m, then continue up scree for 10m to a short chimney and slab. Climb these for 30m to a scree slope. The upper buttress lies above on the left; climb its crest in two steep pitches for 75m. Scrambling leads to the final slopes.
Winter: 240m   II   (1935)
An interesting climb on snow with some short ice pitches. Take the right branch of Central Gully to the middle terrace, where a choice of lines leads to the top. Care should be taken in avalanche conditions.

154   Jubilation   240m   IV,4 *   (1963)
Follow Jubilee Climb for 75m, then traverse left to an icefall and climb steep ice to a snow bay. Move left into a chimney which leads to the final arete of the buttress.

CENTRAL TRIDENT BUTTRESS

To the right of Jubilee Climb lies an extremely steep, rounded wall of superb-looking rock, which is characterised by a large corner system at its right-hand end. The left arete of this corner is split by a deep crack-line. Left again is an overlapping slabby corner. All the climbs here are good and well worth doing.

155   Steam   90m   HVS **   (1970)

About 25 metres left of the prominent crack in the arete is a large right-facing corner with overlapping slabs on its right wall. Start below this.

1. 25m 4c Climb the corner to an overhang, and turn it on the left to reach a stance.

2. 30m 5a Climb the wall above for 6m, then traverse left into a small corner left of the main line. Follow this to a left-sloping ramp and belay in a corner.

3. 35m 4c Traverse diagonally up right to a sloping ledge on the left. Continue left and climb the steep wall to the top.

156   Mega Route X   70m   VI,6 ***   (1982)

A very steep icefall approximating to the line of Steam. The lowest 5m takes a long time to form, and the icefall often crashes to the ground at about the point it becomes climbable.

1. 40m Climb the icefall directly to a ramp which slants left to a belay in the corner below an overhang.

2. 30m Continue up right to easier ground and a block belay.

157   Heidbanger   90m   E1 *   (1970)

A wandering line to the right of Steam. The route climbs into the cave in the deep crack in the central arete, then continues up the wall above. Start mid-way between Steam and the base of the crack, just left of a steep groove.

1. 40m 5b Surmount a bulge and move right to the top of the groove after 6m. Climb a short corner above onto a slab. Traverse right across this to the arete, which is turned to reach the cave.

2. 20m 5b Take a crack leading out of the cave, then follow a left-trending line of weakness up the wall to the arete.

3. 30m 4c Ascend the big corner-line, then continue up a smaller corner to the top, passing a dubious flake.

157a   Cranium: 25m   E1 5b   (1977)

A direct start to Heidbanger. Climb the deep crack in the arete directly from the ground to the cave.

CENTRAL TRIDENT BUTTRESS

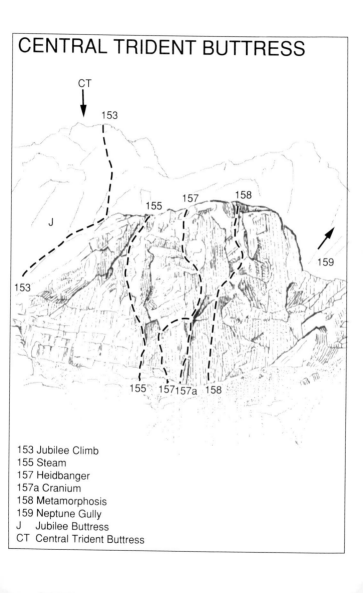

153 Jubilee Climb
155 Steam
157 Heidbanger
157a Cranium
158 Metamorphosis
159 Neptune Gully
J   Jubilee Buttress
CT   Central Trident Buttress

158   Metamorphosis   105m   E1 **   (1971)
The best route on the buttress, and one of the finest of its grade on
the mountain. It follows the hanging corner right of the cracked arete
of Heidbanger. Start just left of the overhanging crack at the right-hand
end of the face.
1. 35m 5b Move right up the wall to join the crack below a bulge.
Surmount this and follow the crack-line to below a corner. Go right and
up to the corner, and follow this to a ledge.
2. 30m 5a Continue up the corner past a recess to a ledge. Traverse
right, then go up to a poor stance beneath a prominent flake.
3. 25m 4c Follow the flake and crack above, then trend right to easier
ground.
4. 15m Finish by a corner and the wall above.

NORTH TRIDENT BUTTRESS

North Trident Buttress is the furthest right of the Trident Buttresses. It
is easy-angled at its base, but higher up it steepens into twin ridges
separated by a gully. It is a fine area for winter mountaineering routes.

159   Neptune Gully   155m   III   (1956)
This S-shaped gully splits the right-hand crest of the buttress, and lies
to the left of the North Trident Buttress. Start 10 metres left of Moonlight
Gully and climb the lower snow slopes of North Trident Buttress to an
ice pitch barring access to the gully. Turn this on the right, then climb
a short pitch to the foot of a steep ice step. Turn this on the left wall to
reach a ledge, then continue by a hard corner to regain the gully. Climb
ice-bound rocks on the left, then continue up snow between the steep
buttresses to a 7m ice pitch. Climb this directly to snow slopes which
lead to a large platform overlooking Number Five Gully. Continue
easily to the plateau.

Between Neptune Gully and North Trident Buttress is a 50m wall of
steep rock on the left flank of the buttress. There are two climbs here:

Geotactic   45m   VS 4b   (1993)
Start from a small grassy bay below a prominent left-facing slabby wall
at the left end of the lower tier. Climb a groove to a good ledge, then
continue up the groove and traverse left at a giant flake. Climb up near
the buttress edge before making a rising traverse back right to finish
by an awkward corner directly above the start of the route.

Tuff Nut   45m   HVS 5a *   (1993)
The wall of clean rock on the right side of the lower tier is split by a
prominent crack. Climb the crack, move left at the top and finish by a
short corner.

160   North Trident Buttress   200m   III **   (1904)
A good mixed climb taking the buttress overlooking Moonlight Gully.
The best line is dependent on the conditions, and the description is
for general guidance only. Climb the lower rocks, which are generally
masked with snow, and continue up to the final tower. Turn this to gain
the easy upper section of the buttress. It is possible to start the climb
from snow slopes on the left-hand side of the buttress (Grade III).
There are also a number of short icefalls high up on the buttress, which
are easily reached *via* Moonlight Gully. In summer the buttress is a
rather unsatisfactory climb (200m Very Difficult), but it is possible to
climb the steep chimney on the right side of the lower tier, to the left
of the original route (45m Severe 1935).

   Central Rib Direct (150m IV 1967) takes the central of three narrow
ribs on the right flank of the buttress, and can be gained by a left-rising
traverse from Moonlight Gully. On the first ascent, a considerable
amount of aid was used to climb the exposed right arete on the
imposing final tower.

161   Moonlight Gully   150m   I/II   (1898)
This pleasant snow gully separates North Trident Buttress from Moonlight Gully Buttress. The gully is narrow and straight and ends in the
wide upper funnel of Number Five Gully.

MOONLIGHT GULLY BUTTRESS

This two-tiered buttress separates Moonlight Gully from the lower
reaches of Number Five Gully. The summer routes here are pleasant
and easily accessible and they make a good approach to the climbs
higher up on Number Five Gully Buttress.

162   Diagonal Route   90m   Moderate   (1936)
Start at the foot of Moonlight Gully and traverse up and right to a broad
terrace. Continue by the left-hand of two chimneys to the top of the
first tier. Climb the upper tier by the continuation chimney.
Winter: 90m   III   (1983)
Follow the summer route to the top.

163   Right-Hand Chimney   120m   Very Difficult *   (1943)

Start midway between Moonlight and Number Five Gully, at the foot of the rightmost and better defined of the chimneys splitting the buttress. The route follows the chimney throughout, and is steep and sustained in its lower half. Thereafter, easier climbing leads to the top of the first tier. Climb the upper tier by the continuation of the chimney with little difficulty.

Winter: 120m   III,4 **   (1983)

Follow the summer route by excellent sustained climbing.

Gaslight   90m   Very Difficult   (1984)

Climb the buttress between Right-Hand Chimney and the right edge to a large roof. Step into Right-Hand Chimney to bypass the roof, then traverse right above the roof to reach the right edge of the buttress. Climb the edge to the top.

Winter: 90m   IV,4   (1989)

Follow the summer line throughout.

Moonlight Arete   90m   Very Difficult

The junction of the front and gully faces of the buttress gives a fine scramble, with a 10m overhanging crux.

Phosphorescent Grooves   175m   III,4 *   (1985)

A useful early season route, taking an interesting rising traverse across the Number Five Gully face of the buttress. The climb may largely bank out late in the season. Start at the edge of the buttress just left of the gully entrance. Climb easy rocks to a large ledge. Continue straight up to a steep wall, then follow obvious ledges rightwards to belay below a slabby corner. Climb the corner to a belay above. Continue right, make an awkward move into a vertical 5m chimney, and climb this to a belay. Traverse right, first slightly down, then back up to easy ground just above the lower tier of the buttress.

164   Number Five Gully   450m   I   (1895)

The gully immediately left of Carn Dearg Buttress is wide and shallow in its lower reaches, and higher up it opens out into a small corrie. The cornices can be massive, but the rim is extensive and an exit should always be possible. There is often a large cone of debris at the foot of the gully which testifies to its tendency to avalanche. In summer the gully is straightforward, with some avoidable chockstones low down.

MOONLIGHT GULLY AND NUMBER FIVE GULLY BUTTRESS

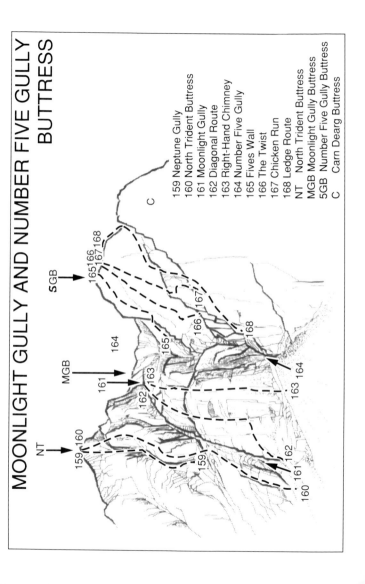

159 Neptune Gully
160 North Trident Buttress
161 Moonlight Gully
162 Diagonal Route
163 Right-Hand Chimney
164 Number Five Gully
165 Fives Wall
166 The Twist
167 Chicken Run
168 Ledge Route
NT   North Trident Buttress
MGB Moonlight Gully Buttress
5GB Number Five Gully Buttress
C   Carn Dearg Buttress

NUMBER FIVE GULLY BUTTRESS

A broad scree ledge leads out right into a large grassy bay from above the lower narrows of Number Five Gully. Above this lies Number Five Gully Buttress which presents steep walls, both to the bay, and to the gully. The rock is generally very good, and the buttress has some fine exposed routes. The ground above the buttress is broken by large steep walls, and route-finding through these can be awkward. Descent is best by Ledge Route. The following three routes lie on the steep gully wall of the buttress.

Lysystrata   55m   HVS   (1971)
The steep V-groove at the left end of the face.
1. 15m 5a Climb a steep corner to a grass terrace.
2. 40m 4c Make a few moves up a groove to an overhang, swing left and climb the groove above with difficulty.

Antigone   55m   HVS   (1971)
Start as for the previous route.
1. 15m 5a Climb a steep corner to a grass terrace.
2. 40m 5a From the foot of the Lysystrata groove, climb another steep groove to a bulge and a slab. Ascend this to a bulge, then move left and back right to a final crack.

Agamemnon   70m   E1 *   (1971)
Start from the curving grass ledge, halfway up the gully face of the buttress.
1. 40m 5a Climb the steep groove just left of an overhanging section, and make a difficult move at its top to exit on a ledge. Go right to a pedestal below a very steep wall.
2. 30m 5b Move up right with difficulty to a hanging slab. Climb the steep wall above and finish up a vertical wall on the right.

165   Fives Wall   60m   Severe   (1953)
Start halfway up the gully face of the buttress at the far end of the curving grass ledge. Climb a groove to a ledge, traverse right past its end, then move up to a large flake. Climb this, then continue up cracks to a large slabby ledge. Traverse left and climb a short crack and wall to a large ledge. Further right a steep crack leads to the top of the buttress.

The Slant   150m   VS *   (1959)

A good exposed route. Start at the lowest point of the buttress.

1. 15m 4a Move up left to a ledge with block belays.
2. 40m 4b Continue by awkward corners to a gangway. At the top step right, then left to a belay below a cracked slab.
3. 25m 4c Climb the slab, then traverse right into a small corner. Climb a short distance to a good belay in a niche.
4. 40m 4c Break out left, traverse left up a slab, then continue left up across a steep wall to a large ledge.
5. 30m Scramble to the top of the buttress.

166   The Twist   140m   VS *   (1962)

This steep and exposed route starts up the gangway of The Slant, then traverses to the edge of the buttress and takes the easiest line to the top. Start at the lowest rocks, under a steep corner.

1. 25m 4c Climb a short steep groove to a ledge at the foot of the gangway. Continue up to a little corner-crack, climb this, then move up to a spike belay.
2. 15m 4a Continue to the top of the gangway and reach a belay at the foot of the cracked slab, as for The Slant.
3. 25m 4c Traverse right to sloping ledges above the overhanging wall. Climb diagonally right over a big flake, then move horizontally along sloping ledges to a belay under an obvious corner.
4. 35m 4b Climb the corner to a block. Traverse right, then move up to a chockstone belay by a pinnacle.
5. 40m 4b Follow the cracks above to the top of a huge pedestal block. Gain the ledge above, climb into a groove on the left, then move out right to a large block. Finish up left to reach a grass ledge, then scramble to the top of the buttress.

167   Chicken Run   150m   VS   (1961)

Start about 50m up and right from the lowest point of the buttress, below a steep and nasty-looking crack. Although this initial crack looks poor, the upper section of this climb is on good steep rock. The technical grade is 4b.

1. 25m Climb the steep crack to a ledge (crux).
2. 30m Continue slightly rightwards on shattered rock to an obvious rock ledge. Traverse left along this to a great flake.
3. 10m Climb the wall above to a ledge.
4. 25m Follow cracks and awkward corners to a larger ledge.
5. 60m The angle now relents. Climb easily to the top of the buttress.

Turkish   180m   HVS   (1967)

A poor route up the left wall of the great corner which dominates the northern face of the buttress. Start below a prominent wide crack below and left of the great corner.

1. 40m Climb the crack, then move left over short walls to belay on a ramp.

2. 35m Move up the ramp, surmount an awkward corner, then move up to the foot of the great corner.

3. 30m Trend left across the left wall, then avoid some large loose blocks by tensioning left for 3m from a peg to reach a ledge. Continue directly up to a platform and belay.

4. 35m Move left, climb a short wall, then ascend a short gully.

5. 40m Continue to the foot of the final wall, then bear hard right for 30m to belay on the crest of the buttress.

The small gully which separates the main face from the smaller wall leading out right is **Fives Gully** (35m Very Difficult 1959). It holds little snow in winter. There are several other short climbs on this wall. **Crack and Chimney** (35m Very Difficult 1958) follows the crack and chimney line about 25 metres right of the gully. The twin chimney-cracks 45 metres right of the gully give a poor Moderate climb called **Easy Chimney**. It is grade II in winter (35m 1959). Between Crack and Chimney and Easy Chimney is a large crack which gives the line of **Five Card Trick** (40m VS 1981). All these climbs are short, but are useful fillers-in after climbing on the main Carn Dearg Buttress.

168   Ledge Route   450m   Easy ***   (1895)

A superb expedition. The climbing is little more than scrambling, but the situation and scenery are magnificent. It is also the best descent route from climbs on Carn Dearg Buttress. Start up Number Five Gully, and break out right on the first ledge from the foot of the gully proper. Follow this until it becomes impracticable, where a shallow gully can be seen leading up and slightly left to a higher ledge. Follow the higher ledge to the right to reach the easy-angled crest of the Great Buttress of Carn Dearg by a large cairn. Follow the crest of the buttress to the top.

Winter: 450m   II ***   *5. 3. 05 E Chris Darby*   (1897)

Probably the best route of its grade on the mountain, with sustained interest and magnificent situations. Start up Number Five Gully, but leave it by a right-slanting ramp soon after it becomes a gully proper. Follow the ramp over The Curtain to a broad almost horizontal ledge which fades out on the right. Before the ledge narrows, leave it by a left-slanting gully which comes out on a broad snow shelf. Pass a large pinnacle block before rounding the corner to reach a platform. Continue up the ridge, narrow in places, to the north-west summit of Carn Dearg. In good visibility, Ledge Route can be used for descent. From the top, follow the narrow ridge down to the top of Carn Dearg Buttress, then take the broad highest shelf (marked by the pinnacle block) to reach Number Five Gully. Instead of descending the gully (which may contain a short ice pitch), continue to the far side where another broad shelf leads gradually down from the large ledge at the top of Moonlight Gully Buttress towards Lochan na Ciste.

CARN DEARG
1221m   (Map Ref 158 719)

This is the highest point on the north-west spur of Ben Nevis. Viewed from the C.I.C. Hut, its most outstanding feature is the great rock buttress on its eastern flank.

CARN DEARG BUTTRESS

The mighty Carn Dearg Buttress lies to the right of Number Five Gully. The rock architecture of its magnificent front face, consisting of overlapping slabs, huge corners, and sweeping overhangs, is unequalled anywhere else in the British Isles. The right-hand end of the buttress is defined by an impressive vertical wall, with a long gully to its right. The rock on the buttress is superb, rough and solid, and receives much sun.

Carn Dearg is the location of some of the most celebrated routes in Scotland, many of which are long and of a quality which would make them classics anywhere. Although many are in the higher grades, there are some fine lower grade climbs too. They are visited less frequently than the well known classics, but are still well worth doing. Reliable rock climbing is possible on the buttress from mid-April, though it can be a bit cold. Some of the more persistent weeps can take until August to dry out. The infrequency of perfect conditions means that many of the harder rock climbs might be found to be rather stiff for their grades.

Splitting the face in the middle of the buttress is a huge open book corner, narrowing as it rises until it becomes a fault line running into a long line of overhangs on the upper buttress. This is the line of Centurion. Towards the right-hand end of the buttress, to the left of the arete formed by the front face of the buttress and the extremely steep side wall, is the long deep chimney line of Sassenach. The steep wall is Titan's Wall, which is bounded on its right by a line of chimneys formed at the junction of the face and a huge flake. Further right again is Waterfall Gully, a long wet gully which defines the right end of the buttress.

The best descent is to follow Ledge Route into Number Five Gully. This often carries snow until late summer, and care should be taken descending in rock boots. Much of the gully can be outflanked by climbing down wet slabs on either side.

Carn Dearg is an inspiring place in winter, and almost without exception the routes tend to be hard mixed climbs. Most of the climbs are of high quality, but are not often in condition. Optimum conditions occur after a heavy snowfall, followed by a sustained freeze. However, The Curtain (the huge icefall down the left-hand side of the buttress) is often in condition.

169   The Curtain Rail   80m   IV,4 *   (1988)
The groove and icefall left of and parallel to The Curtain offers a good alternative when the queues are too long. Beware of falling ice and other debris!
1. 30m Follow the groove to the foot of the icefall.
2. 50m Climb the icefall on the right to reach Ledge Route. An easier alternative is to continue up the groove on steep snow (50m II).

170   The Curtain   110m   IV,5 ***   (1965)
This magnificent exercise in ice climbing is an excellent introduction to the steeper routes. It probably receives more ascents than any other route of its grade on the mountain. Start at the foot of the huge iced slab at the left end of the buttress.
1. 40m Climb the slab to a cave belay at its top.
2. 30m Move left and climb the bulging wall above to reach an exposed stance under a rock wall, immediately left of a steep iced wall.
3. 40m Climb the wall trending right to gain an icy groove leading to Ledge Route. Belay well back.

In summer, the line of The Curtain is taken by **Mourning Slab** (110m VS 1961). It gives a fair climb when dry, but such conditions are extremely rare, and there is normally a stream of water running down the route.

Near the left-hand side of the cliff, above a curving subsidiary buttress, is a long deep chimney which runs up to join Ledge Route. This is the line of Route I.

171   Route I   215m   Very Difficult **   (1931)

One of the finest chimney climbs on the mountain, calling for determined use of an armoury of bridging and back and foot techniques, with the crux right at the top. Start left of the lowest rocks of the subsidiary buttress.

1. 35m Climb up to a ledge at 15m, then follow the right edge above to a larger ledge.

2. 10m Scramble up grassy cracks to the left to a large block belay.

3. 30m Traverse left and follow grooves to a recess. Continue up to the right, then move left to a platform. The Direct Start joins here.

4. 35m Scramble to the top of the subsidiary buttress and walk right to the foot of the upper chimney of Route I.

5. 20m Climb the chimney, finishing by a grassy groove to reach a recess.

6. 5m Climb the right wall to a belay.

7. 15m Regain the chimney and climb it to a stance and spike belay.

8. 20m Move left onto an exposed slab and climb it to the foot of the final chimney. Climb the chimney to a broad ledge.

9. 45m Walk right and climb easy rock to the top.

Direct Start: 70m   Very Difficult **   (1941)

This requires a more delicate touch than the original route. Start at the lowest point of the subsidiary buttress and climb its right edge, then a groove on the right wall, to gain the ledge below the upper chimney.

Winter: 175m   V,6 ***   (1972)

From the foot of The Curtain follow the obvious ledge right for 60 metres to the foot of the chimney. The first pitch is difficult, and the final chimney may call for some cunning. If it proves too tight a squeeze, it is possible to avoid it by steep moves on the right wall.

Winter Direct Start: 80m   VI,6 **   (1984)

Start just right of the rib taken by the summer Direct Start below a right-facing corner. Climb the corner, first by its right wall then its left, to gain the rib. Follow this to the ledge leading right to the upper chimney.

CARN DEARG BUTTRESS

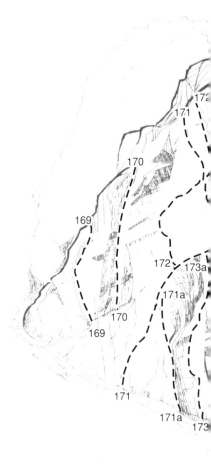

172   P.M.   110m   VS *   (1966)
A good climb with enjoyable slab climbing followed by an unlikely and wild finish. Start on the ledge below the upper buttress, left of the chimney of Route I, where a groove forms a break in the overhangs.
1. 15m 4c Move left around a bulge to gain the groove. Climb this to a grass ledge below a slabby corner.
2. 35m 4b Trend up and left across the slabs, cross an overlap and reach a flake belay.
3. 30m 4b Move up and cross the slab on the right. Climb a steep grassy crack for 6m, then move up and right to a spike belay below the final chimney of Route I.
4. 30m 4b Go right and climb a fearsome-looking bulging corner, then continue up the crack above on gigantic holds.

Sod's Law   110m   V,6   (1985)
Start on the terrace 5 metres left of the chimney of Route I. Make a hard move up a steep crack to reach a line of turf. Climb the turf to below the final overhangs (55m), then traverse right into the top pitch of Route I (20m), and follow this to the top.

173   Route II   265m   Severe **   (1943)
A superb outing, climbing through some fantastic ground for the grade. The original route follows the lower pitches of Route I, but the best line includes the Direct Start. Start as for Route I at the left of the lowest rocks of the subsidiary buttress.
1 to 4. 110m Follow the first four pitches of Route I to below its upper chimney. The Direct Start joins here.
5. 15m Climb the chimney for 10m, then traverse the slab on the right to reach a small stance and good belay.
6. 25m Move right to a large flake beneath the great overhangs.
4. 10m Traverse the flake (6m), then climb a rock rib to a thread belay on a platform. The same point can be reached by climbing directly above the flake and traversing right on vegetation, but this is not as good.
5. 40m Traverse right across the buttress, following the obvious line of weakness, to gain a platform on the edge of the buttress.
6. 30m Scramble up the edge.
7. 35m Enter a groove, and follow this mainly on the right wall to the buttress crest.

Direct Start: 80m   Very Difficult ***   (1962)
Immediately right of the rib taken by the Direct Start to Route I is a
right-facing corner. Start on a grass ledge below its slabby right wall.
1. 30m Climb the centre of the smooth slab to a small ledge. Step
right to a wall, then take a small slanting corner and traverse left to a
stance. Finish up a small black crack to a flake belay.
2. 25m Continue straight up to a large block below a groove. Climb
the groove, then traverse right, round an arete, to a shattered ledge.
3. 25m Move up to easier ground and a belay below the upper
chimney of Route I.

Route II Direct   265m   VI,6 ***   (1978)
This magnificent climb is one of the finest mixed routes on the
mountain. Start below the deep corner just right of the summer Direct
Start. Climb the corner, traverse left below an overhang, move up to
a large block and continue up the groove above. Traverse right round
an arete and climb the bulge above to reach the traverse ledge. Take
a diagonal line across the slabs beneath the overhangs, to reach a
groove on the far edge of the buttress. Follow this up the crest to easy
ground. It is possible to avoid the lower section of the buttress
altogether and reach the top of the Direct Start by traversing in from
the foot of The Curtain (200m V,6 1978).

Dissection   165m   HVS   (1971)
This direct line starts between the Direct Start to Route II and The
Shadow, then cuts through the midriff of P.M. on the upper wall. An
airy route with good positions. Pitch 1 is often wet.
1. 30m 4b Climb the crack just right of the Direct Start to Route II.
2. 20m Continue up the crack to a shelf to the right of the arete,
avoided by the Direct Start to Route II.
3. 25m 4c Go left of the arete, initially awkward, then climb more easily
to the terrace.
4. 30m 4c From the back of the terrace, pull over a steep wall to the
right of the groove of P.M. and climb slabs overlooking the groove to
a belay below a steep groove.
5. 20m 4c Climb slabs on the right to a junction with P.M. (It may be
better to run pitch 4 and 5 together).
6. 20m 5a Climb a crack to a steeper groove in the overhangs. Climb
this and step out left to a spectacular stance.
7. 20m 5a Move left round the overhangs to a fine crack in the wall
and finish up this.

Ring the Alarm   270m   VI,5 ***   (1986)
A brilliant route in an unlikely situation. Start below the crack just right
of the Direct Start to Route II, as for Dissection.
1. 45m Climb the crack, as for Dissection.
2. 30m Follow Route II Direct for 10m, then traverse across The
Shadow to a stance on the edge of the slab.
3. 45m Traverse the lip of the slab (very exposed) to reach a groove
(on Cowslip). Climb this, then pull over an overlap to a stance.
4. 30m Climb the icefall and icy slab above (The Weep) to reach Route
II.
5 to 7. 120m Follow Route II to the top.
Overload Finish   155m   VI,6   (1988)
1. 45m From the top of pitch 3 climb the icefall and icy slab, then
traverse right to join Centurion.
2. 30m Surmount the steep step above and traverse horizontally right
above the overlap to the buttress edge. (Junction with The Bat).
3. 20m Continue up the groove above to join Route II.
4. 60m Finish up Route II.

174   The Shadow   265m   VS *   (1959)
A fair outing at a reasonable standard, taking a parallel line to Route
II. The technical grade is 4b. Start 3 metres right of Dissection, at the
foot of a thin crack.
1. 40m Climb the crack, then traverse right to a belay. Surmount the
block above, move round a corner, then follow a little groove to a grass
ledge.
2. 25m Climb the wall above and step right to enter a grassy groove.
3. 35m Follow the groove until it widens, then traverse 10 metres right
to block belays.
4. 40m Move up, then traverse left below a black slab to break through
the overlap. Continue to a small corner.
5. 40m Make an ascending traverse right across a wet streak to the
grassy groove of Centurion.
6. 35m Continue up and right to belay in a grassy corner on the crest
of the buttress.
7. 25m Climb the right wall of the corner, then traverse left across
another slab to a ledge.
8. 25m Finish by the groove above.

Winter: 265m   VII,6 **   (1979)
A sustained, and high standard mixed climb approximating to the summer line. Start 10 metres right of Route II Direct and follow a crack line and groove to a belay (20m). Traverse right to the obvious line of overhangs below the traverse line of Route II. Continue traversing right to join Centurion (40m). Cross the line of Centurion and move up and right to below a large overhang (20m). Climb an exposed broken crack-line through the right side of the overhang to reach a snowy recess on the arete (15m). Continue up an overhanging groove until a difficult step left can be made onto an icy rib. Climb the rib with difficulty, then move slightly left to join the final grooves of Sassenach.
Right-Hand Start: 40m   VI,6 *   (1989)
Start at the foot of a groove just right of the original route. Climb the groove, surmount a block, and make a difficult move left on thin ice to join the original line.

175   The Bullroar   285m   HVS ***   (1961)
One of the best rock climbs on Nevis. It is not as popular as its better known neighbours, but its relative lack of attention only adds to its attraction. It takes a committing rising traverse across the great central slabs in the centre of the face. The wet streak on the main slab dries early in the day, but returns by mid to late afternoon. Start 30 metres right of the Direct Start to Route II, at a large right-facing corner with some large boulders at its foot.
1. 25m 5a Pull over an awkward bulge into a widening groove, then continue to a flake belay.
2. 15m 4b Move left into a parallel groove and climb this until 5m below the overlap at the top of the central slabs.
3. 15m 4a Traverse right along the slab under the overlap to a crack and climb this to a belay.
4. 45m 5a Descend slightly, then traverse right across the slab, passing a possible stance, to reach a descending traverse which leads to a belay above pitch 3 of Centurion.
5. 25m 4c Climb the crack above, then traverse right to a belay under the overlaps.
6. 30m 4b Traverse right under the overlaps on excellent small flake holds to easier ground. Climb this to a large terrace above the chimneys of The Bat and Sassenach.
7. 10m From the left end of the terrace, traverse left to an area of shattered rock beneath an undercut groove.

8 to 10. 120m 4c Climb the groove and continue by a series of corners and slabby grooves to the top of the buttress.

The Groove Variation: 15m   HVS   (1962)
From the belay at the top of pitch 1, climb directly over the bulge, so avoiding the left traverse. Harder and not as good as the original line.

176   Adrenalin Rush   240m   E3 *   (1978)
A technical route taking a direct line through the overlaps left of Torro. Start at a large boulder some 10 metres right of the start of The Bullroar.
1. 15m 5b Climb a crack on the left-hand side of the boulder, continue up the groove above, then step left onto a ledge.
2. 35m 6a Step up, then move right to enter a groove directly above the belay. Follow the groove to a roof, move right, then pull over the roof to a slab. Move 8 metres diagonally right, then move back left along the lip of the next overlap to a belay below a corner.
3. 40m 4c Follow the corner-line, passing an overhang after 10m. Continue up the crack-line to belay in a large corner 10m below a big roof.
4. 35m 4c Move onto a rib on the left, then climb it until it is possible to traverse right along the lip of a roof. Pull onto a hanging slab and cross this to a poorish belay on its right edge.
5. 25m 5c Step down and traverse steeply right for 10m to the foot of a shallow groove. Climb this for 6m, step left, then move up a corner and cross a slab on the right to belay below a wide diagonal crack (junction with Centurion).
6. 35m 5b Cross the slab on the left to a corner, then traverse across its left wall to a slabby rib. Climb the slab to finish up an undercut groove on the left.
7 and 8. 55m Finish as for Centurion.

177   Cowslip   190m   E2   (1970)
This route follows the line of the Weep, the great dark streak which emanates from the garden patch on Route II. A good line, but rarely wholly dry, and probably unrepeated. The technical grade is thought to be 5c. Start just left of Torro, and take a smooth groove up and left to a small stance beneath a bank of overhangs. Climb up into a steep groove, gain a slab on the left (awkward), then traverse delicately left to an overlap which is followed to its lowest point. Pull onto the small

The Curtain, Ben Nevis

slab above and move up to climb the black overhanging corner above (poor protection). Continue more easily by the slabs above to reach the traverse line of Route II. Finish as for Centurion.

178 Torro 215m E2 ***   (1962)
This brilliant route takes a complex but natural line up the sweep of slabs left of Centurion. Start just left of the foot of the rib which forms the left wall of the great corner of Centurion.
1. 30m 5b Climb the overhanging groove to a flake. Continue up the groove to a larger flake, then climb it on its right-hand side. Move back left and continue up the groove to a good stance.
2. 25m 5b Continue up the widening fault above, then work up and left to the edge of a slab. Make a descending traverse left across the slab, move round an arete, then go up an overhanging groove through the overlap to a stance below and right of twin overlaps.
3. 25m 5a Move diagonally right round a bulge to a crack above. Climb this for 6m, then move slightly right and go up a slab to a good stance.
4. 20m 5c Climb a slight crack for 6m, step left onto a higher slab, cross this for 3m and pull over the overhang above trending left. Take the groove above to a stance.
5. 35m 5a Follow the fault for 5m, traverse right across a slab to a crack and climb this to an overhang. Climb through the overhang trending left, then finish by a groove to reach a grassy stance.
6. 15m 4b Continue up the fault to a grass ledge below the long band of overhangs. Junction with Route II and Centurion.
7. 30m 5a Follow Centurion pitch 6 through the upper overhangs.
8. 35m 5b Traverse left to a steep black corner, then climb this to a grass terrace at the top. The sting in the tail!

179 Red Rag 220m E2 *   (1991)
A good climb linking the line of grooves and corners between Torro and Centurion.
1. 15m 5b Climb the cracked wall left of Centurion pitch 1 to a platform.
2. 15m 5a Continue up the V-groove directly behind the belay to a stance by a jammed spike in a crevasse.
3. 25m 5b Step left and follow Torro pitch 2 to the edge of the slab. At this point Torro continues left. Instead, move horizontally right into a groove with a perched loose block, pull over an overhang, and make

Caligula, Ben Nevis (Climber, Ken Johnstone)

a difficult step down and right into a second groove. Belay here (hanging stance).

4. 20m 5a Climb the groove and exit up a wall on the right through an overlap to a belay overlooking Centurion.

5. 25m 5a Ascend the right-facing corner above, step left onto a slab, and follow cracks to a foothold stance beneath the second great overlap at its widest point.

6. 10m 5c Surmount the overlap on the right (Friend 3 1/2 runner on lip), pull onto the arete and move up to a slab. Climb easily up to a ledge and stance. (Centurion emerges here from a corner on the right).

7. 30m 5a Trend up and left to a crack-line and follow it through an overhang to belay on ledges below a small broken overlap.

8. 25m 4a Continue easily to the Route II traverse.

9 and 10. 55m Finish as for Centurion.

180   Centurion   190m   HVS *   (1956)**

An outstanding route - the classic of the crag. It follows a superlative line up the great corner in the centre of the buttress. It takes its name from the smooth overlapping slabs which flank the route on the right, which bring to mind the armour on a Roman centurion. The route is very popular, and on a good day it is not unusual for six or seven parties strung out along the climb. The first pitch sometimes causes more problems than the harder pitches above, and the penultimate pitch breaks through the unlikely-looking upper overhangs by some superb moves. The second pitch is often wet but the seeps are normally avoidable. Start at the foot of the corner.

1. 15m 4c Climb the left wall of the corner by an awkward crack to a fine stance on top of the rib.

2. 35m 5a Traverse into the corner and climb it to a belay on a slab in an overhung bay. A brilliant pitch - the holds just keep coming!

3. 25m 4b Traverse left onto the edge. Climb easy grooves until level with the lip of a big overhang, then step back right onto the lip and move up to a stance.

4. 20m 4b Move back into the corner. Traverse left up across the wall to below an overhanging crack. Climb the arete to a stance.

5. 40m 4a Climb slabby grooves in the same line past a block, then continue up easier ground to join the Route II traverse.

6. 30m 5a Climb up to the overhang. Move left onto a steep slab, and head up and left to another overhang. Step from a detached flake and traverse delicately left onto a big slab. Climb easily up and right to a stance below the second tier of overhangs.

7. 25m 4c Traverse right for 6m and climb a spiky arete to a bulge. Surmount this, step left into an easy groove and climb this to the terrace at the top.
Winter: 190m   VIII,8 **   (1986)
A very sustained and extremely difficult mixed climb. The route is not often in accepted winter condition, and consists of hard technical climbing on snowed-up rock. Follow the summer route for five pitches to the Route II traverse, then finish up Route II. The first ascent took two days with a bivouac after pitch 4. One rest point was used on pitch 2.

181   King Kong   275m   E2 ***   (1964)
This superb climb takes an intricate and improbable line through the overlapping slabs to the right of Centurion. The route can be divided into three distinct sections. The first three pitches follow an indefensibly indirect line through the overlaps at the base of the slabs. These are rarely climbed and can be easily bypassed by following the second pitch of The Bat (as described). The central section through overlapping slabs of immaculate rough red rock contains some of the finest climbing on the mountain. The final section follows the crack and corner system to the left of the final chimneys of The Bat. The route is long and sustained and should not be underestimated. The route-finding, especially in the crucial central section, can be a considerable challenge in itself.
1. 15m 4c Climb Centurion pitch 1.
2. 15m 4c Follow the Centurion corner for 6m, then traverse right across a pink slab to belay on a perched block.
3. 30m 5c Move up and left onto a slab, climb an overlap and continue up to a crack. Traverse left on underclings and move up onto a higher slab. Climb this for 5m to a high runner, then hand traverse down and right along a thin crack to a foothold below a smooth left-facing corner. Move up and right from here to a corner-bulge. Swing round this and take a hanging stance on the left side of a small pinnacle.
4. 35m 5b From the top of the pinnacle, climb the slab on the left and pull up and right through a roof. Move up easily to the base of a shallow crack-line on the left side of the large red wall. Climb the crack and move right along the ledge at the top. Move up to belay at the top of The Bat corner.
5. 40m 5b The route now follows the crack and corner system 10 metres left of The Bat. Move up from the stance, then traverse 5 metres

left to the crack system. Follow this over several bulges to a grassy bay.

6. 30m Move easily up the grassy bay to the foot of a steep crack cut by a roof.

7. 40m 5a Climb the crack through the roof and continue up the corner on the left to belay below a corner-crack. Junction with Route II.

8. 40m 4c Climb the corner, swing across to a spike, move left, then climb up to a stance and spike belay.

9. 30m Continue slightly right, then climb up to a grassy groove. Move left, then finish directly above.

Original Start: 70m   E3   (1964)

Often wet and rarely climbed.

1. 15m 4c Climb Centurion pitch 1.

2. 20m 6a Move out right on the slabs for 6m, then descend 3m to a lower slab. Traverse right to an open corner and belay.

3. 35m 5b Climb the corner to a sloping slab. Move up to a corner and follow this to a junction with The Bat. Make a descending left traverse past the block belay at the end of The Bat pitch 2, and take a stance on the large perched block.

182   The Bat   270m   E2 ***   (1959)

This great classic takes the slim hanging corner to the right of central slabs, reached by an intricate traverse from above the first pitch of Centurion. It was named after the great swooping falls taken on the first ascent, much of which was reputedly climbed at night.

1. 15m 4c Climb Centurion, pitch 1.

2. 35m 5a Follow the Centurion corner for 6m, then traverse right across a pink slab to a perched block. Continue moving right along a shelf to a block belay.

3. 25m 5a Descend to the right for 3m to enter a bottomless groove, and climb a short wall to a triangular slab. Follow the V-groove above, then trend right along slabs to a belay beneath the left edge of the deep chimney of Sassenach.

4. 15m 5b The Hoodie Groove. Climb a steep shallow groove on the left of the chimney, then enter the main corner.

5. 30m 5b Climb the corner to the overhang, then launch into the wide corner-crack above. Continue boldly to a ledge and belay, trying not to emulate Haston.

6. 35m 4b Climb the groove to the left end of a large terrace. For those

not wishing to continue to the top of the buttress, it is possible to traverse right from here and abseil down Titan's Wall.

7 to 9. 120m Continue up the line of grooves above to the top of the buttress.

183 Sassenach 270m E1 ** (1954)

This magnificent, old-fashioned classic takes the prominent chimney line towards the right-hand end of the front face. It was the first of the big routes to be climbed on the buttress, but it is somewhat neglected nowadays, which adds to its considerable atmosphere. The E1 grade assumes aid is used to enter the chimneys, otherwise the route goes free at E3 6a. It is also possible to reach the base of the great chimney by taking the Patey Traverse (75m VS 1953) across Titan's Wall from Waterfall Gully. Start below and right of a great chimney-corner where a large slab of rock leans against the face.

1. 35m 4c From just left of the slab climb sloping mossy ledges until it is possible to step right onto a nose. Traverse left to the foot of a crack and climb this to a stance.

2. 25m 5a Climb the corner above (often wet, 2 slings for aid), then traverse up and left beneath the overhang to a belay at the foot of the chimney. This pitch can be climbed free at 6a.

3 and 4. 50m 5a Climb the great chimney for two pitches to a grassy terrace. Good old-fashioned climbing; beware of several large loose spikes.

5. 20m Move up right along the terrace to the foot of a V-groove capped by an overhang.

6. 35m 4b Climb the groove for 10m, then move out left onto a ledge. Continue up the crack above to enter a further groove.

7. 15m Climb the groove and step right at its top.

8 and 9. 90m Continue up grooves to the top of the buttress.

184 The Banana Groove 105m E4 ** (1983)

The buttress between Sassenach and the left edge of Titan's Wall is cut by two grooves. This excellent route, which had been eyed by many climbers over the years, takes the left-hand groove. Start as for Titan's Wall.

1. 35m 5b Follow Titan's Wall pitch 1 to a belay on the long ledge near the left edge.

2. 10m 4c Traverse left round the edge and cross slabs to a ledge below the groove.

3. 45m 6a Climb directly up the corner (possible detour onto the left wall at one point). Where the corner fades, climb the wall *via* cracks to a very precarious block. Pull up and right across a small overlap into a small right-facing groove. Pull out left onto a flat hold, then take a crack leading to a ledge. A stunning pitch.

4. 15m 5c Climb the overhanging crack above to the terrace. From here, either continue up Titan's Wall to join the final pitches of Sassenach, or abseil down Titan's Wall.

Caligula   110m   E3 **   (1978)
The original climb on this section of cliff, taking the most natural line of weakness between Sassenach and Agrippa. The route starts up The Banana Groove, before moving out right to climb a crack on its right wall.

1. 35m 5b Climb Titan's Wall pitch 1 to a belay on the long ledge near the left edge.

2. 10m 4c Follow The Banana Groove to a ledge below the groove.

3. 25m 5c Climb the corner (possible detour onto the left wall at one point). After 20m there is a small overlap. Traverse right from here to a small ledge and belay.

4. 40m 5c Step up and left to a thin diagonal crack. Climb this and the overhang above, then continue along a right-trending ramp to a crack. Climb the crack and continue to a stance and belay at the top of Titan's Wall. From here, either continue up Titan's Wall to join the final pitches of Sassenach, or abseil down Titan's Wall.

Caligula Direct   60m   E3 **
A more direct version of Caligula. It is very sustained and often climbed in mistake for the original line. Start from the stance at the top of pitch 2 of the normal line.

1. 50m 6a Climb the normal route, but instead of traversing out right after 20m, continue up The Banana Groove. A little way below the little overlap and right-facing groove of The Banana Groove, make a hard step down and right onto a slabby wall. Move across this and climb a corner to a ledge.

2. 10m Climb easily up the wall above to the Titan's Wall stance. From here, either continue up Titan's Wall to join the final pitches of Sassenach, or abseil down Titan's Wall.

Agrippa 85m E5 *** (1983)

This bold and sustained route tackles the overhanging edge left of Titan's Wall; not for the faint-hearted! Start below the slabby rib left of Titan's Wall.

1. 35m 5c Climb the rib for 15m to a small overhang. Gain the sloping ledge above, then follow a groove to a shelf below a further overhang. Climb directly over this to the belay ledge at the top of pitch 1 of Titan's Wall.

2. 25m 6b Follow the short slim groove on the left side of the edge, then climb a crack to gain better holds leading to a large dubious block. From a standing position on the block move precariously round onto the left wall of the arete and climb this with difficulty to a good ledge and belay.

3. 25m 5c Climb a slight groove on the right for a few metres, then move up left across the wall to a flake crack in the arete. Climb this to good holds, then move right to the ledge at the top of Titan's Wall (poorly protected). From here, either continue up Titan's Wall to join the final pitches of Sassenach, or abseil down Titan's Wall.

185 Titan's Wall 245m E3 *** (1959/1977)

A brilliant route with two outstanding pitches following the line of cracks up the centre of the vertical wall on the right side of the buttress. The second pitch is strenuous and very sustained, and overall the climb is high in the grade. It was first climbed as an aid route, and the first free ascent was a major milestone in Scottish rock climbing. It is normal to abseil down the line of the route after completing the first two pitches. Start below the line of cracks 10 metres from the left edge of the wall.

1. 35m 5b Follow the central crack line to an overhang at 15m. Pull over this and continue up the line of cracks, trending right, to a ledge. Traverse left along the ledge to a belay.

2. 45m 5c Return right to the end of the ledge and arrange protection which will be good for a sideways pull. Climb the steep and sustained crack above, over a number of small bulges, until it eases. Continue directly to the top of the wall following the vertical crack with sustained interest.

3. 30m Climb up to the left, then move right to a groove. Follow this to the upper pitches of Sassenach.

4 to 6. 135m 4b Continue up Sassenach to the top.

Boadicea   100m   E4 *   (1989)

This sustained climb takes the thin crack to the right of Titan's Wall. It is well protected with small wires.

1. 35m 5b Follow Titan's Wall pitch 1 to a belay on the long ledge near the left arete.

2. 20m 5a From the foot of the Titan's Wall crack, follow a right-curving crack to a stance on The Shield Direct.

3. 40m 6a Return left to the crack, which now becomes vertical. Climb it, thin at first, to reach an easier section by some flakes. Continue up the smooth section above (crux) to a stance.

4. 5m A short descent to the left leads to the abseil slings at the top of Titan's Wall.

186   The Shield Direct   215m   HVS *   (1956/1962)

The line of chimneys formed by the junction of Titan's Wall and the huge flake on its right was originally climbed in 1956. The route avoided the lower fault line, and traversed into the upper fault from Waterfall Gully. The direct line, as described, is far superior, and although it is rarely completely dry, it is still worth climbing. Start 5 metres right of Titan's Wall, just left of the deeply cut cracks in the corner. The technical grade is 5a.

1. 25m Climb the wall for 4m, traverse right into the crack, then climb up to a belay.

2. 35m Follow the crack until a metre or so under the great roof. Move onto the left wall and climb a thin crack (often wet - several pegs aid) to surmount the left edge of the roof (crux). Climb a short chimney to a stance, then continue by the line of the chimney to a block belay.

3. 30m Take the steep groove above, then traverse right into the chimney of the upper fault line. Follow the chimney until it is possible to step left into a small cave.

4. 40m Regain the chimney and follow it to a difficult bulge. Climb this and continue up to a belay.

5. 35m Continue in the line of the increasingly grassy chimney to the top of the flake.

6. 50m Finish up the final pitch of Evening Wall.

Winter: 285m   VII,7 ***   (1979)

An outstanding route which combines very steep ice with sustained and technical mixed climbing. It is rarely in condition, and the initial groove is often bare. Start at an ice groove directly below the chimney of The Shield.

1. 50m Climb the ice groove and continue over two bulges to gain a large ledge on the right at the foot of the chimney section of The Shield.
2. 30m Climb the ice chimney and continue up steep ice to a cave stance on the left.
3. 35m Follow the line of icy grooves to easier climbing in the now wider chimney.
4. 40m Continue in the same line to the top of the chimney flake.
5. 45m Move up left onto a flake, cross the bulge above trending right and continue by the easiest line to ledges.
6. 35m Climb up and right to a left-slanting ledge line. Follow this to the crest of the buttress.
7. 50m Follow the arete to its top and a junction with Ledge Route.

Evening Wall   210m   Very Difficult *   (1940)
A fine route up the easier-angled wall right of The Shield Direct. Start at the foot of a clean-cut chimney, 10 metres right of Waterfall Gully.
1. 25m Climb the chimney, exit by the left wall, and climb up to a block belay.
2. 30m Continue for 6m, then traverse across Waterfall Gully on the left. Climb the far wall by a difficult edge, followed by slabs to grass.
3. 35m Climb an easy-angled chimney for 15m, then continue up a right-trending groove cutting through the wall above to a line of slanting slabs which lead to the base of an enormous flake.
4. 10m Follow a chimney to the top of the flake.
5. 30m Traverse left over grass and easy rocks to a flake belay.
6. 20m Gain the crest of the buttress, climb up left, then make a short traverse right and move up to a large ledge.
7 and 8. 60m Move left along the ledge, and descend slightly to the foot of twin grooves. Climb the right-hand groove for 10m to a stance, then continue in the groove to the top of the buttress.

187 Gemini   300m   VI,6 ***   (1979)
One of the most interesting and atmospheric ice climbs on the mountain. Climb a steep ice groove just left of the first pitch of Waterfall Gully to join the right-trending groove of Evening Wall after 70m. Follow this to the enormous detached flake. Climb the very steep ice smear on the left wall of the flake to reach a ledge below some right-sloping grooves. Follow these for 60m to the foot of obvious twin grooves. Climb either groove to a broad ledge. Traverse right along the ledge for 15m and climb iced slabs for 45m to easier ground.

CARN DEARG TO CASTLE RIDGE

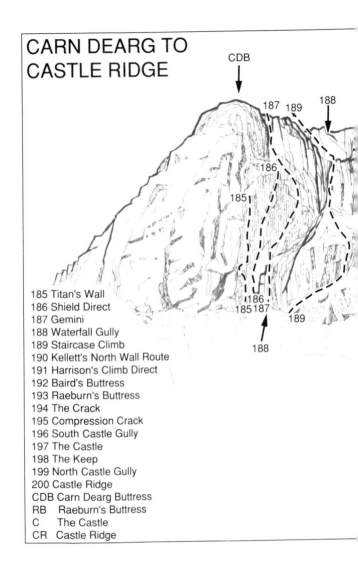

CDB

187 189 188

186

185

186
185 187
189

188

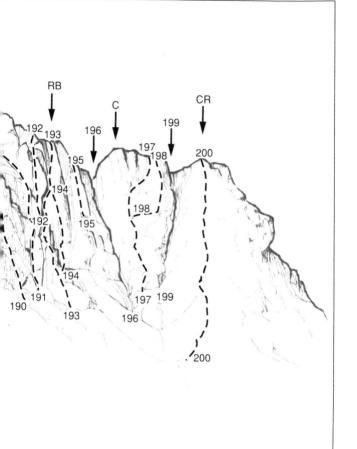

Left-Hand Finish: 130m   V,5 **   (1988)
Start from the ledge below the right-sloping grooves.
1. 45m Climb the steep groove on the left to a ledge. Traverse blindly left, then continue directly up steep mixed ground.
2. 50m Trend right by an ice scoop, then traverse left along a narrow ledge to a shallow cave.
3. 35m Move left up ice into an open slabby corner which leads to the top.

188   Waterfall Gully   215m   IV,4 **   (1959)
The prominent gully which defines the right flank of Carn Dearg Buttress provides a good and varied winter climb. The foot of the gully readily develops into a large icefall, which provides the main interest of the route. Climb the icefall (40m) to its top where the angle eases. Follow the bed of the gully for 200m to a cave or possible through-route on the right. Exit right (sometimes difficult) onto mixed ground and follow this up left for three pitches to join Ledge Route. Care should be taken on the slabby rocks in the exit area which may present a hazard in avalanche conditions.
True Finish: 200m   VI,6 **   (1984)
Although the difficulties are short-lived, this is an excellent and very worthwhile route. At the point where Waterfall Gully swings right, climb the steep crack on the left wall and continue up the narrow chimney above to a small snow basin (40m). Either finish by the line of the crack or exit left onto easier ground to join Ledge Route.

189   Staircase Climb   215m   Very Difficult   (1898)
Start to the right of Evening Wall, and take the higher of two shelves which slope up round a corner to the right. Once around the corner, follow the stepped slab up right to the foot of a clean-cut crack in a corner. Climb the crack, then continue up a short wall above to a platform. Climb the chimney above to easy ground. Scramble up the crest of the buttress towards a conspicuous pinnacle. Turn the pinnacle on the left, descend a short distance into Waterfall Gully, then move up to a steep slab which leads to the saddle beyond the pinnacle. Climb the left-hand of two chimneys above to reach a ridge. Climb easily up and left to gain the upper rocks of Carn Dearg Buttress.

Three variations have been recorded. Straight Chimney Variation (40m Severe 1944) climbs the steep chimney to the right of the start of the original route. Raeburn's Variation (45m Very Difficult 1903)

moves left from the platform above the clean-cut crack and climbs a
deep-cut chimney to reach easier rocks leading to the pinnacle. Deep
Chimney Variation (40m Difficult 1944) climbs the right-hand of the
twin chimneys above the saddle.
Winter: IV,5 *   (1957)
This good, but rarely done mixed climb, follows the summer line, and
maintains its interest throughout. The lower section can be especially
hard, and turning the pinnacle under light snow cover can be difficult.

   The line of crags some distance below the main cliff of Carn Dearg
provide good practice in steep ice climbing up frozen watercourses.
There is also one good rock climb.

The Trial   45m   E3 5c *   (1988)
To the right of the main watercourse, on the right-hand side of the
buttress, there is an area of dry rock. At the right side of the steepest
section of the cliff is a corner which starts from a grass ledge. The
route climbs the cracked arete in the smooth wall left of the corner.
Start directly below the arete. Climb the clean wall to the arete, and
follow this to the top. An excellent pitch.

NORTH WALL OF CARN DEARG

This is the name given to the northern flank of Carn Dearg Buttress.
Although it is traversed by several large ledges, the intervening walls
are impressively steep and provide fine climbing.
   Slightly to the right of the toe of the buttress, a grassy rake leads
up left to the first of the large ledges. The rake is Easy Way, and the
ledge it gains is Broad Terrace, which slants up gradually from left to
right. The next ledge is Flake Terrace, which runs up across the face
from the lower reaches of Harrison's Climb. It is gained via a series of
easy chimneys. The ledge above Flake Terrace is Diagonal Terrace,
and the final ledge below the top of the buttress is Green Terrace.
None of these ledges present any great difficulty and may be used as
a means of access or descent.

Macphee's Route   100m   Very Difficult   (1931)
From the lowest point of the wall follow a grass shelf on the crest to a
vegetated chimney, and climb it to a grass ledge. Continue up the
chimney above, and make a hard exit to the left end of Broad Terrace.

Climb the broken crack on the left, traverse left onto the slab-rib, and continue by slabs to a belay on Flake Terrace. (The broken crack may be climbed direct, but this misses out the finest situations on the climb). The steep wall above is unclimbed and the route now traverses Flake Terrace, with an awkward descent behind a large flake, to reach the Crevasse. Either continue to the top by Kellett's North Wall Route or descend the continuation of Flake Terrace to reach the first pitch of Harrison's Climb.

Zagzig 55m Severe (1959)
On the steep wall below Easy Way is an obvious zigzag fault. Start below the fault, about 30m from the left edge of the wall.
1. 25m Climb up to the grassy lower crack, then traverse it to a stance.
2. 30m Move right up the chimney by a stomach traverse until forced onto the wall at the halfway point. Finish by making an awkward exit from a cave to reach Easy Way. Descend this or continue upwards by Macphee's Route.

190 Kellett's North Wall Route 180m Severe * (1943)
A tremendous climb, but often greasy. Each pitch was recorded as a separate route by Kellett during his exploration of the face in the summer of 1943, but they link together to form a logical line which runs the entire height of the wall. Start right of the grassy rake of Easy Way, below a large flake with a deep chimney to the right.
1. 30m Flake Chimney. Climb the chimney to exit by a window in the flake, then scramble up to Broad Terrace.
2. 20m Direct Start to Route B. Climb to the foot of a conspicuous crack which leads to the crest of Flake Terrace.
3. 30m Route B. About 6m right of the secondary point of the flake gain a groove in the steep wall above and climb to a large grass recess. Make an exposed traverse right onto a rib, then climb directly up a crack to a block belay on Diagonal Terrace.
4. 15m Route A. Traverse right to an open corner.
5. 35m Route A. Climb up right of the corner and reach a ledge beneath a steep exposed slab with two thin cracks. Move up, then gain the cracks by a difficult step left. Continue directly for 15m, then move easily up to the right to below a right-angled corner.
6. 50m Route A. Bridge up the corner to reach a terrace. Continue up easy slabs to the top of the buttress.

Caterpillar Crawl Variation: 45m   Severe   (1949)
A variation to the upper part of Kellett's North Wall Route, with a
different type of climbing to that found on the original climb. Start at
the top of pitch 5 below the right-angled corner.
1. 15m Descend a metre or so and traverse right along a narrow ledge
until it is possible to stand. Continue delicately to a spike belay.
2. 30m Move right until the short wall above can be climbed, then
follow a line of holds up left to a stance behind a block. Climb the wall
above to a mossy recess, descend a short distance round the rib on
the left, then move up to enter a series of grooves on the right which
lead to the top.

Winter: 200m **   VII,7   (1991)
This sustained and technical mixed climb approximates to the lower
section of the summer route. It starts up Flake Chimney, then follows
Route B before finishing along Diagonal Terrace to reach Waterfall
Gully. Pitch 3 is both hard and serious, but has good belays. Start right
of Easy Way below a large flake with a deep chimney to the right.
1. 25m Climb the chimney, exit by a window, and continue up to Broad
Terrace.
2. 20m Climb a corner to the left of the conspicuous crack of the Direct
Start to Route B to reach Flake Terrace.
3. 30m Traverse 6m right along the terrace and move up to a recess.
Move right to a steep groove and climb this to join Diagonal Terrace.
Good belay.
4. 30m Move up left along Diagonal Terrace and continue up a steep
turfy groove-line.
5 and 6. 95m Exit left into Waterfall Gully and follow this to the top.

The Shroud   200m   VII,6 **   (1993)
In exceptional conditions an impressive icefall forms down the steep
wall to the left of Harrison's Direct. On the first ascent the free-hanging
fang was 1m short of connecting with the belay ledge.
1. 50m Start up an ice gully and continue up the slope above to belay
on the right side of the icefall.
2. 25m Climb the centre of the icefall and belay on a narrow ice ledge
right of the free-hanging fang.
3. 25m Follow the fang to the upper ice wall. Semi-hanging belay on
screws.
4. 50m Continue up the ice wall above to easier-angled ice.
5. 50m Climb the ice step above to easier ground.

Harrison's Climb   275m   Difficult   (1929)
The deep chimney which defines the right-hand edge of the face, and
separates the North Wall of Carn Dearg from Cousin's Buttress, gives
a pleasant but non-distinguished summer climb. Start 10 metres left
of the chimney at a small platform of rock. Climb easily up and right
to enter the deep chimney, and follow this to the saddle behind the top
of Cousin's Buttress. Traverse left below a smooth wall to gain a grass
ledge which leads to easy ground. Scramble up this for 100m to a wide
corrie. Follow the right edge of a watercourse in the centre of the corrie
to the foot of a chimney leading through the final rocks. Pass the first
chockstone via a through-route, and turn the second on the right to
gain a shallow gully. Climb an overhanging pitch by two huge flakes,
turn a final chockstone on the right, and continue easily to the top.
   There are two variations. The Chimney Start (20m Very Difficult
1931) climbs the initial chimney in its entirety, and the Dungeon
Variation (90m Very Difficult 1949) moves out right from the saddle,
climbs a grassy chimney, then follows a gully to the summit rocks.
Winter: 275m   III **   (1962)
A very good route, although the Direct is an even finer line. The
approach to the chimney is normally banked out, but there can on
occasion be a large build-up of ice on this section. Continue up a
superb ice corner to the saddle, then traverse left to a 30m icefall.
Climb this by its right edge, then follow easier ground to the upper
corrie from which there is a variety of exits.

191   Harrison's Climb Direct   275m   IV,4 ***   (1976)
A superb climb, which gives some of the best ice climbing of its grade
on the mountain. Start at the right-hand end of the face, below the
deep chimney-gully which separates the North Wall of Carn Dearg
from Cousin's Buttress. Climb a steep ice pitch (The Chimney Start),
then continue up the icy corner of the original route to reach the saddle.
Traverse left to the 30m icefall, then take a rising line up the buttress
on the right, to gain the edge overlooking Raeburn's Buttress. Follow
this for two pitches to the upper corrie, where a selection of routes lead
to the top.

COUSIN'S BUTTRESS

The buttress has the appearance of a huge flake or pinnacle some
60m high, butting against the North Wall of Carn Dearg. It is separated
from the main wall by deep chimneys on either side, and presents a

steep narrow face to the right, and a less steep wall broken by two large grass ledges on its front face. These ledges continue right to join the approach gully of Raeburn's Buttress which lies further right.

Cousin's Buttress 225m Very Difficult (1904)
Climb the gully on the right side of the buttress on water-worn rocks for 20m, then traverse left onto the second grass ledge. Climb directly by steep rocks for 10m, then scramble to the top of the buttress (30m). Descend to the saddle behind the buttress, then gain the wall beyond and traverse left past an awkward corner to a grass ledge. A few metres along the ledge, break up right and climb a rock rib for 60m to a large scree slope. Scramble up to the steep rocks under the summit of Carn Dearg. Climb these, exiting slightly right of the summit.
Direct Start: 60m Severe (1944)
This variation ascends the front face of the buttress, and avoids the gully taken by the original route. Climb up to the first of the two big grass ledges on the north face.
1. 30m Start by climbing up to the second ledge from the right, but after 10m traverse left by a slab to a crack in the corner. Follow the crack to the left end of the second grass ledge.
2. 30m Climb the steep rocks on the left to a small flake which is visible from the ledge. Climb a bulge onto the top of the flake, traverse left, surmount a short wall, then scramble to the top of the buttress.
Winter: 275m III * (1935)
Climb the initial gully on the right side of the buttress, with one short ice pitch, to the saddle, then continue up Harrison's Climb to the top.

CARN DEARG SUMMIT BUTTRESS

Above Cousin's and Raeburn's buttresses is a small hanging corrie. The upper face leads almost to the summit of Carn Dearg and contains several gullies and buttresses which can be used as a logical continuation to the routes on the North Wall of Carn Dearg. The corrie can also be reached by descending into the basin from the upper reaches of Ledge Route. This is a fine and remote part of the mountain in winter, but the corrie is prone to avalanche and should be avoided after heavy snowfall. The climbs finish near the summit of Carn Dearg.

Colando Gully 180m II (1958)
The winding gully on the left consists of steep snow with the occasional short ice pitch.

Arch Buttress   180m   III *   (1959)
The buttress to the right of Colando Gully. Climb the crest for 45m,
then move right into a groove. At the top make an awkward move left
to a platform, then continue for 30m to a snow patch. Move right, climb
the chimney, then make a long stride up and left into the centre of three
chimneys. Easy climbing leads to the summit.

Arch Gully   180m   I   (1958)
The central gully separating the buttresses gives a steep snow climb
of no great difficulty. The arch is formed by a huge chockstone.

Surprise Buttress   240m   III *   (1959)
The right-hand buttress. Traverse onto the buttress from the foot of
Arch Gully, climb a short groove, then traverse back to the left edge
of the buttress. Follow this as closely as possible to a steep wall above
the huge chockstone in Arch Gully. Traverse right beneath the wall
until above Surprise Gully, then climb short walls slightly left to a small
ledge and block belay about 10m above the traverse. Step down and
right, climb a steep groove, and finish by easier climbing.

Surprise Gully   180m   II   (1958)
The right-hand gully has a rock rib splitting the lower section. Climb
easily for 150m to shoulder, and finish by an icy groove on the left.

192   Baird's Buttress   90m   Very Difficult   (1938)
This buttress lies on the right edge of the corrie, just before the rocks
merge with the upper section of Raeburn's Buttress. Start from a large
ledge below a crack which splits the front of the buttress. Climb the
crack in two steep sections, then continue up the steep wall above
which leads to easier climbing and the top of the buttress.
Winter: 90m   IV,4   (1977)
Follow the summer line to the top. A worthwhile finish to Boomer's
Requiem or Continuation Wall.

RAEBURN'S BUTTRESS

Between Carn Dearg and The Castle lies a tall slender buttress of
generally good rock which appears as a pinnacle from some angles.
This is Raeburn's Buttress, and gives good climbing in both summer
and winter. The left side of the buttress is defined by a gully system
which splits into two chimneys after 60m, and the right side is bounded

by South Castle Gully. The buttress is cut by a terrace at 140m which is followed by the Girdle Traverse. The front face of the buttress is impressively steep and split by a prominent crack.

Boomer's Requiem   180m   V,5 ***   (1973)
This excellent route starts up the left branch of the gully system to the left of Raeburn's Buttress to reach the icefall which plunges from the hanging corrie to meet the lower section of the buttress. It has a daunting crux on very steep ice, and was originally graded IV and regarded as the test-piece for the grade! Follow the initial gully of Raeburn's Buttress to the bifurcation, where the left-hand fork is barred by an impressively steep icefall. Climb this in two pitches and continue up snow slopes into the hanging corrie. Either finish up one of the routes on Carn Dearg Summit Buttress or descend Ledge Route.

Continuation Wall   180m   IV,4   (1977)
Start as for Boomer's Requiem and climb up to the bifurcation. Continue up the continuation chimney, and surmount a short ice step above. This leads up and right to a steepening snow gully which finishes on the Girdle Traverse Ledge. Either traverse easily left into the hanging corrie and finish up one of the routes on Carn Dearg Summit Buttress, or move up and right and continue up Baird's Buttress. The first part of the winter line follows the summer route (140m Severe 1951) which finishes on the Girdle Traverse ledge.

193   Raeburn's Buttress   230m   Very Difficult *   (1908)
A good climb, and although the route is not entirely clean or solid, it is still worth doing. Start below the gully on the left side of the buttress, and climb easy water-worn rocks to a point where the gully splits into two chimneys. Take the right branch to a cave and belay. Exit by the right wall and gain a chockstone, then traverse into the chimney-gully on the right. Follow the gully to the Girdle Traverse terrace on the neck of the buttress. Alternatively, traverse right onto the crest of the buttress and climb up to the terrace. Climb the crest of the buttress and finish by a narrow arete.
Winter: 230m   IV,5 **   (1959)
An excellent and sustained mixed climb. Climb the introductory gully to the bifurcation, and follow the right branch to the cave. The short right wall above the cave belay will be very hard if insufficiently iced. Follow the gully above to the buttress crest, and continue up the arete to the top.

Direct Start: 65m   IV,4 *   (1979)
Gain the buttress crest as soon as possible from the introductory gully,
and follow it to join the original route.
Intermediate Gully Finish: 140m   IV,4 ***   (1938)
Easier than the summer line, and more often in condition. Instead of
climbing the right wall of the cave, continue up the gully to a steep exit
at the top. Continue up grooves to the left of the final arete to the top.

   The following three routes lie on the steep front face of the buttress
which is cut by the prominent line of The Crack.

Saxifrage   90m   VS   (1984)
This route follows the thin groove 10 metres left of The Crack.
1. 20m 4c Climb the first pitch of The Crack.
2. 40m Continue up the grooved arete above to a belay on slabs
below some steep cracked blocks.
3. 30m Climb over the blocks, then move up and left to join Raeburn's
Buttress.

194   The Crack   85m   HVS *   (1946)
This daunting and atmospheric climb takes the conspicuous crack
which splits the front face of the buttress. Good but hard.
1. 20m 4c Start at the foot of the introductory gully of Raeburn's
Buttress, and scramble up right making for the foot of the crack. Access
is barred by deceptive looking slabs. Climb these trending right to gain
a ledge and traverse right to a block belay.
2. 35m 5a Climb the crack, surmount an overhang, and reach a
platform on the right. Continue up the crack to a chockstone, climb
another overhang, then more easily to a ledge and belay on the left.
3. 30m 4b Follow the crack to easier ground and a junction with
Raeburn's Buttress.

Teufel Grooves   95m   HVS   (1969)
The route follows the groove system to the right of The Crack on the
front face of the buttress.
1. 30m 4c Follow the first pitch of The Crack, then move right for 10m
to a belay below the obvious corner.
2. 40m 5a Climb the wall and crack above, move right to a ledge, and
continue up the stepped corner above.
3. 25m 4b Move left across a slab, then climb a groove to finish on
the left arete.

195 Compression Crack   120m   Very Difficult *   (1940)
Halfway along the steep right wall of the final section of Raeburn's Buttress is a steep chimney-corner. This can be reached by scrambling up easy slabs and grass ledges above the left wall of South Castle Gully to reach the well-defined Girdle Traverse ledge. This point can also be gained by following the ledge from beneath the final arete of Raeburn's Buttress. Climb the chimney, which becomes progressively steeper, on clean water-worn rock (35m), then break up left over slabs to reach the top of the buttress.
Winter: 130m   V,5 *   (1985)
In winter, the summer line is often masked by a series of imposing ice smears which give the line of the route. Climb the prominent icefall below Raeburn's Buttress and make a long traverse right to the iced chimney-corner. Climb a steep ice pitch in the first corner (15m), then continue up the second corner for 20m to snow slopes. Follow these to the top.

Winter Chimneys   125m   Severe   (1962)
Follow the terrace beyond Compression Crack for 30m to the foot of a deep chimney topped by a huge capstone. Climb the chimney, and those succeeding it, and finish by a through-route under a large chockstone.
Winter: 135m   IV,4   (1960)
Climb the icefall as for Compression Crack, then continue the traverse to the next icefall. Climb the chimney on ice, then traverse right to a bulging crack. Follow this to a stance above the great capstone. Continue up the chimney line for 20m, then traverse left to enter the fan-shaped corrie which leads to the Carn Dearg summit slopes.

THE CASTLE

The deep recess of Castle Corrie contains the buttress of The Castle, which is well demarcated by South and North Castle gullies.

196 South Castle Gully   210m   I   (1896)
This gully divides Raeburn's Buttress from the recessed buttress of The Castle on the right. Extreme care should be taken after a heavy snowfall, as the outward-sloping rock strata makes the gully avalanche prone. The gully is normally an uncomplicated snow ascent. However, in very lean conditions at the start of the season it may be Grade III.

Near the top, on the left wall of the gully, is a short but obvious icefall. This is **Plum Duff** (60m IV,4 1984). In summer the gully is loose and not recommended (210m Very Difficult 1911). The Left Wall Variation (Very Difficult 1935) climbs the third pitch by a slanting ledge on the left wall.

The Castle is the distinctive undercut buttress which lies high up on the back wall of Castle Corrie. It is contained within a V-shape formed by South Castle Gully on the left and North Castle Gully on the right. The rock is basically sound, although it is rather messy in the easier-angled lower section. In winter the slabby lower part of the buttress and the gullies on either side have a tendency to avalanche, and the area has produced some huge slides.

197   The Castle   215m   Very Difficult *   (1898)
Start beneath the undercut nose of the buttress at a slabby break.
1. 10m Climb overhanging rock on good holds for 4m, then continue more easily to a belay.
2 to 4. 120m Scramble up, bearing slightly left to reach a shallow gully which leads to a grass terrace under the upper slabs.
5. 40m Climb the slabs bearing slightly right, then left, by an awkward corner. Move left into a chimney and follow this to a chockstone belay.
6. 35m Break out by the right wall past an awkward corner, then climb slabs to a shallow gully leading to a grass bay. Climb slabs on the right, followed by a short chimney.
7. 10m Continue up the slabs on the right which lead to a short wall and the top of the buttress.
Winter: 215m   III *   (1896)
A good route, but conditions must be carefully assessed and the route should be avoided if avalanche conditions prevail. A cone of avalanche debris often masks the initial strenuous moves of the first pitch making it straightforward. Continue up steep snow in the centre of the buttress, trend left, then climb a steep groove until beneath the final steep wall. Exit right on slabs, which can be awkward if not well covered by snow.

Turret Cracks   60m   HVS   (1965)
This climb follows a thin crack-line to the left of the prominent line of chimneys on the final tower of the buttress. Follow the original route to the start of pitch 5 at a ledge immediately under the chimneys. From a large pinnacle follow a line of corners trending left to reach a pedestal slab (5a). Climb steep cracks above for two pitches to the top (4b).

198 The Keep 75m Severe (1958)
Follow The Castle for four pitches to the exit from the shallow gully, where a grass terrace leads right under the upper slabs. Traverse down to a corner and a block belay.
1. 30m Climb above the belay to a ledge, move right, and follow a groove to a grass ledge. Climb onto a projecting block and continue to a good stance and belay.
2. 20m Climb a groove, surmount a bulge, then continue to easier climbing and a flake belay.
3. 30m The groove continues above, but it is better to finish by the slab edge on the left.

199 North Castle Gully 230m II (1896)
The gully to the right of The Castle contains several short chockstone pitches which are normally completely covered, giving an uncomplicated snow ascent. The cornice is seldom large. It is loose and best avoided in summer (230m Difficult 1904).

CASTLE RIDGE

Castle Ridge is the final great ridge on the north face of Ben Nevis. It is the easiest of the four ridges, and while not in the same class as the others, it does have a distinct quality of its own, mainly derived from the tremendous views out over Lochaber. The huge North Wall of Castle Ridge has yielded some excellent winter climbs, along with a few rock routes.

An easy descent can be made down the extensive boulder field on the north side of Carn Dearg to reach Lochan Meall an t-Suidhe. From the top of Castle Ridge it is important to first head due west for 300m before descending, to avoid the North Wall of Castle Ridge.

200 Castle Ridge 275m Moderate * (1899)
A worthwhile excursion, but mainly scrambling with a few moderate pitches. Start from the lowest point of the buttress, and climb fairly directly, crossing a succession of slabs, to reach some huge detached blocks (90m). Continue up steeper rock to an almost level section of the ridge (75m). This point can be reached more easily from the foot of North Castle Gully. Climb the steep section above by taking two 10m chimneys to where the ridge narrows. Climb a steep rib by twin cracks, then scramble to the top of the buttress.

Winter: 275m III ** (1895)

A good climb which is possible in most conditions, although it should be avoided after heavy snowfall as the approach slopes are prone to avalanche. Gain the ridge from below the Castle gullies, and follow the easiest line until the crest is blocked by a steep wall. Traverse up and right, and climb an awkward flaky chimney to a good ledge. Climb another difficult pitch to gain the upper part of the ridge, which leads to the top with no further difficulty.

NORTH WALL OF CASTLE RIDGE

To the right of Castle Ridge, a huge broken face extends for about 600m to the west until the cliffs merge with the hillside. There are some superb winter climbs here, and the prominent curving shelf of The Serpent which slants diagonally across the wall from left to right is easily seen from the Allt a'Mhuilinn path. There are a number of difficult summer and winter routes on the steep buttress high up on the left side of the face. Approach to this is awkward, and in summer it is probably easiest to traverse in from Castle Ridge, although the correct line is difficult to locate.

American Pie 770m V,5 ** (1978)

This fine mountaineering expedition is one of the longest winter climbs in the British Isles, but unfortunately it is rarely in condition. Start to the left of The Serpent, below a large prominent ice smear.

1. 30m Climb snow and ice to the foot of a steep, narrow and hidden ice chimney which slants up to the right.
2. 30m Climb the chimney to a small snow bay.
3. 10m Continue up the small twisting ice chimney above.
4 and 5. 60m Break out of the corner onto the buttress edge and continue straight up to a snow bay.
6. 15m Climb the short icy groove above to the foot of a ramp.
7 to 14. 420m Follow the ramp up and right across the face to the upper amphitheatre.
15 and 16. 100m Continue up and left over mixed ground to a rock band.
18. 30m Climb through the rock band on the left.
19 and 20. 75m Traverse up and right to exit just below the top of Castle Ridge.

201   The Serpent   300m   II   (1959)
This steep snow climb is the easiest route on the face, but it is quite committing and has difficult route-finding. Start near the left edge of the face at a small gully above a prominent boulder called the Lunching Stone. Climb the gully, then follow a curving shelf leading right to reach the lower section of a second gully (150m). Climb this to the shoulder of Carn Dearg.

202   The Moat   500m   II *   (1972)
The huge ledge which crosses the face above the line of The Serpent gives a straightforward climb with fine situations on high angle snow. Climb The Serpent for 70m, then move left to the ledge. Follow the ledge to its end and finish up a steep gully.

The following routes lie on the steep buttress high up on the left side of the face. On the left side of the buttress, tucked under Castle Ridge, is a steep pale grey wall with a distinctive overhang on its right and two more lower down on the left. The right side of the wall is cut by a prominent groove system taken by Lobby Dancer. There are three rock climbs on the wall, but it is unlikely that they have been repeated, and the grades should be treated with caution.

203   Camanachd Heroes   215m   E1   (1992)
At the left end of the steep grey wall there are two prominent over-hangs. This route works diagonally right between the overhangs, then follows a gangway across the 'brow' of the wall to finish directly *via* an amphitheatre onto Castle Ridge. Start below a right-trending crack at the left end of the wall which ends in a bottomless chimney just left of the lower overhang.
1. 25m Climb the wall and crack (crux) to a belay just short of the chimney.
2. 40m Enter the chimney, and ascend the open corner to its top.
3. 40m Traverse along the gangway, overcoming a short wall *en route*, to reach a prominent crack.
4. 35m Climb the crack to the amphitheatre.
5. 40m Climb slabby cracks and the corner above to a large ledge.
6. 35m Enter the final corner by a wall, and climb this to Castle Ridge.

204 Prodigal Boys 150m HVS (1991)
This route starts just left of Plastic Max, below a long groove which
loses itself in roofs and overhangs at 40m. It then goes directly through
the square-cut roofs which are a dominant feature of the route.
1. 35m Climb the groove, bypassing an overhang at 25m on the right.
2. 40m Climb the crack above to a roof. Traverse left, climb a crack,
then continue by a slab and crack to an overhang. Surmount this and
trend right to a large grass ledge.
3. 45m Continue by parallel cracks and another overhang to a stance.
4. 30m Climb up to Castle Ridge.

Plastic Max 150m VS (1971)
Start below the prominent groove system to the right of the large roof
at the right-hand end of the grey wall.
1. 45m Climb straight up to belay in a niche.
2. 35m Continue up a water-worn wall to a jammed block, then
traverse left for 10m to a stance.
3. 40m Climb a groove, then move left on small holds. Climb straight
up the grooves above, then move left to a ledge.
4. 30m Move up over blocks by an awkward mantelshelf, and
scramble up to Castle Ridge.

205 Lobby Dancer 280m VI,6 *** (1977)
This good winter climb has seen few ascents. It follows the prominent
groove on the right side of the wall taken by the lower section of Plastic
Max. Climb directly up to the foot of the groove by a series of ice
pitches, or traverse in from the left along the diagonal ledge line of The
Serpent. Follow the groove for three pitches to belay below the barrier
wall. Gain the continuation of the groove above the wall (1 peg aid),
then climb up to a block belay on the right. Move left to finish on the
crest of Castle Ridge.

Alchemist 270m VI,5 ** (1979)
The groove system just to the right of Lobby Dancer gives another
impressive winter line. Start as for Lobby Dancer to reach the foot of
the grooves. Follow the groove system with minor deviations to below
the overhanging barrier near the top of the buttress. On the right wall,
about 10m right of Lobby Dancer, is a huge flake. Climb this and use
aid to enter the narrow iced chimney above. From its top climb up left,
then traverse right to a cave and block belay. Climb right, go round an
arete, and follow the groove above to exit on Castle Ridge.

NORTH WALL OF CASTLE RIDGE

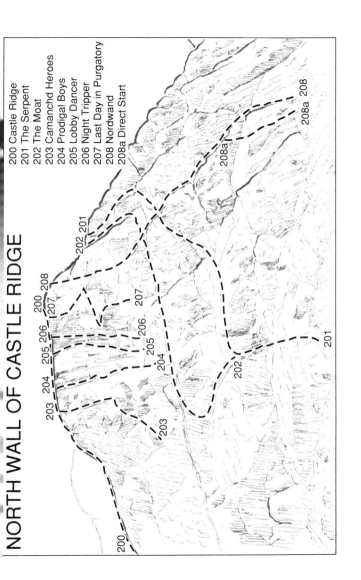

200 Castle Ridge
201 The Serpent
202 The Moat
203 Camanchd Heroes
204 Prodigal Boys
205 Lobby Dancer
206 Night Tripper
207 Last Day in Purgatory
208 Nordwand
208a Direct Start

Mist Dancer Variation: 50m   VI,5   (1988)
To the right of the huge flake is a chimney-groove which provides a
free alternative to the original line. Climb the chimney-groove (poorly
protected), exit left, then traverse left to rejoin the final groove of
Alchemist.

206   Night Tripper   185m   VS   (1971)
Start 20 metres right of Plastic Max below a groove system with a
series of square-cut roofs at two-thirds height.
1. 45m Climb the open groove to a steepening and move out right
around the overhang to a belay above.
2. 40m Continue up the corner to a glacis, then take the cracked wet
wall above to reach the continuation of the groove on the left. Step
into this and go up to a large stance below some overhangs.
3. 45m Move up the corner until a series of handholds lead left under
the overhangs. Step left round an overlap onto a slab which leads up
right to a comfortable stance.
4. 45m Climb a black slabby corner on the left to the final corner. Climb
this directly at first, then move out left at the top.
5. 10m Move up and left to the final belay on boulder-strewn ledges,
and scramble up to the crest of Castle Ridge.

207   Last Day in Purgatory   330m   V,5 **   (1979)
This route takes a steep zigzag line up the wall to the right of Lobby
Dancer. At first it climbs the wall directly, then moves left to a ledge
line which traverses the wall diagonally right. From here it moves back
diagonally left to finish directly at the left-hand end of the wall. Follow
the approach section of Lobby Dancer and traverse right to a point
midway along the wall where it is criss-crossed by several prominent
ledges. Climb grooves to beneath a steep wall, then traverse left and
climb a small chimney. At its top exit left onto a slab, continue left, then
move directly up to a large ledge (crux). Traverse right along the ledge,
descend a short section, then climb a wall. Continue the traverse until
it is possible to join a ledge line which heads back diagonally left.
Traverse left under the headwall for 50m, then move across to a
snowfield overlooking the upper section of Lobby Dancer. Climb short
steep cracks to a belay, and continue more easily (as for Alchemist)
to the top.

208   Nordwand   430m   III *   (1959)
A worthwhile mixed route, especially if climbed by the Direct Start.
Start in a small gully near the right edge of the face. After 25m, break
out left onto the buttress, or alternatively continue by an ice pitch in
the gully. Traverse left to gain the natural line of ascent and follow this
until about 200m up the face. At this point the rising shelf of The
Serpent comes in from the left. Cross this and continue up steep snow
to the foot of the summit rocks. Climb these by a series of walls and
traverses leading to the left, to gain the final rocks of Castle Ridge.
Direct Start: 100m   IV,4 **   (1989)
Start just left of the original route and climb an open icy corner-groove
for two long and poorly protected pitches.

Casino Royale   190m   VI,5 *   (1988)
Start at the foot of a thin gully just left of the obvious gully of La Petite.
Climb a wall to a snow basin, then continue up an icefall to an open
gully. Follow this, then climb steep thin ice to below a roof. Move left
with difficulty to a thin ice seam in a corner, and climb this to the top.
Trend right up a diagonal snow slope to finish.

La Petite   185m   III   (1959)
This route follows the prominent gully near the right edge of the face.
Start 30 metres right of Nordwand, climb ice for 25m, then continue
for 15m up steep ice-glazed rock to enter the gully. Follow the gully
which trends right to finish on the shoulder of Carn Dearg.

Le Méchant   140   IV,4   (1991)
About 50 metres right of La Petite is a thin gully cutting through a wall.
1. 35m Climb a small buttress to a belay below the gully.
2. 45m Surmount a slab to enter the gully, and follow it over an icy
bulge.
3. 45m Continue up an icy slab and groove to the crest of the buttress.
4. 35m Climb the crest easily to the shoulder of Carn Dearg.

The obvious gully which splits the small buttress well to the right of
the main crag is **Red Gully** (120m II 1959).

GIRDLE TRAVERSES

The Girdle Traverse   4000m   Severe   (1941)
This monster expedition takes the natural line along the shelf which
cuts across the entire north face of the mountain. The climbing is
straightforward except for the section approaching Point Five Gully.
Start from the Carn Mor Dearg Arete, cross to the second platform of
North-East Buttress, take the V-traverse to The Basin on Orion Face,
and cross Zero Gully to reach Observatory Ridge. Follow a curving
ledge across Point Five Gully to above Rubicon Wall on Observatory
Buttress. Traverse the shelf under Psychedelic Wall, and walk across
to the foot of the Great Tower on Tower Ridge. Cross Glover's
Chimney, traverse to Number Two Gully, ascend Hesperides Ledge,
and move across to Green Gully and so on to Number Three Gully.
Cross Creag Coire na Ciste to Number Four Gully, then move up
slopes to cross the Trident Buttress and Carn Dearg face. Continue
along to South Castle Gully, The Castle, North Castle Gully and finish
at the top of Castle Ridge.

The Winter Girdle   1500m   IV,4   (1959)
A winter traverse from right to left from Observatory Gully to the Carn
Mor Dearg Arete. From the foot of Gardyloo Gully traverse under
Psychedelic Wall and cross Observatory Buttress to enter Point Five
Gully. Climb up a short distance, then cross thinly iced slabs to reach
easier ground leading to Observatory Ridge. Cross Zero Gully, descend to The Basin on Orion Face, then follow the slanting snow ramp
of the V-Traverse to the crest of North-East Buttress. Continue along
an ascending traverse which leads around the buttress to the final
slopes of the Carn Mor Dearg Arete.

Third Time Lucky   600m   VI,6   (1979)
This unusual winter traverse of the Minus Face is probably unrepeated. From the First Platform, follow North-East Buttress and take
the snowy ledge on to the upper part of Minus Two Buttress. An abseil
from a spike leads to a snow patch in the centre of the buttress 25m
below, giving access to a traverse line into Minus Two Gully. Continue
to Minus One Gully, and move across to The Basin on Orion Face.
The last section is very difficult and several aid points were used on
the first ascent. The climbing becomes progressively easier as the
route crosses Orion Face to finish up Zero Gully.

Marathon 610m HVS * (1966)

Although contrived, this long rising traverse of the Minus and Orion faces links together several fine pitches, and passes through some of the most impressive rock scenery on Ben Nevis. The route deserves to receive more ascents. The technical grade is 5a. Start by following the Clough Variation to Left-Hand Route on Minus Two Buttress. From the junction with the original route traverse right below the overhangs of Central Route to the edge of the corner of Right-Hand Route. Make a short abseil and climb the crux of Right-Hand Route. From the belay above traverse right to climb the upper grooves of Subtraction to a grassy ledge on the edge of Minus Two Gully. Cross the gully to a small platform, descend slightly and cross to the plinth on Minus One Direct. Follow Minus One Direct (pitch 4) up right to the edge of Minus One Gully. Climb up a short distance and traverse delicately right to a stance and corner belay on Astronomy. Make a slightly descending traverse into the corner formed by the Great Slab Rib of The Long Climb, then follow this to a grass ledge. Continue as for The Long Climb to the foot of the Second Slab Rib. Slant obliquely right across slabs, and continue in the same general line, finishing near the final part of Slav Route by a chimney to the right of a prominent prow.

The Orgy 670m HVS (1961)

A mammoth, but very contrived mid-level girdle of Carn Dearg Buttress. It involves a significant amount of descent of some of the best routes on the buttress! Several pegs were used for aid on the first ascent.

1 to 4. 110m Climb the subsidiary buttress of Route I to the start of the chimney.

5. 25m Traverse up and right to a groove. Descend 2m, then follow a gangway between the overlaps to a belay.

6. 15m Move right to a grassy groove and descend to a spike.

7. 15m Regain the traverse line and continue, rising slightly, to reach another groove. Descend a little, then cross to a grass ledge and belay on Centurion.

8. 50m Descend Centurion to the stance at the top of pitch 3.

9. 25m Traverse horizontally right between the overlaps for 15m. Move up right, descend a crack for 3m, then move right to a stance on the nose overlooking the corner of The Bat.

10. 35m Climb the slab up and right across The Bat to the left edge of the great chimney of Sassenach. Climb a bulge and continue near the edge to the grassy terrace at the top of Sassenach pitch 4.

11. 50m Descend the great chimney of Sassenach.

12. 20m Move right along The Patey Traverse and descend to the belay at the top of the first pitch of Titan's Wall.

13. 35m Continue rightwards along the ledge, then make a hard move into the corner-crack of The Shield Direct. Climb the crack to a large block belay.

14. 20m Climb directly for 6m to a wide ledge, then traverse into The Shield Direct.

15 and 16. 125m Climb The Shield Direct to its junction with Evening Wall.

17. 40m Move up and left and follow a zigzag line of gangways and short walls to a grass ledge. Belay at a large block below a bulging corner.

18. 30m Climb the crack above and continue easily to a scree-covered terrace.

19 and 20. 75m Easy climbing leads to the top.

The High Girdle 400m Severe (1961)

A high level girdle of Carn Dearg Buttress based on the natural rising traverse line of Route II.

1 and 2. 60m Climb the easy groove left of Mourning slab (The Curtain Rail) and belay on the left edge.

3. 20m Continue to a grass ledge on the edge above on the right, traverse up into the foot of a corner, then move down to a ledge on Mourning Slab.

4. 20m Traverse up and right to a diagonal crack, climb it, then descend to a small stance. Move up a little, then traverse right to a grass ledge.

5. 15m Cross the chimney of Route I and descend to the junction with Route II.

6 and 7. 90m Follow Route II to the outer edge of the buttress.

8. 30m Continue by a grassy traverse to Evening Wall.

9. 40m Follow a broad ledge, under a blank wall, passing a series of large blocks to join The Orgy.

10. 20m Go round the corner, then move up and left by a series of ledges to belay at a large block below a bulging corner.

11. 30m Climb the crack above and continue easily to a scree-covered terrace.

12. 75m Easy climbing leads to the top.

Gemini, Ben Nevis (Climber, John Main)

The Mamores and the Aonachs

This chapter describes the excellent and varied climbing to be found in the mountains surrounding Ben Nevis. Many of the crags have been developed quite recently and, with characteristics quite distinct from those of Ben Nevis, they provide a host of climbs which are often in good condition before there has been a substantial build up of snow and ice. Also included are the deep and impressive gullies which rise out of Glen Nevis on the flanks of Ben Nevis itself.

GLEN NEVIS

From the Glen Nevis road, several gullies can be seen etched into the western flank of Ben Nevis. They are primarily summer expeditions that offer sport of varying degrees of aquatic interest, but included in their ranks is Surgeon's Gully, one of the finest examples of its kind. The buttresses between the gullies are composed of steep slabs which are difficult to descend, but a path crossing the face at 600m provides a useful exit route. corner line

The only gully recorded on the steep slope of Meall an t-Suidhe above the Tourist Track car park (Map Ref 123 731) is **Achintee Gully** (120m Difficult 1946). It has a number of pitches but only one provides any real difficulty. The right branch at the top gives a further 60m of climbing. After a heavy snowfall and a prolonged freeze it can provide an enjoyable winter climb, suitable for a short day (120m II/III 1904).

Five Finger Gully (150m Difficult 1946) is the first major gully south of the Red Burn. It is a cascading river course with several waterfalls and other 'interesting' pitches. To the right is **Antler Gully** (120m Very Difficult 1947) which starts above the old graveyard. Further right is Surgeon's Gully, which cuts very deeply into the hillside. The route finishes at the traverse path, but the gully splits into three branches above. Although each branch has been thoroughly explored it is unlikely that the entire gully has been climbed in one push. A direct ascent of the barrier pitch combined with the intriguing central branch would produce the longest and most difficult gully climb in Scotland.

Stirling Bridge, Aonach Mor (Climber, Steve Kennedy)

Surgeon's Gully   450m   VS   (1947)
Rarely climbed, but an absolute must for the connoisseur of summer gully climbing! Start by following the prominent stone wall up the hillside to the mouth of the gully, and climb a series of short slabby pitches to the base of the first major chockstone pitch.

1. 20m Climb to the cave and exit by a slab on the right.

2. 10m After an awkward start, back and foot to the top of a chockstone and exit on the left.

3. 20m Climb directly for 10m, then back and foot to turn the chockstone by the right wall.

4. Follow the gully easily to the barrier pitch, a magnificent section over 30m high, with a large chockstone in its upper reaches. Although the chockstone has been climbed directly, the easiest line takes the right wall 10m from the back of the gully.

5. Climb the vegetated right wall, finishing by an open chimney. Traverse up and left and descend into the gully after a further 30m.

6. 10m Climb a sloping rake on the left on good holds.

7. 5m Surmount the chockstone.

8. 10m The first waterfall pitch. Start up the left side, then traverse right into the waterfall and climb it direct.

9. 5m The next chockstone pitch is best climbed back and foot.

10 and 11. 15m Two more waterfalls!

12. 10m An easier-angled sloping pitch.

13. The crux section now looms above, where a large chockstone and attendant waterfall block the exit. Start a few metres back on the right wall and climb the smooth groove above (delicate). Move right to a small ledge (runner) and continue 3m to a stance and peg belay.

14. Go up 3m, surmount the nose on the left, then traverse left into the waterfall to climb into a cave beneath the exit chockstone. From a good runner climb the chockstone to a thread belay 8m higher.

15 to 17. Climb the rake on the left (10m), turn the chockstone with difficulty (10m), and climb the central groove (5m).

18. 5m Continue up the smooth groove on the extreme right.

19. 20m Another waterfall pitch. Start on the right and work obliquely left, then climb straight up the bed of the fall from the halfway point.

20. 35m Climb the gully bed above (normally very wet!) and exit by a large chockstone.

21. 15m Climb up to the chockstone and turn it on the left.

22. 10m Continue by the gully bed to the final pitch which contains the largest chockstone in the gully. Climb it either on the left or right to finish on the horizontal traverse path (the highpoint of the original

ascent). Above, the gully opens out to form three branches. The left is a simple scramble, the central very steep and apparently difficult and the right patently more possible.

Easy Gully lies just right of Surgeon's Gully and is a useful descent route. To the right, **Polldubh Gully** (600m Severe 1947) starts with moderate slabs which can be avoided by grassy slopes on either side. After 100m the gully closes in, and three awkward pitches lead to a point where the gully splits into two. After a 10m waterfall pitch, the left branch becomes a dry watercourse running towards the top of Easy Gully. The right branch is open on the hillside for 50m before closing in again for a succession of chockstones and wet pitches which eventually lead to the traverse path.

Christmas Gully (225m Very Difficult 1946) is on the right side of the face and can be recognised by a prominent waterfall low down. It consists of three sections. The first climbs the waterfall to halfway, then traverses right to enter the gully higher up. The central section ascends a series of grassy pitches to where the gully narrows again. The final 150m section, known as 'The Gorge', is climbed by a series of short awkward pitches, then leaves the gully on the left to rejoin it higher up above a fork.

Much further up Glen Nevis is **Steall Gully** (150m II 1946) which lies on the south-east flank of Ben Nevis, almost in line with the summit when viewed from the Steall Hut. It consists of a series of short ice pitches and is best approached by the burn which descends from the col between Ben Nevis and Meall Cumhann.

There are many crags at Polldubh and in the Glen Nevis gorge. The rough mica schist is studded with quartz and provides high quality, technical rock climbing. The routes have become very popular and are fully described in the *Highland Outcrops* guide. In very cold weather, a number of water weeps can freeze to give low-level fun.

The Steall Waterfall   120m   III **   (1963)

After a prolonged cold spell, the large waterfall above the Steall Hut (Map Ref 177 683) freezes to form an impressive cataract of ice. It is considerably easier than it looks if climbed by the line of least resistance. The best descent is to abseil down through the trees on the left (east) side.

STOB BAN
999m   (Map Ref 147 654)

The attractive profile of Stob Ban, with its distinctive summit cone, can be seen from many points in Glen Nevis. The main peak is comprised of quartzite, but the two northern tops are mica schist. The rock is too broken for good rock climbing, but in winter conditions the north-east face provides an interesting selection of medium grade routes.

The cliffs can be divided into three principal buttresses. South Buttress is the large mass of quartzite directly below the main summit which is split by two wide snow gullies. Central Buttress lies north-east of the summit and is set forward from, and at a lower level than South Buttress. It is distinguished by a large triangular front face, and a slanting shelf and gully which separates it from South Buttress. North Buttress is mica schist, and lies approximately 600 metres north of the summit directly below a small top at Map Ref 146 659.

Approach from Glen Nevis by following a good path on the east bank of Allt Coire a'Mhusgain until opposite the cliffs, then descend to cross the stream and strike up snow slopes to the foot of the routes (1½ hours). The shortest descent is by the exposed north ridge which drops steeply over two subsidiary summits to reach more open slopes after 2 km. It is best to head north-west from here to avoid a series of rocky outcrops. It is also possible to descend the steep east ridge for about 1 km before heading north to reach the ascent path.

SOUTH BUTTRESS

The two gullies either side of the steep central wall are **South Gully** (150m I) on the left and North Gully (150m I) on the right. The wall itself is breached by **North Ridge Route** (120m Very Difficult 1948) which takes the spur in the centre of the face and finishes a few metres right of the summit. The first 50m are the most difficult. The buttress to the left of South Gully is known as the **East Wing**. It was climbed in 1948 with the lower section providing the greatest difficulties.

CENTRAL BUTTRESS

The three gully lines on the left flank of the buttress are bordered on the right by the prominent line of Skyline Rib, which forms the left edge of the broad triangular front face of the buttress. A short arete giving about 150m of easy climbing links the top of Central Buttress to the main ridge some 200m north of the summit.

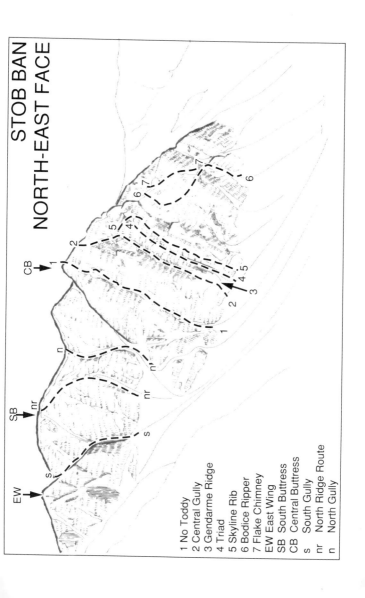

STOB BAN
NORTH-EAST FACE

1 No Toddy
2 Central Gully
3 Gendarme Ridge
4 Triad
5 Skyline Rib
6 Bodice Ripper
7 Flake Chimney
EW East Wing
SB South Buttress
CB Central Buttress
s South Gully
nr North Ridge Route
n North Gully

1   No Toddy   150m   III,4   (1986)
The left-hand gully. Start at a small snowfield some distance up the
left flank of the buttress. Climb a steep ice pitch (crux) to easier ground
and a stance on the right. Move back left and ascend the gully easily
to where a possible escape slants right. Instead, traverse left and
bridge up the continuation of the lower line. Continue up mixed ground
to the top of the buttress.

2   Central Gully   150m   IV,4   (1969)
An uneven climb. Most of the gully is Grade I, except for a steep 25m
section at the start. At the top of the gully move left along an easy ramp
to the crest of the ridge, which leads easily to the top.

3   Gendarme Ridge   150m   IV,4   (1904)
The slender buttress right of Central Gully has what appears to be a
gendarme near its foot, but this is actually part of the buttress. Climb
up to the supposed gendarme, and continue steeply for 60m to where
the angle eases. The upper part of the buttress is straightforward.
Finish along the left-slanting ramp as for Central Gully.

4   Triad   150m   III   (1986)
The right-hand gully is defined by a narrow rock buttress on the left
and Skyline Rib on the right. The gully gradually steepens and narrows
to a chimney which leads to the final stance of Skyline Rib. Follow a
snow ramp on the right, then traverse left along a narrow ledge to the
crest of the buttress. Join the easy left-slanting ramp above and finish
as for Central Gully.

5   Skyline Rib   120m   IV,4   (1987)
Follow the crest of the narrow buttress, taking care with several loose
blocks, and continue to the top *via* the ramp of Triad.

6   Bodice Ripper   150m   IV,4 *   (1984)
A good but fairly serious route up the large triangular front face of
Central Buttress. Start right of centre at the foot of the obvious
right-slanting gully. Climb easily to a prominent left-slanting ramp.
Follow this until it fades and take a stance (poor belay) at the foot of
a steep and narrow right-slanting slab. Gain the slab with difficulty and
climb to its top (crux), then zigzag up to the snowfield above. Continue
to the top of the snowfield and ascend the obvious gully with interest.

At its top, squeeze up a narrow chimney (the bodice ripper!) which leads right to the broad ramp of Triad. Follow this to the top.

7   Flake Chimney   150m   III   (1985)
Climb the entry pitch of Bodice Ripper to a bay. Follow a chimney on the right to a notch behind a giant flake, then traverse right across a slab and two left-trending grooves to reach a second chimney which slants up to the right. Climb this to easy ground.

NORTH BUTTRESS

East Ridge   200m   II/III   (1895)
A fine mountaineering route with an excellent finish along the fine arete at the top. It is best approached as for the routes on Central Buttress, followed by a traverse right across the corrie floor.

SGORR AN IUBHAIR
1001m   (Map Ref 165 655)

There are three climbs in the north-west corrie of Sgorr an Iubhair, which may be worth doing if one happens to be in the area with a rope and gear. **Let Loose** (55m Very Difficult 1970) takes the west-facing edge of the slab just south of the summit, and is extremely loose. **Applause** (50m Severe 1970) lies further west and lower down about halfway along the series of slabs just left of the steepest and largest slab. Climb a short wall to a vertical groove which leads to the top. The third route, **Three Fingers** (30m Very Difficult) follows the line of least resistance on the best-looking slab below and slightly right of the top.

SGURR A'MHAIM
1099m   (Map Ref 165 667)

In the centre of Coire nan Cnamh is a prominent band of quartzite in which the strata are contorted into a spectacular fold. Five routes have been recorded on the largest section of clean rock, and there is scope for several more. Approach from Glen Nevis by ascending the steep vegetated hillside behind the Steall Hut (1½ hours from car park). The climbs are described from left to right. The first four routes are reached by scrambling up to the second grass ledge.

Heart of Glass   30m   E2 5a   (1990)
Start on the left side of the main crag and climb the crack just right of
a vegetated groove. Hard to protect.

Around the Bend   30m   HVS 5a   (1990)
Ascend the crack in the centre of the main crag with an obvious
mantelshelf finish.

Strata-Sphere   25m   E2 5b   (1990)
Climb the main crag right of centre and finish up broken cracks.

Bananafishbones   25m   E1 5a   (1990)
Climb the crack on the right side of the main crag, surmount an overlap
at half-height and finish up a crack.

Clam-Jam   40m   E1 5b **   (1990)
Start from the lower grass ledge and climb the clean slab immediately
right of the main crag.

THE AONACHS

The broad ridge of the Aonachs runs north to south and is sandwiched
between the Grey Corries to the east and Carn Mor Dearg to the west.
Each side of the ridge is cut by wild and remote corries, and the peaks
demand respect, especially in wild weather. They provide excellent
climbing of surprising variety. The altitude of the hills, second only to
Ben Nevis in this guide, means that they offer some of the most reliable
winter climbing in the area.

AONACH MOR
1221m   (Map Ref 193 730)

At first glance, the great rounded bulk of Aonach Mor would seem to
be an unlikely climbing ground, since the crags on the east and west
faces of the mountain are hidden from many viewpoints. The cliffs of
Coire an Lochain can be seen from Spean Bridge, but they are dwarfed
by the vast scale of the mountain's eastern aspect. Lying close to Ben
Nevis, development of these crags has been slow, and it is only in the
late 1980s that they were systematically explored.

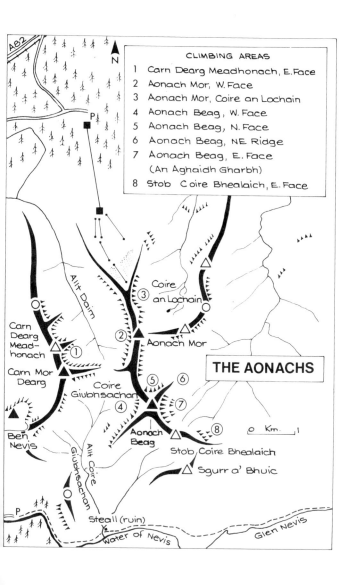

CLIMBING AREAS

1 Carn Dearg Meadhonach, E.Face
2 Aonach Mor, W.Face
3 Aonach Mor, Coire an Lochain
4 Aonach Beag, W.Face
5 Aonach Beag, N.Face
6 Aonach Beag, NE Ridge
7 Aonach Beag, E.Face
  (An Aghaidh Gharbh)
8 Stob Coire Bhealaich, E.Face

THE AONACHS

The rock is good quality granite, which is too vegetated to provide any worthwhile summer routes. In winter however, the vegetation and high altitude mean that the cliffs come into condition and provide quality climbing when other crags in the west are too low to be properly frozen. Early in the season, they can provide an alternative to Ben Nevis, which may have insufficient ice for good climbing.

The cliffs used to be the sole preserve of the mountaineer who favoured solitude and long walks, but completion of the Gondola and ski development in 1990 made Coire an Lochain the most accessible winter cliff in Scotland. It is now a mere 150 metres walk from the top ski tow to the descent gully, and the promise of a winter route or two followed by an exhilarating ski descent at the end of the day has made climbing in the corrie very popular.

The climbs are described anti-clockwise around the mountain, starting from the Aonach Mor-Aonach Beag col (Map Ref 194 719).

AN CUL CHOIRE   (Map Ref 194 723)

The corrie formed by the south and east ridges of Aonach Mor contains a prominent schist buttress, a conspicuous feature when viewed from the Aonach Mor-Aonach Beag col. Two summer routes have been recorded. **Route 1** (120m Difficult 1945) starts in the centre of the buttress, and heads for a narrow neck before reaching easier rocks. **Route 2** (120m Difficult 1945) starts 10 metres right of Route 1 and follows, in part, the edge overlooking the gully on the right. The rock is loose in places and neither route has much to recommend it. In winter the ridge provides a short but worthwhile mixed climb. The best approach is to contour down and right from the Aonach Mor-Aonach Beag col to reach a large ledge at the start of the main difficulties.

Aonach Seang   120m   III *

A fine route, based on the summer line of Route 1. It is described well by its Gaelic name - Slender Ridge. From the ledge, climb the shallow chimney-groove which leads to a steep corner pitch on the left side of the buttress (crux). Above, climb more easily on the crest to a narrow neck, followed by broken rocks which lead to the plateau.

COIRE AN LOCHAIN   (Map Ref 192 737)

Coire an Lochain, on the east face of Aonach Mor, presents a long line of granite cliffs up to 150m high. Their base is very high (starting above 1000m), and the rock is generally well vegetated. This means that the routes come into condition rapidly and provide good climbing with the first snows of winter. Facing east, and sheltered from southerly and westerly gales, the crag receives the morning sunshine and readily forms ice. Convenient descents at either end of the cliffs allow several climbs to be done in a day, and the general feel of the place is similar to Coire an t-Sneachda in the Northern Corries of Cairn Gorm.

Under heavy snow conditions, and with the frequent westerly gales, the corrie cornices easily. It is important to bear in mind that late in the season the cornices can reach monstrous proportions and make direct exits from some of the routes impossible. However, many of the climbs finish on relatively easy ground, across which it is possible to traverse to places with less pronounced cornices.

The rock is excellent fine-grained granite that has been fractured along a vertical plane, resulting in many cracks, chimneys and gullies. The buttress routes are generally well protected, but the rock on the side walls of the major fault lines is often quite compact, so belays in the gullies can be harder to find.

The corrie forms part of an almost perfect spherical bowl, centred around the lochan at Map Ref 198 739. The apex of the corrie rim is cut by a broad snow gully which lies almost due east of the lochan. This is Easy Gully, which provides the easiest descent from the plateau into the corrie, and is a convenient reference point for describing the climbs. Left of Easy Gully, the south side of the corrie contains a series of north-east facing buttresses, which, although shorter than those further to the north, are less exposed to the sun and stay in condition later into the season. Most of the climbing is on the most prominent buttress, The Prow. Right of Easy Gully the climbs can be divided into four main sections. First are the Ribbed Walls, which are divided into a series of grooves and ribs and are separated from Central Buttress by the deep gully of Tunnel Vision. Further right are two narrow buttresses separated by three deep gullies. This is the Twins Area. The left-hand buttress can be recognised by the deep cleft of The Split, which is a useful landmark in poor visibility. Further right is North Buttress, which terminates with a wide gully left of the ridge bounding the north end of the corrie.

Access

There are two main approaches on foot from the valley. Either drive to Leanachan (Map Ref 219 786) and follow forest tracks towards Allt Choille-rais (boggy) which lead up to the base of the cliffs in Coire an Lochain. The O.S. Mountainmaster, Outdoor Leisure 32, 1:25000 map is useful for this approach. The climbs are quite hard to locate in poor visibility. If in doubt, head straight uphill from the lochan. (3 to 3½ hours).

Alternatively, follow the signposts and drive to the Gondola car park then take a rather indistinct path up through the cleared area under the cables. This joins a forestry track which takes a sharp right turn and leads to a small dam. Now head uphill on a rather better path and follow it to the Gondola station (1½ hours). The same point can be reached rather more quickly by mechanical means when the Gondola is running; check by phoning Nevis Range at Fort William (0397) 705825.

The easiest way to the cliffs from the Gondola station is to take the chairlift and tows, but skis are essential. On foot, the quickest way is to follow the line of the ski tows directly up the side of the main ski run, then alongside the summit ski tow to its end (3 hours in total). This point, marked by a small shack and a large cairn, is 150 metres south from the rim of Easy Gully (185 degrees grid). In poor visibility it may be difficult to locate the top of the gully, and extreme caution should be exercised as the cornices can be very large. It is normally possible to enter the gully by its northern edge, which appears to escape much of the cornicing. Skis can be used as a convenient belay in case it is necessary to abseil.

In doubtful weather, or after heavy snowfall (which is likely to make Easy Gully and the slopes beneath hideously avalanche-prone) a more circuitous but safer approach is to contour east below Aonach an Nid, then to take a gently rising line southwards to reach a minor col high on the ridge which bounds the north side of Coire an Lochain (about 3½ hours in total). All the approaches involve traversing steep avalanche-prone slopes below the routes. In heavy snow conditions, or if a high category avalanche warning report has been issued, climbing should be avoided in the corrie. The best climbing conditions are likely to be found early in the season before the more traditional areas in this guide have come into condition. It is worth noting however, that avalanche conditions may occur here even in November, before the regular avalanche warning reports have started for the winter.

Easy Gully is the most commonly used descent back into the corrie. It is also possible to descend just to the north of the north bounding ridge of the corrie. This is a useful approach for the climbs on North Buttress. The best way off the mountain after finishing climbing is to descend the ski slopes to the valley.

NORTH-EAST FACE

1   Hidden Gully   120m   II *   (1989)
An attractive-looking route up the narrow twisting couloir in the centre
of the slabby buttress which defines the southern edge of the corrie.
It may bank out under heavy snow conditions.

The following climbs are located on The Prow, which is approximately 100 metres left of Easy Gully. This distinctive buttress, which
lies left of a deep gully (suitable descent late in the season), is
characterised by a rock prow high in the centre. The obvious line of
Stirling Bridge takes the right-angled corner near the right edge, and
the short corner immediately left of the twin parallel grooves on the
front face of the buttress is **Riptide** (IV,4 60m 1990). The groove a
short distance further left gives a short climb (45m III 1990).

2   The Betrayal   90m   IV,4   (1990)
The left-hand of the two parallel grooves on the front of the buttress.
Climb the groove over a series of bulges to a small snow bay
immediately under the prow. Steep awkward moves out left lead to
easier ground and the cornice.

The Guardian   90m   IV,5 *   (1990)
The right-hand of the two parallel grooves leads to a prominent
flake-chimney. Climb the chimney to steep but easier ground.

3   Stirling Bridge   70m   VI,7 **   (1990)
An excellent route with a memorable first pitch. Climb the prominent
right-angled corner (steep and strenuous) close to the right edge of
the buttress, and pull out right near the top. Continue up a short groove
to a large block belay on the left. Easier ground leads to the cornice.

4   Easy Gully   100m   I
This broad snow gully cuts deep into the plateau, and gives the best
descent route back to the corrie. The cornice can normally be avoided
on the right.

There are two routes on the broken buttress left of Easy Gully. **The
Web** (100m II/III 1989) climbs the chimney about 30 metres left of the
gully, and **Nausea** (90m II/III 1989) takes the icefall 20 metres further
left. Both routes bank out late in the season.

AONACH MOR
COIRE AN LOCHAIN

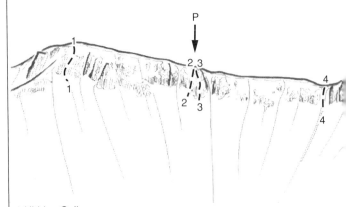

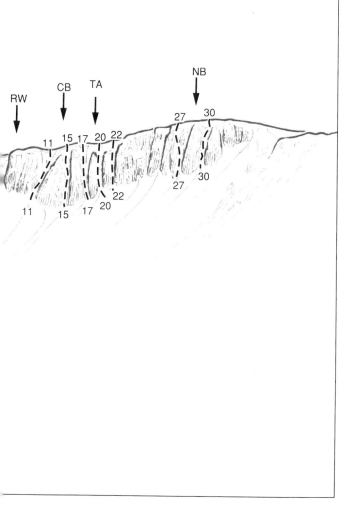

THE RIBBED WALLS

This section is characterised by a series of vertical ribs seamed by grooves. The most obvious feature near the left end of the face is the deep cleft of Temperance Union Blues and further right are several icefalls which provide the best pure ice climbing on the mountain. Just left of the broad gully of Tunnel Vision is a prominent tower taken by Gondola with the Wind. Late in the season the first pitch of many of the routes can bank out, and a large cornice often forms over the entire length of the cliff. This is best avoided at its right-hand end, just left of the final tower of Gondola with the Wind.

5   Muddy Waters   90m   III   (1990)
About 10 metres right of Easy Gully is an obvious chimney high on the buttress. Climb easy mixed ground to the foot of the chimney, and follow it trending right to the cornice. The lower section completely banks out late in the season.

6   Barrel Buttress   60m   IV,4   (1993)
Between Muddy Waters and the Temperance Union Blues is a small recess defined on the right by a sharp narrow arete, and on the left by a broad buttress. Start just right of the foot of the buttress and climb it directly, avoiding the steep wall at the top on the left.

Nid Arete   90m   IV,5 *   (1993)
This good and well protected mixed route takes the groove line on the left side of the narrow arete to the right of Barrel Buttress. Climb the groove directly, then follow the furthest corner on the right (overlooking the final section of Temperance Union Blues) to the top.

7   Temperance Union Blues   90m   III   (1989)
The cliff is split by a deep cleft at half-height about 50 metres right of Easy Gully.
1. 45m Take either of two converging lines to the bottom of the cleft.
2. 45m Climb the cleft to where it steepens, then exit by a ramp to reach the cornice.

Pernille   70m   III   (1990)
The buttress immediately right of the deep cleft of Temperance Union Blues. Climb into an obvious scoop just right of the cleft, and continue up right to a steep left-trending ramp which leads to a snow bay. Exit right to reach the cornice.

At the right end of the Ribbed Walls, immediately to the left of the wide gully of Tunnel Vision, are two buttresses separated by a snowy amphitheatre. The better defined right-hand buttress is taken by the fine line of Gondola with the Wind. The main feature of the left-hand buttress is a pair of icefalls which form down its left side.

Aquafresh   100m   IV,4 *   *18.2.01, č Trevor.*   (1990)
Start 40 metres left of Tunnel Vision, and climb the left-hand icefall, trending left mixed ground at the top.

8   White Shark   110m   IV,4 ***   (1990)
The right-hand icefall gives an excellent route. Climb the shallow gully, characterised by a steep slabby corner at half-height, to a ledge. Continue up the steep icefall which forms down the corner to an exit onto easier ground.

9   Tinsel Town   110m   V,4 **   (1991)
An elegant climb up the groove line left of Gondola with the Wind. Start 10 metres right of White Shark.
1. 40m Climb a system of grooves just right of the buttress crest, then continue up a chimney to a stance on the left.
2. 50m Move back right into the main groove and climb steep mixed ground to a belay below the cornice.
3. 20m The cornice can be huge. On the first ascent it was outflanked by a long traverse to the right.

Remora   100m   III,4   (1990)
Climb the first pitch of Tinsel Town, then continue up and left below the steep crest of the upper buttress to a belay above the icefall of White Shark. Finish up the easy gully above.

10   Gondola with the Wind   125m   IV,5 **   (1990)
A good mixed climb up the right side of the buttress, just left of Tunnel Vision. The steep tower immediately below the plateau provides an exciting finish.
1. 45m Start up a short groove 8 metres left of Tunnel Vision. Climb to a small amphitheatre, then exit on the right.
2. 35m Follow a system of shallow grooves close to the edge of the buttress, and spiral right, round the side of the tower, to a steep corner.
3. 45m Climb the corner (hard) and continue up the snow slopes above.

11   Tunnel Vision   120m   III   (1989)

The wide gully between the Ribbed Walls and Central Buttress. An initial narrows leads to a snow bay with three possible exits. The Central Finish climbs ice smears up the back wall, in an exposed position, to a steep cornice finish. In full conditions this wall may bank out to a frightening angle with an impassable cornice. The Left Branch provides a steep and technical alternative (50m III,4 1990), and it should always be possible to climb the right branch to reach the upper easy section of Morwind.

CENTRAL BUTTRESS

This buttress lies between the gullies of Tunnel Vision on the left and Left Twin to its right. It is the highest section of crag in the corrie, and it provides some of the finest mixed routes on the mountain. The two most prominent lines are Morwind, which takes the fault line up the left crest of the buttress, and Typhoon, which climbs the left-facing corner system on the right side of the front face. The cornices on this buttress are often large and unbroken, but a vague snow arete on the final snow slopes can normally be relied on to provide a safe way through. If the cornice is impassable, it is possible to traverse right for 50 metres and descend the gully of Forgotten Twin.

Shelf Route   110m   III   (1990)

Start in a small bay up and left of the lowest point of the buttress and climb up and right to reach a steep groove. Climb the groove to a narrow shelf left of the buttress crest, overlooking Tunnel Vision. Follow this until a break on the right leads to the buttress crest. Continue up Morwind to the top.

12   Morwind   150m   III,4 ***   (1988)

This fine mixed route was the first to be recorded in the corrie, and has rapidly become a classic. Start at the toe of the buttress and climb a short gully to enter a shallow chimney line. Follow this for two pitches to a small bay beneath a cave. Exit right up mixed ground to reach snow slopes and the summit cornice.

13   Turf Walk   150m   III,4 *   (1989)

An interesting mixed climb taking the right-slanting fault line that crosses the left side of the front face of the buttress. Start 15 metres right of Morwind and follow a left-slanting gully to a belay in a bay below the fault. Follow the fault up and right to ledges leading rightwards. Step right, then climb up and back left to belay below steep grooves left of the central depression. Climb the groove on the left, step left onto the exposed prow, and continue to easier ground and the top.

14   Roaring Forties   140m   IV,4 *   (1991)
This fine route takes the icefall which forms in the depression in the centre of the face. Good and varied, but not in condition as often as other routes on the buttress. Start 5 metres left of the corner line of Typhoon.
1. 45m Follow icy grooves into a recess.
2. 25m Climb the steep back wall by a groove on the right.
3. 50m Climb the icefall above to reach the final snow slopes.
4. 20m Easy climbing leads to the cornice.

15   Typhoon   130m   IV,4 ***   (1989)
An excellent climb, taking a direct line up the left facing chimney-groove on the right side of the front face. Start 15 metres left of the deep gully of Left Twin.
1. 40m Climb the lower slabby grooves to belay at the base of a chimney.
2. 30m Climb the chimney and groove past an overhang.
3. 40m Continue straight up on steep ice to exit onto the final snow slopes.
4. 20m Easy climbing leads to the cornice.

16   Hurricane Arete   140m   VI,7 **   (1989)
This technical mixed climb weaves an intricate and unlikely line through the overhangs just left of the right arete of Central Buttress. Start midway between Typhoon and Left Twin.
1. 50m Take iced slabs for 30m to reach a short left-slanting gully. Climb this, then move up right along a narrow ramp to a small ledge. Belay beneath a prominent overhang, just left of a right-facing corner that is capped by yet another overhang.
2. 20m Pull over the roof directly above the belay onto a steep slab, then follow a left-slanting crack to a prominent spike. Move right below an overhanging wall, then climb very steeply into a small snow bay. A difficult and sustained pitch.
3. 50m Climb the groove on the left to the final overhangs. Bridge up and exit on the left and continue up easier ground.
4. 20m Snow slopes lead to the cornice.

AONACH MOR
RIBBED WALLS TO NORTH
BUTTRESS

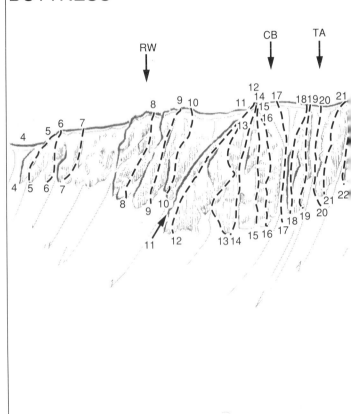

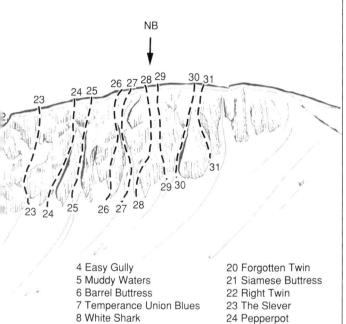

NB

4 Easy Gully	20 Forgotten Twin
5 Muddy Waters	21 Siamese Buttress
6 Barrel Buttress	22 Right Twin
7 Temperance Union Blues	23 The Slever
8 White Shark	24 Pepperpot
9 Tinsel Town	25 Molar Canal
10 Gondola with the Wind	26 Grooved Arete
11 Tunnel Vision	27 Icicle Gully
12 Morwind	28 Force Ten Buttress
13 Turf Walk	29 Solar Wind
14 Roaring Forties	30 Jet Stream
15 Typhoon	31 North Buttress Route
16 Hurricane Arete	RW Ribbed Walls
17 Left Twin	CB Central Buttress
18 The Split	TA Twins Area
19 Lickety Split	NB North Buttress

TWINS AREA

To the right of Central Buttress are two steep and narrow buttresses, Split Buttress and Siamese Buttress, which are bordered by three deep gullies. The gullies are rather confusingly known as 'The Twins'. The left side of Split Buttress is cut by the deep chimney of the Split. This is a useful point of reference in poor visibility which can be easily recognised by its large jammed blocks.

17   Left Twin   120m   III ***   (1989)
The deep gully immediately right of Central Buttress is the best traditional gully climb in the corrie. It is similar in difficulty and quality to SC Gully in Stob Coire nan Lochan (Glen Coe).

18   The Split   130m   III,4 **   (1989)
The prominent chimney, which almost slices Split Buttress in two, provides a climb of character and interest.
1. 25m Start at the foot of the buttress and climb the introductory gully to enter the chimney.
2. 45m Climb the chimney passing beneath several large jammed blocks until it is possible to exit left, 4m below the capping roof. Continue up the arete to belay.
3. 60m Easy snow leads up and left to finish as for Left Twin.

19   Lickety Split   130m   IV,5 **   (1989)
This fine varied mixed climb starts by climbing the icefall directly below the gully of Forgotten Twin and continues up the clean right-facing corner on the right side of the lower half of Split Buttress.
1. 30m Climb the icefall to a stance below the corner.
2. 20m Follow the corner to a good stance.
3. 20m Continue up the steep wall above, passing two overhangs, to reach a rock ridge overlooking the gully of Left Twin.
4. 60m Follow the ridge to the final snow slopes and plateau.

Slick Mick's Groove   130m   IV,5 *   (1992)
A good technical climb to the left of Lickety Split.
1. 30m Lickety Split, pitch 1.
2. 40m Move up left around the rib and to gain the small left-facing groove to the left of the crux corner of Lickety Split. Climb this with increasing difficulty and make a difficult exit onto a ledge. Continue to the final ridge of Lickety Split.
3. 60m Follow the ridge to the top.

20   Forgotten Twin   120m   I/II   (1989)
The gully between Split Buttress and Siamese Buttress provides the
easiest climb on the face. Start *via* a short ramp leading left from the
foot of Right Twin.

21   Siamese Buttress   120m   II *   (1989)
The well-defined buttress left of Right Twin gives an enjoyable
scramble. It is easiest if started from the right, but Grade III if started
up the steep corners on the left.

22   Right Twin   120m   II **   (1989)
A good traditional gully, narrow and well-defined, with steep sections
at the bottom and at mid-height. Exit left at the top.

There are a number of narrow ribs to the left of North Buttress. The
following four routes start in a large bay about 50 metres left of
Grooved Arete.

23   The Slever   100m   III,4   (1991)
A large icefall forms the left-hand margin of the bay. Climb it in one
long pitch to reach easy snow slopes above. Move right into a small
gully, and continue easily to the cornice.

24   Pepperpot   100m   III,4   (1990)
Just right of The Slever, and tucked away in the top left-hand corner
of the bay, is a steep icy chimney. Climb this, and finish by the gully
on the left.

Golden Promise   100m   VI,7   (1992)
This difficult mixed route climbs the steep groove-line situated at the
top right-hand side of the bay.
1. 45m The lower part of the groove is a straightforward snow gully
which leads to a large block belay on the right below the main
difficulties.
2. 45m Climb the steep groove above, and pull over a large bulge at
20m to reach a small *cul-de-sac*. Exit by a groove on the left and follow
easier grooves above to belay just short of the upper gully of Molar
Canal.
3. 10m Follow the gully to the top.

25   Molar Canal 100m   III   (1990)
About 35 metres left of Grooved Arete is a gully which becomes deep
and wide in its upper reaches. Start up a short icefall, and continue up
grooves into the gully. At the top it may be necessary to outflank the
cornice away to the left.

NORTH BUTTRESS
The last continuous section of crag at the northern end of the corrie is
separated from the deep gully of Molar Canal by two narrow ribs. It is
made up of three distinct buttresses, divided by the deep Icicle Gully
on the left and the clean-cut ice groove of Jet Stream on the right. The
routes here are among the finest in the corrie.

26   Grooved Arete   130m   IV,5 ***   (1988)
A superb mixed route up the narrow buttress immediately left of Icicle
Gully. Technically hard for the grade, but well protected. A little gem!
1. 45m Start at the foot of the gully and gain the arete to the left. Follow
this, easily at first, then with increasing difficulty up grooves on its left
side. Move back right to belay below a steep tower.
2. 35m Climb a series of grooves on the crest of the tower, step left
to a ledge and continue up a vertical corner. An excellent pitch.
3. 50m Easy climbing on the crest leads to the plateau.

27   Icicle Gully   130m   III   (1988)
The gully between Grooved Arete and Force Ten Buttress.
1. 50m Climb the gully to a belay on the right.
2. 50m Continue up the wider right-hand line to where it narrows.
Climb the icicle to a snow bay.
3. 30m Follow mixed ground to the cornice.

28   Force Ten Buttress   140m   III,4 **   (1988)
An excellent mixed route up the buttress between Icicle Gully and Jet
Stream. It tackles some surprising ground, but is well protected.
1. 45m Start up mixed ground just left of the crest, then move right to
a belay at the foot of a steep chimney where the buttress steepens.
2. 30m Climb the chimney, step right and climb a short difficult crack.
3. 40m Continue up interesting mixed ground to the right of the crest
to join a gully. Follow the gully to a col where the buttress merges into
the final snow slopes.
4. 25m Easy snow leads to the cornice.

Between Force Ten Buttress and North Buttress route is a small bay which contains two prominent gully lines. They form ice readily, lie in the shade until late in the season, and are often in condition throughout the winter.

29   Solar Wind   110m   IV,4 *   (1992)
1. 45m Start hard under Force Ten Buttress, and climb the well-defined left-hand chimney to a snow patch.
2. 40m Above is a steep square-cut groove. Climb this, exiting left near the top to reach the continuation gully. Follow this to belay where Force Ten Buttress merges into the final snow slopes.
3. 25m Easy snow leads to the cornice.

30   Jet Stream   100m   IV,4 ***   (1988)
The striking right-hand chimney immediately left of North Buttress Route is one of the finest ice routes on the mountain, especially early in the season before the first pitch banks out.
1. 45m Climb the chimney over several steep sections to a snow ledge.
2. 45m Either exit right up a steep wall to reach easier ground, or take the Direct Finish (45m IV,5 1990) directly up the headwall above.
3. 10m Easy climbing leads to the cornice.

The subsidiary chimney right of the first pitch of Solar Wind is **Guide's Variation** (45m IV,4 1992). It can be used as an alternative start to either of the previous two routes.

31   North Buttress Route   85m   II/III   (1990)
The short buttress at the north end of the corrie provides a quick route for the end of the day. Avoid the steep lower section, which is characterised by a prominent icefall, and start in a bay about 20m up and right from the base of the buttress. Follow grooves up left to the crest, then follow this to the top.

WEST FACE   *(Map Ref 189 729)*

For those seeking solitude away from the bustle of Coire an Lochain and the ski area, the crags on the west face of Aonach Mor are in a truly wild and remote setting. They consist of a number of long granite ridges, the steepest of which lie directly below the summit. The routes are over 500m long and finish just by the summit cairn. They provide enjoyable mountaineering expeditions that are possible in a variety of conditions. There are four main ridge lines, the most distinctive being the third from the left, which contains a prominent slab at half-height. The quickest approach is to contour round into the Allt Daim from the gondola station (1 to 1½ hours). The routes lie in a slightly recessed bay and are not visible until just past the prominent east ridge of Carn Dearg Meadhonach. Alternatively, approach as for the west face of Aonach Beag and continue to the col between Carn Mor Dearg and Aonach Mor (1½ to 2 hours). The routes can be reached from here in 20 minutes.

Golden Oldy   500m   II   *15.2.97 E Ben.*   (1979)
Follow the leftmost buttress, which becomes better defined higher up.

Western Rib   500m   II/III *   *23.2.99. E Paul Mc.*   (1988)
From below, the second buttress from the left appears as a flying buttress to the one on its right. It is in fact distinct and gives the best route on the face.

Daim Buttress   500m   II/III *   (1989)
The third buttress from the left. Follow snow and rocky corners for 200m to the base of the prominent slab. Move left, climb cracks on the left edge of the slab to a platform (50m), and continue up the cracks and corners above (50m). A further 200m of scrambling leads to the summit cairn.

Solitaire   500m   II   (1990)
The right-hand ridge, which starts just left of a deep gully, is slightly easier than the other two routes on the face, but an enjoyable excursion nonetheless. It provides a fine scramble in summer (Difficult 1989).

CARN DEARG MEADHONACH
1179m   (Map Ref 176 726)

The long pinnacled east ridge of this peak is a fine Grade II climb if the crest is followed throughout. The main pinnacle is not as difficult as it looks, and continuing along the Carn Mor Dearg arete to the summit of Ben Nevis results in an excellent mountaineering expedition. Approach along the Allt Daim as for the west face of Aonach Mor.

AONACH BEAG
1234m   (Map Ref 197 714)

Nestling deep between Aonach Mor and Carn Mor Dearg, this se-
cluded and rather secretive mountain is the second highest in the
Central Highlands. It boasts several crags which retain an air of
remoteness despite the nearby ski development on Aonach Mor. The
three principal climbing grounds lie on the north, east and west faces.
All are primarily winter climbing areas, although the west face does
have two excellent rock routes.

In contrast to Aonach Mor, the rock on Aonach Beag is schist rather
than granite, and the routes are generally more serious. This is
particularly true of the north face which has a number of superb, but
poorly protected, ice routes. On the west face however, the rock is a
little less compact, and has sufficient holds to allow good well protected
mixed climbing.

The Aonach Mor-Aonach Beag col is the key to approaching many
of the routes on the mountain, and can easily be reached from the
summit of Aonach Mor in about 15 minutes. If an early start is required,
the Aonach Mor Gondola is unlikely to be open, and the col is best
reached on foot from Glen Nevis. From the car park at the end of the
public road, follow the path through the gorge to the ruins of Old Steall.
Leave the main valley here and head north up the hillside on the west
bank of the Allt Guibhsachan. After 250m of ascent the angle eases,
and a vague path leads towards the unnamed bealach between Carn
Mor Dearg and Aonach Mor.

At the head of the glen strike up the steep slope to the east which
eventually leads to the col between Aonach Mor and Aonach Beag
after a gruelling climb of 550m (3 to 3½ hours). About 30 minutes can
be saved on this approach by taking the brutally steep short-cut over
the Bealach Cumhann. This is best approached by taking the true right
bank of the small stream which descends from the col, starting from
where it cuts the upper minor path through the Glen Nevis gorge.

The summit plateau, ringed by giant cornices on the east and north
faces, is a serious place in winter. The small summit cairn lies
perilously close to the cornice edge and is often buried by snow. After
finishing a route, it is best to locate the sharp north ridge of the
mountain, and descend this to the safety of the Aonach Mor-Aonach
Beag col.

NORTH FACE   *(Map Ref 196 718)*

The large triangular face between the Aonach Mor-Aonach Beag col and the North-East Ridge provides several excellent ice routes in a remote setting. The rock is difficult to protect, so a good selection of pegs and a ice screws should be carried on the harder routes. Good conditions are likely to be found here when the Psychedelic Wall area on Ben Nevis is well iced, although it is rare for good ice to remain after March.

The face has a rock wall and steep buttress nearest the col, a gully area in the centre, and the lower rocky part of the North-East Ridge on the left. Except for Mayfly, which climbs a broad gully on the left side of the face, the climbs are concentrated on the rock wall and buttress near the col.

The climbs are usually approached by descending from the Aonach Mor-Aonach Beag col, but care should be taken with the large cornice and avalanche-prone slopes which occasionally form on the east side. The cornice can normally be negotiated by descending snow or mixed slopes at the south end of the col. The traditional approach to the North-East Ridge, from Old Steall in Glen Nevis, is described in the preamble for that climb.

The climbs are described from right to left as one descends from the Aonach Mor-Aonach Beag col. The first major line of weakness is reached after 100m, and takes the form of a wide icefall which splits into two Y-shaped branches below a steep rock headwall. Whiteout starts up the icefall, but avoids the steepest section of the headwall by taking the right branch. The challenge of the headwall itself is met by two routes. Stand and Deliver climbs the prominent icefall which hangs down the steep central section of the wall, and Blackout takes the narrow ice chimney 15 metres to the right.

1   Whiteout   150m   II   (1985)
Climb the icefall for 50m to a snowfield. At its top, trend right below the headwall *via* short ice steps to reach a snow ramp. This leads to a steep buttress which is cut by the deep chimney of Blackout on its left side. Climb the right side of the buttress to the final snow slopes.

2   Blackout   120m   IV,5 *   (1987)
The icy chimney passed by Whiteout provides a fine technical pitch. Approach *via* Whiteout and climb the chimney using the left wall.

AONACH BEAG NORTH FACE

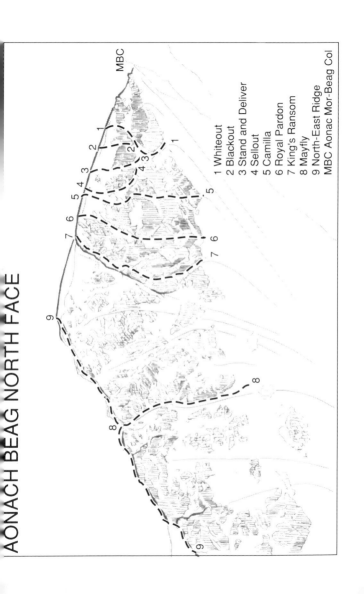

1 Whiteout
2 Blackout
3 Stand and Deliver
4 Sellout
5 Camilla
6 Royal Pardon
7 King's Ransom
8 Mayfly
9 North-East Ridge
MBC Aonac Mor-Beag Col

3   Stand and Deliver   120m   V,5 *   (1989)
The imposing icefall directly above the initial gully of Whiteout provides
a long and sustained ice pitch which leads to the final snow slopes.

4   Sellout   150m   III   (1989)
A left-hand finish to Whiteout. From beneath the icefall of Stand and
Deliver, traverse left below the headwall to reach an ice pitch. Climb
this for 30m to easier mixed ground and the snow slopes above.

About 100m down and left of Whiteout, the rocks steepen into an
impressive buttress of compact schist which provides the finest ice
routes on the mountain.

5   Camilla   230m   V,5 **   (1993)
This serious ice route climbs the twin icicles which hang down the
overhanging wall at mid-height on the right side of the face. Start at
the toe of the buttress, about 25 metres right of the prominent icefall
taken by Royal Pardon.
1. 40m Climb snow trending left to beneath steeper rocks. Work back
right, then climb steep ice to reach the crest of the buttress.
2. 50m Continue up the snow slope above and follow a shallow icy
gully to below the twin icicles. Move past or behind these to rock belays
high on the right.
3. 50m Step down to climb the upper part of the right-hand icicle, then
continue up easier-angled ice to the crest of the buttress.
4. 50m Continue up ice on the left to reach a snowfield.
5. 40m Climb snow to the top.

6   Royal Pardon   220m   VI,6 ***   (1987)
This tremendous ice climb takes the thin ice smear which hangs down
from the shallow depression in the centre of the buttress. A serious
route, comparable in quality to the steeper ice climbs on The Ben.
1. 50m Climb a series of icefalls to a flake belay at the bottom right
side of the smear.
2. 40m Climb the smear, passing two vertical sections, to a poor peg
belay on the right.
3. 20m A short pitch up the final ice wall leads to a broad snow couloir.
4 to 6. 110m Follow the couloir for 50m to where it steepens into an
icy gully which trends up and left. Two good ice pitches up this lead to
the top.

7 King's Ransom 250m VI,6 ** (1987)

A varied and exciting route. It starts up the narrow gully which cuts deep into the left flank of the buttress, before breaking out right across difficult mixed ground to reach the crest.

1. 20m Start about 40 metres left of Royal Pardon, beneath the gully, and climb easy-angled ice to its start.

2. 50m Climb the gully, passing behind a large chockstone, and climb the vertical free-standing ice pillar above. An excellent pitch.

3. 40m Continue up the gully to its end. Belay on a spike below the impending wall on the left edge of the buttress.

4. 20m It is possible to escape left from here onto easier ground, but this avoids the challenge of the upper pillar. Instead, follow the ramp line on the right to where it fades, and pull over the steep wall above (peg for aid) to reach a second ramp. Climb this for 10m (delicate) to reach the crest of the buttress.

5 to 7. 120m A fine snow arete and easier mixed ground lead to the plateau.

8 Mayfly 210m III (1979)

About 300 metres left of the steep buttress climbed by Royal Pardon, and just left of the centre of the face, is an initially wide gully which leads to a point above the pinnacles of the North-East Ridge. It is marked on its lower right by a rock rib. Climb the gully for 90m to reach an icefall 20m high and equally wide. Climb this on the right and continue up the narrower gully above *via* a steep ice pitch to the easier top section. Finish along the North-East Ridge.

9 North-East Ridge 460m III ** (1895)

This classic mountaineering expedition finishes virtually on the summit of the mountain. Although not quite in the same class as the great Nevis ridges, this route is in a wild and remote setting and well worth the 3-hour walk.

The traditional approach is from Glen Nevis. From Old Steall, continue along the glen for 2km before heading north up the hillside to bealach 731m (Map Ref 211 705) which lies just west of Sgurr Choinnich Beag. Descend 100m, then head north-north-west, cross three burns (the second and third are small ravines) to reach a fourth stream line. The start of the ridge is now immediately above. (3 hours from Glen Nevis; the final section from the bealach is very rough underfoot and will take at least 1 hour).

The lower section of the ridge is broad, broken and open to much variation, but after 100m the climbing becomes steeper. Turn the pinnacles at half-height on their right, regain the crest of the ridge, and pass an overhung nose on its left. The knife-edge snow ridge above leads to the easier and broader upper section and the summit.

STOB COIRE BHEALAICH   *(Map Ref 207 710)*

This prominent buttress lies on the south-east ridge of Aonach Beag, and is attached to the summit of unnamed top 1048m (Map Ref 206 709) by a sharp ridge. The steep profile of its front face can be seen from Aonach Mor. The best climbs lie on the steep wall to the left of the prominent narrow slanting snowfield of The Ramp, which cuts diagonally across this face from left to right to a spectacular finish on the sharp ridge. Approach from Glen Nevis as for the North-East Ridge. From bealach 731m, traverse left across broken ground to the foot of the face (2 hours). The routes are described from left to right.

The Clare Effect   120m   IV,3 *   (1989)
High up on the left side of the face, above The Ramp, is a prominent right-angled corner line. Approach by The Ramp and enter the corner by a steep ice pitch. Follow it on ice to the usually large cornice.

Sideslip   180m   IV,4   (1991)
Start 10 metres right of The Clare Effect and climb the obvious corner up right for 60m. Climb an iced slab on the left before moving back right to reach the fault line which crosses the upper part of the face. Traverse right along the fault for 10 metres to a large spike, then move up and left to a large recessed area. Continue up to open snow slopes on the right, which are followed to the final narrow ridge of The Ramp.

Helter Skelter   240m   IV,4 *   (1993)
A serious route taking a wandering line up the steep face to the right of Sideslip. Frozen turf and route finding ability are essential! Start a few metres left of The Ramp and take the first line leading right onto the face. Climb up and right towards a prominent rocky beak (belay), then follow a vague groove line above to a shallow cave. Climb up to a rock band running across the face, then follow a hidden ramp leading back left. Climb back up and right below a second rock band before

The Grey Corries from Coire an Lochain, Aonach Mor

pulling out left above by a narrow shelf. Continue up broken mixed ground to a grassy shelf which leads to an exposed finish on the narrow ridge of The Ramp.

The Ramp   300m   II *   (1975)
Left of the crest of the buttress, a long tapering snow ramp leads through the fairly steep face to the top of the buttress (230m). The exposed ridge above is rarely corniced, and provides a fine finish.

Blinker's Buttress   300m   II   (1989)
A snow gully 50 metres right of the start of The Ramp leads to a snow bay and the crest of the buttress. The same point can be reached by taking the Direct Start which climbs a steep ice pitch a little to the left (50m IV,4 1989). Above, a series of grooves just to the right of the crest lead to easier ground. Follow the ridge to the top, joining the upper part of The Ramp.

AN AGHAIDH GHARBH   *(Map Ref 198 714)*

The east face of Aonach Beag deserves its Gaelic name - the rough face. Only one route has been climbed in its great eastern corrie, which is bounded on its right by the North-East Ridge. A long approach and severe cornice difficulties have deterred all subsequent explorers.

Anabasis   240m   III   (1973)
This climb takes the steep buttress high in the corrie, from which a band of more broken rocks slant up rightwards to just below the summit. The buttress lies above a basin which is reached by a long approach up steep snow slopes broken by deep gullies and rocky outcrops. Climb the gully at the lowest point of the buttress to where it ends at a deep cave beneath overhangs. Traverse right along a snow shelf until an open groove can be climbed to a snow bay (50m). Mixed ground on the left leads to the upper snow slopes. The massive cornice can be breached by climbing a rock nose directly beneath the summit.

WEST FACE   *(Map Ref 193 713)*

High on the west face of Aonach Beag, a line of crags runs southwards for about 800 metres from the Aonach Mor-Aonach Beag col. Many

Chandelle, Aonach Beag (Climber, Roger Everett)

icefalls form here, but the best routes have been found on the buttresses where the rock is well suited to mixed climbing, with good turf and protectable cracks.

Broken Axe Buttress lies at the northern end of the face, just left of a deep easy gully which slants up from the right. The slopes to its right include several rocky outcrops, and a number of icefalls form down the broken mixed ground between. Some 500m from the col, just to the left of a broad snow gully, is the prominent Raw Egg Buttress. Further right are more crags which look good from afar, but unfortunately they are rather broken and prove to be disappointing.

All the approaches to the west face are long. The easiest approach to Broken Axe Buttress is to contour south from the Aonach Mor-Aonach Beag col. The base of the buttress is about 150 metres south of, and approximately 50m below, the level of the col. The climbs on Raw Egg Buttress are best approached from Glen Nevis, by following the Allt Guibhsachan from the ruins of Old Steall (2 to 2½ hours from Glen Nevis car park). If avalanche conditions prevail, great care should be taken when climbing the long snow gully which leads to the foot of the buttress from the glen floor.

The climbs are described from left to right (southwards from the Aonach Mor-Aonach Beag col).

BROKEN AXE BUTTRESS *(Map Ref 193 717)*

Broken Axe Buttress takes the form of a right-angled triangle set forward from the main face. Its upright left edge is a well-defined crest, and a deep slanting snow gully running behind the buttress defines the sloping right side.

10   Twinkle   150m   IV,5 **   (1988)

This delightful mixed route follows the steep left edge of the buttress. It is technically hard for the grade, but well protected with several escapes possible onto easier ground. Gain the foot of the buttress from the deep set gully on the right, and move left past a small snow bay to reach a steep wall.

1. 30m Climb a chimney-groove to the left of the steep wall, then move right to belay above the wall.

2. 40m Continue up the open groove above to a small ledge, step right and climb the continuation groove to a small col.

3 and 4. 80m Step right to a steep corner. Climb this and the overhanging chimney above, and continue directly to reach a delicate snow arete which leads to the top.

AONACH BEAG WEST FACE

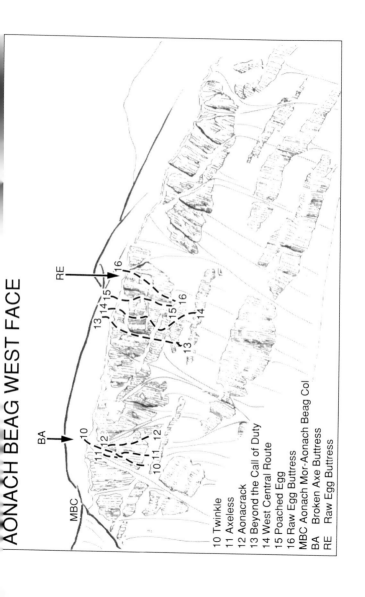

10 Twinkle
11 Axeless
12 Aonacrack
13 Beyond the Call of Duty
14 West Central Route
15 Poached Egg
16 Raw Egg Buttress
MBC Aonach Mor-Aonach Beag Col
BA   Broken Axe Buttress
RE   Raw Egg Buttress

11 Axeless 150m III * (1988)

A varied and interesting route taking the line of least resistance up the buttress. Start below the steep wall a few metres right of Twinkle and take a groove on the right to a ledge. Step right and climb a steep ice pitch to reach snow which leads back left to the crest of the buttress at a col (junction with Twinkle). Move left to avoid the steep step above, then trend back right to gain the final snow arete of Twinkle.

12 Aonacrack 150m IV,5 * (1993)

This good mixed climb takes the prominent crack on the right side of the buttress. Start near the top of the small snow bay to the right of Axeless.

1. 15m Pull awkwardly onto a ramp which leads left to the base of the crack.
2. 25m Climb the crack, passing a steep bulge after 15m to reach a ledge below a huge perched upright block. Climb a crack on the left and belay on top of the block.
3. 40m Continue up the crack and exit by a steep bulging groove to reach a ledge.
4. 40m Climb easily along the broken ridge to the snow arete of Twinkle.
5. 30m Follow the arete to where it merges with the summit slopes.

13 Beyond the Call of Duty 150m III,4 (1988)

This climb takes the three-tiered icefall, which is the central and most prominent in the series of icefalls between Raw Egg and Broken Axe buttresses. The first step is easy-angled, the second is a standing pillar best approached from the right, and the third starts steeply but eases higher up. Snow slopes then lead to the top.

14 West Central Route 150m II (1988)

An enjoyable open mountaineering line. Follow open grooves to belay at the right end of a rock wall to the right of the second pitch of Beyond the Call of Duty. Climb the icefall to the right, then follow snow to a right-facing groove high on the face. Climb this and continue up snow to the top. The route banks out under heavy snow conditions.

15 Poached Egg 150m II (1987)

Immediately left of Raw Egg Buttress is an icy couloir. Follow this over several short steps, trending left to snow slopes below the plateau.

Variation: Eggsclamation   100m   II   (1987)
Leave the main line at one third height and continue more steeply and directly to finish next to the final rocks of the buttress.

RAW EGG BUTTRESS   *(Map Ref 191 711)*

This superb buttress boasts several excellent summer and winter routes. The three winter routes on the front face all provide technical but well protected mixed climbing, while the south-west wall, one of the most impressive rock features in the area, has two excellent summer routes.

16   Raw Egg Buttress   180m   IV,4 **   (1987)
This good and well protected mixed climb takes the obvious right-trending line of weakness up the front face. The winter line approximates to the summer route, which is very vegetated and not recommended (180m Very Difficult 1938). Start at the left end of the buttress.

1. 30m Climb an icy groove to below an overhanging corner, then traverse right below a steep wall until it is possible to climb it at its right-hand end.

2. 50m Trend up and left over mixed ground to belay next to a notch formed by a tower with a prominent perched block in the ridge on the left.

3 and 4. 85m Follow the icy groove line above for two long pitches, always trending right over several steep steps and corners.

5. 15m The steep corner to the left of a steep wall leads to a difficult exit.

Aonach Wall   150m   V,6 *   (1988)
A technical mixed climb with the crux at the very top, taking a line just right of the left arete of the buttress. Start left of Raw Egg Buttress, directly below the steep tower with the prominent perched block.

1 and 2. 55m Climb the arete and avoid the tower on the right to gain the notch; junction with Raw Egg Buttress.

3. 40m Continue up the short corner above to arrive at a snow patch below a longer corner, which leads to the arete.

4. 20m Easy snow leads to the base of the headwall.

5. 20m Climb a groove, and the wide crack above, to a ledge.

6. 15m Move right to a steep V-groove which is the only weakness in the final wall. Climb this with difficulty to the top.

Salmonella   125m   VII,8 **   (1991)

This strenuous and demanding climb follows the crack and chimney system between Raw Egg Buttress and the left edge of the Chandelle wall. The stances are good, and the protection mostly excellent - a technician's dream! Start about 30m up and right of Raw Egg Buttress, and 40m down and left of Chandelle, below a prominent right-facing corner which cuts the lower tier. Moderate mixed ground leads to its foot. Peg belay on the right.

1. 35m Climb the corner, which continuously overhangs for the first 20m, and continue more reasonably to a belay on easy ground above. (Possible escape down the rake on right).

2. 15m Scramble up to the obvious V-groove above, with an off-width crack at its back.

3. 40m Climb the groove to a ledge, and follow the continuation chimney to a peg belay below a prominent overhanging off-width (well seen from below).

4. 10m Climb the off-width to a ledge (bold to start, but not quite as hard as it looks).

5. 25m Reach an alcove, and pull over an overhanging block to easy ground.

Well up and right of the previous routes is an impressive 100m wall of good solid schist, which provides the only worthwhile rock climbing on the mountain. Facing south-west and receiving little drainage, the climbs dry quicker than their altitude suggests.

17   Chandelle   90m   E3 ***   (1988)

A magnificent climb up the left side of the wall.

1. 25m 5c From the left end of a grass ledge at the foot of the wall, climb a short groove to a platform. Traverse left along a ledge to a small spike. Climb the crack above (sustained), passing a small overlap, and continue up the wall on the right to a belay in a prominent quartz cave.

2. 10m 5c Bridge up the mouth of the cave then swing left onto the wall. Move left to a crack, and climb this to a horizontal break. Move left to belay on a good ledge on the left arete.

3. 25m 5b Move back right along the horizontal break to some large blocks. Climb the crack above for 6m, then traverse left and go up to a ledge beneath an overhang.

4. 30m 4c Climb the wall on the left to a ledge. Move right to a steep corner, and follow this and the groove above to the top.

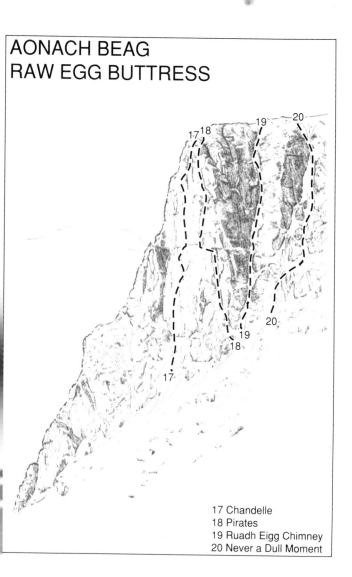

AONACH BEAG
RAW EGG BUTTRESS

17 Chandelle
18 Pirates
19 Ruadh Eigg Chimney
20 Never a Dull Moment

18   Pirates   90m   E2 **   (1988)
Another superb route taking the right side of the wall.
1. 30m 4c Start in a scoop at the right end of the wall and climb up
and right to the arete, which is followed until a step left can be made
onto a stance beneath an overhang.
2. 30m 5c Hand traverse left along the horizontal break until beneath
the obvious impending jam crack. Climb this to a stance at its top.
3. 30m 5c Trend left to the prominent nose. Pull onto the nose and
climb straight up the final wall in an exposed position to finish.

19   Ruadh Eigg Chimney   60m   IV,5 *   (1992)
The right edge of the Chandelle wall is defined by a deep gully which
steepens into a narrow chimney, capped by a bridge formed by three
giant chockstones. Short but good.
1. 30m Start up snow, surmount a short step and move up to belay
at the base of the chimney.
2. 30m Back and foot up the chimney until it is possible to step onto
the bridge. Cross the bridge and climb ice on the left wall to reach the
easier continuation gully above.

20   Never a Dull Moment   70m   IV,6   (1990)
Right of Ruadh Eigg Chimney is another gully which has a steep step
at half-height. In lean conditions this provides a short but technical
pitch, but it can bank out under heavy snow.
1. 30m The gully line leads to an amphitheatre where the steep step
prevents further progress.
2. 15m Take the rock groove to the right of the gully and break back
left to easier ground.
3. 15m Follow the continuation gully up and left to the top.

In the bay about 100 metres south of Raw Egg Buttress there are
two summer routes which climb the buttresses either side of a prominent chimney. **North Buttress** (100m Difficult 1951) takes the buttress
to the left, and **Crevassed Rib** (100m Very Difficult 1951) climbs the
buttress on the right, finishing by the steep upper slab.

The Central Highlands

This chapter describes the the climbs south and north of the A86, including Ben Alder, remotely situated in the centre of the great tract of wilderness to the west of Loch Ericht. Creag Meagaidh is the main climbing ground in this area, and is justifiably recognised for the stature of its winter climbs. The other mountain crags are remote and rarely visited, and the majority of the routes await second ascents.

SGURR INNSE
809m   (Map Ref 290 748)

The crags on this steep and rocky hill are too broken for much good rock climbing, but one route has been recorded on the south-west face. The easiest descent is *via* a shelf on the north-west face.

Headjam   50m   Severe   (1970)
The obvious groove on the summit cliff facing the Lairig Leacach Bothy.
1. 35m Climb a crack in the groove and its right wall for 15m, then continue up steeper ground to an overhang split by a narrow chimney-crack. Climb this to a platform on the left.
2. 15m Continue up the right-trending groove above and scramble up easy ground to the summit of the Sgurr.

MEALL GARBH
977m   (Map Ref 374 727)

CREAGAN COIRE NAM CNAMH

Situated 10km south of Loch Laggan, Coire nam Cnamh lies on the east face of Meall Garbh, the southerly top of Chno Dearg (1047m). Facing east, ice builds up readily from a wealth of drainage and the crag provides a variety of winter routes, mainly in the lower grades. The best conditions are normally found in the first half of the winter, when the cliff may be a useful alternative when the higher climbing areas in this guide are out of condition. The rock is a form of gneiss, quite solid, and blade pegs should be carried for runners and belays.

The cliff is too vegetated to provide good rock climbing, and only two summer routes have been recorded.

Access is fairly long. In good visibility and on a day with little snow, the quickest route is on a bearing from Fersit to the slight col between Chno Dearg and Meall Garbh. In most other conditions it is best to follow the forestry track which leaves the A86 some 25km east of Spean Bridge. Cross the bridge over the River Spean at Map Ref 432 830 and follow the track into Strath Ossian. After 10km, at the bridge at Map Ref 398 730, leave the track and follow a good path up the left bank of Allt Feith Thuill. From the point where the path fords the stream, head north-west uphill into the corrie. A bicycle is useful for the forestry track. If approaching on foot, it may be quicker to reach the second bridge by following the hill path from Fersit into Strath Ossian.

The main buttress is split by the deep gash of Central Gully, which contains two giant chockstones. The buttress is bounded on the right by Broad Gully, the entrance to which is barred by an ice pitch, and on the left by the deep chimney of The Frozen Vice. To the left is the steep wall taken by Inspiration. The small Terminal Buttress lies at the left end of the crag. The climbs are described from left to right.

1   Foxes' Gully   80m   I   (1976)
The upper gully on the left side of Terminal Buttress. It starts with a 5m ice pitch.

2   The Cushion   140m   II/III   (1977)
Start on the left side of the buttress, about 90m below Foxes Gully and 10 metres left of steep slabs. Follow a short steep fault which leads to ice walls and bulges. Climb these, trending first right then left.

3   Terminal Buttress   150m   II   (1976)
Follow a left-trending ramp onto the buttress, then climb a fault line to the top.

4   Nash's Gully   120m   I   (1976)
The first obvious gully to the right of Terminal Buttress. There is an alternative finish up the small cleft on the left.

5   Dickinson's Route   150m   II   (1977)
Climb Nash's Gully for 30m and exit by ice bulges on the right. Continue up the groove above, trending right to the top.

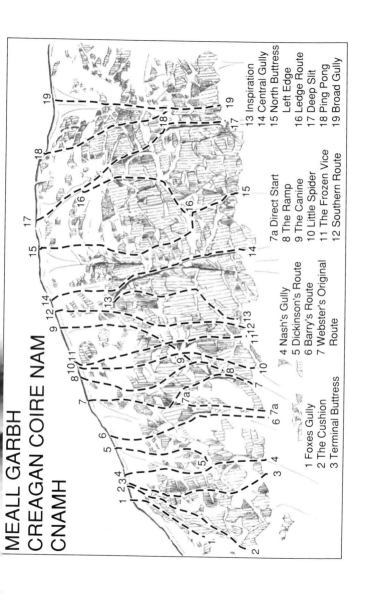

MEALL GARBH
CREAGAN COIRE NAM
CNAMH

1 Foxes Gully
2 The Cushion
3 Terminal Buttress

4 Nash's Gully
5 Dickinson's Route
6 Barry's Route
7 Webster's Original
Route

7a Direct Start
8 The Ramp
9 The Canine
10 Little Spider
11 The Frozen Vice
12 Southern Route

13 Inspiration
14 Central Gully
15 North Buttress
Left Edge
16 Ledge Route
17 Deep Slit
18 Ping Pong
19 Broad Gully

6 Barry's Route 150m I   (1976)
The left-trending gully 60 metres right of Nash's Gully.

The following four routes lie on the broad buttress between the gullies of Barry's Route and The Frozen Vice. A blue icicle often forms low down on the right side of the buttress.

7 Webster's Original Route 200m II/III   (1976)
Start just left of the icicle in a prominent cleft.
1. 40m Climb small ice bulges in the cleft and continue left to a steep corner.
2. 40m At the top of the corner, traverse down into the gully on the left. Continue up the gully for 10m to a belay. The same point can be reached by taking the Direct Start (45m II 1976) which takes the icy corner 45 metres left of and 30m above the blue icicle.
3 to 5. 120m Continue up the gully, which has two main ice pitches.

8 The Ramp 180m II/III   (1976)
The obvious left-trending ramp system. Start as for Webster's Original Route.
1. 45m Traverse right above a steep 6m ice wall, then climb up to the first ramp.
2 to 4. 135m Halfway along the ramp, an ice step leads to a second ramp. Follow this, trending left to the top of Webster's Original Route. *The Direct Variation* (III) climbs the steep 6m ice wall to reach the initial traverse, and higher up takes the 15m ice wall on the right at the end of the second ramp.

9 The Canine 230m I/II   (1977)
Start as for The Ramp, and follow the right-slanting ramp line which crosses Little Spider and The Frozen Vice.

10 Little Spider 140m IV,4 *   (1977)
1. 30m Climb the blue icicle, trending right to below a rocky rib.
2. 40m Continue up ice on either the left or right side of the rib to reach the foot of the left-hand chimney.
3. 35m Climb the chimney (crux), breaking out left onto the snowfield above The Ramp.
4. 35m Take the right-hand chimney to the summit snowfield.

11   The Frozen Vice   180m   .IV,4 *   (1976)
Start below the obvious deep corner 30 metres right of the blue icicle.
1. 45m Climb the corner to easier ground.
2. 45m Cross the easy ground to the base of the huge chimney.
3. 45m Climb the chimney (crux).
4. 45m Ascend the summit snowfield.

12   Southern Route   220m   III,4   (1977)
Start just right of The Frozen Vice and climb a 25m ice pitch which
leads into a gully. Follow the gully to its end and finish up the buttress
on the right.

13   Inspiration   120m   Severe   (1964)
The best of the two summer lines on the cliff. Start just right of The
Frozen Vice and scramble up for 10m, moving left past a steep wall,
to the lower end of a grassy ramp which slopes gently up to the right.
Follow the ramp to a split corner and climb this for 8m. Trend left to an
obvious corner and follow this to a grass ledge (30m). Continue up
more grass, then surmount a large obvious block to gain the ridge on
the right (30m). Climb this to where it steepens (crux), then finish up
easier rocks to the top.
Winter: 185m   IV,5 ***   (1987)
A fine technical mixed route loosely based on the summer line. Start
at the lower end of the grassy ramp which slants up to the right.
1. 30m Directly above is a flake crack with two chockstones. Climb
this and move right to the base of twin corners, the left being an
obvious wide layback crack.
2. 10m Start up the right-hand corner and pull left to the base of the
layback crack. Step back into the right-hand corner and follow it to a
big ledge (crux).
3. 40m Continue diagonally right up grassy slabby ground, passing a
large block. Climb a steep icy turf scoop to belay on the left.
4. 45m Above is a steep wall with a diagonal crack and two old pegs.
Traverse left, then climb two turf-topped walls to the base of a corner.
Start up the corner, then go left and back right to rejoin it. Finish up
the corner to reach easy ground.
5 and 6. 60m Finish up snow which steepens at the cornice.

Central Gully, with its two caves formed by huge chockstones, is the
most obvious feature in the centre of the highest section of the cliff. At
its foot it splits into an obvious inverted 'V' formation. **Watcher's Wall**

(220m Severe 1964) takes the left-hand leg, traverses right under the first cave at the apex of the 'V', and continues up cracks and chimneys to the right of the gully.

14   Central Gully   220m   IV,5 ***   (1977)
An excellent route. Start up the deep gash of the right-hand leg of the 'V'. A steep ice pitch often forms below the second chockstone, and a high runner can be arranged in the roof of the cave to protect the exit (crux). Above, easier ground leads to the summit snowfield.

15   North Buttress Left Edge   230m   IV,4 *   (1977)
An interesting mixed route based on the crack and chimney system taken by the upper section of Watcher's Wall.
1. 40m Start 45 metres right of Central Gully and climb the obvious easy corner to a large ledge, where there is a huge detached flake.
2. 30m Traverse left for 10 metres along the ledge to reach a narrow chimney. Climb this to where it becomes vertical and move left to a ledge overlooking Central Gully.
3 and 4. 80m Continue up walls and chimney-cracks to the right of a prominent corner.
5 and 6. 80m Climb the corner and ascend snow slopes to the top.

16   Ledge Route   230m   II   (1977)
Start as for North Buttress Left Edge to reach the large ledge, then traverse 45m right to a deep overhanging gully. Climb left of the gully at first, and then follow it, exiting right at the top.

17   Deep Slit   140m   III *   (1976)
Start 25 metres left of Broad Gully in a deep narrow gully. The first 50m contains two good ice pitches. Above, trend left up the continuation gully to where it splits, and follow the easier left-hand exit. The cornice can be large and is best avoided on the right.

18   Ping Pong   140m   III ***   (1976)
One of the most enjoyable ice routes on the crag.
1. 45m Either climb the initial icefall of Broad Gully, or take a leftward trending shallow gully for 30m and move back right into Broad Gully (easier and not as good).
2. 45m Take the icy gully on the left and continue up short ice steps between Deep Slit and Broad Gully.
3. 50m Follow the upper continuation gully of Deep Slit, and finish by the right-hand exit.

19 Broad Gully 140m III ** (1976)

The straight broad gully right of the main buttress starts with a steep ice pitch, interrupted by a snow bay at mid-height. Another short ice pitch leads to straightforward snow slopes above.

Y-Gully 150m II (1977)

The obvious wide gully 50 metres right of Broad Gully can be quite icy with a steepening at two-thirds height.

BINNEIN SHUAS
747m (Map Ref 463 826)

This crag is primarily a rock climbing venue and is fully described in the *Highland Outcrops* guide. However, several winter routes have been recorded, which might be worth considering for a short day. The base of the cliff is at an altitude of 500m, so a prolonged freeze is required to bring the routes into good winter condition.

All the winter routes lie on the two-tiered East Sector which is separated from the prominent buttress of the Fortress by the slanting line of **Hidden Gully** (120m III 1965). On the upper tier of the East Sector, **Scotch on the Rocks** (150m IV,4 1987) follows the summer line of Usquebaugh to the terrace, and then takes the icefall on the right. Further right, the summer line of **Eastern Chimney** (140m IV,5 1987) provides an excellent route. Three icefalls form on the lower tier. **Foxtrot** (70m IV,4 1982) follows the central and largest icefall in two pitches to finish on the terrace.

BEINN A' CHAORAINN
1052m (Map Ref 386 851)

The narrow east ridge of the central summit provides a fine 300m Grade I scramble. The best route through the extensive forest which guards the southern aspect of the mountain starts from Roughburn (Map Ref 377 812). Follow the forestry track north-west for 1km to a junction, then take the right fork for 3km to the Allt na h-Uamha, which leads up to the foot of the ridge.

CREAG MEAGAIDH

1128m   (Map Ref 418 875)

COIRE ARDAIR

Creag Meagaidh is situated north of Loch Laggan in the Moy Forest. It is a large and sprawling mountain, with an extensive summit plateau and several ridges that enclose a number of deep corries. The finest of these is the north-east facing Coire Ardair, which lies 1 km east of the summit. Over 3km long, and nearly 500m high, its cliffs are among the highest in Britain. The rock is mica schist and very vegetated and, to date, no worthwhile summer routes have been found. In winter however, the quality and scale of the climbing puts Coire Ardair into the same class as Ben Nevis.

The rock strata lies horizontally and slopes inwards, which results in a large number of snow-holding ledges. The shattered nature of the rock allows both pegs and nuts to be placed for runners and belays. Ice screws are essential for the steeper ice routes and they can also be placed with surprising security in the huge swards of grass and moss draped all over the cliff.

The cliff holds plenty of snow, and the majority of the routes come into condition most winters. Since it is centrally placed, Creag Meagaidh often avoids the worst of the weather in the west. Although the gullies can provide good climbing on water ice during a period of cold weather early in the season, the best conditions are likely to be found during a cold and sunny spell in February or March following a heavy snow fall. It should be noted, however, that the corrie is particularly prone to severe avalanche conditions and should be avoided during a thaw or immediately after a heavy fall of snow.

Access

The approach starts from the A86 road, at the track to Aberarder Farm, where there is a convenient lay-by and small car park. Take the track to the farm, passing through a gate just east of the buildings and continue by a path on the north side of the Allt Coire Ardair. The path stays well above and parallel to the burn as the glen takes a great curve to the west, at which point the cliffs come into view. The path eventually descends to the floor of the glen, about 500 metres before the Lochan a' Choire Ardair, and it continues to the north-east corner of the Lochan by a small box containing rescue equipment. The total

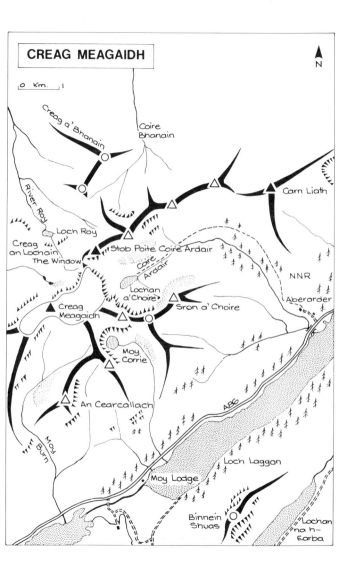

distance is about 7km and takes $1\frac{1}{2}$ to 2 hours under normal conditions. In heavy snow, the path may be obliterated and progress then becomes very laborious and time-consuming. The most useful map of the area is the O.S. 1:50000 sheet 34.

Descent

The summit plateau of Creag Meagaidh is very flat and featureless, and great care is necessary when navigating in poor visibility. Many climbers have been benighted, or have inadvertently descended to Glen Roy. In good conditions, descent by Raeburn's Gully or Easy Gully is feasible. The ridge of Sron a' Choire, which leads back to Aberarder, may also be used and is the easiest descent from the Bellevue Buttress or Pinnacle Buttress areas in poor conditions. Otherwise, descent is best made by the Window, which leads to the Inner Corrie and so to the Lochan. There is a line of old fence posts running down to the Window, and a little rock buttress which has to be avoided on the left. These are useful identity features in poor visibility.

From the Lochan a' Choire Ardair, there is an excellent panoramic view of the cliffs. High on the left is Bellevue Buttress, which is separated from the magnificent, towering Pinnacle Buttress by the left-trending line of Raeburn's Gully. To the right of Pinnacle Buttress are the gentler slopes of Easy Gully, above which rises the Post Face with its four great gullies, or Posts. A prominent feature of Bellevue Buttress, Pinnacle Buttress and the Post Face is a virtually continuous ledge line which crosses their upper half. This gives the line of the unique Creag Meagaidh Girdle Traverse, which to some extent detracts from the seriousness of the main routes, as it provides a possible escape. Right of the Post Face, the crags turn in to form the Inner Corrie, whose features are not clearly distinguished when viewed from the Lochan. The Inner Corrie terminates at the Window, the name given to the very prominent bealach between Creag Meagaidh on the left and Stob Poite Coire Ardair, 1055m (Map Ref 426 886 - unnamed on the O.S. map), to the right. The climbs are described from left to right.

BELLEVUE BUTTRESS

At the extreme left end of the cliffs left of Raeburn's Gully there are two buttresses. The larger buttress, which tapers towards the plateau on the left, is called Bellevue Buttress, and the narrower one to the right is Raeburn's Gully Buttress. Bellevue Buttress reaches a maximum height of 300m, and is characterised in its lower section by a huge roof.

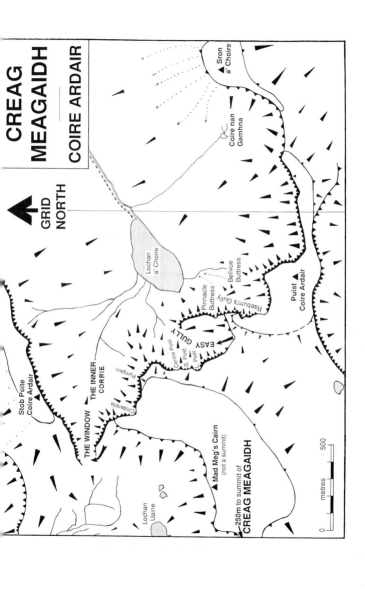

CREAG MEAGAIDH

COIRE ARDAIR

GRID NORTH

Sron a' Choire

Coire nan Gamhna

Lochan a' Choire

Bellvue Buttress

Pinnacle Buttress

Raeburn's Gully

Puist Coire Ardair

Centre Post

S. Post

EASY GULLY

Stob Poite Coire Ardair

THE WINDOW

THE INNER CORRIE

Pumpkin

Cinderella

Mad Meg's Cairn
(not a summit)

Lochan Uaine

250m to summit of
CREAG MEAGAIDH

0   500
metres

Two short routes have been climbed on the left side of the buttress.
The Snail (105m II 1969) climbs the gully on the extreme left-hand
side, and **Lotsavu** (105m II 1970) takes the rib to its right.

1   The Scene   450m   II *   (1966)
This is the first part of the Girdle Traverse of Coire Ardair. The route
follows an obvious horizontal ledge from left to right across Bellevue
Buttress, about 120m below the plateau. For the first 300m, the ledge
is both narrow and spectacularly exposed. The remaining 150m cross
the open snow slopes above Raeburn's Gully Buttress into Raeburn's
Gully.

Naevueata   120m   IV,4 *   (1966)
A steep ice route taking a direct line up the left flank of Bellevue
Buttress. Start just left of The Scene and climb steep snow, followed
by a 30m ice pitch to reach a second snowfield. Directly above, climb
the right-hand of two ice pitches and continue up high-angled snow-ice
to the cornice, which can be very large.

2   Fifteen A   210m   III   (1966)
This route follows a diagonal line trending right across the buttress.
Start 40m below The Scene and traverse up and right, crossing The
Scene, to belay on the right side of a prominent icefall (90m). Climb
this trending left and exit onto a steep snowfield. At its top traverse
right below a rock wall, then climb diagonally up right to the plateau.
The cornice can normally be avoided on the right.

3   Eastern Corner   300m   III **   (1961)
The deep corner which separates Bellevue Buttress from Raeburn's
Gully Buttress is the most accessible route in the corrie and passes
through some fine rock scenery. The first 150m provide interesting
climbing, followed by 150m of steep snow which leads to the plateau
and possible cornice difficulties.

Raeburn's Gully Buttress   450m   III   (1976)
Start on the right side of the buttress and follow easy grooves to a
horizontal ledge, which is just below the level of the true beginning of
Raeburn's Gully. Traverse left along the ledge for 60m to a large block,
then return right for 25m to the crest of the buttress. Climb the crest,
trending left where possible. The final 300m can be climbed anywhere
at an easier standard.

4   Raeburn's Gully   360m   I *   (1903)
The gully which slants up left beneath the impressive left side of
Pinnacle Buttress gives a straightforward snow ascent. If the snow is
deep, the upper section of Raeburn's Gully Buttress can be taken after
the first 150m. The gully is sometimes used in descent and also gives
access to Ritchie's and Smith's gullies.

PINNACLE BUTTRESS

The great buttress between Raeburn's Gully and Easy Gully is nearly
500m high and at least as far across. The broad, triangular frontal face
which tapers towards Easy Gully on the right, is bounded on the left
by a steep wall which towers above Raeburn's Gully. This is one of the
highest continuously steep cliffs in the British Isles, and exposure on
the upper part of the face is both bewildering and Dolomitic.

The summit tower of the buttress is bounded on its right by the
prominent exit gully of 1959 Face Route which rises from the central
snow patches. The Raeburn's Gully wall has three parallel slits rising
from the middle section of the gully. From left to right these are the
lines of Ritchie's Gully, Smith's Gully and The Fly. There are three
ledge lines which cross this section of the face. The upper ledge is
unnamed and unclimbed. The middle line is taken by the exposed
Appolyon Ledge, and the lower line, which is gained by a difficult 30m
traverse from 15m up Smith's Gully, is **Vanishing Ledge** (360m IV,5
1976). Lower down, starting from the foot of Raeburn's Gully, is the
diagonal line of Raeburn's Ledge which is taken by the initial pitches
of Nordwander.

Two summer climbs have been recorded on the buttress. **Red Scar
Route** (450m Severe 1936) approximates to the winter line of 1959
Face Route, and **Edge Route** (450m 1930) follows a line near the right
edge of the buttress. It is extremely unlikely that either route has been
repeated. Appolyon Ledge has also been traversed in summer (1936).

The first four routes are gained from the middle part of Raeburn's
Gully.

5   Appolyon Ledge   500m   II **   (1966)
The second section of the Girdle Traverse of Coire Ardair is started
from Raeburn's Gully about 90m below the plateau. The climbing is
continuously spectacular throughout its length, particularly at a point
just over halfway where the ledge virtually disappears and leaves only
a horizontal slit in the otherwise holdless wall. Once the ledge is
crossed, 180m of easy climbing across the upper slopes of Easy Gully

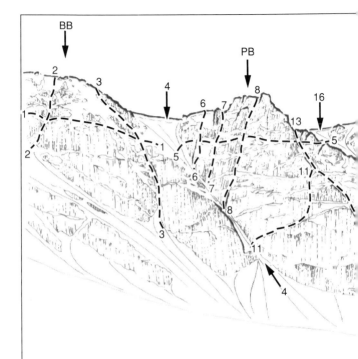

1 The Scene
2 Fifteen A
3 Eastern Corner
4 Raeburn's Gully
5 Appolyon Ledge
6 Ritchie's Gully
7 Smith's Gully
8 The Fly Direct
11 Nordwander
13 1959 Face Route
16 Easy Gully
17 Last Post
18 Post Horn Gallop

19 South Post Direct
20 Centre Post
20a Centre Post Direct
21 North Post
22 Postman Pat
23 Staghorn Gully
24 South Pipe Direct
26 Trespasser Buttress
BB Bellevue Buttress
PB Pinnacle Buttress
GB Great Buttress
PF Post Face
IC Inner Corrie

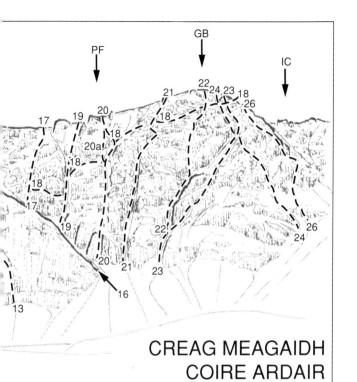

CREAG MEAGAIDH
COIRE ARDAIR

leads to the foot of the Post Face. March's Variation (105m III 1972) leaves the main ledge a little before it is cut by The Fly, and climbs gradually rightwards across a series of ledges to gain the steep snow ramp which crosses the final wall above Appolyon Ledge. A narrow ledge then leads around the skyline to reach easy ground 45m below the plateau.

6   Ritchie's Gully   165m   IV,4 **   (1957)
The shortest and furthest left of the three parallel slits on the Raeburn's Gully face. A fine and varied route, although snow build-up can affect the length of the lower part of the climb. Climb a steep icefall, turning an overhang by a right traverse, and continue up to Appolyon Ledge.
  The initial icefall can be avoided by traversing right along Appolyon Ledge. Continue up the gully to the cornice which can sometimes be difficult. The **Blue Icicle** (35m V,5 1976) takes the steep pillar of ice 30 metres left of the initial icefall.

7   Smith's Gully   180m   V ***   (1959)
The central gully on the Raeburn's Gully face gives a tremendous climb of great character, continuously steep and sustained. Despite the passage of time, it is still considered to be one of the hardest traditional Scottish gullies. The route takes a while to come into condition and pitch 4 can be particularly difficult if unconsolidated.
1. 35m Climb the gully and exit left at the top chockstone to belay on the left above a snow bay.
2. 20m A short steep ice wall leads to a belay in a second small snow bay.
3. 45m Continue up the steep groove to where Appolyon Ledge crosses the gully.
4. 45m Climb the vertical ice wall above (crux) to easier ground.
5. 35m Snow slopes lead to the cornice, which can normally be avoided on the right.

8   The Fly Direct   240m   VII,6 ***   (1983)
The narrow gully to the right of Smith's Gully is one of Scotland's most sought-after ice climbs. The route is serious and very sustained, and although it is not often in condition there have been a number of repeats. The third pitch is probably the crux and can be very intimidating if thinly iced.

1. 20m Start 7 metres left of the gully line and climb steep mixed ground trending up and right to reach the base of the gully proper, which is guarded by a bulge split by a wide crack. This point can also be reached by starting in a niche 10 metres right of the gully line, then climbing a steep groove on the right wall for 5m, before traversing left under a roof to gain the foot of the gully.

2. 30m Step out above the belay, and bridge the wide crack for 5m, then continue up steep snow-ice in the depression above to a good block belay.

3. 50m Climb the steep icefall for 20m to where it eases. Continue straight up and step right into a niche (good peg belay).

4. 30m Move easily up to Apployon Ledge. Belay on the right.

5. 30m Climb the open chimney above and exit right under a big roof. Go diagonally right for 5m by to belay by an icicle (old peg).

6. 30m Climb the icicle and continue up the steep icefall above. Belay on the left in an exposed and awkward situation.

7. 20m Climb the icefall above.

8. 30m Move left to reach an easy snow groove which leads to the plateau.

9 The Midge 400m VI,5 **   (1983)
Another superb route, tackling the huge wall to the right of The Fly. It is probably climbable quite often, the only critical factors being ice in the initial corner and the presence of the icefall in the upper section of The Fly Direct. Start at the snow fan near the foot of Raeburn's Gully, where Raeburn's Ledge slants up to the right.

1 and 2. 80m Climb straight up a steep icy corner to reach the left end of a big snow patch.

3 and 4. 60m Continue up the short groove above, then move left and climb iced slabs to the right of a big right-facing corner (which holds little ice) to reach Vanishing Ledge.

5. 40m Traverse left and belay below a second right-facing corner which initially leans to the right.

6. 50m Climb the corner, passing an old peg, and exit left at the top. Move up to belay under a roof.

7. 40m Pass the roof on its immediate right, then move left for 3m before trending right to Appolyon Ledge.

8 to 11. 130m Traverse left for 30 metres to join pitch 5 of The Fly Direct, which offers the easiest way through the upper rocks.

10   The White Spider 300m   IV,4 *   (1976)
A direct line up the lower part of Pinnacle Face. Start at the same point
as The Midge and traverse Raeburn's Ledge for 30m to the foot of a
corner. Climb this for 40m to a snowfield. Continue straight up for 40m,
then take a 20m ice pitch on the left to reach a second snowfield.
Traverse right for 60m and climb a 20m ice pitch to exit onto Vanishing
Ledge. Finish up the exit gully of 1959 Face Route.

11   Nordwander 300m   IV,4 *   (1972)
Starting near the foot of Raeburn's Gully, this route takes the diagonal
line of Raeburn's Ledge across Pinnacle Buttress, to finish by the exit
gully of 1959 Face Route. Start as for The White Spider and traverse
along Raeburn's Ledge for one pitch, then break through the snow
walls above to reach easier iced grooves which lead to the central
snow patches and the exit gully.

12   Pinnacle Buttress Direct 360m   VI,5 **   (1984)
In an exceptional winter, an icefall forms down the face below the exit
gully of 1959 Face Route to reach the left toe of the buttress at the
base of Raeburn's Gully. When the icefall fails to reach the ground it
can be reached from a horizontal ledge leading across the face from
45m up Raeburn's Gully.
1. 45m Traverse the ledge to a peg belay below the icefall.
2. 40m Climb the icicle and continue up vertical ice above to a short
iced slab. Peg belay.
3. 45m Follow the steepening slab on the left to reach a faint vertical
groove which leads to a thread belay.
4. 45m Climb the ice smear above to join Nordwander.
5 to 8. 185m Finish as for 1959 Face Route.

13   1959 Face Route 450m   V,4 **   (1959)
A good mixed route with exciting situations which takes an intricate
line up the front face of Pinnacle Buttress leading to the prominent
gully to the right of the summit tower. Start at a small bay about 80
metres right of Raeburn's Gully. From the bay, a depression leads up
to a shallow gully, which develops into a series of icy chimneys higher
up. Climb the depression for 60m, then continue up the shallow gully
for another 60m to a point 50m below the base of the first chimney.
Traverse left for 60m to the foot of a left-slanting chimney-groove with
an obvious chockstone. Climb the groove for 90m to the large snow

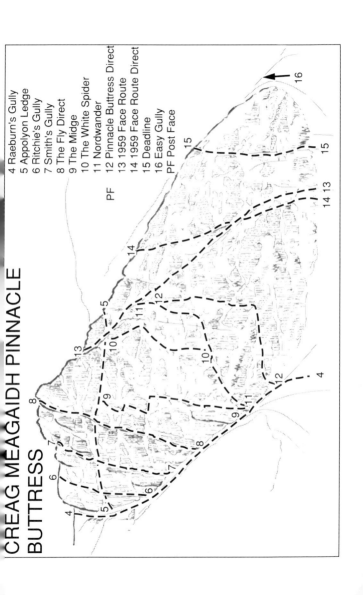

CREAG MEAGAIDH PINNACLE BUTTRESS

4 Raeburn's Gully
5 Appolyon Ledge
6 Ritchie's Gully
7 Smith's Gully
8 The Fly Direct
9 The Midge
10 The White Spider
11 Nordwander
12 Pinnacle Buttress Direct
13 1959 Face Route
14 1959 Face Route Direct
15 Deadline
16 Easy Gully
PF Post Face

patches in the centre of the face. Go up left to the foot of the prominent exit gully with its 30m barrier icefall, then climb this to the buttress crest. 60m of easy climbing leads to the top.

14   1959 Face Route Direct   240m   VI,6 *   (1981)
Start just left of the previous route and climb two pitches up thinly iced slabs to where the normal route trends left. Continue up the series of icy chimneys above, and climb a steep tapering icefall (crux) followed by a corner to reach the buttress crest.

15   Deadline   180m   VI,5 *   (1991)
Just to the right of 1959 Face Route, a large rib is bounded on its right side by a prominent right-facing corner system which curves up from left to right.
1. 40m Climb increasingly steep ice covered slabs to enter the corner and belay above the initial steepening where the ground eases.
2. 40m Continue up the corner and bulging slabs above to reach a well-defined chimney.
3. 40m Climb the chimney.
4 and 5. 60m Finish by easy snow and mixed ground to reach Easy Gully.

THE POST FACE

The Post Face stretches from Easy Gully on the left to Staghorn Gully where the angle is formed as the cliffs turn in to the Inner Corrie. Its most prominent features are the four parallel slits of the Posts, separated by well-defined buttresses, known as the Pillars. As Easy Gully rises, the Post Face diminishes in height. Last Post is the leftmost and North Post the furthest right of the four gullies. From the foot of Great Buttress, which lies right of North Post, two parallel shelves slant up right to the foot of two smaller gullies, known as the Pipes. The face is very prone to avalanche and should be avoided after heavy snow fall.

Four summer routes have been recorded on the face. They are all poor climbs and not recommended. South Pillar (250m 1906), Central Pillar (400m 1934) and North Post (400m 1936) follow the same lines as their winter counterparts, and **Amustoavoid** (60m Very Difficult 1966) takes the steep buttress to the right of the North Pipe of Staghorn Gully.

16   Easy Gully   450m   I   (1896)
This is the easiest route in the corrie. It lies right of Pinnacle Buttress
and slants up left under the Post Face. The lower part of the gully is
narrow, but it widens in its upper section and variations on the left are
possible. In descent, keep well out from the Post Face initially, then
cut back in below it at mid-height.

Missed the Post   220m   IV,4   (1985)
A narrower and almost parallel line to Last Post. Start in Easy Gully at
an obvious icefall about 20m up from Last Post.
1. 50m Climb the icefall to a steep ramp leading to easier snow.
2. 50m Easy snow leads over two short steps to a snowfield.
3. 50m Cross the snowfield to a short steep chimney, then move up
to a smaller snowfield.
4. 40m Climb the shallow icy chimney above (crux).
5. 30m Easy ground leads to the top.

17   Last Post   240m   V,5 ***   (1962)
This excellent ice climb, the leftmost of the Posts, starts as an
impressive icefall (crux) halfway up Easy Gully. Above, a snowfield
steepens to a second icefall, which is climbed in two pitches. Easy
snow then leads to another 30m icefall, which is followed by easy
ground to the plateau. For maximum value, all the icefalls should be
climbed direct. The route is Grade IV,4 if the left side of the first icefall
and the right side of the second are climbed. The third icefall can also
be avoided on the left.

18   Post Horn Gallop   600m   IV,4   (1962)
The third section of the Girdle Traverse crosses the Post Face
diagonally from left to right. Climb the first pitch of Last Post, then break
out right to reach a narrow ledge which enters South Post below its
second main pitch. Go up slightly, then exit awkwardly onto a broad
snow ledge circling Central Pillar. This turns into Centre Post below its
great ice pitch. Cross by the traverse of the ordinary route, and
continue on a diagonal line to the spectacular easy balcony crossing
well above the small upper enclosure of North Post. Thereafter 150m
of exposed climbing leads to the upper snow bowl of Staghorn Gully.

South Pillar   250m   IV,4   (1972)
Climb the icy groove between Last Post and South Post Direct and
continue up the buttress above. Avoid the final tower on the right.

19   South Post Direct 400m   V,4 **   (1956)
An excellent climb, often in condition. This is the second Post from the
left, and has two steep and exposed ice pitches linked by an easier
section. The first pitch is a steep tapering icefall, although it can bank
out substantially in a year of heavy snow. Continue up the icy couloir
above to the foot of the long second ice pitch. Climb this from left to
right (crux) and follow the gully, with one more ice pitch, to the plateau.
The route is Grade III if the initial steep icefall is avoided by traversing
up and left from the foot of Centre Post. The crux pitch can also be
avoided by climbing on the left and regaining the gully line above.

Central Pillar 400m   IV,4   (1936)
The buttress between South and Centre Posts gives a fine climb and,
like the other Pillars, is a good alternative to the Posts when conditions
are poor. Climb a steep pitch to a snowfield and follow the left side of
the buttress to a prominent right-sloping ledge at 250m. Continue up
the 30m arete which forms the right edge of the steep wall above, then
follow a snowfield right of the crest, before moving across left and
finishing left of the final bulge.

20   Centre Post 400m   III ***   (1937)
The third Post from the left provides a magnificent climb of alpine
proportions. The lower 250m is a steep snowfield which leads, with
one ice pitch, to the foot of the impressive icefall taken by Centre Post
Direct. Turn this on the right, by making a steep and airy traverse up
and across the right wall to gain a snowfield, then move back left
around a rock outcrop to rejoin the main gully. Much variation is
possible after the traverse. The ordinary route continues up the gully
without further difficulty, and the Skidrowe Finish (150m III 1965)
climbs the narrow gully after the traverse.

20a   Centre Post Direct 60m   V,5   (1964)
The impressive icefall at just over half-height in Centre Post is a
spectacular feature which was recognised as a 'last great problem' for
many years. Depending on the build up of snow, the pitch may vary
from 45m to 60m, with the first half being the steepest. It eases only
slightly in the upper half.

North Pillar 400m   IV,4 *   (1965)
The buttress between the Centre and North Posts is perhaps the best
of the Pillars. Snow slopes lead to the steep central section (120m).
This is climbed directly for three pitches to exit by a steep ice wall (crux)
to the left of the buttress crest. Above, snow slopes lead to the plateau.

21 North Post 400m V,5 ** (1960)

This is the rightmost and narrowest of the Posts. It is an excellent climb, but it is rarely in good condition. Steep snow leads to a narrow chute and a chockstone pitch (crux). Where the gully above widens, a vertical chimney in the left corner gives access to an easy ledge leading to a large platform on the right. Cross back left across the terminal face overlooking the gully by an exposed 25m traverse. A further 30m, first right, then back left, leads to an easy open couloir and the top.

Direct Finish: 60m VI,5 ***

Avoid the vertical chimney by climbing a short steep ice pillar directly above the snow gully to reach the terrace of Post Horn Gallop. A thin ice sheet on the upper wall leads to the top.

There are three routes on Great Buttress, the large wide buttress to the right of North Post. Easter Pillar climbs the left edge overlooking North Post, and is the longest route on the Post Face. Great Buttress Route takes a line left of centre, and Postman Pat follows the steep icicles on the right flank of the buttress overlooking the lower shelf of Staghorn Gully.

Easter Pillar 420m IV,4 (1975)

Start right of North Post at the lowest point of the face and climb easy ground on the left side of the buttress until it steepens (90m). Climb steep mixed ground just right of the left edge for 200m to reach the terrace of Post Horn Gallop. Traverse right for 30 metres, then move back left and continue more easily to the top.

Great Buttress Route 410m IV,4 (1979)

A sustained mixed climb which will be considerably eased by a good covering of snow and ice. Start at the lowest point of the cliff as for Easter Pillar.

1 and 2. 90m Climb easy mixed ground to the foot of the buttress proper.

3 to 7. 210m Attack the buttress approximately 60 metres right of The North Post, and follow the line of least resistance to reach the ledge of Post Horn Gallop. Good belays at regular intervals.

8. 30m From the ledge, climb the steep buttress directly above (crux).

9 and 10. 110m Easy snow slopes lead to the plateau.

22   Postman Pat   300m   VII,7 **   (1991)

A demanding route combining steep ice with technical mixed climbing. To the right of the upper mixed section of Great Buttress is a shallow wide gully undercut by a steep wall. Below this is a sloping shelf and overhanging wall. Two icicles hang down the overhanging wall from the shelf.

1. 45m   Climb the left-hand icicle to the shelf. Go up this to belay just below a narrow turf ledge on the steep retaining wall.

2. 45m   Traverse left along the ledge for 5 metres, then climb up steeply to reach the shallow wide gully.

3 and 4. 100m   Continue up the gully for two pitches to the Post Horn Gallop terrace.

5, 6 and 7. 110m   An icy runnel leads to the upper snowfields.

23   Staghorn Gully   400m   III ***   (1934)

This excellent and popular climb is often in condition. As the cliff bends round from the Post Face into the Inner Corrie, there are two parallel gullies on the upper part of the crag. These are the South and North Pipes and they can be approached by the long partially hidden shelf which slants up right from near the foot of North Post. The North Pipe, which is better known as Staghorn Gully, is the right-hand and easier of the two gullies, and leads by a series of short ice pitches to a snow bowl below the plateau.

Direct Start: 130m   III   (1960)

The shallow gully to the right, which leads directly to the foot of the Pipes. It begins well up and right of the shelf of the ordinary start, and although shorter, it gives a route of more uniform difficulty.

24   South Pipe Direct   250m   IV,4 **   (1935/1960)

The Direct Start to Staghorn Gully combined with the South Pipe gives a fine sustained climb in its own right, but it is less often in condition than Staghorn Gully.

THE INNER CORRIE

The Inner Corrie stretches from Staghorn Gully to the Window. The climbs here are mostly shorter and less serious than those on the other faces, but their higher altitude and more northerly aspect means they stay in condition until late in the season. The main features from left

Ritchie's Gully, Creag Meagaidh   (Climber, Bish Macara)

to right are: the well-defined Trespasser Buttress; the deep ice corner
of The Pumpkin; then a narrow gully leading to the twin icefalls of The
Wand and Diadem. Right of this lie broken rocks with a central
snowfield, bounding the left side of the gully taken by Cinderella. Two
further gullies cut the rocks between Cinderella and the Window.

The Last Lap   900m   IV,4 **   (1966)
The fourth and last section of the Girdle Traverse is an interesting
expedition in its own right. Be warned - it has a sting in the tail! The
best approach is by the shelf of Staghorn Gully. From below the Pipes
traverse right on a series of snow and ice ledges, descend part of The
Sash, cross beneath the icefalls of Diadem and The Wand and ascend
rightwards to the prominent central snowfield. (To link Post Horn
Gallop with The Last Lap, descend the upper part of The Sash from
the snow bowl of Staghorn Gully.) Traverse the snowfield, descend
into Cinderella, and climb The Prow to within 30m of the plateau. Cross
into Crescent Gully and descend this to above its ice pitch. Now cross
the vertical right wall by a spectacular narrow ledge, and continue
across the traverse of Quasimodo to finish above the Window.

26   Trespasser Buttress   300m   IV,5 *   (1969)
An interesting mixed climb. The buttress to the right of the Direct Start
to Staghorn Gully has a well-defined narrow chimney system which
slants up from left to right. Start from a shelf below the left corner of
the buttress and climb up steeply to gain the chimney, which leads to
a snow bay. Go right to a short chimney and climb this to an overhung
bay. Make a long step right to reach an exposed ledge known as the
Diving Board, then continue more easily to the top of the first step.
Follow the chimney line above to the top of the next step on the left.
Start the upper buttress by a chimney on the right, then traverse left
to the crest and follow it to where it tapers into the face. Finish by a
small chimney to reach easier ground and the top.

27   The Pumpkin   300m   V,4 ***   (1968)
A classic - the longest and most popular of the Inner Corrie ice routes.
It climbs the long ice corner right of Trespasser Buttress and comes
into condition for long periods most winters. The first pitches are poorly
protected, and can feel difficult in poor conditions.
1 and 2. 90m Climb the corner to easier ground.

The Fly Direct, Creag Meagaidh (Climber, Robin Clothier)

CREAG MEAGAIDH
THE INNER CORRIE

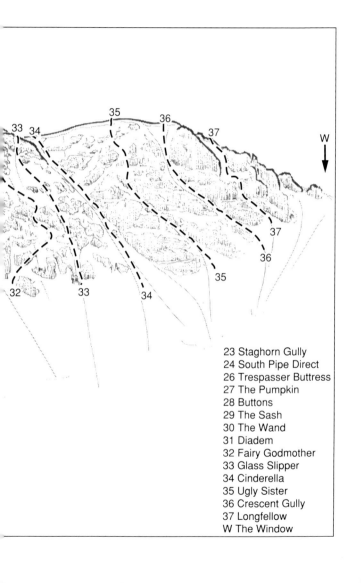

23 Staghorn Gully
24 South Pipe Direct
26 Trespasser Buttress
27 The Pumpkin
28 Buttons
29 The Sash
30 The Wand
31 Diadem
32 Fairy Godmother
33 Glass Slipper
34 Cinderella
35 Ugly Sister
36 Crescent Gully
37 Longfellow
W The Window

3. 45m Snow leads to a steep left-slanting chimney.
4. 35m Climb the chimney with an awkward bulge at 20m.
5 to 7. 130m Continue up the chimney over easy ice and snow to the summit plateau. The cornice can sometimes be very difficult. An easier alternative finish traverses left from below the foot of the left-slanting chimney and climbs the deep gully to the right of the final tower of Trespasser Buttress.

28   Buttons 280m III,4   (1988)
The broad triangular buttress between The Pumpkin and The Sash is cut by a prominent ramp which slants up from left to right in its steep lower section.
1 and 2. 90m Start in the short gully which leads up to the ramp, and follow it for two rope lengths to its end.
3 and 4. 100m Trend left up snow and mixed ground for two long pitches to reach a broad triangular buttress (junction with The Sash).
5. 50m Climb the buttress just right of centre (crux) to reach easier ground.
6. 40m Snow leads to the cornice.

29   The Sash 240m II *   (1963)
A pleasant route which is often in condition. Start in the narrow ice gully which leads up to the two parallel icefalls of The Wand and Diadem. From below the icefalls, follow a line of shelves up and left, underneath the final buttress of Buttons, to reach the plateau.

30   The Wand 210m V,5 **   (1969)
The left-hand of the prominent twin icefalls provides a sustained ice route that is often in condition. Climb the snow gully of The Sash to the foot of the icefall. The next section varies in height between 45m and 60m, depending on conditions, and is best climbed by keeping close to the right wall. Above, the angle eases and the line of least resistance is followed to the plateau.

31   Diadem 210m V,4 *   (1964)
Another fine ice climb which follows the right-hand icefall. It is slightly easier than its twin to the left, but is less often in condition as it forms a funnel which collects fresh snow. Approach as for The Wand and climb the icefall and easy ground above to the foot of a long ice corner. Follow this to easy-angled snow and the top.

Between the gullies of The Sash and Cinderella is a broken buttress with a large central snowfield. Near the right end of this buttress is a steep narrow chimney taken by Glass Slipper. **Will o' the Wisp** (210m III 1963) is a rather wandering line which starts to the left of Cinderella, traverses left above the chimney of Glass Slipper to reach the snow-field, and finishes up the furthest left of the three obvious breaks in the upper cliff.

32   Fairy Godmother   210m   III *   (1970)
A good varied route - probably the best on this section of the cliff. Start midway between The Sash and the narrow chimney of Glass Slipper, at a rightward sloping ramp. Follow the ramp for one pitch, then trend up and left by a series of ramps and walls to reach the central snowfield. Climb the obvious short gully someway left of the Will o' the Wisp exit, then go left up a ramp to an airy perch overlooking Diadem. Finish by the steep tower above.

33   Glass Slipper   210m   III *   (1964)
The steep narrow chimney just left of Cinderella leads to the central snowfield in two pitches. Above, climb the central break, with one ice pitch, to the top.

34   Cinderella   210m   II *   (1963)
The prominent straight snow gully in the centre of the corrie gives a pleasant climb on snow. There may be one or two short ice pitches early in the season. **The Prow** (110m III 1963) is a variation finish which leaves the gully just below mid-height. The route slants steeply up the side of the spur on the right by a ramp, then follows the crest to the cornice which can sometimes be very large.

35   Ugly Sister   210m   III   (1970)
Well right of Cinderella is the curving line of Crescent Gully. Between the two is a snow ramp slanting up left. Climb the ramp to a saddle, continue up the crest for 6m, and traverse right to a better line leading up left to the crest above The Prow. Finish up snow to the cornice, which may be difficult.

36   Crescent Gully   210m   II   (1958)
This is the curving gully midway between Cinderella and the Window. It has a steep and imposing right wall. Climb up left on snow to an ice pitch, which leads to a snow bowl and the cornice.

Quasimodo   210m   III   (1966)
Start up the steep narrow gully to the right of Crescent Gully, which
curves left by a snow ramp past an overhanging chimney to disappear
in a rock wall. Traverse horizontally right on a narrow, ill-defined ledge
round some awkward bulges, above the overhanging chimney for
45m. Now go straight up a steep spur, then move left to finish on steep
snow to the plateau.

37   Longfellow   210m   II   (1968)
Right of Crescent Gully is another narrow gully. Climb this for 60m,
move right, then left, over a short wall, to gain a groove system on the
left. This leads to the crest of the buttress and the plateau. The Direct
Variation (III 1991) goes straight up, avoiding the detour to the right
and left.

The Crab Crawl   2400m   IV,4 ***   (1969)
The Girdle Traverse of Coire Ardair, immortalised by Tom Patey's bold
solo first ascent, crosses the cliffs of Coire Ardair in four stages. For
much of the way the traverse follows a natural line and is best done
from left to right. Bellevue Buttress is crossed by The Scene, Pinnacle
Buttress by Appolyon Ledge, the Post Face by Post Horn Gallop and
the Inner Corrie by The Last Lap. For a detailed description, refer to
the individual descriptions of the separate sections.

LOCH ROY CORRIE

There are two winter climbing crags in the remote and rarely visited
Loch Roy Corrie, which lies 1 km north-west of the Window. It is best
reached from Glen Roy with Luib-chonnal bothy (Map Ref 394 936)
as a base, which is about 1½ hours' walk from the climbs. Alternatively,
it is possible to approach *via* the Window, but this involves a large
amount of descent and re-ascent. Both crags are about 250m in height
and belays are generally good. The cliff bases are at an altitude of only
600m, so conditions are much less reliable than in Coire Ardair.

CARN DEARG BUTTRESS   (Map Ref 412 895)

This schist crag lies on the east flank of Carn Dearg, the 888m
northerly outlier of Creag Meagaidh. To the right of the broken central
wall there is a series of well-defined gullies and buttresses where most
of the climbs have been found.

Wet Walk   135m   I   (1972)
Follow the left branch of the shallow double gully on the right-hand side of the buttress, with a steep uncorniced section at the top.

The Rough Ride   150m   II   (1972)
To the right of the obvious deep-cut gully of The Spin is a steep right-trending chimney. Start up this, climb over a bulge to reach a ridge, and continue up the buttress edge above to the plateau.

The Spin   165m   I *   (1972)
The most deeply-cut gully in the right-hand section of the buttress gives good situations. It is best to keep to the right near the top where the huge cornice is smallest.

Midnight Crunch   180m   II   (1972)
Between the broken centre wall on the left and the well-defined buttress left of The Spin is a curving gully. Follow this, climbing several short steep ice pitches to reach a snow ridge, then trend left past rocks to the cornice.

Big Red Van   230m   III,4 *   (1972)
A good route on the broken central wall between the big gully on the left and Midnight Crunch on the right, closer to the latter. Climb a short ice gully to a snowfield which leads to shallow steep ice gully. From its top, climb a short vertical pitch on the right, then move back left over steep ground to the start of an obvious right-trending gully-ramp. Steep ice steps above lead to a snow slope and the cornice.

CREAG AN LOCHAIN   (Map Ref 417 890)
This rather sombre north-facing crag is cut by a wide gully which splits the cliff into two distinct halves. The right-hand section is the highest and consists of a series of steep walls cut by terraces. Although shorter, the left-hand section is more impressive, presenting a steep and compact wall of solid gneiss. It takes a lot of drainage from the plateau and ices readily in cold weather.

Loch Roy Gully   180m   IV,4   (1972)
This route lies just right of centre of the right-hand section, starting just right of the lowest rocks. It consists of three distinct steps and finishes by the obvious very narrow chimney-gully. The crux is near the top.

Fox Trot   75m   V,5 *   (1976)
Some 90 metres short of the left edge of the crag is an icefall. It is
composed of three sections which may merge into one great sheet.
Start up the introductory gully below the icefall to gain a ledge and peg
belays, then climb the central fall direct.

CARN DEARG
945m   (Map Ref 635 024)

LOCH DUBH CRAG   *(Map Ref 630 015)*

Very few crags cut the extensive plateau of the Monadhliath, but the
small and compact Loch Dubh Crag on the south-west face of Carn
Dearg is a notable exception. It offers a couple of worthwhile winter
routes in a wild and empty part of the Highlands. The approach from
Glen Banchor above Newtonmore is long and takes about 2 to 2½
hours.

Wee Team Gully   130m   IV,4 **   (1985)
The central deep-set gully gives a fine ice climb if each of its three ice
pitches are climbed direct. It is possible to traverse in above the first
pitch and the third pitch can also be avoided by easier gullies on either
side. With a large build up the route is Grade III.

The Great Trek   100m   IV,4   (1987)
The upper part of the buttress to the left of Wee Team Gully is cut by
a steep shallow gully. Start 20 metres left of Wee Team Gully and climb
a groove to a ledge. Gain the steep gully above by a groove on the
left and finish up the icefall above.

CREAG DHUBH
757m   (Map Ref 678 973)

CREAG DUBH NEWTONMORE   *(Map Ref 670 958)*

This major roadside crag lies 5km south-west of Newtonmore. It is
almost exclusively a summer cliff and is fully described in the *Highland
Outcrops* guide. After a sustained period of hard frost, the summer line
of **Oui Oui** (90m III 1966) freezes to give a very good climb up a great

pillar of ice. It is worth considering for a short day. Conditions can even be assessed from the comfort of your car! Despite at least one determined attempt, the direct finish up the free-hanging icicle still awaits an ascent.

GEAL CHARN
917m   (Map Ref 597 783)

CREAG DHUBH   *(Map Ref 590 792)*

This long, north-facing, and rather broken crag lies on the south bank of Loch Ericht. It boasts a couple of good steep water-ice climbs, but with the base of the cliff at 500m, a hard freeze is required to bring the routes into condition. The quickest approach starts from Balsporran Cottages at Map Ref 628 792 on the A9, and follows the Allt Beul an Sporain to cross the col north of Geal Charn (1 hour).

High on the left side of the crag is a recessed area of rock with two icy corners. These are **Wafer Me** (60m II/III 1987) and **Ice Cream** (60m II 1987). Further right is a large ice sheet taken by The Hex Factor, and at the right end of the crag is an obvious waterfall, which is climbed by Neapolitan.

The Hex Factor   120m   V,4 **   (1987)
A good exposed ice route. Start beneath the ice sheet which runs down a left-facing corner in its steep central section.
1. 35m Climb the initial ice cascades to reach a large shelf.
2. 50m A 7m vertical section leads into the corner. After 30m, traverse left under a steep nose of ice, then move up to an ice cave belay.
3. 35m Traverse right along an exposed ledge and climb the curtain of ice above to easier ground.

Neapolitan   95m   IV,4 *   (1987)
Climb the waterfall on its left side to a shelf at 45m. Continue up the left side of the upper tier to the top.

BEN ALDER
1148m   (Map Ref 496 719)

Ben Alder is one of Scotland's remotest mountains, and is certainly the most inaccessible climbing ground described in this guide. It is a complex mountain, with a vast summit plateau, extensive cliffs on its north face and two great corries on its eastern flank. It is primarily a winter climbing area and has a number of routes of all grades, which will have a strong appeal for those with a keen sense of exploration. Anyone prepared to make the long approach will not be disappointed. Visits will require at least one overnight stop, and in conditions of deep snow, reaching the foot of the routes can be an achievement in itself. The rock is mica schist, and a good selection of pegs should be carried for runners and belays. Ice screws are worth taking for the harder routes.

Access
The best approach starts from Dalwhinnie. Follow the good estate road along the north-west shore of Loch Ericht past Ben Alder Lodge to just before Loch Pattack, where a path on the east bank of the Allt a'Chaoil-reidhe leads to Culra Lodge. Just before reaching the lodge there is a bothy at Map Ref 523 762, which provides a good base. (15km from Dalwhinnie, about 3½ hours). From the bothy it is about 1½ hours to the foot of the climbs.

With its deeply scalloped corries and huge cornices, the summit plateau of Ben Alder is a serious place in winter, and careful navigation is required. The safest descent is to head west-north-west from the summit and descend easy slopes to the Bealach Dubh. In good visibility it is possible to descend the hanging valley just east of Enigmatic Buttress, or alternatively a confident party can descend the Long Leachas.

EAST FACE

The two great corries of Garbh Choire and Garbh-choire Beag, which stretch north from Bealach Breabag for over 2km, can be seen over 20km away from the A9 by Dalwhinnie. Giant cornices form with snow collected from the massive catchment area on the summit plateau, and both corries hold snow into early summer. Garbh-choire Beag is flanked on its right side by the north ridge which is divided into two

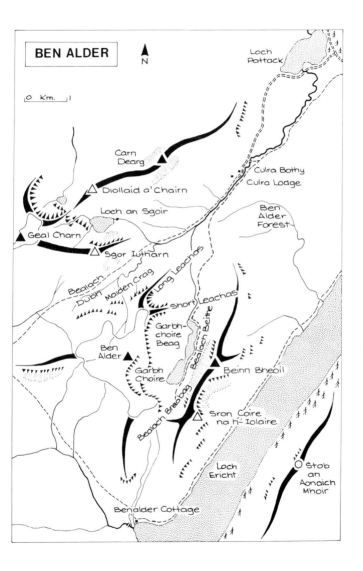

spurs (or legs) known as the Short and Long Leachas. There are no difficult climbs on this side of the mountain, but for a classic winter mountaineering experience, a route on the wild and lonely east face of Ben Alder can scarcely be bettered.

GARBH CHOIRE   (Map Ref 496 714)

This grand and impressive corrie is not steep enough to provide technical winter climbing, but the **Central Gully** (200m I 1896) which cuts the centre of the back wall gives a good snow climb. The ramp to the right, which trends up and right to finish through steeper ground, is Grade II.

The large triangular crag of quartz-feldspar, which faces north-east above the southern end of Lochan a'Bealach Bheithe, is known as the South Buttress of Garbh Choire. The crag is about 200m high and is cut by a broad grass rake for two-thirds of its width, dividing the cliff into two 100m tiers. The rake begins at the far end of Bealach Breabag and lies behind a pinnacled arete on its left. Two chimneys split the 100m wall situated low down at the right end of the lower tier. These are **Left-Hand Chimney** (100m Severe 1950s) and **Uncle's Chimney** (100m Very Difficult 1950s). The prominent diedre in the centre of the upper tier is taken by **Crab Walk** (200m Severe 1966).

In summer this crag may be more conveniently approached from Ben Alder Cottage. About 800 metres north of the cottage is a small crag in the form of an amphitheatre with a vertical wall on the right. The only climb recorded to date is **Vertical Horror** (20m VS 1966) which climbs the steep corner just to the right of three pinnacles.

GARBH-CHOIRE BEAG   (Map Ref 503 721)

The left-hand side of this corrie presents an impressive mixed face which bears some resemblance to an Oberland Nordwand. The face lacks distinct features, but there are three vague gully lines with mixed ground between. Only one route has been recorded to date and there is potential for more.

Alderwand   300m   III ***   (1987)

An excellent mountaineering route in a remote and grand setting. It takes the depression between the two left-hand gullies directly up the centre of the face. Start with an (avoidable) ice pitch to reach a snow terrace, and continue by four long pitches up the icy open groove line above to exit on mixed ground. Snow slopes lead to the cornice.

The Short and Long Leachas are little more than easy scrambles in summer, but in winter they provide sporting 300m Grade I routes to the summit plateau. The **Short Leachas** takes the eastern spur of the north ridge and gives a fine mountaineering route if tackled direct, although most of the difficulties can be avoided on the left. The **Long Leachas** climbs the north-eastern spur at the end of the north ridge and is the nearest part of the mountain to Culra. It follows a narrow ridge in its upper section, and is slightly harder than its neighbour to the left.

NORTH FACE

Nearly 2km of crags overlook the Allt a'Bhealaich Dhuibh, flanked at their left end by the Long Leachas. To the right of this ridge, there is first an area of easy gullies and buttresses, followed by the impressive Maiden Crag which lies to the right of a high pot-shaped corrie. Further right is a deep wide gully which rises in short steps to an open snow slope, then a broken buttress which lies to the left of a high hanging valley which has two Grade I snow gullies. Enigmatic Buttress lies to the right of the hanging valley.

Wingeing Sassenach   300m   II/III   (1986)
To the left of Maiden Crag there is a barrel-shaped buttress which terminates in a short arete. This route climbs the centre of the buttress by a series of icy scoops, then it finishes up the arete.

MAIDEN CRAG   (Map Ref 498 734)
This steep cliff has a prominent icefall on its lower left side which leads up to a diagonal terrace trending right beneath a steep and impressive headwall. Ice Maiden climbs the icefall, and follows the terrace to exit by a prominent hanging groove, the only apparent weakness in the headwall. Further right are a series of steep corners and gullies taken by Witchwhite and Nightshift. The routes are not technically difficult by modern standards, but they earn their grades due to the serious situation and protection which can sometimes be difficult to arrange.

Ice Maiden   280m   V,5 ***   (1987)
An excellent ice route - the best line on the cliff.
1. 30m Start directly below the icefall and climb a snowy gully to its base.
2. 50m Climb the icefall to an open gully.
3 and 4. 90m Follow the gully up and right to reach the diagonal snow terrace below the headwall. Traverse easily along this to a belay to the right of the hanging groove.
5. 35m Climb short thinly iced walls up and left and make an exciting finish up the vertical ice hose above.
6 and 7. 75m Two rope lengths up easy-angled snow slopes lead to the plateau.

Witchwhite   275m   V,4 *   (1988)
This interesting mixed climb follows the gully system in the centre of the face. Start about 30 metres right of Ice Maiden in a small but *well-er-line* snow bay. Take the steep corner out of the left-hand side of the bay, passing a prominent jutting flake, to reach a snow patch. Continue up the open gully line above to the diagonal snow terrace (100m). From a small cave at the apex of the terrace, someway to the right of Ice Maiden, climb a series of short ice steps before moving diagonally left (crux) to finish on the arete overlooking the final groove of Ice Maiden. Easy ground leads to the top.

Nightshift   250m   V,4 *   (1988)
To the right of Witchwhite is an obvious gully leading up to a terrace. Climb the gully for 50m to the terrace, and continue up the wall directly above before moving left to an arete (50m). At the top of the arete move up and right to exit on to the diagonal snow terrace. Traverse right beneath the headwall until a break allows access to a snow gully which is followed to easier ground.

ENIGMATIC BUTTRESS   (Map Ref 490 732)
This buttress was the focus of several exploratory rock climbing attempts in the 1930s, but unfortunately it is less impressive close to than it appears from a distance. It is characterised by a number of ramp-lines that slant from left to right in its steeper lower half. Only one route has been recorded, which takes the first ramp line from the left.

The Walker's Spur   250m   IV,4   (1987)
Start just left of the crest of the buttress and climb the ramp delicately
to reach a snow patch. Move right up a steep groove to a belay below
a well-defined corner just left of the steep rock of the crest. Climb the
corner to easier ground. The final 150m are straightforward.

SGOR IUTHARN
1010m   (Map Ref 488 743)

Directly across the valley from the Long Leachas, a fine narrow ridge
rises to Sgor Iutharn, the eastern shoulder of Geal Charn. This
spectacular feature, well seen from Culra, is known as the **Lancet
Edge.** It is not as difficult as its impressive appearance at first
suggests, and provides a fine scramble in summer and a 300m Grade
I in winter.

The Eastern Traverse, Tower Ridge, Ben Nevis

Graded List of Winter Climbs

This list was compiled with the assistance of a great many people and assumes each route is climbed in optimum conditions. There is no substitute for experience here, and predicting exactly when these occur is one of the great arts of the winter climbing game. Surprisingly, there was a high level of agreement in the ranking of the harder climbs, but the ordering of the middle grade routes (IIIs and IVs) was close to random. This is due to the large number of climbs of this grade spread throughout the area covered by this guide. Many of these are unrepeated, and no one person has done more than a limited fraction of their total number. The list should not be taken too seriously therefore, but if nothing else it will promote lively discussion, and hopefully it will also give an approximate idea of the relative difficulty of your chosen route.

Centurion	Ben Nevis	VIII,8 **
Point Blank	Ben Nevis	VII,6 **
Stormy Petrel	Ben Nevis	VII,6 ***
The Shield Direct	Ben Nevis	VII,7 ***
Salmonella	Aonach Beag	VII,8 **
The Shadow	Ben Nevis	VII,6 **
Pointless	Ben Nevis	VII,6 ***
Postman Pat	Creag Meagaidh	VII,7 **
Albatross	Ben Nevis	VII,6 ***
The Fly Direct	Creag Meagaidh	VII,6 ***
Kellett's North Wall Route	Ben Nevis	VII,7 **
Urban Spaceman	Ben Nevis	VII,6 **
Journey into Space	Ben Nevis	VII,6 **
The Shroud	Ben Nevis	VII,6 **
The Good Groove	Ben Nevis	VII,7 **
The Black Hole	Ben Nevis	VI,6 **
Levitation	Ben Nevis	VI,6 **
Ring the Alarm, Overload Finish	Ben Nevis	VI,6
Fascist Groove	Ben Nevis	VI,6 *
Mickey Mouse Finish	Ben Nevis	VI,6 **
Waterfall Gully, True Finish	Ben Nevis	VI,6 **
Match Point	Ben Nevis	VI,6 **
Royal Pardon	Aonach Beag	VI,6 ***
Third Time Lucky	Ben Nevis	VI,6
Kellett's Route	Ben Nevis	VI,6 ***
Minus One Buttress	Ben Nevis	VI,6 ***
Mega Route X	Ben Nevis	VI,6 ***
Gemini	Ben Nevis	VI,6 ***
Albatross, Right-Hand Start	Ben Nevis	VI,6
King's Ransom	Aonach Beag	VI,6 **
Ring the Alarm	Ben Nevis	VI,5 ***

Central Route	Ben Nevis	VI,7
Eastern Block	Ben Nevis	VI,6
Galactic Hitchhiker	Ben Nevis	VI,5 **
Riders on the Storm	Ben Nevis	VI,5 ***
Alchemist, Mist Dancer Variation	Ben Nevis	VI,5
Zybernaught	Ben Nevis	VI,5
The Great Glen	Ben Nevis	VI,5 *
Left-Hand Route	Ben Nevis	VI,6 ***
Astronomy, Direct Finish	Ben Nevis	VI,5 ***
Route I, Direct Start	Ben Nevis	VI,6 **
Interstellar Overdrive	Ben Nevis	VI,5 *
Astronomy	Ben Nevis	VI,5 ***
Lobby Dancer	Ben Nevis	VI,6 ***
The Midge	Creag Meagaidh	VI,5 **
Left Edge, Gardyloo Buttress	Ben Nevis	VI,5 *
Alchemist	Ben Nevis	VI,5 **
Route II Direct	Ben Nevis	VI,6 ***
Le Panthere Rose	Ben Nevis	VI,6 *
Right-Hand Route	Ben Nevis	VI,6 **
Don't Die of Ignorance	Ben Nevis	VI,6
Une Journee Ordinaire	Ben Nevis	VI,6
Pinnacle Buttress Direct	Creag Meagaidh	VI,5 **
Minus One Gully	Ben Nevis	VI,6 ***
Psychedelic Wall	Ben Nevis	VI,5 ***
North Post, Direct Finish	Creag Meagaidh	VI,5 ***
The Flight of the Condor	Ben Nevis	VI,5 **
Casino Royale	Ben Nevis	VI,5 *
Slav Route	Ben Nevis	VI,5 ***
Hurricane Arete	Aonach Mor	VI,7 **
Tower Face of The Comb	Ben Nevis	VI,6 ***
Golden Promise	Aonach Mor	VI,7
Cutlass	Ben Nevis	VI,7 *
Astral Highway	Ben Nevis	VI,5 **
The Shadow, Right-Hand Start	Ben Nevis	VI,6 *
Long Climb Finish	Ben Nevis	VI,5 ***
Pointless, Variation Start	Ben Nevis	VI,5
1959 Face Route Direct	Creag Meagaidh	VI,6 *
Stirling Bridge	Aonach Mor	VI,7 **
Deadline	Creag Meagaidh	VI,5 *
Route I	Ben Nevis	V,6 ***
Clefthanger	Ben Nevis	V,6 *
Echo Traverse, Wet Spring Start	Ben Nevis	V,6
North-West Face Icefall	Ben Nevis	V,6
Last Day in Purgatory	Ben Nevis	V,5 **
Left Edge Route	Ben Nevis	V,5 **
Rubicon Wall	Ben Nevis	V,5 **

Smith's Gully	Creag Meagaidh	V,5 ***
Beta Route	Ben Nevis	V,5
Smith's Route	Ben Nevis	V,5 ***
Gemini, Left-Hand Finish	Ben Nevis	V,5 **
Smith-Holt Route	Ben Nevis	V,5 **
Centre Post Direct	Creag Meagaidh	V,5
Left Edge Route, Direct Finish	Ben Nevis	V,5 **
Galactic Hitchhiker, Left-Hand Start	Ben Nevis	V,5
Sod's Law	Ben Nevis	V,6
Orion Direct, Direct Start	Ben Nevis	V,5 *
Minus One Gully, Direct Finish	Ben Nevis	V,5 **
Caledonia	Ben Nevis	V,5 *
Orion Direct	Ben Nevis	V,5 ***
Aonach Wall	Aonach Beag	V,6 *
The Groove Climb	Ben Nevis	V,6 *
Camilla	Aonach Beag	V,5 **
Down to the Wire	Ben Nevis	V,6
Compression Crack	Ben Nevis	V,5 *
American Pie	Ben Nevis	V,5 **
Two-Step Corner	Ben Nevis	V,5 ***
Sickle	Ben Nevis	V,5 ***
Kellett's Route, Augean Alley Finish	Ben Nevis	V,5
Quickstep	Ben Nevis	V,5 **
Boomer's Requiem	Ben Nevis	V,5 ***
The Blue Icicle	Creag Meagaidh	V,5
Indicator Right-Hand	Ben Nevis	V,5 **
Minus Two Buttress	Ben Nevis	V,5 **
Point Five Gully	Ben Nevis	V,5 ***
Ice Maiden	Ben Alder	V,5 ***
Minus Two Gully	Ben Nevis	V,5 ***
North Post	Creag Meagaidh	V,5 **
Satanic Verses	Ben Nevis	V,5
Smith's Route, Icicle Variation	Ben Nevis	V,5 ***
Diana	Ben Nevis	V,5 *
Pinnacle Buttress Direct	Ben Nevis	V,5 **
Stand and Deliver	Ben Nevis	V,5 *
Vanishing Gully	Ben Nevis	V,5 ***
Vade Mecum	Ben Nevis	V,5 **
Shot in the Dark	Ben Nevis	V,5 **
Tower Face of the Comb, Left-Hand Start	Ben Nevis	V,5
Hadrian's Wall Direct	Ben Nevis	V,5 **
Witchwhite	Ben Alder	V,4 *
Fish Eye Chimney	Ben Nevis	V,5
Observatory Buttress	Ben Nevis	V,5 ***
Venus	Ben Nevis	V,5 *
Running Hot	Ben Nevis	V,5

Bydand	Ben Nevis	V,5 *
Fox Trot	Creag Meagaidh	V,5 *
Indicator Wall	Ben Nevis	V,4 ***
1959 Face Route	Creag Meagaidh	V,4 **
Zero Gully	Ben Nevis	V,4 ***
The Wand	Creag Meagaidh	V,5 **
Nightshift	Ben Alder	V,4 *
Last Post	Creag Meagaidh	V,5 **
The Chute	Ben Nevis	V,4 **
The Pumpkin	Creag Meagaidh	V,4 ***
The Hex Factor	Creag Dhubh	V,4 **
Tinsel Town	Aonach Mor	V,4 **
Diadem	Creag Meagaidh	V,4 *
South Post Direct	Creag Meagaidh	V,4 **
Antonine Wall	Ben Nevis	IV,4 *
Winter Chimney	Ben Nevis	IV,5 *
Vanishing Ledge	Creag Meagaidh	IV,5
The Winter Girdle	Ben Nevis	IV,4
West Face Lower Route	Ben Nevis	IV,5 **
Pigott's Route	Ben Nevis	IV,5 *
Shot in the Light	Ben Nevis	IV,5
Eastern Chimney	Binnein Shuas	IV,5
North-West Face Route, Douglas Boulder	Ben Nevis	IV,5
Blackout	Aonach Beag	IV,5 *
The Upper Cascade	Ben Nevis	IV,5
Slick Mick's Groove	Aonach Mor	IV,5.*
The Curtain	Ben Nevis	IV,5 ***
Inspiration	Meall Garbh	IV,5 ***
Helter Skelter	Aonach Beag	IV,4 *
Continuation Wall	Ben Nevis	IV,4
Gondola with the Wind	Aonach Mor	IV,5 **
Grooved Arete	Aonach Mor	IV,5 ***
Aonacrack	Aonach Beag	IV,5 *
Mercury	Ben Nevis	IV,4 **
Lickety Split	Aonach Mor	IV,5 **
The Great Chimney	Ben Nevis	IV,5 *
Never a Dull Moment	Aonach Beag	IV,6
Trespasser Buttress	Creag Meagaidh	IV,5 *
Raeburn's Arete	Ben Nevis	IV,5 ***
Twinkle	Aonach Beag	IV,5 **
North-West Face, Observatory Buttress	Ben Nevis	IV,4 *
The Clanger	Ben Nevis	IV,5 **
Roaring Forties	Ben Nevis	IV,5 **
Bodice Ripper	Stob Ban	IV,4 *

Raw Egg Buttress	Aonach Beag	IV,4 **
Silverside	Ben Nevis	IV,4
Lost the Place	Ben Nevis	IV,4
Rogue's Rib	Ben Nevis	IV,4
Burrito's Groove	Ben Nevis	IV,5 **
The Crab Crawl	Creag Meagaidh	IV,4 ***
Pirate	Ben Nevis	IV,4
Raeburn's Buttress, Intermediate Gully Finish	Ben Nevis	IV,4 ***
Staircase Climb	Ben Nevis	IV,5 *
Observatory Buttress Direct	Ben Nevis	IV,4 *
Neapolitan	Creag Dhubh	IV,4 *
Tramp	Ben Nevis	IV,4 *
Sideslip	Aonach Beag	IV,4
Thompson's Route	Ben Nevis	IV,4 ***
Ruadh Eigg Chimney	Aonach Beag	IV,5 *
Baird's Buttress	Ben Nevis	IV,4
Chimney Groove	Ben Nevis	IV,6
Aphrodite	Ben Nevis	IV,4 **
Newbigging's 80 Minute Route	Ben Nevis	IV,4
Skyline Rib	Stob Ban	IV,4
Gargoyle Wall	Ben Nevis	IV,5 *
The Cascade	Ben Nevis	IV,5 **
The Guardian	Aonach Mor	IV,5 *
Wagroochimsla	Ben Nevis	IV,4
Raeburn's Buttress, Direct Start	Ben Nevis	IV,4 *
North Pillar	Creag Meagaidh	IV,4 *
Minus Three Gully	Ben Nevis	IV,4 ***
Wendigo	Ben Nevis	IV,4 **
Ritchie's Gully	Creag Meagaidh	IV,4 **
Typhoon	Aonach Mor	IV,4 ***
Roaring Forties	Aonach Mor	IV,4 *
Right-Hand Wall Route	Ben Nevis	IV,5
Missed the Post	Creag Meagaidh	IV,4
Pinnacle Buttress	Ben Nevis	IV,4
Central Pillar	Creag Meagaidh	IV,4
Plum Duff	Ben Nevis	IV,4
Easter Pillar	Creag Meagaidh	IV,4
Ruddy Rocks	Ben Nevis	IV,4
Nid Arete	Aonach Mor	IV,5 *
Abacus	Ben Nevis	IV,4
Observatory Wall	Ben Nevis	IV,4
The White Spider	Creag Meagaidh	IV,4 *
Slab Rib Variation	Ben Nevis	IV,5 *
Rain Trip	Ben Nevis	IV,4
Direct Route, Douglas Boulder	Ben Nevis	IV,4 *

Central Gully, Right-Hand	Ben Nevis	IV,4 *
Aquafresh	Aonach Mor	IV,4 *
The Betrayal	Aonach Mor	IV,5
Blinker's Buttress, Direct Start	Aonach Beag	IV,4
Jet Stream	Aonach Mor	IV,4 ***
Newbigging's Route, Far Right-Hand Variation	Ben Nevis	IV,4 **
Scotch on the Rocks	Binnein Shuas	IV,4
Le Mechant	Ben Nevis	IV,4
Nordwand, Direct Start	Ben Nevis	IV,4 **
Foxtrot	Binnein Shuas	IV,4
Central Gully	Meall Garbh	IV,5 ***
Raeburn's Buttress	Ben Nevis	IV,5 **
Western Grooves, Douglas Boulder	Ben Nevis	IV,5
Left-Hand Chimney, Douglas Boulder	Ben Nevis	IV,4
Naevuata	Creag Meagaidh	IV,4 *
Barrel Buttress	Aonach Mor	IV,4
The Last Lap	Creag Meagaidh	IV,4 **
Pinnacle Arete	Ben Nevis	IV,4 **
White Shark	Aonach Mor	IV,4 ***
Platform's Rib	Ben Nevis	IV,4 *
Winter Chimneys	Ben Nevis	IV,4
Wee Team Gully	Carn Dearg	IV,4 **
South Pillar	Creag Meagaidh	IV,4
Nordwander	Creag Meagaidh	IV,4 *
The Great Trek	Carn Dearg	IV,4
Observatory Ridge	Ben Nevis	IV,4 ***
Gutless	Ben Nevis	IV,5
Pigott's Route, Tower Ridge	Ben Nevis	IV,4
Great Buttress Route	Creag Meagaidh	IV,4
Solar Wind	Aonach Mor	IV,4 *
Point Five Gully, Right-Hand Finish	Ben Nevis	IV,4
North Buttress, Left Edge	Meall Garbh	IV,4 *
Little Spider	Meall Garbh	IV,4 *
Rip Off	Ben Nevis	IV,4 *
Post Horn Gallop	Creag Meagaidh	IV,4
Riptide	Aonach Mor	IV,4
Green Hollow Route	Ben Nevis	IV,4 *
The Walker's Spur	Ben Alder	IV,4
Comb Gully Buttress, Variation Finish	Ben Nevis	IV,4 **
South Pipe Direct	Creag Meagaidh	IV,4 **
Comb Gully Buttress	Ben Nevis	IV,4 **
East Face, Observatory Ridge	Ben Nevis	IV,5 *
The Comb, Left Flank	Ben Nevis	IV,4 *
Green Gully	Ben Nevis	IV,4 ***
Five Finger Discount	Ben Nevis	IV,4 **
The Clare Effect	Aonach Beag	IV,3 *

Route Major	Ben Nevis	IV,3 ***
Comb Gully	Ben Nevis	IV,4 ***
Loch Roy Gully	Creag Meagaidh	IV,4
Italian Right-Hand	Ben Nevis	IV,4 ***
Moonwalk	Ben Nevis	IV,3 **
Point Five Gully, Left-Hand Finish	Ben Nevis	IV,4
No Toddy	Stob Ban	IV,4 *
Harrison's Climb Direct	Ben Nevis	IV,4 ***
Central Gully	Stob Ban	IV,4
North-East Buttress	Ben Nevis	IV,4 ***
Gaslight	Ben Nevis	IV,4
The Frozen Vice	Meall Garbh	IV,4 *
Gendarme Ridge	Stob Ban	IV,4
Waterfall Gully	Ben Nevis	IV,4 **
Guide's Variation	Aonach Mor	IV,4
The Curtain Rail	Ben Nevis	IV,4 *
Jubilation	Ben Nevis	IV,4 *
Four Play	Ben Nevis	IV,4
Force Ten Buttress	Aonach Mor	III,4 **
Turf Walk	Aonach Mor	III,4 *
Recess Route	Ben Nevis	III,4
Remora	Aonach Mor	III,4
Morwind	Aonach Mor	III,4 ***
Right-Hand Chimney, Moonlight Gully Buttress	Ben Nevis	III,4 **
The Split	Aonach Mor	III,4 **
Glover's Chimney	Ben Nevis	III,4 **
Tunnel Vision, Left Branch	Aonach Mor	III,4
The Slever	Aonach Mor	III,4
Phosphorescent Grooves	Ben Nevis	III,4 *
Pinnacle Buttress of the Tower	Ben Nevis	III,4 *
Buttons	Creag Meagaidh	III,4
Big Red Van	Carn Dearg	III,4 *
Southern Route	Meall Garbh	III,4
Good Friday Climb, Left-Hand Finish	Ben Nevis	III,4
Central Rib	Ben Nevis	III,4 *
Beyond the Call of Duty	Aonach Beag	III,4
The Western Traverse	Ben Nevis	III,4 **
Broad Gully	Meall Garbh	III,4 **
Pepperpot	Aonach Mor	III,4

Route II, Carn Dearg Buttress, Ben Nevis

Graded List of Rock Climbs

The majority of climbs on this list are on Ben Nevis. They have been graded assuming that the rock is warm and dry, but with such a short summer climbing season this may not always be the case. Wet cracks, damp vegetation and cold temperatures may add considerably to the difficulty. On unfrequented routes, which generally have fewer stars, loose rock may also be a problem. The majority of the grades have been checked by contacting people who have climbed them, but be prepared for a few surprises. It is possible that there are a few 'Scottish VS's' lurking near the bottom of the list!

Agrippa	E5 5c,6b,5c ***
The Banana Groove	E4 5b,4c,6a,5c **
Boadicea	E4 5b,5a,6a,- *
Titan's Wall	E3 5b,5c,-,-,4b,- ***
Caligula Direct	E3 6a,- **
Chandelle	E3 5c,5c,5b,4c ***
Adrenalin Rush	E3 5b,6a,4c,4c,5c,5b,5a,4c *
King Kong, Original Start	E3 4c,6a,5b
Caligula	E3 5b,4c,5c,5c **
The Trial	E3 5c *
King Kong	E2 4c,4c,5c,5b,5b,-,5a,4c,- **
The Bat	E2 4c,5a,5a,5b,5b,4b,-,-,- **
Cowslip	E2 5c
Red Rag	E2 5b,5a,5b,5a,5a,5c,5a,4a,5a,4c *
Pirates	E2 4c,5c,5c **
Subtraction	E2 -,5b,-,-,-,5c,-,- **
Orient Express	E2 5c,5a *
Heart of Glass	E2 5a
Strata-Sphere	E2 5b
Torro	E2 5b,5b,5a,5c,5a,4b,5a,5b ***
Metamorphosis	E1 5b,5a,4c,- **
Heidbanger	E1 5b,5b,4c *
Cranium	E1 5b
Agamemnon	E1 5a,5b *
Camanachd Heroes	E1
The Urchin	E1 5a,5b
Bananafishbones	E1 5a
Clam-Jam	E1 5b **
Sassenach	E1 4c,5a,5a,5a,-,4b,-,-,- **
Minus One, Arete Variation	HVS 4c,5b,4c ***
The Orgy	HVS
Last Stand	HVS -,5a,5a **
The Shield Direct	HVS 5a *
Minus One, Serendipity Variation	HVS 5a,4c,5a ***
Arthur	HVS -,4b,5a,4c,-

The Bullroar	HVS 5a,4b,4a,5a,4c,4b,-,4c,-,- ***
Steam	HVS 4c,5a,4c **
Rolling Stones	HVS
Tuff Nut	HVS 5a *
Centurion	HVS 4c,5a,4b,4b,4a,5a,4c ***
The Knuckleduster	HVS 4c,5a,5a,4c **
The Brass Monkey	HVS 5a
Prodigal Boys	HVS
Sioux Wall	HVS -,5a,5a,- **
Central Route	HVS 4a,4a,5a,-,-,-,-,- *
Turret Cracks	HVS -,5a,4b
Kellett's Route	HVS 4b,5a,4c,-
Steam Train	HVS 5a,5a,-
Clefthanger	HVS -,5a,-
Marathon	HVS 5a *
Antigone	HVS 5a,5a
Chinook	HVS 5a,- *
Gutbuster	HVS 4c,5a,4c *
Dissection	HVS 4b,-,4c,4c,4c,5a,5a
The Crack	HVS 4c,5a,4b *
Teufel Grooves	HVS 4c,5a,4b
Lysystrata	HVS 5a,4c
Minus One Direct	HVS -,4b,4c,5b,4b,4a,4b,4b,- **
Turkish	HVS
Around the Bend	HVS 5a
Surgeon's Gully	VS
The Banshee	VS
Pointless	VS 4c
Left Edge Route	VS 4c *
Night Tripper	VS
Plastic Max	VS
North-Eastern Grooves	VS -,4b,4c,-,-,4b,4c,4b,- *
Strident Edge	VS -,4b,4c,4b **
Psychedelic Wall	VS 4c
Astronomy	VS 4b,-,4b,4a,4a,-,-,-,- *
Right-Hand Route	VS -,4b,4b,-,-,-,-,- **
Left-Hand Route	VS 4a,4a,4b,4b,-,-,-,- **
P.M.	VS 4c,4b,4b,4b *
The Twist	VS 4c,4a,4c,4b,4b *
The Slant	VS 4a,4b,4c,4c,- *
Sidewinder	VS -,4c,4b,- *
Left-Hand Route, Left Edge Variation	VS 4b,4c,4b ***
Spartacus	VS 4b,4b,4b,- *
The Long Climb	VS -,-,4a,-,-,-,4b,-,-,-,- ***
Chicken Run	VS 4b

The Shadow	VS 4b *
Cutlass	VS -,4b,-,- *
Beta Route, Direct Variation	VS 4c
Saxifrage	VS 4c
Left-Hand Route, Clough Variation	VS *
The Minge	VS -,4c,4b
Beta Route	VS 4b,4c,4a,4a
Reprobate's Rib	VS -,4b,-,4b,- *
Geotactic	VS 4b
Wagroochimsla	VS 4b,4b,-,-

List of First Ascents

This list includes all the known first ascents in the area, but despite determined research the origin of some routes has remained elusive. Unravelling the historical background of the region has proved to be a fascinating task. In the case of Ben Nevis, some discrepancies were found between various guidebooks for the first ascent dates of a few routes. When this was the case, Ken Crocket's authoritative book, *Ben Nevis* (SMT 1986) was used as the final arbiter. It also came to light that several routes were climbed prior to the recorded first ascent, and these have been noted when known. Any aid used on the first ascent has been listed. It should be remembered that until the early 1970s it was common practice to use ice pegs to assist in step-cutting, and the amount of aid used on a winter climb was never systematically reported. All routes now go free, except where noted in the text which describes the freest version to date, and first free ascents have been listed when known. The following abbreviations have been used:

S	Summer
W	Winter
FFA	First free ascent
PA	Peg for aid or tension

BEN NEVIS

S 1892   3 Sep   Tower Ridge   J.Hopkinson, E.Hopkinson, B.Hopkinson, C.Hopkinson
> *The Hopkinsons descended Tower Ridge only. The Ridge was not ascended until the first winter ascent two years later.*

Great Tower Variations:
  Recess Route by W.W.Naismith, G.Thomson 27 Sep 1894.
  Cracked Slabs Route by J.W.Macgregor Apr 1896.
  The Western Traverse by W.W.Naismith, G.Thomson 27 Sep 1894.
  The Eastern Traverse by W.W.Naismith, A.E.Robertson 6 Sep 1900.
  Pigott's Route by A.S.Pigott, J.Wilding 23 Sep 1921.
  Bell's Route by J.H.B.Bell, E.E.Roberts 18 Aug 1929.
  Macphee's Route by G.G.Macphee, G.R.Speaker 1 Sep 1935.
  Rotten Chimney by H.I.Ogilvy, N.P.Piercy 20 Jun 1940.
  Ogilvy's Route by H.I.Ogilvy, N.P.Piercy 23 Jun 1940.

S 1892   6 Sep   North-East Buttress   J.Hopkinson, E.Hopkinson, B.Hopkinson, C.Hopkinson
  First Platform Traverse Variation by G.C.Williams, J.L.Aikman 14 Jul 1929.
  Direct Ridge Variation by D.W.Robinson, J.G.Robinson, J.G.MacLean, A.R.Lillie 26 Sep 1930.
  Tough-Brown Variant by W.Brown, W.Tough 25 May 1895.

W 1894   30 Mar   Tower Ridge   J.N.Collie, G.A.Solly, J.Collier
Great Tower Variations:
  The Western Traverse by J.N.Collie, G.A.Solly, J.Collier 30 Mar 1894.

Pigott's Route by J.R.Marshall and party Winter 1958.

Recess Route by D.J.Bennet, J.Rendell 21 Mar 1950.

W 1895   12 Apr Castle Ridge   J.N.Collie, W.W.Naismith, G.Thomson,
                                       M.W.Travers

W 1895   Apr Number Three Gully   J.N.Collie, M.W.Travers

This was the first recorded ascent. The gully had certainly been climbed as early as 1870.

W 1895   Apr Number Four Gully   A.E.Maylard, W.W.Naismith,
                                       F.C.Squance

W 1895   Apr Number Five Gully   J.N.Collie and party

It is likely that these two gullies had received earlier ascents in the 1870s.

S 1895   2 Jun Slingsby's Chimney   G.Hastings, H.Priestman,
                                       W.Cecil Slingsby

Chockstone Variation by F.Greig, A.E.McKenzie and A.N.Other 18 Sep 1904.

S 1895   8 Jun Green and Napier's   E.W.Green, R.G.Napier
                 Route

S 1895   9 Jun Ledge Route   J.S.Napier, R.G.Napier, E.W.Green

W 1896   Apr The Castle   W.Brown, J.MacLay, W.W.Naismith,
                                       G.Thomson

An advanced route for the time.

W 1896   Apr Number Two Gully   J.Collier, G.Hastings, W.C.Slingsby

W 1896   1 Apr South Castle Gully   W.Brunskill, W.W.King, W.W.Naismith

W 1896   3 Apr North-East Buttress   W.W.Naismith, W.Brunskill,
                                       A.B.W.Kennedy, W.W.King,
                                       F.C.Squance

S 1896   3 Apr Direct Route,   W.Brown, L.Hinxman, H.Raeburn,
                 Douglas Boulder   W.Douglas

W 1896   4 Apr North Castle Gully   J.H.Bell, R.G.Napier

S 1896   6 Apr East Ridge,   J.H.Bell, R.G.Napier
                 Douglas Boulder

Variation Start by J.Y.MacDonald, H.W.Turnbull 17 Mar 1931.

W 1896   Apr The Castle   W.Brown, J.MacLay, W.W.Naismith,
                                       G.Thomson

An advanced route for the time.

W 1897 Easter   Ledge Route   SMC party

W 1897   25 Apr Tower Gully   G.Hastings, E.L.W.Haskett-Smith,
                                       W.P.Haskett-Smith

Logically, this should have been named Number One Gully.

W 1897   26 Apr Gardyloo Gully   G.Hastings, W.P.Haskett-Smith

The Observatory rubbish chute. The name is a corruption of the French 'gardez l'eau'- the warning cry of Edinburgh householders as they were about to tip rubbish into the street.

W 1898   3 Jan Moonlight Gully   W.Inglis Clark, T.Gibson

Nine hours of sustained step cutting were required, and the party finished the route by the light of the full moon.

S 1898   12 Jul Staircase Climb   J.H.Bell, J.Maclay, W.W.Naismith
Raeburn's Variation by H.Raeburn, A.E.Robertson 6 Jul 1903.
Straight Chimney Variation by B.P.Kellett, C.M.Plackett, R.L.Plackett
22 Jun 1944.
Deep Chimney Variation by B.P.Kellett, C.M.Plackett, R.L.Plackett
22 Jun 1944.
S 1898   11 Sep The Castle   H.Raeburn, T.Gibson
S 1899   May Castle Ridge   J.G.Inglis, J.W.Inglis, C.Inglis Clark,
                                        W.Inglis Clark
S 1901   22 Jun Observatory Ridge   H.Raeburn
Direct Variation by G.C.Williams, J.L.Aikman, A.R.Lillie 31 Aug 1930.
Combined tactics used. FFA: A.T.Hargreaves, H.V.Hughes, G.G.Macphee
16 Jun 1931. Left-Hand Start by J.H.B.Bell.
S 1901   23 Jun Raeburn's 18 Minute   H.Raeburn, C.Inglis Clark,
                 Route   W.Inglis Clark
S 1902   27 Jun Glover's Chimney   G.T.Glover, C.Inglis Clark,
                                        W.Inglis Clark
Originally called Tower Gap West Gully.
S 1902   28 Jun Pinnacle Buttress of   G.T.Glover, W.Inglis Clark
                 the Tower
S 1902   28 Jun Observatory Buttress   H.Raeburn
A bold solo by Raeburn on his third attempt on the route.
S 1902   29 Jun Pinnacle Arete   H.Raeburn, C.Inglis Clark,
                                        W.Inglis Clark
S 1902   29 Jun Number Three Gully   H.Raeburn, C.Inglis Clark,
                 Buttress   W.Inglis Clark
S 1902   30 Jun Raeburn's Arete   H.Raeburn, C.Inglis Clark,
                                        W.Inglis Clark
*'From a climbing point of view, this route ranks amongst the steepest on Ben
Nevis, and would be impossible but for the magnificent nature of the rock' A
bold lead by Raeburn on a route that was years ahead of its time.*
1931 Variation by A.T.Hargreaves, G.G.Macphee, H.V.Hughes 20 Jun 1931.
1949 Variation by S.Tewnion, J.Black, H.Convey Apr 1949.
S 1902   21 Aug Newbigging's 80   W.C.Newbigging and a Swiss
                 Minute Route   companion.
The name was a dig at Raeburn's meticulous timekeeping on ascents.
W 1904   1 Jan North Trident   J.Maclay, H.Raeburn, C.W.Walker,
                 Buttress   H.Walker
Direct Start by D.Haston and party.
W 1904   Jan Eastern Traverse   H.Raeburn, J.Rennie, J.H.Wigner
                 from Tower Gully
W 1904   Apr Central Gully, South   H.Raeburn, C.Inglis Clark,
                 Trident Buttress   W.Inglis Clark
Icefall Variation by L.S.Lovat, K.Bryan 11 Mar 1956.
S 1904   11 Jun Cousin's Buttress   C.W.Walker, H.Walker
Direct Start by B.P.Kellett 20 Aug 1944

S 1904 4 Aug South-West Ridge, J.W.Burns, W.A.Morrison,
Douglas Boulder W.C.Newbigging, A.E.Robertson
S 1904 19 Sep North Castle Gully F.Greig, A.E.McKenzie, A.N.Other
W 1906 Apr Green Gully H.Raeburn, E.Phildius
'...I must confess to a feeling of helplessness for a moment as I stood on my ice-axe, driven horizontally into the vertical snow wall, some hundreds of feet of little less than vertical ice-plastered rocks stretching away down into the depths of the mist beneath, while my fingers slid helplessly from the glassy surface of the cornice neve...' A futuristic ascent by Raeburn.
W 1907 28 Dec Goodeve's Route T.E.Goodeve, C.Inglis Clark,
J.H.A.McIntyre
The result of an epic escape by a belated party on Tower Ridge. After The Western Traverse, the party down-climbed Glover's Chimney, but understandably baulked at the large icefall. They then took to the snowed up rocks to the right of the chimney, to complete their epic escape to the plateau. They eventually returned to Fort William some 30 hours after leaving. They may have had less trouble forcing the Ridge! The first complete ascent was recorded as The White Line by M.G.Geddes and H.Gillespie 18 Mar 1971.
S 1908 28 Sep Raeburn's Buttress H.Raeburn, H.MacRobert, D.S.Arthur
S 1911 15 Jul South Castle Gully H.MacRobert, R.E.Workman,
C.Inglis Clark, W.Inglis Clark
Left Wall Variation by G.G.MacPhee, A.G.Murray 29 Sep 1935.
S 1911 28 Sep Raeburn's Easy H.Raeburn, A.W.Russell
Route
W 1920 Apr Observatory Ridge H.Raeburn, F.S.Goggs, W.A.Mounsey
The most significant Scottish winter ascent of the 1920s. A magnificent lead by Raeburn.
W 1920 Apr Raeburn's Easy SMC party, names not recorded
Route
Direct Finish by R.Harvey, A.Meekin Winter 1986.
S 1921 24 Sep Pigott's Route A.S.Pigott, J.Wilding
A poor route. It was rejected by Raeburn as a possible rock climb in 1903.
W 1929 1 Jan Number Four Gully J.H.B.Bell
Buttress
S 1929 29 Mar East Wall Route C.W.Parry, G.Murray, G.M.Lawson,
M.Matheson, S.F.M.Cumming
S 1929 12 Jun Harrison's Climb A.Harrison, G.M.Lawson, W.N.Allan
Chimney Start by A.Horn, H.V.Hughes 25 Jun 1931.
Dungeon Variation by I.M.Brooker, A.D.Lyall 2 Jul 1949.
S 1929 16 Sep Right-Hand Wall N.W.Mowbray, D.Hotchkin, S.J.Jack
Route, Minus Three
Buttress
Slab Rib Variation by J.Jackson, A.G.Murray, D.J.S.Harvey, W.L.Coats
5 May 1935.

S 1931   Mar 1931 Route   J.Y.MacDonald, H.W.Turnbull
Left-Hand Chimney Variation by B.P.Kellett 19 Jun 1943.
Central Rib Variation by I.S.Clough 18 Apr 1959.
S 1931 17 Jun Route I   A.T.Hargreaves, G.G.Macphee,
                                          H.V.Hughes
Direct Start by R.L.Plackett, W.W.Campbell 31 Aug 1941.
S 1931 19 Jun Observatory   A.T.Hargreaves, G.G.Macphee,
                 Buttress Direct   H.V.Hughes
Slab Variation by W.M.MacKenzie, A.M.MacAlpine, W.H.Murray,
J.K.W.Dunn 30 Aug 1936.
S 1931 24 Jun Macphee's Route   G.G.Macphee, H.V.Hughes
S 1933   6 Apr Green Hollow Route   M.S.Cumming, E.J.A.Leslie, P.D.Baird
S 1933 13 Sep Rubicon Wall   A.T.Hargreaves, F.G.Heap, R.E.Heap
'For the next two hundred feet we decribed a curving course over the
slab-sea, cautiously balancing up from one rounded hold to another, rarely
if ever finding a notch and never an edge or splinter for grasping fingers.' A
committing route, heralding a new style of balance and friction climbing. For
several years it was considered the hardest rock climb on the mountain.
S 1933   8 Oct Garadh Buttress   G.G.Macphee, G.C.Williams,
                                         P.Ghiglione
Originally known as the East Ridge of Garadh na Ciste.
W 1934 24 Mar North Gully   J.Y.MacDonald, H.W.Turnbull
Left Fork by D.Bathgate, J.Knight, A.McKeith Feb 1964.
W 1934   Mar South-West Ridge,   J.Y.MacDonald, H.W.Turnbull
                  Douglas Boulder
W 1934   Mar 1934 Route, Second-   J.Y.MacDonald, H.W.Turnbull
                  ary Tower Ridge
S 1934 24 Jun 1934 Route, South   G.G.Macphee, G.C.Williams
                 Trident Buttress
Direct Finish by A.B.Black, A.Swan 12 Jun 1954.
S 1934 16 Sep Slav Route   E Derzag, M.Debelak,
                                         E.A.M.Wedderburn
S 1934 30 Sep Platforms Rib   J.H.B.Bell, C.M.Allan, M.B.Stewart
W 1935 17 Mar Glover's Chimney   G.G.Macphee, G.C.Williams,
                                         D.Henderson
'The entire chimney was sheeted with ice and there was no place where the
leader could take a proper rest, much less to which he could bring me up.
It was a thrilling experience for the second and third, straining their eyes in
the darkness watching their leader's figure dimly silhouetted against the sky
as he got nearer to the Tower Gap.' A significant ascent that had an
inspirational effect on the young climbers of the day.
W 1935   Apr Cousin's Buttress   G.G.Macphee, G.F.Todd
The route was climbed in thaw conditions and left unrecorded at the time.

Wee Team Gully, Carn Dearg, Monadhliath (Climber, James Grosset)

W 1935   5 May   Jubilee Climb   G.G.Macphee, G.C.Williams,
                                                    D.Henderson
Climbed under snow cover with only a small rock section at the 3m wall.
S 1935   6 May   North Trident   G.G.Macphee, J.Jackson, A.G.Murray,
                 Buttress, Direct   D.J.S.Harvey
                 Variation
S 1935 15 Jun   Ruddy Rocks   G.G.Macphee, G.C.Williams
S 1935 22 Jun   The Eastern Climb   G.G.Macphee, G.C.Williams
S 1935   5 Aug   Gardyloo Gully   G.G.Macphee, R.C.Frost
S 1935 28 Sep   The Great Chimney   G.G.Macphee, A.G.Murray
S 1935 29 Sep   North Gully   G.G.Macphee, A.G.Murray
S 1935 30 Sep   Bayonet Route   G.G.Macphee, A.G.Murray
   Main Overhang Variation by B.P.Kellett May 1943.
   Direct Start by J.R.Marshall, J.Stenhouse Aug 1959.
W 1936 10 Apr   South Gully   G.G.Macphee
S 1936 10 May   North-West Face   W.G.McClymont, J.H.B.Bell
                 Route, Douglas
                 Boulder
S 1936 10 May   1936 Route   W.G.McClymont, J.H.B.Bell
S 1936   1 Aug   Diagonal Route   J.H.Ogilvie, J.Ward
S 1936 13 Sep   Left Edge Route,   C.M.Allan, J.H.B.Bell,
                 Observatory   E.A.M.Wedderburn
                 Buttress
S 1937 11 Jul   West Face Upper   J.F.Hamilton, J.H.B.Bell
                 Route
W 1938 12 Apr   Comb Gully   F.G.Stangle, R.Morsley, P.A.Small
S 1938 18 Jun   Baird's Buttress   E.J.A.Leslie, P.D.Baird
S 1938 19 Jun   Newbigging's Route,   P.D.Baird, E.J.A.Leslie
                 Right-Hand Variation
S 1938   7 Jul   Newbigging's Route,   N.Ridyard, A.Smith, N.Forsyth, J.Smith
                 Far Right Variation
   Overhang Variation by G.H.Wiltshire, R.W.Cahn, L.Young Jul 1945
S 1938 12 Jun   North-West Face,   E.J.A.Leslie, W.H.Murray,
                 Observatory Buttress   E.A.M.Wedderburn, J.H.B.Bell
W 1939   7 Apr   Good Friday Climb   G.G.Macphee, R.W.Lovel,
                                                    H.R.Shepherd, D.Edwards
S 1940 14 Jun   The Long Climb   J.H.B.Bell, J.D.B.Wilson
   Variation Alpha by J.H.B.Bell, G.Dwyer Aug 1940.
   Epsilon Chimney by J.H.B.Bell, J.E.McEwan Jun 1940.
   Variation Zeta by J.H.B.Bell, V.P.Roy Jul 1935.
   V-Traverse by J.H.B.Bell, G.Dwyer Aug 1943.
   V-Traverse Continuation by B.P.Kellett Aug 1943.

Alderwand, Ben Alder (Climber, Roger Everett)

S 1940 16 Jun Hesperides Ledge   J.H.B.Bell, J.D.B.Wilson
'It is a steeply inclined, curving shelf and is a perfect garden of mossy and lush vegetation...there are several exceedingly delicate corners to negotiate with a most precipitous drop on the right. The vegetation is loosely anchored, the rocks are rather loose, and there are practically no positive holds...'

S 1940 19 Jun Evening Wall   C.F.Rolland, H.I.Ogilvy
S 1940 21 Jun Compression Crack   C.F.Rolland, H.I.Ogilvy
S 1940 22 Jun Tower Face of the   H.I.Ogilvy, C.F.Rolland, J.R.Hewitt
               Comb
'Owing to the nature of the rock and moss encountered we suggest Quisling Wall as a name.'
Chimney Variation by G.Dwyer, J.H.B.Bell 6 Aug 1940.
Central Wall Variation by B.P.Kellett 18 Jul 1943.
Left-Hand Variation by J.R.Marshall, J.Stenhouse Jul 1958.

S 1940   Aug Beta Route   J.H.B.Bell, G.Dwyer
Direct Variation by B.P.Kellett 17 Jun 1944.

S 1941 10 Jul Central Rib   M.W.Erlebach, E.C.Pyatt
Tower Finish by B.P.Kellett 10 Jul 1943.

S 1941 11 Jul Indicator Wall   J.F.Scott, J.T.Austin, W.Moore
Direct Variation by B.P.Kellett 1 Aug 1943.

S 1941 21 Sep The Girdle Traverse   J.H.B.Bell, J.D.B.Wilson
Wilson stopped after The Comb and Bell continued alone across Coire na Ciste.

S 1941 23 Sep Thompson's Route   S.Thompson, B.P.Thompson
S 1942 30 Aug Number Two Gully   B.P.Kellett, J.A.Dunster
Probably the hardest summer gully after Point Five.

S 1943 29 May Lower East Wall   B.P.Kellett
               Route

S 1943   9 Jun Route II   B.P.Kellett, W.A.Russell
Direct Start by B.W.Robertson, G.Chisholm 19 May 1962.

S 1943 24 Jul Italian Climb   B.P.Kellett
S 1943 24 Jul Broad Gully   B.P.Kellett
S 1943 25 Jul Right-Hand Chimney,   G.Scott, E.M.Hanlon, B.P.Kellett
               Moonlight Gully
               Buttress

S 1943 25 Jul The Groove Climb   B.P.Kellett
S 1943   Jul Comb Gully Buttress   B.P.Kellett
S 1943 Summer Kellett's North Wall Route:
Route A by B.P.Kellett 2 Jul 1943.
Flake Chimney by B.P.Kellett 10 Aug 1943.
Route B by B.P.Kellett, J.H.B.Bell, M.Forsyth 11 Aug 1943.
Direct Start to Route B by B.P.Kellett, C.M.Plackett Summer 1943.
Caterpillar Crawl Variation by B.Ritchie, J.Mills, C.Pattinson, R.Hill 24 Jun 1949.
Routes were climbed on this wall by E.Luscher in 1920, and Nelstrop and Bryom in 1940, but their accounts are impossible to reconcile with the actual buttress.

S 1944 20 Jun Left-Hand Route, B.P.Kellett, R.L.Plackett, C.M.Plackett
Minus Two Buttress

One of Kellett's finest discoveries on Nevis.
Clough Variation by I.S.Clough, D.G.Roberts, C.Grandison, D.Miller 1 Jun 1963.
Left Edge Variation by N.Richardson, R.T.Richardson, A.Walker 11 Jun 1988.

S 1944 21 Jun Left-Hand Chimney, B.P.Kellett
Douglas Boulder

S 1944 8 Jul West Face Lower B.P.Kellett
Route

S 1944 16 Jul Tower Face Crack B.P.Kellett

S 1944 18 Jul Right-Hand Chimney, B.P.Kellett
Douglas Boulder

S 1944 20 Jul Right-Hand Route, B.P.Kellett
Minus Two Buttress

Kellett lost his trousers on the approach. Another bold solo!

S 1944 22 Jul Kellett's Route, B.P.Kellett
Gardyloo Buttress

Kellett's finest hour. A fine solution to a long-standing problem.
Variation Finish by D.Haston, J.Stenhouse 14 Sep 1958.

S 1944 30 Jul 1944 Route B.P.Kellett

S 1944 30 Jul The Slab Climb B.P.Kellett

S 1946 16 Jun The Crack H.A.Carsten, T.McGuinness

'The first Crack pitch is 50ft long and is really a chimney. It overhangs and is undercut and the entry is rotten...' A formidably steep route.

S 1947 2 Aug Number Two Gully J.D.B.Wilson, G.A.Collie
Buttress

W 1949 19 Feb Tower Cleft G.Pratt, J.Francis

W 1950 Apr Slingsby's Chimney C.Donaldson, J.Russell

Probably climbed earlier but this is the first recorded ascent.

S 1950 28 Aug Gargoyle Wall W.Peascod, B.L.Dodson, C.H.Peckett,
J.Renwick, G.G.Macphee

S 1950 29 Aug Minus Two Gully B.L.Dodson, W.Peascod

S 1951 7 Oct Continuation Wall T.Weir, I McNicol, A McNicol

W 1952 23 Mar Observatory Buttress D.D.Stewart, W.M.Foster
Direct

A difficult route hinting at the winter advance soon to come.

W 1952 Mar Raeburn's 18 Minute E.U.M.C. party
Route

S 1953 Sep Fives Wall J.R.Marshall, C.L.Donaldson

S 1954 18 Apr Sassenach J.Brown, D.D.Whillans

Carn Dearg Buttress eventually climbed, but by an English team to the chagrin of the Scots.
Patey Traverse to foot of Great Chimney by T.W.Patey, W.Brooker, W.Smith 1953 on an unsuccessful first ascent attempt.
FFA: R.Anderson, M.Hamilton 21 Aug 1983

S 1954   3 Oct The Gutter   C.G.M.Slesser, G.Waldie, S.Paterson
S 1955   Jun North-Eastern   R.O.Downes, M.J.O'Hara,
                Grooves   E.D.G.Langmuir
  Climbed over 2 days. 1 PA.
  FFA: R.O.Downes, M.J.O'Hara, M.Prestige 11 Jun 1960.
S 1955 27 Aug Zero Gully   W.Smith, G.McIntosh, M.Noon
S 1955 28 Aug Point Five Gully   M.Noon, G.McIntosh
  The Creag Dhu snatch summer ascents of the two prestigious Nevis gullies.
W 1956 15 Feb Neptune Gully   A.J.Bennet, J.Clarkson
S 1956   1 Apr Rogue's Rib   T.W.Patey, J.Smith
  The initial section was avoided by taking the snow gully of Italian Climb.
  Complete ascent by K.Bryan, N.Harthill 1956.
S 1956 11 Jun Minus One Direct   R.O.Downes, M.J.O'Hara,
                                       M.Prestige (1 PA).
  Plinth Variation by P.F.Macdonald, I.G.Rowe Jun 1967.
  Serendipity Variation by K.V.Crocket, I.Fulton 27 Aug 1972.
  Arete Variation by S.Abbott, D.N.Williams 28 Aug 1983. 1 PA.
  FFA: W.Jeffrey, D.N.Williams 6 Jul 1984.
S 1956 15 Jul Echo Traverse   L.S.Lovat, K.Bryan, N.Harthill
S 1956 30 Aug Centurion   D.D.Whillans, R.O.Downes
  Another great line on Carn Dearg falls to Whillans. Attempted in the 1940s.
S 1956   1 Sep The Shield   D.D.Whillans, R.O.Downes
  Direct Start by J.R.Marshall, R.Marshall, G.J.Ritchie Jun 1962. Several PA.
  A neglected route nowadays, but considered by Marshall to be as good as
  Centurion.
W 1957 16 Feb Cresta   T.W.Patey, L.S.Lovat, A.G.Nicol
  W.H.Murray suggested the line to Patey. 'Although a rock climber's midden
  in summer, like many similar faces it seemed to offer glorious winter climbing
  - a miniature Scottish Brenva, in fact.'
  Direct Finish by M.Slesser, N.Tennent 18 Feb 1957.
  Variation Start by I.S.Clough, J.M.Alexander 27 Jan 1959.
W 1957 18 Feb Zero Gully   H.MacInnes, A.G.Nicol, T.W.Patey
  The subject of intense competition and many attempts. Conditions were very
  good that day - 'It was exhilarating climbing on reliable snow although the
  extreme angle and long runouts did not encourage any liberties.' J.H.B.Bell
  and C.M.Allan had climbed most of the gully as early as Apr 1936, but
  avoided the crucial section by ascending the iced rocks of Slav Route.
W 1957 18 Feb Number Three Gully   L.S.Lovat, D.J.Bennet
                Buttress
W 1957   Feb Staircase Climb   D.Haston, J.Stenhouse
S 1957 21 Jun The Chute   CUMC party
  Originally called The Ruritanian Climb.
W 1957 17 Nov Pinnacle Buttress   D.J.Bennet, A.Tait
                of the Tower
W 1958   Jan Italian Climb   J.R.Marshall, A.McCorquodale,
                                       G.J.Ritchie

W 1958 16 Feb Garadh Gully   I.S.Clough, M.Bucke
    Indirect Finish by M.Duff, D.McCallum 4 Dec 1980.
W 1958 16 Feb Broad Gully   I.S.Clough, M.Bucke
W 1958 23 Mar Number Two Gully   J.R.Marshall, L.S.Lovat, A.H.Hendry
                Buttress
    Variation Finish by I.S.Clough, S.Stebbing, P.Cresswell, W.Reid, N.Bull,
    D.Ducker 1 Apr 1960.
S 1958   8 Apr Crack and Chimney I.S.Clough, P.Nicholson
W 1958 12 Apr Colando Gully   I.S.Clough, D.Pipes
W 1958 12 Apr Arch Gully   I.S.Clough, D.Pipes
W 1958 12 Apr Surprise Gully   I.S.Clough, D.Pipes
W 1958   Apr Frost Bite   I.S.Clough, D.Pipes, J.M.Alexander,
                                    P.A.Hannon, M.Bucke
W 1958   Direct Route,   J.R.Marshall and party
                Douglas Boulder
    The route was verglassed only and the ascent was left unrecorded at the
    time. Climbed in full winter condition in late 1960s.
S 1958 29 Jun Comb Gully   I.S.Clough, J.M.Alexander
S 1958 29 Jun The Keep   J.M.Alexander, I.S.Clough
S 1958   5 Jul Minus One Gully   I.S.Clough, D.Pipes
    Some aid was used.
S 1958   6 Jul Green Gully   D.Pipes, I.S.Clough
W 1959   1 Jan Tower Face of the   R.Smith, R.K.Holt
                Comb
    One of Smith's finest routes - a demanding mixed climb with no known
    repeats until the mid 1980s.
    Left-Hand Start by R.Clothier, A.Shand Winter 1987.
W 1959   3 Jan Surprise Buttress   I.S.Clough, B.Halpin
W 1959   3 Jan Arch Buttress   D.Pipes, A.Flegg
W 1959   6 Jan Slalom   I.S.Clough, D.Pipes, R.Shaw,
                                    J.M.Alexander, A.Flegg
W 1959   8 Jan Waterfall Gully   D.Pipes, I.S.Clough, J.M.Alexander,
                                    R.Shaw, A.Flegg
    Climbed over two days using fixed ropes.
    True Finish by D.Cuthbertson, C.Fraser 3 Mar 1984.
W 1959 16 Jan Point Five Gully   J.M.Alexander, I.S.Clough,
                                    D.Pipes, R.Shaw
    After many attempts, this famous route succumbed after a six-day siege.
    'Every night they recuperated in the C.I.C Hut - a disqualification in the
    opinion of a puritan minority (who alleged, furthermore, that a rest day had
    allowed the party to replenish their stocks from a Fort William blacksmith's).
    Whether Point Five can be climbed in a day, using conventional technique,
    remains to be seen.' The first one-day, and second overall ascent was made
    by J.R.Marshall, R.Smith 10 Feb 1960. 'No artificial aids apart from two ice
    axes were used.'
    Left-Hand Finish by R.Clothier, R.Webb Jan 1988.

W 1959   28 Jan   Central Gully, Creag   I.S.Clough, J.M.Alexander
                    Coire na Ciste
   Central Gully Right-Hand by I.MacEacheran, J.Knight
W 1959   31 Jan   Raeburn's Buttress   W.D.Brooker, J.M.Taylor
   Intermediate Gully Finish by R.Ashley, G.G.I.S.Clough, C.H.Oakes
   14 Apr 1938.
   Direct Start by D.Gardner, T.Walne, C.Higgins Apr 1979.
W 1959   31 Jan   The Winter Girdle   J.R.Marshall, T.W.Patey
   *Patey was modest about this bold and lengthy expedition. 'This was not such
   a tour de force as one might suppose; there is a natural traversing line most
   of the way,and the difficulties are not extreme.' In an interesting contrast of
   styles, Marshall wore crampons, and Patey used nails.*
W 1959   Jan   Smith-Holt Route   R.Smith, R.K.Holt
   *The first winter route to venture onto the Orion Face. 'This twelve hour climb
   was perhaps the finest performance of the season.'*
W 1959   1 Feb   West Face Lower   W.D.Brooker, J.R.Marshall, T.W.Patey
                    Route
   1 PA. Also known as Hadrian's Wall. Patey wanted to name the route 0.25!
   Summer line followed by K.V.Crocket, C.Stead 12 Mar 1972.
W 1959   1 Feb   Pinnacle Arete   R.H.Sellars, J.Smith
W 1959   10 Feb   Bob-Run   I.S.Clough, H.Fisher, B.Small, D.Pipes,
                    J.Porter, F.Jones
W 1959   10 Feb   Fives Gully   I.S.Clough
W 1959   10 Feb   Easy Chimney   I.S.Clough
W 1959   11 Feb   Minus Two Gully   J.R.Marshall, J.Stenhouse, D.Haston
   *A magnificent tour de force. Haston was impressed - 'For Stenhouse and
   me it was both a stunner and a mind-awakener. We were supposed to share
   leads, but after we followed Jimmy over the bulge it became apparent that
   his experience and ability were still beyond ours. We were taking as long to
   second as he was to lead.'*
W 1959   11 Feb   Nordwand   I.S.Clough, D.Pipes, B.Sarll, F.Jones,
                    J.Porter
   Direct Start by G.Suzca and party Winter 1989.
W 1959   11 Feb   Red Gully   D.Pipes, I.S.Clough, J.Porter, B.Sarll,
                    H.Fisher
W 1959   11 Feb   La Petite   I.S.Clough, D.Pipes, J.Porter
W 1959   12 Feb   Hesperides Ledge   J.R.Marshall, J.Stenhouse, D.Haston
W 1959   12 Feb   The Serpent   I.S.Clough, D.Pipes, J.Porter
W 1959   8 Mar   Platforms Rib   H.MacInnes, T.Sullivan, M.White,
                    I.S.Clough
   Several PA were used on the steep wall.
S 1959   18 Apr   Vagabond's Rib   I.S.Clough
S 1959   18 Apr   Lady's Day   I.S.Clough, C.MacInnes, E.Buckley
S 1959   19 Apr   Titan's Wall   I.S.Clough, H.MacInnes
   *Climbed as an aid route. A very dim view was taken by the SMC Committee
   - '...pegs shouldn't replace skill or supplement a blatant lack of shame.'*

FFA: M.Fowler, P.Thomas Jun 1977, but attempted free in the late 1960s.
Direct Finish (as described) by D.Cuthbertson, M.Hamilton Jun 1977.

S	1959	20 May	Beggar's Groove	I.S.Clough, J.Pickering, C.Anderson R.Henson, P.Brocklehurst, R.Porteus
S	1959	28 May	Zagzig	I.S.Clough, R.Porteus, P.Brocklehurst, R.Henson
S	1959	Aug	Subtraction	J.McLean, W.Smith
S	1959	19 Sep	The Shadow	T.Sullivan, N.Collingham
S	1959	19 Sep	The Slant	T.Sullivan, N.Collingham
S	1959	Sep	The Bat	D.Haston, R.Smith

Despite some aid, an important ascent, with Scottish pride at long last restored on the cliff. The final pitches of Sassenach were followed to the top. The name referred to the 'various swoopings out of the corner and the amount of night climbing involved.'
Independent Finish by D.Haston, J.R.Marshall Sep 1959.

W	1960	2 Jan	Rogue's Rib	I.S.Clough, G.Grandison
W	1960	8 Jan	Comb Gully Buttress	I.S.Clough, J.M.Alexander

Variation Finish by I.Fulton, D.Gardner 3 Jan 1971

W	1960	29 Jan	Winter Chimneys	I.S.Clough, R.Sefton

Several PA used to surmount the great capstone.

W	1960	6 Feb	The Great Chimney	J.R.Marshall, R.Smith

Sling for aid on the great chockstone.

W	1960	7 Feb	Minus Three Gully	R.Smith, J.R.Marshall
W	1960	8 Feb	Smith's Route	R.Smith, J.R.Marshall

'In the current Nevis Guide, the summer climb ranks second to Sassenach for difficulty - perhaps a generous assessment but not a recommendation for crampons.' 'Then I lost the grip of the axe and it started somersaulting in the air with both my arms windmilling trying to grab it and my feet scarting about in crumbly holds.' A very steep ice route, unrepeated for 11 years.
Icicle Variation by K.V.Crocket, C.Gilmore Feb 1975.

W	1960	9 Feb	Observatory Buttress	J.R.Marshall, R.Smith

Originally left unrecorded, in the mistaken belief that Raeburn's ascent was made under winter conditions. A winter ascent had in fact been attempted as far back as 1901 by Raeburn, Ling, Douglas and Rennie - hard men!

W	1960	12 Feb	Pigott's Route	J.R.Marshall, R.Smith

Despite many attempts, this was the last of the Smith-Marshall climbs to receive a second ascent.

W	1960	13 Feb	Orion Direct	J.R.Marshall, R.Smith

'Probably the most formidable route of its kind in Scotland.' The climax of a magnificent week's climbing by Smith and Marshall, and the highpoint of the step-cutting era.
Direct Start by S.Docherty, N.Muir Mar 1971 on an unsuccessful second ascent attempt.

S	1960	May	Central Route, Minus Two Buttress	R.Smith, J.Hawkshaw

Smith's last new route on the mountain.

W 1961   4 Jan Tower Scoop   I.S.Clough, G.Grandison
W 1961   15 Jan Vanishing Gully   R.Marshall, G.Tiso
   One of the best winter routes of the 1960s.
W 1961   21 Jan 1931 Route   G.Wallace, R.Shaw
S 1961   30 May The Bullroar   J.R.Marshall, J.Stenhouse
   Possibly Marshall's finest summer contribution to Nevis.
   The Groove Variation by J.McLean, W.Smith Jun 1962
S 1961   30 May Chicken Run   J.R.Marshall, J.Stenhouse
S 1961   31 May The Brass Monkey   J.R.Marshall, J.Stenhouse
   2 PA used to gain the base of the crack on pitch 2.
   Upper Crack Direct by J.McLean, W.Smith 1962.
S 1961   31 May The Orgy   I.S.Clough, K.Sutcliffe
   Several PA.
S 1961   1 Jun Mourning Slab   I.S.Clough, K.Sutcliffe
S 1961   1 Jun The High Girdle   I.S.Clough, K.Sutcliffe
W 1962   Winter Harrison's Climb   C.G.M.Slesser, N.Tennent
S 1962   11 Jun Winter Chimneys   I.S.Clough, G.Grandison
S 1962   12 Jun Spartacus   I.S.Clough, G.Grandison
S 1962   13 Jun Astronomy   I.S.Clough, G.Grandison
S 1962   14 Jun The Twist   I.S.Clough, G.Grandison
S 1962   Jun Left Edge Route,   J.R.Marshall, G.J.Ritchie, R.Marshall
                 Gardyloo Buttress
   A long-standing problem.
S 1962   25 Jul Torro   J.McLean, W.Smith, W.Gordon (1PA)
   FFA: I.Nicolson, I.Fulton Jun 1970.
W 1963   24 Feb Wendigo   T.W.Patey, J.Brown
   Patey's last new route on Ben Nevis.
W 1963   Mar Winter Chimney   D.Haston, D.Gray
S 1963   6 Jul Cutlass   E.Cairns, F.Harper
W 1963   Dec Jubilation   R.Marshall, J.R.Marshall, J.Stenhouse
W 1963   Dec Thompson's Route   R.Marshall, J.R.Marshall, J.Stenhouse
S 1964   Jun The Clanger   J.R.Marshall, J.Stenhouse
S 1964   Jun Sidewinder   J.R.Marshall, R.Marshall, A.Wightman
S 1964   Jun Wagroochimsla   D.Haston, R.N.Campbell
   All is revealed by the name - WAll GROOve CHIMney SLAb!
S 1964   Jul Minus Three Gully   J.R.Marshall, G.J.Ritchie
   The last summer gully to receive an ascent - 'It apparently embraces all the
   horrors typical of wet Nevis grooves.'
S 1964   2 Sep King Kong   B.W.Robertson, J.Graham
   Climbed over 2 days using much aid, but a bold attempt at a futuristic line.
   FFA: N.Muir, I.Nicolson Jun 1970 using entry from The Bat.
   FFA of complete lower section by K.Johnstone, A.Grigg 10 Jul 1977.
W 1965   Feb Green Hollow Route   J.R.Marshall, J.Moriarty
W 1965   Feb The Chute   J.R.Marshall, R.N.Campbell, R.Holt
W 1965   Feb The Curtain   J.Knight, D.Bathgate
S 1965   16 Jun Turret Cracks   I.S.Clough, D.G.Roberts

S 1965   Aug Rolling Stones   J.Cunningham, C.Higgins
W 1966   Feb East Wall Route   J.R.Marshall, R.Marshall
     1 PA on the thin slab.
W 1966   Feb Echo Traverse   J.R.Marshall, R.Marshall (1PA)
     Wet Spring Start by R.Clothier, B.Goodlad Apr 1993.
S 1966   4 Sep Pointless   R.Marshall, J.R.Marshall
S 1966   4 Sep The Knuckleduster   J.R.Marshall, R.Marshall
S 1966 21 Sep P.M.   G.Farquhar, I.S.Clough
S 1966 22 Sep Marathon   G.Farquhar, I.S.Clough
W 1967 18 Feb Central Rib Direct   P.Macdonald, A.McKeith
     A considerable amount of aid was used on the final tower.
W 1967 25 Feb Newbigging's   J.R.Marshall, R.N.Campbell
                 80 Minute Route
W 1967   Mar The Clanger   J.R.Marshall, R.Marshall,
                                          R.N.Campbell
     *An earlier attempt by Marshall finished after a spectacular fall by Stenhouse.
     'Eli streaks out of the groove head down like a 225lb torpedo, my eyes are
     on stalks as he smashes a crater from the ledge and bounces into orbit. I
     wrap the rope tight and think of the 500ft drop below...'*
W 1967   Mar Ruddy Rocks   J.R.Marshall, R.Marshall,
                                          R.N.Campbell
S 1967   Jun Turkish   J.Ferguson, C.Higgins (1 PA)
S 1967   Sep Psychedelic Wall   R.Marshall, J.R.Jackson
S 1967 Summer Direct Route II,   D.Browning, H.Small
                 Douglas Boulder
W 1969 16 Feb Route Major   I.S.Clough, H.MacInnes
S 1969 13 Sep Teufel Grooves   D.Bathgate, J.Porteus
W 1970   Feb Garadh Buttress   N.Muir, G.Whitten
     Possibly climbed before.
W 1970   Mar Central Rib   R.N.Campbell, J.R.Marshall
S 1970   Apr Cowslip   R.Carrington, I.Nicolson
     *'The Weep isn't a rock feature, it is a vast streak of black gunge which
     emanates from a huge clump of moss on the traverse line of Route II, then
     oozes its way down over slabs and overlaps before drying up 60ft from the
     foot of the crag.' A well known problem, Carrington and Nicolson snatched
     their ascent early in the season,with the Weep still dry from the winter frosts.*
S 1970   9 Jun Heidbanger   N.Muir, I.Nicolson
S 1970   Jun Gutless   R.N.Campbell, F.Harper
S 1970 Summer Steam   S.Docherty, B.Gorman
W 1971   Feb Joyful Chimneys   R.N.Campbell, J.R.Marshall
W 1971 15 Mar Aphrodite   M.G.Geddes, J.C.Higham
W 1971   Mar Astronomy   A.Fyffe, H.MacInnes, K.Spence (1PA)
     A major ascent on which the second and third men jumared.
     Direct Finish C.Fraser, M.Thompson 16 Feb 1986, but possibly climbed in
     the late 1970s by R.Baxter-Jones and T.Jepson.
W 1971   Apr Hadrian's Wall Direct M.G.Geddes, G.E.Little (1 PA)

S	1971	7 Jul	Nutless	M.Horsburgh, K.Schwartz
S	1971	10 Jul	Plastic Max	D.Bathgate, G.Anderson
S	1971	Aug	Metamorphosis	S.Docherty, D.Gardner

One of the best finds of the 1970s.

S	1971	12 Sep	Arthur	K.Schwartz, G.Webster (1 PA)
S	1971	12 Sep	Night Tripper	N.Muir, R.Schipper
S	1971	30 Sep	Dissection	M.Cundy, P.Nunn
S	1971	7 Oct	Lysystrata	P.Braithwaite, P.Nunn
S	1971	7 Oct	Antigone	P.Braithwaite, P.Nunn
S	1971	7 Oct	Agamemnon	P.Braithwaite, P.Nunn

'We were going well' - A productive day for the English pair!

W	1972	24 Jan	Wagroochimsla	S.Docherty, G.Adam

Sling for aid on overhanging corner.

W	1972	30 Jan	Left-Hand Route, Minus Two Buttress	S.Docherty, N.Muir (1PA)

The first modern ice route on the Minus Face.

W	1972	8 Feb	The Moat	I.Sykes, I.Rae, I.Dewar
W	1972	Feb	Newbigging's Route, Far Right Variation	R.N.Campbell, R.Carrington, J.R.Marshall
W	1972	Feb	Left-Hand Chimney, Douglas Boulder	R.Carrington, J.R.Marshall

Carrington was so impressed by Marshall's performance that he temporarily discarded his curved pick gear and reverted to step cutting with one axe!

W	1972	Mar	Right-Hand Route, Minus Two Buttress	R.Carrington, A.Rouse
W	1972	7 Mar	Right-Hand Wall Route, Minus Three Buttress	R.Ferguson, J.Higham

Slab Rib Variation by C.D.Grant, C.Stead 22 Mar 1982.

W	1972	Winter	Route I	D.Knowles, D.Wilson

Climbed in semi-winter conditions by D.D.Stewart and party in late 1950s.
Direct Start by D.Cuthbertson and J.Sylvester Mar 1984.

S	1972	Jul	Strident Edge	N.Muir, D.Regan
S	1972	1 Aug	Joyful Chimneys	J.R.Marshall, R.R.Rodger
S	1972	4 Sep	Sioux Wall	I.B.Nicolson, G.Grassam
S	1972	Sep	Nosepicker	R.N.Campbell, J.R.Marshall
S	1972	Oct	Gutbuster	R.N.Campbell, D.Palmer
W	1973	Feb	Italian Right-Hand	I.Fulton, S.Belk
W	1973	Feb	Boomer's Requiem	C.Higgins, D.MacArthur
W	1973	Mar	Moonwalk	K.Hughes, J.Mothersele
W	1974	23 Feb	Minus One Gully	K.V.Crocket, C.Stead

After 26 failed attempts, the last Nevis winter gully climbed at last!

W	1974	3 Mar	East Face, Observatory Ridge	B.Dunn, C.Higgins
W	1974	5 Mar	Minus Two Buttress	B.Dunn, C.Higgins, D.MacArthur

W 1974   9 Mar Left Edge Route,   D.F.Lang, N.W Quinn
                Observatory Buttress
    Direct Finish by D.Wilkinson, M.Burt 8 Mar 1980.
W 1974 23 Mar Slav Route   D.F.Lang, N.W.Quinn
    Several days earlier B.Dunn, C.Higgins and D.MacArthur climbed to within
    15m of the summit plateau, but were forced to traverse into Zero Gully just
    25m from the top.
W 1974 25 Mar Lower East Wall   K.V.Crocket, C.Gilmore
                Route
W 1974   Mar   Vade Mecum   D.Knowles, D.Wilson and party
    Originally known as West Face Direct. The lower section to the base of the
    ice pillar was climbed by K.V.Crocket, C.Stead as a variation to West Face
    Lower Route.
W 1975   Feb   Indicator Wall   G.Smith, T.King
W 1975   Feb   Indicator Right-Hand   D.F.Lang, N.W.Quinn
W 1975 21 Mar North-West Face,   F.Craddock, C.Stead
                Observatory Buttress
W 1975   Mar   Two Step Corner   D.Kirtley, D.Montgomery
W 1976   7 Feb Harrison's Climb   K.V.Crocket, C.Gilmore
                Direct
W 1976   Mar   Left Edge Route,   R.Carrington, A.Rouse (1PA)
                Gardyloo Buttress
W 1976   Mar   Pinnacle Buttress   R.Carrington, B.Hall
W 1976   Mar   Rip Off   P.Braithwaite, J.Lowe
    Both climbers neglected to rope up and soloed the route in tandem.
W 1976 28 Dec Astral Highway   C.Higgins, A.Kimber
    The left-hand groove on the final section was followed to finish below the
    '40ft corner.'
W 1977   Jan   Right Edge   R.Milward, F.von Gement
W 1977 28 Feb Lobby Dancer   C.Higgins, A.Kimber (1 PA)
W 1977   Feb   Continuation Wall   B.Dunn, D.Gardner
W 1977   Feb   Baird's Buttress   B.Dunn, D.Gardner
    Climbed on the same day as a finish to Continuation Wall.
W 1977   5 Apr Minus One Buttress   N.Muir, A.Paul
    A brilliantly timed ascent to snatch one of the mountain's finest winter prizes.
W 1977 14 Apr Rubicon Wall   N.Muir, A.Paul
W 1977 17 Apr Silverside   B.Dunn, D.Gardner
S 1977 19 Jun Cranium   N.Muir, A.Paul
W 1977 27 Nov Abacus   N.Muir, A.Paul
W 1977   3 Dec Antonine Wall   N.Muir, A.Paul
W 1977 29 Dec Sickle   M.G.Geddes, B.P.Hall
W 1977   Dec   Gargoyle Wall   R.Carrington, I.Nicolson
W 1978 21 Jan Albatross   M.G.Geddes, C.Higgins
    Fascist Groove Start by C.Rice, R.Webb 12 Feb 1983.
    Right-Hand Start by a Newcastle party Winter 1989.

W 1978 22 Jan Psychedelic Wall   N.Muir, A.Paul
Direct Finish by C.Cartwright, R.Clothier, N.Wilson 1 Apr 1989.
Probably climbed before.
W 1978   4 Feb Five Finger Discount M.G.Geddes, C.Higgins
W 1978 11 Feb Shot in the Dark   M.G.Geddes, A.Rouse
W 1978 12 Feb The Great Glen   P.Braithwaite, P.Moores
W 1978 12 Feb Route II   M.Geddes, A.Rouse
'Then the headlamp came off. The wire tangled with slings, the slings tangled with the axe, and panic threatened.' Despite an early start the climb was finished in the dark. Three pegs for tension were used, but an important ascent and probably Geddes's finest contribution to Nevis.
W 1978 15 Feb Route II Direct   G.Smith, I.Sykes
W 1978 18 Feb Caledonia   D.Gardner, A.Paul
W 1978 18 Feb American Pie   D.F.Lang, N.W.Quinn
W 1978 19 Feb Pointless   N.Banks, G.Smith
Variation Start by M.Fowler, A.V.Saunders 29 Mar 1986.
W 1978   8 Apr Burrito's Groove   M.G.Geddes, C.Higgins
W 1978 14 Apr Galactic Hitchhiker   M.G.Geddes, C.Higgins
A tied-off knifeblade was used to enter the corner at the start of pitch 4. 'Up and down I went on that awful peg, searching for adequate holds until my strength and warmth were almost gone. Finally I found enough...'
S 1978   2 Jun Caligula   D.Cuthbertson, D.Mullin W.Todd
An impressive line that had defeated several previous attempts.
S 1978 18 Jun Adrenalin Rush   K.Johnstone, W.Todd
S 1978   Jun East Face,   C.Higgins, H.Woods
         Observatory Ridge
S 1978 23 Jul Rain Trip   M.Birch, C.M.Kenyon, J.Mackenzie
W 1979 15 Mar The Shield Direct   M.Fowler, A.Saunders
The first winter route to be graded VI in an SMC guide.
W 1979 15 Mar Gutless   P.McKenna, D.Sanderson
W 1979 18 Mar Central Route,   A.Nisbet, B.Sprunt
         Minus Two Buttress
2 PA, 1 NA, but nevertheless, a technically advanced mixed route.
W 1979 23 Mar Gemini   A.Paul, D.Sanderson
The initial ice groove was avoided by starting up Waterfall Gully.
Complete ascent as described by A.Kimber, A.McIntyre 1 Apr 1979.
Left-Hand Finish by A.Fanshawe, A.Orgler, G.E.Little, R.Sailer 16 Feb 1988.
W 1979 26 Mar The Shadow   P.Braithwaite, D.Pearce
Right-Hand Start by R.Clothier, D.Heselden Feb 1989.
W 1979 26 Mar Alchemist   A.Paul, D.Sanderson
Aid was used to gain the narrow iced chimney.
Mist Dancer Variation by R.Clothier, C.Cartwright Winter 1988.
W 1979   8 Apr Last Day in Purgatory C.Higgins, M.G.Geddes
Geddes's last contribution to Ben Nevis
W 1979   8 Apr Western Grooves,   T.Anderson, G.E.Little
         Douglas Boulder

W 1979 Winter Third Time Lucky   R.Milward, S.Parr
Two prior attempts by S.Digler and R.Milward traversed the Little Brenva Face to reach the First Platform, but then failed to cross the Minus Buttresses. The successful ascent started up Slingsby's Chimney and then utilised 2 abseils and several aid points to cross the Minus Face.
W 1980s Winter Zybernaught   A.Paul, D.Hawthorn
W 1980 Winter Kellett's Route,   A.Paul, K.Leinster
                Gardyloo Buttress
    Augean Alley Finish by K.Leinster, A.Paul, G.Reilly Mar 1981.
W 1980   Feb North-West Face   A.Slater, G.Grassam
                Route, Douglas
                Boulder
W 1980   8 Mar Journey Into Space   A.Kimber, C.Higgins
W 1980   2 Apr Fawlty Towers   T.McAuley, N.Muir
W 1980 12 Apr Interstellar Overdrive I.Kennedy, R.Anderson
A frightening ascent climbed in bad thaw conditions.
W 1981 21 Feb The Comb, Left Flank G.E.Little, R.T.Richardson
S 1981   1 Aug Five Card Trick   T.McAuley, N.Muir
S 1981   2 Aug The Minge   T.McAuley, N.Muir
W 1982 28 Jan Venus   M.Duff, A.Nisbet
W 1982   7 Mar Bayonet Route   I.Griffiths, E.Jackson, C.Stead
W 1982 18 Dec Mega Route X   J.Murphy, A.Cain
A ferociously steep route, climbed in two sections over two days. First complete ascent M.Lawrence, R.Webb Dec 1982.
W 1983 19 Feb Stormy Petrel   D.Cuthbertson, R.Kane
W 1983   Mar Long Climb Finish   A.Cain, R.Clothier
W 1983 26 Mar Quickstep   T.Bray, R.Townsend
W 1983 12 Apr Urban Spaceman   D.Hawthorn, A.Paul
W 1983 Winter Shot in the Light   A.Saunders, P.Thornhill
S 1983 21 Aug The Banana Groove   M.Hamilton, R.Anderson
S 1983 29 Aug Agrippa   P.Whillance, R.Anderson
An impressive lead by Whillance of an improbable line in very cold and windy weather.
W 1983 17 Dec Right-Hand Chimney,   D.Hawthorn, C.MacLean A.Paul
                Moonlight Gully
                Buttress
Possibly climbed by D.Haston, R.Smith in the 1960s.
W 1983 17 Dec Diagonal Route   D.Hawthorn, C.MacLean, A.Paul
W 1984   Feb Plum Duff   D.Hawthorn, J.Murphy
S 1984   May Observatory Wall   D.Hawthorn, N.Muir
S 1984   2 Jul Last Stand   D.Hawthorn, A.Paul
S 1984   3 Jul Clefthanger   D.Hawthorn, A.Paul
S 1984   3 Jul The Urchin   D.Hawthorn, A.Paul
S 1984   4 Jul Chinook   D.Hawthorn, A.Paul
S 1984   4 Jul Saxifrage   D.Hawthorn, A.Paul
S 1984 19 Jul Gaslight   G.Adam, N.Muir

S	1984	20 Jul	Militant Chimney	G.Adam, N.Muir
S	1984	20 Jul	Direct Route III, Douglas Boulder	G.Adam, N.Muir
S	1984	11 Aug	The Rattler	G.Adam, N.Muir
S	1984	11 Aug	The Banshee	G.Adam, N.Muir
S	1984	12 Aug	Vanishing Glories	G.Adam, N.Muir

Probably climbed by R.N.Campbell, J.R.Marshall early 1970s but left unrecorded.

S	1984	Summer	Orient Express	J.Grant, D.Hawthorn
S	1984	Summer	Steam Train	D.Hawthorn, D.N.Williams
S	1984	Summer	The Ramp	D.Hawthorn, N.Muir
W	1985	1 Jan	Clefthanger	D.Hawthorn, A.Paul
W	1985	19 Jan	Sod's Law	J.Tinker, M.Duff

B.Hall and A.Rouse climbed a winter version of P.M. on 10 Feb 1986, but their line is thought to coincide with this route.

W	1985	26 Jan	Mercury	M.Hind, J.Christie
W	1985	9 Feb	Compression Crack	M.Hind, C.Rice
W	1985	16 Feb	Diana	M.Duff, J.Tinker

Also known as Direct Route and Liz's Route.

W	1985	Nov	Observatory Wall	D.Hawthorn, A.Paul
W	1985	22 Dec	Phosphorescent Grooves	K.V.Crocket, A.Walker, R.T.Richardson
W	1986	3 Jan	Pirate	M.Duff, A.Nisbet
W	1986	25 Jan	Raeburn's Arete	D.F.Lang, C.Stead
W	1986	31 Jan	Bydand	M.Duff, M.Aldridge, J.Woods
W	1986	1 Feb	Ring the Alarm	M.Duff, J.Tinker

Overload Finish by R.Clothier, D.Heselden 27 Feb 1988

| W | 1986 | 8 Feb | Running Hot | M.Duff, J.Tinker, R.Nowack |
| W | 1986 | 9 Feb | Centurion | J.McKenzie, K.Spence |

Climbed over 2 days with a bivouac. 1 rest point was used at top of pitch 2. This pitch had previously been climbed free by two previous attempts on the route. The upper pitches were avoided by following the traverse of Route II. A solo ascent by R.Milward over 2 days in winter 1975 used a considerable amount of aid.

| W | 1986 | 29 Mar | Match Point | S.M.Richardson, E.Hart |
| W | 1986 | 5 Apr | The Black Hole | A.Saunders, M.Fowler |

Several pitches had been climbed before.

W	1986	11 Apr	Riders on the Storm	D.Hawthorn, E.Todd
S	1986	13 Sep	The Black Douglas	K.V.Crocket, A.Walker
W	1987	Jan	Eastern Block	G.Livingston, M.Charlton
W	1987	Jan	Fish Eye Chimney	N.Holmes, D.Lampard
W	1987	Jan	Tramp	R.Clothier, C.Cartwright

Climbed in error for Aphrodite. Predates the ascent recorded in SMCJ 181.

| W | 1987 | 14 Feb | Rain Trip | G.Hornby, J.Fisher |

W 1987	Feb	Don't Die of Ignorance	A.Cave, S.Yates
W 1987	Mar	Beam Me Up Scotty	R.G.Reid, I.Crofton
S 1987	25 Aug	Blue-Nosed Baboon	K.V.Crocket, A.Walker

Probably climbed by R.N.Campbell, J.R.Marshall early 1970s but left unrecorded.

S 1987	25 Aug	Cryotherapy	K.V.Crocket, A.Walker

Could be the same route as Vanishing Glories.

W 1988	31 Jan	The Curtain Rail	D.F.Lang, R.T.Richardson, C.Stead
W 1988	24 Feb	Point Blank	M.Duff, R.Nowack

A previous attempt by M.Duff, J.Tinker on 4 Mar 1984 avoided the crux groove by climbing Point Five Gully for a short way.

W 1988	28 Feb	Roaring Forties	D.F.Lang, C.Stead
W 1988	29 Feb	Casino Royale	M.Duff, R.Nowack, A.Bond
S 1988	19 Jun	The Trial	W.Young, A.Tibbs, A.Frazer
W 1988	17 Dec	Lost the Place	C.Cartwright, R.Clothier
W 1989	8 Feb	Gaslight	M.Duff, R.Parsley
W 1989	23 Mar	Cutlass	A.Clarke, J.Main
W 1989	Mar	Pinnacle Buttress Direct	R.Clothier, G.Armstrong
W 1989	7 Apr	Satanic Verses	C.Cartwright, R.Clothier
W 1989	Winter	Icefalls right of North-West Face, Observatory Buttress	G.Perroux and party
S 1989	Jun	Boadicea	W.Todd, A.Cain
S 1989	Jun	Reprobate's Rib	R.Carchrie, N.Richardson, R.T.Richardson, B.Shackleton, A.Walker
W 1991	1 Feb	Kellett's North Wall Route	M.Charlton, M.Burrows-Smith
W 1991	9 Feb	Le Mechant	A.Perkins, M.Duff
W 1991	Apr	The Upper Cascade	G.Perroux, J-P Desterke
S 1991	7 Jul	Red Rag	S.M.Richardson, G.Muhlemann
S 1991	8 Sep	Prodigal Boys	T.McAuley, C.Higgins
S 1992	7 Jun	Camanachd Heroes	T.McAuley, C.Higgins
W 1992	22 Dec	The Groove Climb	J.Main, A.Clarke
W 1993	2 Feb	The Shroud	A.Clarke, J.Main
W 1993	13 Feb	Four Play	J.Raitt, D.Gibson

Almost certainly climbed before but never recorded.

W 1993	27 Feb	Chimney Groove	C.Stead, D.Lang
W 1993	23 Mar	Down to the Wire	B.Goodlad, J.Turner
W 1993	27 Mar	The Good Groove	S.M.Richardson, R.D.Everett

1 rest point was taken on pitch 3.

W 1993	11 Apr	Le Panthere Rose	R.Clothier, B.Goodlad, G.Perroux, F.Bossier

| W 1993 | 15 Apr | Une Journée Ordinaire dans un Enfer Quotidien | G.Perroux, F.Bossier, J.Douay |
| W 1993 | 17 Apr | The Flight of the Condor | S.M.Richardson, J.Ashbridge |

Mickey Mouse Finish by R.Clothier, D.McGimpsey 17 Apr 1993.

W 1993	20 Apr	Levitation	D.Cuthbertson, J.George
S 1993	18 Jul	Tuff Nut	S.Abbott, W.Jeffrey, D.N.Williams
S 1993	18 Jul	Geotactic	D.N.Williams, S.Abbott

GLEN NEVIS

| W 1904 | Winter | Achintee Gully | J.W.Burns, W.C.Newbigging, H.Raeburn |
| S 1946 | 23 Mar | Five Finger Gully | J.Ness, B.Ellison, A.Mackenzie |

Originally called Five Funnel Gully.

S 1946	22 Jun	Achintee Gully	D.G.Duff, J.Ness, A.Burgon
S 1946	16 Dec	Christmas Gully	J.G.Parish, H.Bull, H.G.Nicol
W 1946	17 Dec	Steall Gully	C.G.M.Slesser, J.G.Parish, E.Place, I.Paul, H.G.Nicol, J.Bainton
S 1947	10 Apr	Polldubh Gully	J.G.Parish, J.Ness
S 1947	30 May	Antler Gully	D.G.Duff, R.Murphie, J.Ness
S 1947	15 Aug	Surgeon's Gully	D.H.Haworth, G.Ritchie

D.G.Duff, J.Ness and J.G.Parish had climbed most of the gully earlier in 1947.

| W 1963 | 1 Jan | The Steall Waterfall | I.G.Rowe |

Climbing solo, Rowe stepped on to a mini iceberg on the pool at the top and almost fell back down the route!

STOB BAN

| W 1895 | Apr | East Ridge, North Buttress | W.Brown, W.Tough, L.Hinxman, W.Douglas |
| W 1904 | 4 Jan | Gendarme Ridge | J.Maclay, Parr |

A remarkably difficult route for the time.

S 1948	18 Apr	North Ridge Route	D.Scott, R.Anderson, C.Henderson
S 1948	18 Apr	East Wing Route	G.Allison, J.Black
W 1969	Winter	Central Gully	J.Grieve, C.MacNaughton
W 1984	31 Mar	Bodice Ripper	J.Murphy, D.N.Williams
W 1985	Mar	Flake Chimney	R.N.Campbell, M.Naftalin
W 1986	Feb	No Toddy	M.Creasey and party

Final pitch added by D.Hawthorn, R.Lee, D.N.Williams 10 Apr 1986.

| W 1986 | 10 Apr | Triad | D.Hawthorn, R.Lee, D.N.Williams |
| W 1987 | 13 Feb | Skyline Rib | R.G.Webb, B.A.Mattock |

SGOR AN IUBHAIR

S 1970 21 Aug Let Loose   P.T.Logan, K.Schwartz
S 1970 21 Aug Applause   P.T.Logan, K.Schwartz

SGURR A'MHAIM

S 1990 2 Jul Heart of Glass   C.Smith, J.Williamson
S 1990 2 Jul Around the Bend   J.Williamson, C.Smith
S 1990 2 Jul Strata-Sphere   C.Smith, J.Williamson
S 1990 2 Jul Bananafishbones   C.Smith, J.Williamson
S 1990 2 Jul Clam-Jam   J.Williamson, C.Smith

AONACH MOR

S 1945 20 Sep Route 1   K.Anderson, J.G.Fraser
S 1945 20 Sep Route 2   F.Baird, V.G.A.Freeman, J.Rutherford
W 1979 21 Dec Golden Oldy   A.Kimber
W 1988 10 Jan Morwind   R.D.Everett, S.M.Richardson
    *'The rising storm added increasing interest to the enjoyable hack up steep,
    but well vegetated granite grooves' - the first route to be recorded on the
    extensive cliffs of Coire an Lochain.*
W 1988 26 Nov Icicle Gully   R.D.Everett, S.M.Richardson
W 1988 26 Nov Grooved Arete   S.M.Richardson, R.D.Everett
W 1988 3 Dec Force Ten Buttress R.D.Everett, S.M.Richardson
W 1988 3 Dec Jet Stream   R.D.Everett, S.M.Richardson
    Direct Finish by C.Grant, C.Rice 27 Jan 1990.
W 1988 17 Dec Western Rib   S.M.Richardson, R.D.Everett
W 1989 14 Jan Typhoon   R.D.Everett, S.M.Richardson
    Wind speeds of 220 kph were recorded that day!
W 1989 21 Jan Hidden Gully   R.G.Webb, C.Rice
W 1989 22 Jan Right Twin   S.M.Richardson, R.D.Everett
W 1989 22 Jan Left Twin   R.D.Everett, S.M.Richardson
W 1989 22 Jan Tunnel Vision   S.M.Richardson, R.D.Everett
    Left Branch by S.Kennedy S.Thirgood Winter 1990.
W 1989 22 Jan Forgotten Twin   R.D.Everett, S.M.Richardson
    *Lean conditions that weekend focussed attention on the gullies. These may
    have been climbed by RAF Mountain Rescue Team members in the 1960s,
    but never recorded.*
W 1989 18 Feb Temperance Union   S.Richards, G.Armstrong, C.Millar,
              Blues   J.Owens
W 1989 19 Feb The Split   S.M.Richardson, R.D.Everett
W 1989 19 Feb Siamese Buttress   S.M.Richardson, R.D.Everett
W 1989 25 Feb Daim Buttress   R.D.Everett, N.Barrett, S.M.Richardson
W 1989 4 Mar Hurricane Arete   S.M.Richardson, R.D.Everett
S 1989 1 Oct Solitaire   R.D.Everett
W 1989 25 Nov Nausea   J.Naismith, C.Watkins

W 1989	25 Nov	The Web	S.Kennedy, C.Grindley
W 1989	25 Nov	Turf Walk	C.Grant, R.D.Everett
W 1989	2 Dec	Lickety Split	G.Mulhemann, S.M.Richardson
W 1989	30 Dec	Gondola with the Wind	S.Kennedy, S.Thirgood
W 1990	1 Jan	Solitaire	R.D.Everett, S.M.Richardson
W 1990	25 Jan	Molar Canal	C.Jones, S.Kennedy, B.Williamson
W 1990	25 Jan	North Buttress Route	S.Kennedy, B.Williamson
W 1990	27 Jan	White Shark	C.Millar, R.G.Webb

Pre-dates Colgate Tripper recorded in SMCJ 181.

W 1990	Jan	Pepperpot	R.Lee, N.Wright
W 1990	24 Feb	Remora	R.G.Reid, R.G.Webb
W 1990	9 Mar	Shelf Route	S.Kennedy, S.Thirgood
W 1990	26 Mar	Aquafresh	N.Marshall, D.Ritchie
W 1990	27 Mar	Pernille	C.Jones, A.Taylor
W 1990	28 Mar	The Betrayal	S.Kennedy, D.Ritchie
W 1990	28 Mar	The Guardian	S.Kennedy, D.Ritchie
W 1990	28 Mar	Riptide	T.Gilchrist, E.McGlashan, S.McLean
W 1990	Mar	Left Flank of Prow	D.Ritchie
W 1990	4 Apr	Stirling Bridge	S.Kennedy, D.Ritchie
W 1990	17 Nov	Muddy Waters	C.Jones, S.Kennedy, D.Ritchie
W 1991	3 Feb	Tinsel Town	S.Kennedy, P.Mills
W 1991	2 Mar	The Slever	S.Kennedy, D.Ritchie
W 1991	2 Mar	Roaring Forties	S.M.Richardson, R.D.Everett, J.C.Wilkinson
W 1992	23 Feb	Golden Promise	B.Davison, S.Kennedy, S.Venables
W 1992	27 Feb	Slick Mick's Groove	N.Hitchins, M.Hardwick, A.V.Saunders
W 1992	Feb	Guide's Variation	S.Allan, D.Etherington

Mistaken for Jet Stream on a guide's assessment course!

W 1992	8 Mar	Solar Wind	S.M.Richardson, R.D.Everett
W 1993	7 Feb	Barrel Buttress	S.Kennedy, S.Thirgood
W 1993	7 Feb	Nid Arete	S.Kennedy, S.Thirgood

AONACH BEAG

W 1895	Apr	North-East Ridge	J.Maclay, W.Naismith, G.Thomson

'The best arete in Scotland.' - The high point of the 1895 SMC Fort William meet.

S 1938	May	Raw Egg Buttress	J.A.Brown, B.H.Humble, T.D.MacKinnon
S 1951	Sep	Crevassed Rib	G.S.Johnstone, M. Johnstone

Upper slab by J.Smith, G.S.Johnstone on a subsequent ascent.

S 1951	Sep	North Buttress	M.Coventry, W.V.Thomas
W 1973	22 Apr	Anabasis	R.A.Croft, J.R.Sutcliffe
W 1975	8 Feb	The Ramp	K.V.Crocket, R.Hockey, B.E.H.Maden, R.Miller, R.Pillinger

Climbed in mistake for the North-East Ridge.

W 1979   9 May Mayfly   K.Schwartz
W 1985 30 Nov Whiteout   S.M.Richardson, R.G.Webb
    The start of a renewed interest in the mountain.
W 1987 14 Feb King's Ransom   S.M.Richardson, R.G.Webb (1 PA)
W 1987 18 Feb Royal Pardon   R.G.Webb, S.M.Richardson
    A prominent line that had been attempted earlier by an unknown party.
W 1987 21 Feb Blackout   J.Dunn, R.G.Webb
W 1987 21 Feb Poached Egg   R.G.Webb, J.Dunn
    Eggsclamation Variation by S.M.Richardson, R.D.Everett 5 April 1987.
W 1987   5 Apr Raw Egg Buttress   R.D.Everett, S.M.Richardson
W 1988 16 Jan West Central Route   R.D.Everett, R.G.Webb
W 1988 16 Jan Axeless   R.G.Webb, R.D.Everett
W 1988 20 Feb Twinkle   R.D.Everett, S.M.Richardson
W 1988 20 Feb Beyond The Call of   R.D.Everett, S.M.Richardson
                Duty
W 1988 27 Mar Aonach Wall   R.D.Everett, S.M.Richardson
S 1988 11 Jun Chandelle   R.D.Everett, S.M.Richardson
S 1988 11 Jun Pirates   R.G.Webb, C.Rice
W 1989 26 Feb Blinker's Buttress   R.D.Everett, N.Barrett, S.M.Richardson
    Direct Start by R.D.Everett, N.Barrett, S.M.Richardson 26 Feb 1989
W 1989 17 Mar The Clare Effect   S.Kennedy, L.Skoudas
    1 point of aid used when tunnelling the cornice.
W 1989 15 Apr Sellout   R.G.Webb, S.M.Richardson
W 1989 16 Apr Stand and Deliver   C.Cartwright, R.Clothier
W 1990   1 Jan Never a Dull Moment   S.M.Richardson, R.D.Everett
W 1991 16 Feb Sideslip   S.Kennedy, D.Ritchie
W 1991 23 Mar Salmonella   S.M.Richardson, R.D.Everett
    *'Every part of pick, adze and hammer was battered or delicately manoeuvred
    into cracks and pockets, while front points worked precision edging on the
    rugosities of the walls. Ice streaks and hoar gave it true winter flavour, but
    it was so steep that the ensuing pump was reminiscent of a steep limestone
    rock climb.'*
W 1992 28 Mar Ruadh Eigg Chimney R.D.Everett, S.M.Richardson,
                                      G.Muhlemann
W 1993 31 Jan Camilla   S.M.Richardson, R.D.Everett
W 1993 21 Feb Helter Skelter   S.Kennedy, D.Ritchie
W 1993 21 Mar Aonacrack   J.Ashbridge, S.M.Richardson

SGURR INNSE

S 1970   2 Jun Headjam   S.J.Crymble, K.Schwartz

MEALL GARBH

S 1964 10 Oct Watcher's Wall   P.Tranter, I.G.Rowe

S 1964 10 Oct Inspiration   A.Park, W.Fraser
   'Credit for the discovery of this cliff must go to P.Tranter who nearly fell over
   it. The crag, some 500 ft high, seems to have escaped the notice of both
   climbers and the OS with complete justification.'
W 1976   3 Feb The Ramp   A.L.Wielochowski
W 1976   4 Feb Deep Slit   A.L.Wielochowski
W 1976   4 Feb Nash's Gully   J.P.Nash
W 1976 18 Feb Webster's Original   P.C.Webster and J.S.M.T.C. party
                 Route
   Direct Start by P.Webster 20 Feb 1976.
W 1976 20 Feb Barry's Route   B.Gisborne and J.S.M.T.C. party
W 1976 20 Mar The Frozen Vice   A.L.Wielochowski, G.Thomas
W 1976 30 Mar Foxes Gully   A.L.Wielochowski
W 1976 30 Mar Ping Pong   A.L.Wielochowski
W 1976   1 Apr Terminal Buttress   A.L.Wielochowski, M.Rutherford,
                                        B.H.Parker, J.Crowden
W 1976   1 Apr Broad Gully   A.L.Wielochowski, J.Crowden
W 1977   9 Jan The Canine   H.Davies and party
W 1977   9 Jan Y-Gully   P.C.Webster, D.Robinson, J.A.Taylor
W 1977   6 Feb Southern Route   P.C.Webster, H.R.Thomas, P.Chatterley
W 1977   8 Feb Central Gully   P.Moores, T.Walker and party
   Aid used to exit from the second cave.
   FFA: A.Nisbet, B.Clough 13 Jan 1985.
W 1977 10 Feb Dickinson's Route   K.Dickinson and party
W 1977 12 Feb Little Spider   H.Davies, R.Pelly
W 1977 19 Feb The Cushion   H.Davies and party
W 1977 28 Feb North Buttress Left   P.C.Webster, P.Thomas
                 Edge
W 1977   Feb Ledge Route   H.Davies
W 1987 24 Mar Inspiration   A.Nisbet, J.Grosset

BINNEIN SHUAS

W 1965   Feb Hidden Gully   J.Brown, J.Heron, T.Patey
W 1982   Jan Foxtrot   J.Jeffrey, S.Kennedy, C.Macleod,
                                        M.Sclater
W 1987 18 Jan Scotch on the Rocks   M.Charlton, G.Kinsey
W 1987 18 Jan Eastern Chimney   K.Howett, A.Moist

CREAG MEAGAIDH

W 1896   Apr Easy Gully   W.Tough, W.Douglas, H.Raeburn
W 1903 31 Oct Raeburn's Gully   H.Raeburn, C.Walker, H.Walker
S 1906   Jun South Pillar   H.Raeburn, F.S.Goggs
   Originally called A Buttress.
S 1930   8 Jun Edge Route   J.H.B.Bell, D.C.Macdonald

W 1934   29 Apr   Staghorn Gully   C.M.Allan, J.H.B Bell, H.M.Kelly,
                                          H.Cooper
   Direct Start by J.H.Deacon, T.W.Patey 7 Feb 1960.
S 1934   27 May   Central Pillar   C.M.Allan, J.H.B.Bell, Miss Keay
   *Originally called B Buttress. The upper section of the route had previously
   been climbed by H. Raeburn and C.Walker 1 Nov 1903, who traversed left
   on to the Pillar after climbing halfway up Centre Post.*
W 1935   Jan   South Pipe   J.H.B.Bell, V.Roy
W 1936   21 Mar   Central Pillar   J.H.B.Bell, Martin, Spence, Thomson
S 1936   May   Red Scar Route   J.H.B.Bell, E.A.M.Wedderburn
S 1936   May   Appolyon Ledge   J.H.B.Bell, E.A.M.Wedderburn
S 1936   Jun   North Post   C.M.Allan, J.H.B.Bell, C.Gorrie, I.Ogilvie
W 1937   21 Mar   Centre Post   C.M.Allan, J.H.B.Bell
   Centre Post Direct by B.W.Robertson, F.Harper, E.Cairns 22 Feb 1964.
   *A confident ascent (Tom Patey and Joe Brown had failed the day before) of
   what was considered to be one of the last great problems of Scottish
   mountaineering. 'We were in no doubt that, if ripe, it would be picked like a
   plum from under the very eye of the SMC and Creag Dubh hard men.'*
   Skidrowe Finish by I.Rowe, A.McKeith Feb 1965.
W 1956   10 Feb   South Post   N.S.Tennent, C.G.M Slesser
   The first ice pitch was avoided by traversing in from the right.
   First Pitch Direct by T.W.Patey, R.F.Brooke 5 Mar 1962.
   Third Pitch Direct by A.MacEacheran, J.Knight Mar 1964.
W 1957   Feb   Ritchie's Gully   J.R.Marshall, G.J.Ritchie
   *The initial icefall was avoided by traversing in from the left along Appolyon
   Ledge.*
   Complete ascent by G.N.Hunter, N.Quinn Mar 1969.
W 1958   17 Feb   Crescent Gully   J.Clarkson, R.J.Tanton
W 1959   8 Feb   Smith's Gully   J.R.Marshall, G.Tiso
   *A step-cutting tour de force. The strain began to show on the final pitch -
   '...the familiar flapping axe, spent arms, and frantic, stomping front-points
   were all in evidence...' The name was a gibe at Robin Smith who had failed
   on the route two years earlier.*
W 1959   9 Feb   1959 Face Route   J.R.Marshall, J.Stenhouse, D.Haston
   *'...a route typical of all that is best in Scottish winter mountaineering -
   complicated route-finding, magnificent situations, and every variety of
   obstacle.' The barrier icefall was avoided by climbing the rocks on the right.*
W 1960   6 Feb   North Post   T.W.Patey, J.H.Deacon, G.R.Mcleod,
                                          P.Danelet
   *Pierre Danelet was a visiting guide from Les Diablerets. 'The spectacle of a
   Swiss guide on a Scottish ice climb was both interesting and instructive. Let
   it be said that he acquitted himself with honour.'*
W 1961   28 Jan   Eastern Corner   C.G.M.Slesser, K.Bryan
W 1962   28 Feb   Post Horn Gallop   T.W.Patey, R.F.Brooke
W 1962   5 Mar   Last Post   T.W.Patey, R.F.Brooke
W 1963   Feb   Cinderella   W.Tout, T.W.Patey

W 1963	Mar	The Sash	T.W.Patey, R.W.Barclay, M.Laverty, E.Attfield
W 1963	Mar	Will o' the Wisp	T.W.Patey, E.Attfield
W 1963	Mar	The Prow	D.Pyper, M.Main
W 1964	19 Feb	Diadem	J.Brown, T.W.Patey
W 1964	Mar	The Glass Slipper	I.A.MacEacheran, J.Knight
W 1965	13 Mar	North Pillar	A.McKeith, G.Warburton
W 1966	15 Jan	The Scene	D.Gray, A.McKeith.
W 1966	16 Jan	Appolyon Ledge	D.Gray, A.McKeith.

March's Variation by W.March Winter 1972.

W 1966	22 Jan	Quasimodo	R.S.Burnett, A.McKeith
W 1966	12 Feb	The Last Lap	A.McKeith, M.Galbraith
W 1966	14 Feb	Fifteen A	A.McKeith, M.Galbraith, M.Shand, G.Millar
W 1966	19 Feb	Naevueata	A.McKeith, G.Anderson, J.Heron
S 1966	24 Aug	Amustoavoid	A.McKeith and party

'A horrible climb, horribly named.'

W 1968	2 Mar	Longfellow	R.McMillan, G.S.Peet

Direct Variation by A.Annandale, J.Fuller Winter 1991.

W 1968	14 Apr	The Pumpkin	R.McMillan, G.S.Peet, N.Quinn
W 1969	2 Feb	The Wand	Q.T.Crichton, D.F.Lang, G.N.Hunter, N.Quinn
W 1969	23 Mar	The Crab Crawl	T.W.Patey

A bold solo of a huge route. Two weeks earlier Patey had failed to interest Whillans in an attempt. '"Look mate," he interrupted, "do you know what you want to do? You want to team up with a crab. It's got claws, walks sideways and it's got a thick 'ead. This isn't a climb, it's a bloody crab-crawl!"

W 1969	Mar	Trespasser Buttress	G.N.Hunter, H.MacInnes, D.F.Lang, N.Quinn
W 1969	14 Dec	The Snail	B.Jones, D.Sharp, B.Taplin
W 1970	6 Feb	Lotsavu	B.J.G.Chambers, K.Schwartz
W 1970	27 Dec	Fairy Godmother	M.G.Geddes, N.C.Rayner
W 1970	28 Dec	Ugly Sister	M.G.Geddes, N.C.Rayner
W 1972	11 Mar	South Pillar	R.Carrington, A.Rouse
W 1972	11 Mar	Nordwander	D.Dinwoodie, B.Lawrie, M.Freeman, D.Stuart
W 1975	30 Mar	Easter Pillar	D.F.Lang, N.Quinn
W 1976	Jan	The Blue Icicle	A.L.Wielochowski, H.Davies
W 1976	16 Feb	The White Spider	A.L.Wielochowski, J.P.Nash
W 1976	22 Feb	Vanishing Ledge	A.L.Wielochowski, J.P.Nash
W 1976	30 Dec	Raeburn's Gully Buttress	P.C.Webster, A.L.Wielochowski
W 1979	12 Feb	Great Buttress Route	P.Braithwaite, C.Brookes
W 1981	Mar	1959 Face Route Direct	D.Cuthbertson, T.Prentice

W 1983 19 Feb The Fly Direct   M.Fowler, A.Saunders
The upper section was climbed by A.L.Wielochowski and D.K.R.Nottidge on 17 Mar 1976 after approaching via Vanishing Ledge. This was their third attempt on the line.
W 1983 19 Feb The Midge   A.Nisbet, G.Harper
A previous attempt by A.Nisbet and B.Sprunt failed in darkness 15m from the plateau.
W 1984 22 Mar Pinnacle Buttress   J.Sylvester, K.Howett
                Direct
The route was started from Raeburn's Gully since the icefall failed to reach the ground.
W 1985   9 Feb Missed the Post   P.Brownsort, P.Smith
A similar line was followed by R.Clothier and partner Winter 1979.
W 1988 12 Mar Buttons   C.Grant, S.M.Richardson
W 1991 13 Jan Deadline   A.Perkins, M.Duff
This was Duff's third attempt on the route.
W 1991 10 Feb Postman Pat   A.Perkins, M Duff
A last great problem. 1 axe rest.

CARN DEARG BUTTRESS, GLEN ROY

W 1972   6 Feb Wet Walk   B.J.G.Chambers, K.Schwartz
W 1972   6 Feb The Rough Ride   B.J.G.Chambers, K.Schwartz
W 1972   6 Feb The Spin   B.J.G.Chambers, K.Schwartz
W 1972   6 Feb Midnight Crunch   B.J.G.Chambers, K.Schwartz
W 1972   7 Feb Big Red Van   J.Mount, K.Schwartz
A good weekend's work despite crashing the van in Glen Roy on the approach.

CREAG AN LOCHAIN, GLEN ROY

W 1972   6 Feb Loch Roy Gully   R.Schipper, J.Mount
W 1976 13 Mar Fox Trot   D.K.R.Nottidge, A.L.Wielochowski
The route was discovered by helicopter on a crag spotting mission by the J.S.M.T.C.

CARN DEARG, MONADHLIATH

W 1985 31 Dec Wee Team Gully   J.Grosset, J.Lyall
W 1987   Jan The Great Trek   J.McKeever, G.Taylor, A.Todd

CREAG DUBH

W 1966 Winter Oui Oui   M.Galbraith, R.Woodcock

CREAG DHUBH, LOCH ERICHT

W	1987	18 Feb	The Hex Factor	R.Wild, J.Lyall
W	1987	21 Feb	Wafer Me	J.Lyall, E.Pirie
W	1987	21 Feb	Ice Cream	J.Lyall, E.Pirie
W	1987	24 Mar	Neapolitan	J.Lyall, S.Spalding

BEN ALDER

W	1896	Apr	Central Gully	A.E.Robertson, Reid
S	1950	Summer	Uncle's Chimney	C.U.M.C. party
S	1950	Summer	Left-Hand Chimney	C.U.M.C. party
S	1966	Jul	Crab Walk	J.R.Mackenzie, P.Vasey, R.Fowlie
S	1966	Jul	Vertical Horror	J.R.Mackenzie, P.Vasey, R.Fowlie
W	1986	1 Jan	Wingeing Sassenach	J.Crummy, I.Sutton

Possibly climbed by R.N.Campbell, A.W.Ewing Feb 1970.

W	1987	31 Jan	Alderwand	R.D.Everett, S.M.Richardson
W	1987	31 Jan	The Walker's Spur	S.M.Richardson, R.D.Everett
W	1987	1 Feb	Ice Maiden	R.D.Everett, S.M.Richardson
W	1988	23 Jan	Witchwhite	S.M.Richardson, R.D.Everett
W	1988	23 Jan	Nightshift	C.Grant, C.Rice, R.G.Webb

Index of Routes

The following list includes the principal routes, but not all the variations.

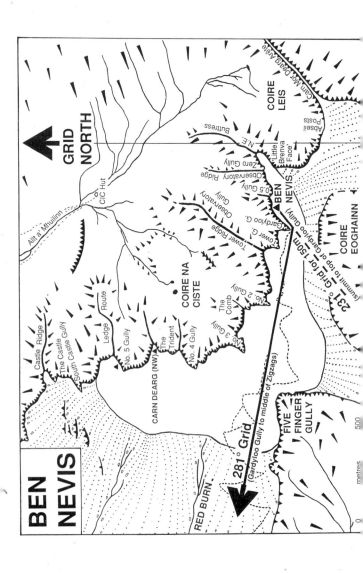

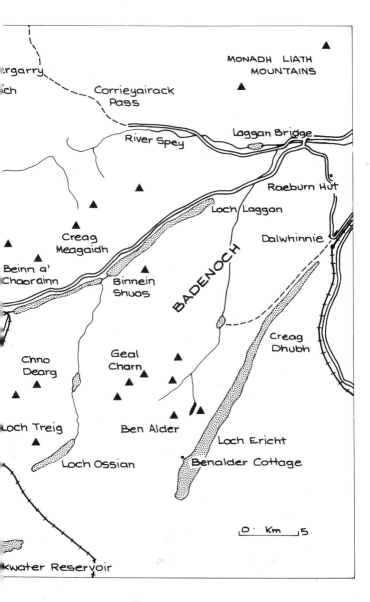